ENTERPRISING WATERS

I0892641

ENTERPRISING WATERS

The History and Art of New York's Erie Canal

Brad L. Utter,

with Ashley Hopkins-Benton and Karen E. Quinn

Foreword by Thomas X. Grasso

excelsior editions

Back cover: *New York and the Erie Canal*, by William Wall, oil on canvas, 1862. *Courtesy of the Arkell Museum at Canajoharie. Gift of Bartlett Arkell, 1934.*

Page ii: Detail from a $5,000 canal stock certificate for the enlargement of the New York State canal system, 1869, shown on page xi. This image served as the inspiration for the signature graphic of the *Enterprising Waters* exhibit, shown on page x. *New York State Museum, Mrs. Arnold B. Barben Canal Collection, H-1988.79.*

Published by
State University of New York Press, Albany

© 2020 New York State Education Department, Albany, NY 12230

All rights reserved

Printed in the United States of America

No part of this book may be used or reproduced in any manner whatsoever without written permission. No part of this book may be stored in a retrieval system or transmitted in any form or by any means including electronic, electrostatic, magnetic tape, mechanical, photocopying, recording, or otherwise without the prior permission in writing of the publisher.

EXCELSIOR EDITIONS is an imprint of STATE UNIVERSITY OF NEW YORK PRESS
For information, contact State University of New York Press, Albany, NY
www.sunypress.edu

Library of Congress Cataloging-in-Publication Data

Names: Utter, Brad L., author. | Hopkins-Benton, Ashley, author. | Quinn, Karen E., author.
Title: Enterprising waters : the history and art of New York's Erie Canal / Brad L. Utter, with Ashley Hopkins-Benton, and Karen E. Quinn.
Description: Albany : Excelsior Editions, [2020] | Includes bibliographical references and index.
Identifiers: LCCN 2019037879 | ISBN 9781438478265 (paperback) | ISBN 9781438478272 (ebook)
Subjects: LCSH: Erie Canal (N.Y.)—History. | Erie Canal Region (N.Y.)—History. | Erie Canal (N.Y.)—In art.
Classification: LCC HE396.E6 U88 2020 | DDC 386/.4809747—dc23
LC record available at https://lccn.loc.gov/2019037879

10 9 8 7 6 5 4 3 2 1

book design, Laurie D. Searl
cover graphic, based on the image on page ii, is by Christopher Havens and Ben Karis-Nix

CONTENTS

FOREWORD

In 1956, when the Erie Canal was a venerable 139 years old, the Canal Society of New York State was formed in Buffalo. By that time the Erie Canal had undergone many of the changes that would ultimately define it, transforming it from "Clinton's Ditch," as it was famously, and derisively, called in its nascence in the early 1820s, to the heavily traveled commercial barge passage of the mid-twentieth century.

So why create a canal society then, in the mid-1950s? In short, the organization formed to share knowledge, serve the public good, and help preserve the canal as well as its epic story—one rich in feats of human ingenuity; in details related to New York's natural history, geology, and geography; and in expressions of the human spirit through music, folklore, literature, and tall tales, some even rooted in reality.

To fully appreciate what an extraordinary thing the Erie Canal is, one must understand a good bit about the America that spurred its creation. The canal was built at a time when the United States was not only a young country but an entirely new idea put into practice, an unprecedented experiment in self-governance and civic participation and responsibility. Moreover, the young republic took root on the eastern edge of a vast, unspoiled continent, the realities of which—including a stunningly varied landscape abundant in natural resources—were being actively discovered.

The idea for a cross-state canal in New York came early, decades before its construction, owing to two things: the desire for better access to the rich resources of the North American interior and the unique opportunity New York's natural landscape presented to achieve it. New York is the only state on the Eastern seaboard that touches both the Atlantic Ocean and the Great Lakes. The Hudson River, flowing from its origin in the Adirondack Mountains down through the Hudson Valley, empties into New York Harbor. The Mohawk River cuts east through a large swath of central New York, joining the Hudson at Cohoes, just north of Albany. Especially significant is the fact that the divide at Rome between the Mohawk River and Wood Creek is the lowest pass in the mountains that form the eastern backbone of North America, stretching from Birmingham, Alabama, to the St. Lawrence River. All this is to say, New York was the logical place to undertake a human-made navigable connector. Dig a channel from Albany to Buffalo and you've got a water route—so much easier for transport than overland hauling—between the Atlantic and Lake Erie, and beyond.

But for all this natural potential, the Erie Canal's creation was not preordained, though its economic success was. Human effort—genius, even—was required, and like nearly all things involving humans, there was conflict. The canal's creation required public approval and state support, and not everyone was on board. The anti-canal faction was strong and dismissed a statewide channel as implausible and therefore wasteful to attempt. Summed up in one allegory: "In the big ditch would be buried the treasury of the state, to be watered by the tears of posterity."

But in 1810, De Witt Clinton, mayor of New York City, took up the cause. By that time, he had already served as a New York State legislator and US senator, and his political clout elevated the advocacy of earlier ardent canal proponents, leading entrepreneurs and statesmen like Jesse Hawley, Joshua Foreman, and Gouverneur Morris. Their efforts paid off, and in 1817 the state legislature passed a bill authorizing the canal's construction.

Winning state support was one hurdle; designing an engineering miracle was another. In 1792 the New York State Legislature had passed an act to explore the development of a canal system and in the process incorporated two entities—the Western and the Northern Inland Lock Navigation companies—to survey and study the possibilities. The Northern Inland Lock Navigation Company (NILNC) set its sights toward Lake Champlain, but little was achieved; the Western Inland Lock Navigation Company (WILNC) was charged in the 1792 legislation with "opening a lock navigation from the now navigable part of Hudson's river to be extended to Lake Ontario, and to the Seneca lake"—virtually the path that would be the Erie Canal thirty years later.

One of the most remarkable of the many remarkable facts about the creation of the Erie Canal is that its engineers were not essentially novices. Although none of the men—Benjamin Wright, James Geddes, Canvass White, John B. Jervis, and others—who contributed to the canal's design had been formally trained, they were in every sense engineers—practical engineers. They learned on the job, acting as surveyors on the WILNC and NILNC projects plus other civil works, and independently studied the achievements of European engineers, in particular the renowned James Brindley of England. His Bridgewater Canal (1761) heavily influenced the design of the Erie Canal in that it more or less followed the natural level contours of the land, hugging the sides of the landscape's picturesque hills and valleys.

Through the efforts of the WILNC, the Erie Canal was preceded by several successes to enable inland navigation. For example, beginning in 1792 the company made improvements to the Mohawk River between Schenectady and Rome, facilitating passage over small rifts and rapids, especially for downbound boats. But getting boats upstream remained a challenge; it was difficult but doable with enough effort and, we imagine, a great deal of profanity. The company also constructed three short canals, all under two miles long: Little Falls Canal (1795), Rome Canal (1797), and German Flatts Canal (1798). These early WILNC projects, and others, incorporated many of the essential features that would go into creating the Erie Canal. These projects also proved important because they functioned as learning labs of a sort, through which the engineers learned by trial and error. Use of construction materials that quickly crumbled, unforeseen maintenance challenges, and too-high tolls all proved to be a barrier when it came to effectively addressing New York's navigation needs. These errors ultimately led to the failure of the NILNC and the absorption of the WILNC by the State in 1820. But by then, construction of the Erie Canal was well under way, overseen by a State-appointed Board of Commissioners that had been created by the 1817 "Canal Act."

Construction of the Erie Canal began on July 4, 1817, at Rome, working east and west, and ended after workers dug through to the western terminus just upstream of Lake Erie on October 25, 1825. The Erie Canal was made real by the backbreaking work of many thousands of laborers, mostly local men and boys, though in future enlargements immigrants, mostly from Ireland (first enlargement) and then Italy (Erie Barge enlargement of the early twentieth century), would carry the brunt of the work, drawn by the promise of work and a new and better life in America.

To mark the canal's completion, De Witt Clinton and other dignitaries boarded the *Seneca Chief* and other vessels at Buffalo to begin the first through journey to New York City. In what has come to be called "the wedding of the waters," on the morning of November 4, 1825, Clinton poured a keg of Lake Erie water into the Atlantic Ocean, consummating the marriage.

This first Erie Canal ran 363 miles, from Albany to Buffalo, and included eighty-three locks and eighteen aqueducts. It was, at the time, the second-longest man-made waterway in the world, second only to the ancient Grand Canal in China. A narrow ribbon of water four feet deep and forty feet wide, it immediately lowered the cost of shipping and transportation, compared to wagons overland, by 90 percent. Boats could carry seventy tons of freight, and the canal became an economic and national wonder. Powered by the income from cargo tolls on the thousands of boats plying the canal, the State payed for its construction and maintenance in just ten years and showed a profit so large that by 1835 it offset the state budget by at least 60 percent. The waterway made New York the "Empire State" and also fostered boomtowns beyond New York—big cities like Detroit, Cleveland, and Chicago.

All this success meant, of course, that New York's thriving commerce quickly outgrew the very canal that created it. Beginning in 1836, the State undertook a series of initiatives to enlarge or improve the canal, the first from 1836 to 1862 and another between 1884 and 1890. Through these enlargement campaigns, the canal grew to a depth of seven feet and width of seventy feet. Longer and wider locks and aqueducts were built, facilitating two-way traffic and curbing the long lines that had become famous for sparking fights between boat crews. Moreover, the expanded canal could handle a new class of boats that could carry up to 240 tons of freight, which further drove down the cost of transporting goods. A third enlargement program began in 1896 but had to be abandoned two years later—when only 40 percent of the project was completed but all of the $9 million allotted for it was spent.

The abandoned project put the Erie Canal in peril. But in 1898 Theodore Roosevelt, as New York's new governor, offered renewed hope as a champion for the canal. Work on "Teddy Roosevelt's Ditch" began in 1905, and it was opened for through traffic on May 15, 1918. This new Barge Canal proved to be a different species of waterway from its nineteenth-century ancestors. It abandoned much of the original route, essentially starving many of the communities that had sprouted and thrived over the previous century. Gone were the "mom and pop" owned and operated canal boats with entire families living aboard. Gone were the animal towing, the manually operated locks, canal-side stores and hotels, and privately owned dry docks and boat yards. In short, a whole way of life vanished with the creation of the new canal.

The Barge Canal fulfilled its purpose over the next few decades, but by midcentury, fatefully, it was eclipsed by modernity. Improved railroads, new oil pipelines, and interstate motor highways made overland hauling easier than was ever imaginable in the nineteenth century. And then, in 1959, the St. Lawrence Seaway opened, allowing ships to pass directly from the Atlantic to the Great Lakes. The days of the Erie Canal as the necessary and vital commercial route were over.

But the Erie Canal's life is not over, and, in fact, it has taken on a new one. Today, the canal has emerged as an economic engine of a different sort, one that is almost entirely recreational and educational (though we are happy to say that we do see some burgeoning local commerce plying the waters, too). In 2000 the US Congress recognized the canal's significance by establishing the Erie Canalway National Heritage Corridor. It is a destination for families, cyclists, heritage tourists, canal enthusiasts and scholars, and people who simply like to explore. As we at the Canal Society of New York State like to say, a visit to the calm waters of the Erie Canal just might be the fastest way to slow down. Let that value not be lost on any of us, in this our era of cyber speed and tech-driven distractions.

The Canal Society's foundational purpose is to share information about New York's canals with the public—people who are interested in canals and, we hope, those not *yet* interested but whose imaginations will be ignited by the stories we convened to steward and share. Together, the existence of the exhibitions *Enterprising Waters* and *Art of the Erie Canal* and this volume take the story of the Erie Canal to a grander scale, allowing for a wider reach to a broader public, to the more than nearly one million adults and children who visited the museum while these exhibitions were in place.

The Canal Society of New York State is immensely proud to have participated in the creation of *Enterprising Waters*, to have lent many of the artifacts, models, and images that brought the canal to life at the New York State Museum for a new generation of inquisitive minds who want to explore the fascinating world of canals both here and abroad.

—Thomas X. Grasso

President Emeritus, Canal Society of New York State

Rochester, New York

August 2018

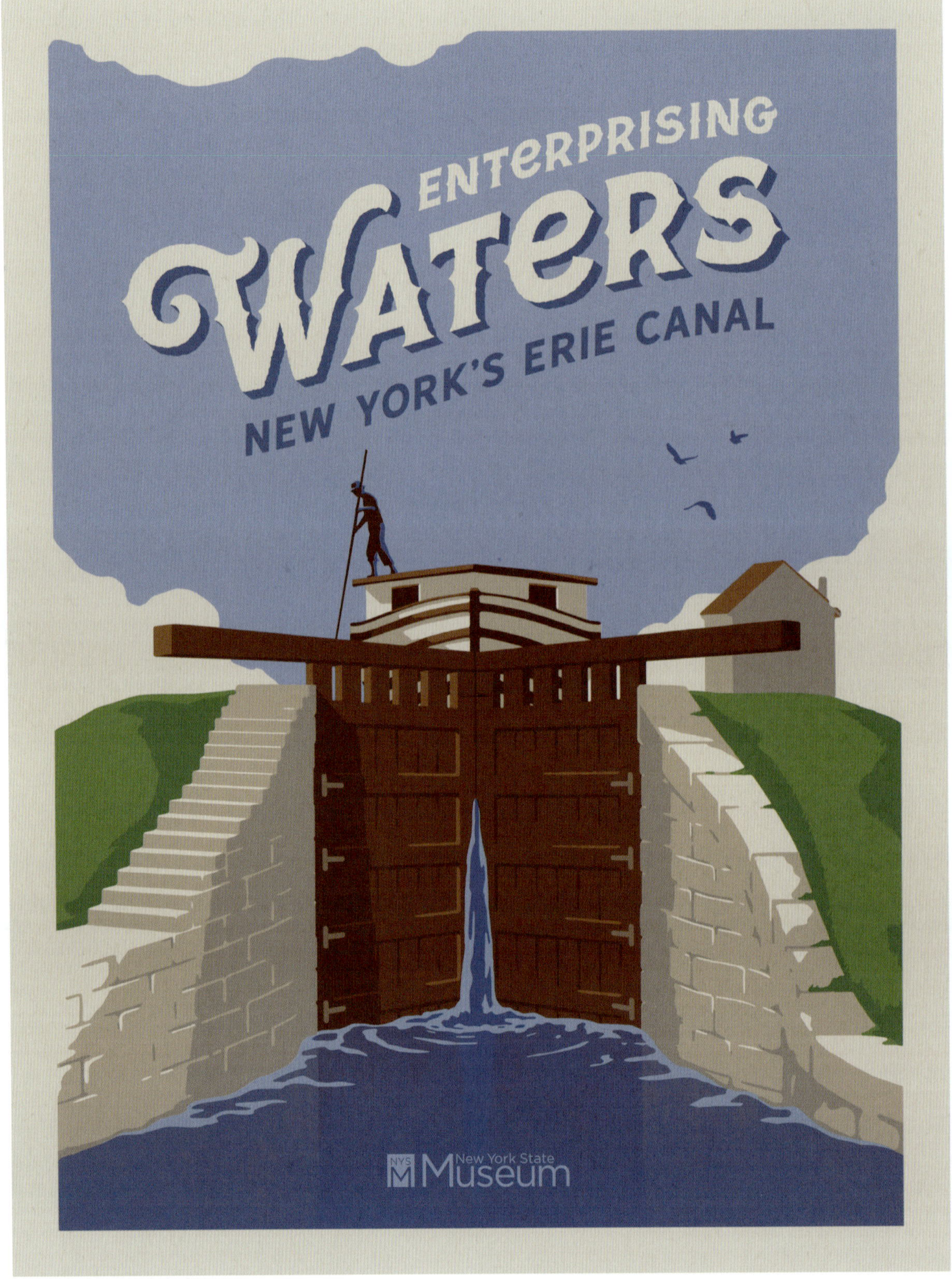

Signature graphic for the exhibit Enterprising Waters: New York's Erie Canal, designed by Christopher Havens and Ben Karis-Nix, New York State Museum, 2016. Inspired by image on page ii.

PREFACE

This catalog is a companion to two related exhibitions at the New York State Museum: *Enterprising Waters: New York's Erie Canal* (on display from September 2017 through October 25, 2020) and *Art of the Erie Canal* (on display from April through September 2018).

Enterprising Waters includes objects and images from the collections of the New York State Museum, Library, and Archives, as well as from more than thirty-five different external institutions and individual lenders. Within a five-part chronological framework presented in the gallery and this volume, from the very kernel of the idea for the Erie Canal through to today, you will see the emergence of three main themes as they relate historically to the canal's existence: politics, engineering, and commerce. These were the forces that shaped every aspect of the canal's creation two hundred years ago. In creating the exhibition, limitations in space and time forced us to make some hard decisions about what to include and what to leave out, with some objects and stories not making it into the gallery. Where possible, we have included that material in this catalog. While the exhibition addresses the canal story from the earliest calls for internal improvements to today, it is impossible to tell every story. As such, we hope that the exhibition and this catalog inspire you to find out more, seek more stories—in general to explore the Erie Canal further.

Interspersed throughout this catalog are works and text from *Art of the Erie Canal*. Some works appeared in both exhibitions. Due to the fragile nature of many of those pieces, they could be on display for only a short time. Therefore, the history exhibition used digital reproductions, and the art installation displayed the original works. In those cases, both labels appear in this catalog, as we feel they add value in different ways. Labels and text from the *Art of the Erie Canal* exhibit can be distinguished by the maroon text.

The exhibition title *Enterprising Waters* was inspired by the many enterprising efforts that it took to make the canal a reality and the endless enterprising ideas and businesses that followed in the wake of its opening. It was the enterprising waters of the Erie Canal that changed America and continue to provide avenues for enterprising people today.

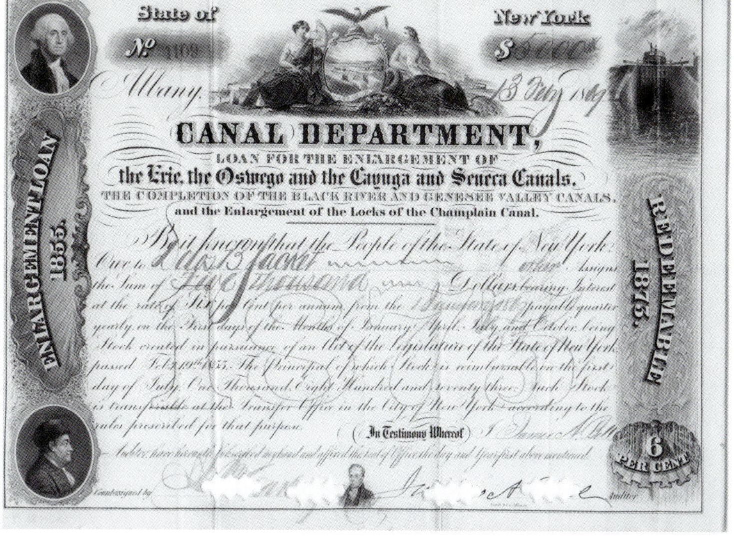

$5,000 canal stock certificate for the enlargement of the New York State canal system, 1869. The inset image in the upper right corner of this document served as the inspiration for the signature graphic of the *Enterprising Waters* exhibit, shown on page x. *New York State Museum, Mrs. Arnold B. Barben Canal Collection, H-1988.79.*

Grand Canal Celebration. Clinton Fire Company No 41. Imbert & Co., hand-colored lithograph, 1826. *New York State Museum, H-1972.123.1.*

ACKNOWLEDGMENTS

Like the Erie Canal itself, the New York State Museum's two exhibitions—*Enterprising Waters: New York's Erie Canal* and *Art of the Erie Canal*—would not have been possible without the work of many.

Starting in the fall of 2014, as we approached the 2017 bicentennial of the beginning of the construction of the canal, a few of us started visiting organizations across the state to plan for how the museum would commemorate this landmark anniversary and highlight for visitors the importance of the canal in the development of New York State and the nation. From New York City to Buffalo we were welcomed by all at every stop of the way, and the experiences proved extremely valuable. As I developed the exhibition concept and script, the works of canal historians Gerard Koeppel, Ronald E. Shaw, and Carol Sheriff proved very insightful, along with those of countless others who have shared the canal story over the past two hundred years. I am also very grateful to retired New York State Museum Senior Historian and Curator Craig Williams, who helped build the museum's wonderful canal collection and who was quick to help whenever I needed it. For me, Craig is the foremost New York State canal system expert around today.

Any exhibit must be more than just words on a wall—without objects you cannot truly bring the story to life. These exhibitions would not have been possible without artifacts, works of art, documents, photographs, and information from our lenders, many of whom we met on that first tour. In addition to our sister institutions, the New York State Library and the New York State Archives, thirty-six lenders contributed to *Enterprising Waters* and thirteen loaned artifacts to *Art of the Erie Canal.* Several people from those organizations went above and beyond to help us, with special thanks to Travis Bowman, John Callaghan, Ronna Dixson, Sue Friedlander, Thomas Hunter, Ashley Maready, Walter Mayer, Christine Olsen, Tom Ragosta, Erin Richardson, Chris Sabick, and Amanda Thompson.

The project also received help in various forms from the following individuals and organizations: Anne W. Brown; David and Elizabeth Beebe, Camillus Erie Canal Park; Christine O'Neil, Chittenango Landing Canal Boat Museum; Thomas Grasso and Dan Ward, Canal Society of New York State; Jean McKay and Bob Radliffe, Erie Canalway National Heritage Corridor; New York State Department of Transportation; Donald Nims, Bergmann Associates; and Brian Stratton, New York State Canal Corporation.

The New York State Library and New York State Archives both hold incredible canal collections. Vicki Weiss and Victor DesRosiers from the library and Andrew Arpy and Keith Swaney from the archives provided endless help in finding appropriate collections and getting them digitized for use in the exhibitions and catalog. Thank you to Julie C. Daniels, director of public broadcasting, New York State Office of Cultural Education; Tom Ruller, New York State archivist; and the late Bernard Margolis, New York State librarian, for your input and support. Two New York State Museum volunteers deserve special thanks for countless hours of help on this project. Paul Schneider assisted with research and was a great brainstorming partner. William "Bill" Schollenberger scanned thousands of canal-related images from our collections over many years, many of which appear in this catalog.

The exhibit design and production staff at the New York State Museum worked together to produce two beautiful exhibitions that enticed many thousands of visitors to step inside the galleries and enjoy and learn from everything we brought together. *Enterprising Waters*—with a giant windlass as a centerpiece—was skillfully designed by exhibit designer Craig Gravina, graphic designers Christopher Havens and Ben Karis-Nix, and the production crew led by museum exhibit specialist Scott Heydrick. The entire team was anchored by exhibit planner Carrie "The Butcher" Ross. Craig and Ben also designed *Art of the Erie Canal*, and Jill Cozzy served as the exhibition planner.

Led by Director of Exhibitions Nancy Kelley, the entire exhibit staff played a role in one or both installations. Many thanks to our colleagues Kelley Feranec, Karen Glaz, Ethan Hacklin, Chelsea Hildebrandt, Chris Kobuskie, Koren Lazarou, Tom Link, Nicholas Lue, Andrew Meier, Steve Michalek, Alan Noble, Corianne Setzer, Daniel Stienstra, Michael Sgambellone, and Tony Temple. Special thanks to John Yost, who came in to do the photography for this catalog—after he retired.

Additional thanks to museum staff, without whom thousands of students and teachers and the wider public in general might not know about this exhibition and the valuable information it is meant to relay: Kathryn Weller, director of education and public programs; Antonia Giuliano, Albert Gnidica, Nicole LaFountain; Hatti Langsford; James Jenkins; and Gina Shahinian.

My deepest thanks to my dedicated colleagues from the museum's research and collections staff and history staff, who helped provide collections and advice and reviewed the exhibition script, including Chief Curator Jennifer Lemak, John Abeel, Kara Chambers, Robert Feranec, Emily Finelli, Robyn Gibson, Ashley Hopkins-Benton, Cornelia Frisbee Houde, Andrea Lain, Devin Lander, Marian Lupulescu, Aaron Noble, Karen Quinn, Candace Sanders, Gwen Saul, and Anne Tyrrell.

Retired history staff members Jeffrey Stringer and Geoffrey Stein joined the team, much to our benefit. Jeffrey made a scale model of the windlass, and Geoffrey provided tremendous insight into the collections. Stephen Loughman, collections manager of our off-site storage warehouse, deserves extra thanks for expertly undertaking the delicate work of transporting the artifacts and art that brought both exhibitions to life.

Special thanks to Bridget Enderle, collections technician. Bridget organized each artifact and image and, working closely with John Abeel, collections technician, ensured each document was scanned or photographed and everything was in its right place at the right time. Simply put, this catalog would not have been possible without Bridget's hard work.

Thank you to Office of Cultural Education Editor Jessica Fisher Neidl for looking over the manuscript for this volume.

Amanda Lanne-Camilli, acquisitions editor at SUNY Press, gave much needed support.

Thank you, Thomas Grasso, president emeritus of the Canal Society of New York State, for writing the foreword for this volume. His years of hard work and dedication to preserving the canal story are inspiring.

A multiyear project of this scope would not be possible without institutional support, including that of the New York State Board of Regents, Chancellor Betty Rosa, and Commissioner of Education MaryEllen Elia. Mark Schaming, director of the New York State Museum and deputy commissioner of cultural education, supported this project from the beginning.

Lastly, I would like to thank my family for their support: my wife, for picking up the slack at home while I traveled across the state working on *Enterprising Waters*. She also endured countless hours of me talking about the canal and my experiences (both good and bad)—all with a smile. To my children, whom I have been dragging to canal sites and events since they were born, I am grateful for their patience and curiosity, their wonder and awe at the real thing, being at the canal. Whether it was watching a boat lock through or enjoying a bounce house alongside the Old Champlain Canal and Lock E2, they experienced many moments that help reinforce that the canal today and in the future is a great thing for our community. I hope I inspire the love of history in my kids that my mother did in me.

Enterprising Waters Lenders

Albany Distillery

Albany Institute of History & Art

Arkell Museum at Canajoharie

Canal Society of New York State*

City of Rome, New York

Clermont State Historic Site

Erie Canal Museum (Syracuse)

Erie Canalway National Heritage Corridor

Fenimore Art Museum

Richard Goodfellow

Lake Champlain Maritime Museum

Library and Archives of Canada

Library of Congress

Memorial Art Gallery

Munson-Williams-Proctor Arts Institute

New-York Historical Society

New York Public Library

New York State Canal Corporation

New York State Office of Parks, Recreation and Historic Preservation, Bureau of Historic Sites

Oneida County History Center

Onondaga Historical Association

Public Art for Public Schools

Rensselaer County Historical Society

Rhode Island School of Design

Rochester Historical Society

Rochester Museum & Science Center

Sackets Harbor Battlefield State Historic Site

---

* Major lender.

Schenectady County Historical Society

Schuyler Mansion State Historic Site

John Scherer

William Skerritt

Len F. Tantillo

The Buffalo History Museum

The Farmers' Museum, Inc.

Waterford Historical Museum and Cultural Center

Watervliet Historical Society

Francis D. Wright III

Art of the Erie Canal grew out of the history exhibition when we realized that we had another story to tell that we couldn't tackle in *Enterprising Waters* because of both space and time constraints. Curators Ashley Hopkins-Benton and Karen Quinn did a tremendous job putting together a wide variety of works that were inspired by the canal and tell the story of its impact in another way.

Art of the Erie Canal LENDERS

Albany Institute of History & Art

Alexandra C. Anderson

Arkell Museum at Canajoharie*

Dolores Elliot

Erie Canal Museum (Syracuse)

Fenimore Art Museum

Memorial Art Gallery of the University of Rochester

Munson-Williams-Proctor Arts Institute

New-York Historical Society

Onondaga Historical Association

Private Collection

Rochester Historical Society

Union College

* Major lender.

INTRODUCTIONS

INTRODUCTION TO *Enterprising Waters: New York's Erie Canal*

> **Why sir, here is a canal for a few miles, projected by George Washington, which if completed, would render this a fine commercial city, which has languished for many years because the small sum of 200,000 dollars necessary to complete it, cannot be obtained from the general government, the state governments, or from individuals—and you talk of making a canal 350 miles through the wilderness—it is a little short of madness to think of it in this day.**
>
> **—Attributed to President Thomas Jefferson, January 1809[1]**

The Erie Canal is the most influential human-made waterway in American history. It opened the way to the North American interior from the Atlantic seaboard and established New York as the leading state in population, industry, and wealth for much of the nineteenth century.

New York and the Erie Canal, by William Wall, oil on canvas, 1862. This is a view of the Mohawk Valley, looking west. Although painted in 1862, this view does not show the railroad, which ran along the northern side of the Mohawk River at that time. The canal is depicted to the left of the river, skirting along the base of the hills as it passes through a break in the mountains. *Courtesy of the Arkell Museum at Canajoharie. Gift of Bartlett Arkell, 1934.*

Two hundred years ago, the United States was a young republic. While most of the population lived along the East Coast, a vast, untapped region lay to the west. Travel into North America's interior was difficult and costly. As citizens called for improved internal trade routes, it was the government of New York State that responded to their calls. In the process, these New Yorkers defined what was possible and, later, expected of their government when it comes to the creation and maintenance of public works.

In a remarkable feat of engineering and grueling labor, the Erie Canal, the combined effort of legislators and laborers, was built from Albany to Buffalo. In eight years, surveyors, engineers, and excavators carved out 363 miles of canal through breaks in the mountain ranges that had previously kept the westward progress of commerce and settlement to a trickle. When the Erie Canal opened in 1825, what had been considered "little short of madness" at its theoretical conception had unlocked the western interior for trade and settlement and solidified New York City as the nation's most powerful commercial center. Indeed, the enterprising waters of the Erie Canal created a new commercial reality in the United States, playing a critical role in the economic, social, and cultural development of the state and the nation.

—Brad L. Utter, Senior Historian and Curator, New York State Museum

INTRODUCTION TO *Art of the Erie Canal*

The Erie Canal, one of the foremost engineering marvels of the nineteenth century, sparked the imagination of artists in America and abroad. This companion exhibition to *Enterprising Waters: New York's Erie Canal* looks at the art inspired by the canal and the opportunities the canal afforded artists both trained and untrained, working in a variety of media.

As the Erie Canal was being constructed, landscape painting in the United States was in its infancy, but distinctly American subjects, such as the Hudson River valley and the Catskills, appealed to a rising romanticism in art and literature. The canal opened passage from Albany to Buffalo, making new vistas and landscapes available to artists. Some of the images these artists created were celebratory, others bucolic, some idealized, and still others showed ambivalence toward this human-made waterway's intrusion upon nature. For some painters, the growth of industry was seen as positive—a harmonious integration of business expanding into the landscape, or a focus on the new structures themselves in increasingly urban surroundings. Later artists featured the fate of the buildings and towns as fortunes declined, and still others looked back upon the heyday of canal prosperity with nostalgia.

The popularity of the canal and increasing tourism led to a demand for souvenirs. Erie Canal images in paintings, prints, and ceramics were soon available to the public—from bird's-eye views of boomtowns to vignettes of natural landmarks such as waterfalls. Increasing affluence along the canal provided new, local patronage for art. Portrait commissions and images of private and commercial property were sought by the rising population of entrepreneurs and others. The selection of works in this exhibition is just a small sample of the wealth of Erie Canal art put forth over the course of its first 150 years.

—Ashley Hopkins-Benton, Senior Historian and Curator, New York State Museum
Karen Quinn, Senior Historian and Curator, New York State Museum

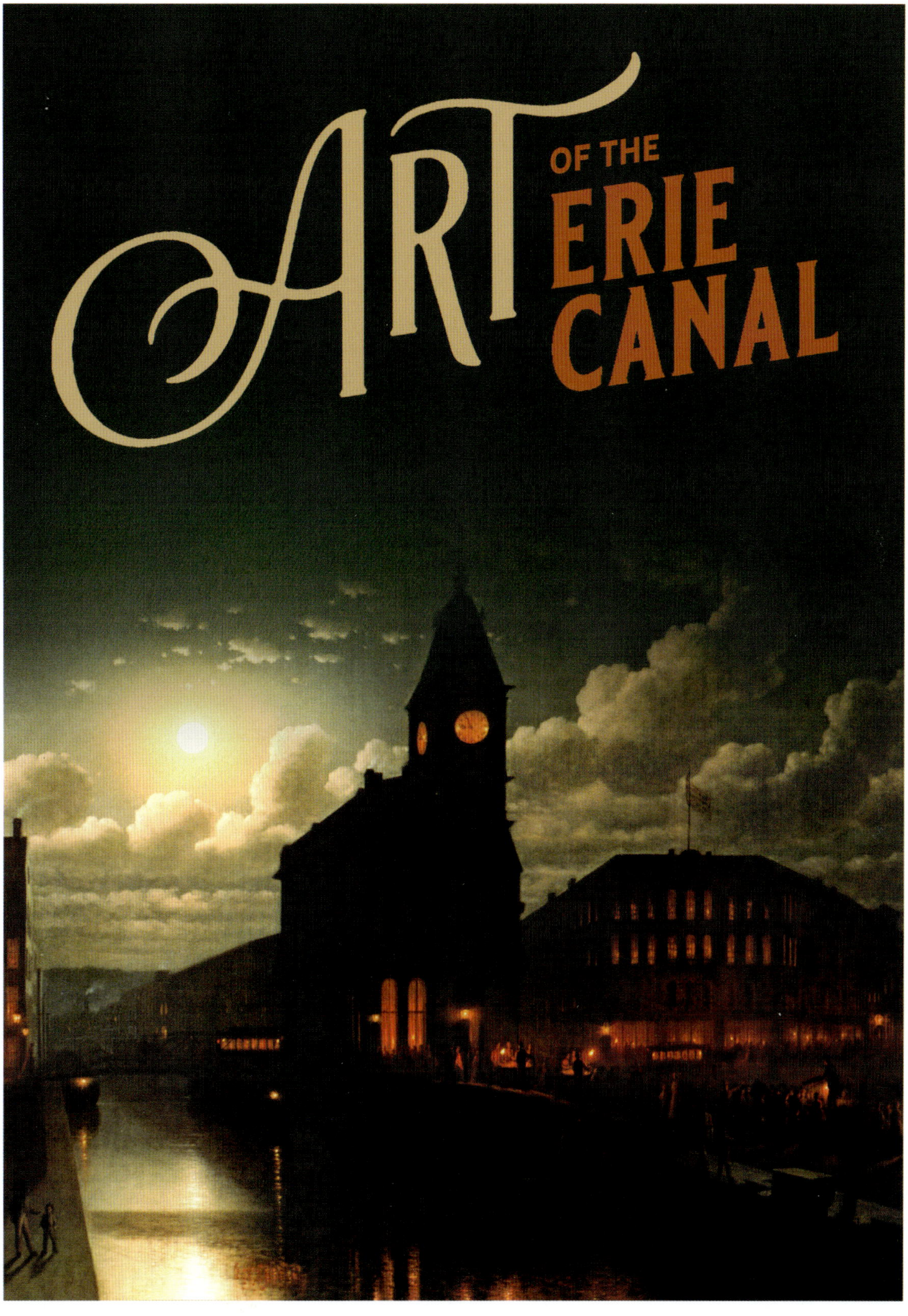

Signature graphic for the exhibit *Art of the Erie Canal*, featuring Clinton Square, Syracuse, New York (Syracuse by Moonlight), ca. 1871, by Johann Mengels Culverhouse.

The Great Water-Fall on the Mohawk River, engraving, artist unknown, ca. 1778. Unlike the Hudson River, the Mohawk River was not deep and had two major waterfalls, Cohoes Falls (pictured above) and Little Falls, which were impossible to navigate. New York State Museum, H-1980.96.17.

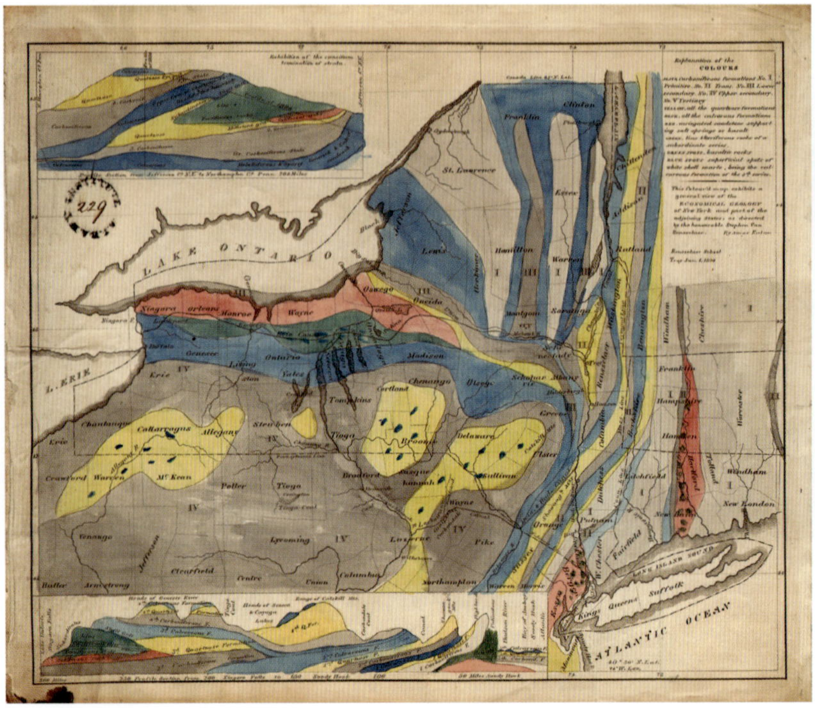

General View of the Economical Geology of New York and Part of Adjoining States, map, Amos Eaton, 1830. Multiple economic surveys were conducted in the state to document the valuable natural resources. This map helps demonstrate the gap in the mountain ranges. Courtesy of the Albany Institute of History & Art, Map 221.

PART I

Before the Canal

> My teams have been out for Albany now 17 days and no tidings of them yet, I am informed the roads were never known to have been as bad as this autumn and winter, indeed some wholly impassable—some wagons would have nine horses before them.
>
> —Samuel S. Forman,
> merchant from Cazenovia, New York, December 25, 1803[1]

New York State's landscape has greatly influenced its history. Its natural waterways afforded Native peoples and early European explorers and settlers with travel and trade routes. These waterways were vital in the military conflicts that raged along the North American frontier during the eighteenth and early nineteenth centuries. New York was frequently at the crossroads for invading armies.

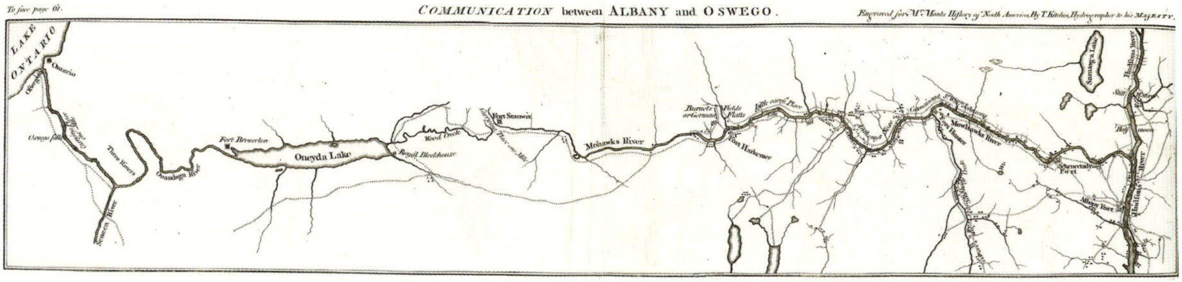

Communication between Albany and Oswego, map, T. Kitchin, 1772. Colonists used ancient Native American trade routes that followed New York's natural waterways. Turnpikes (toll roads) were in use by 1800, but they were not much more than dirt paths. The turnpikes were ill-suited for large-scale commerce by land. *Courtesy of the New York State Library, Manuscripts and Special Collections, V973.26qM29.*

Iron kettles, jaw harp, trade axes, trade beads, metal arrow points, seventeenth and eighteenth centuries.

Beginning in the early seventeenth century, Iroquoian and Algonquian peoples provided beaver pelts to Dutch traders in exchange for European-made objects. Axes, kettles, beads, and other European goods were incorporated into and often modified to fit existing Native cultural practices, such as arrowheads being cut out of copper kettles obtained by trade. *New York State Museum Archeology Collections.*

Copper ring, ca. 1660.
This copper Jesuit trade ring was found in Onondaga County in the early twentieth century. French Jesuit missionaries traveled the Mohawk River valley to proselytize the Haudenosaunee. *New York State Museum, H-XX.200.2.*

Clinton's Brigade at Canajoharie, Edward Buyck, oil on canvas, ca. 1929.
A colonial army travels west through the Mohawk Valley in 1779. The rough terrain and poor roads made the large-scale movement of an army difficult. Note the bateaux on wheels in this painting. *Courtesy of the Arkell Museum at Canajoharie, Gift of Bartlett Arkell, 1929.*

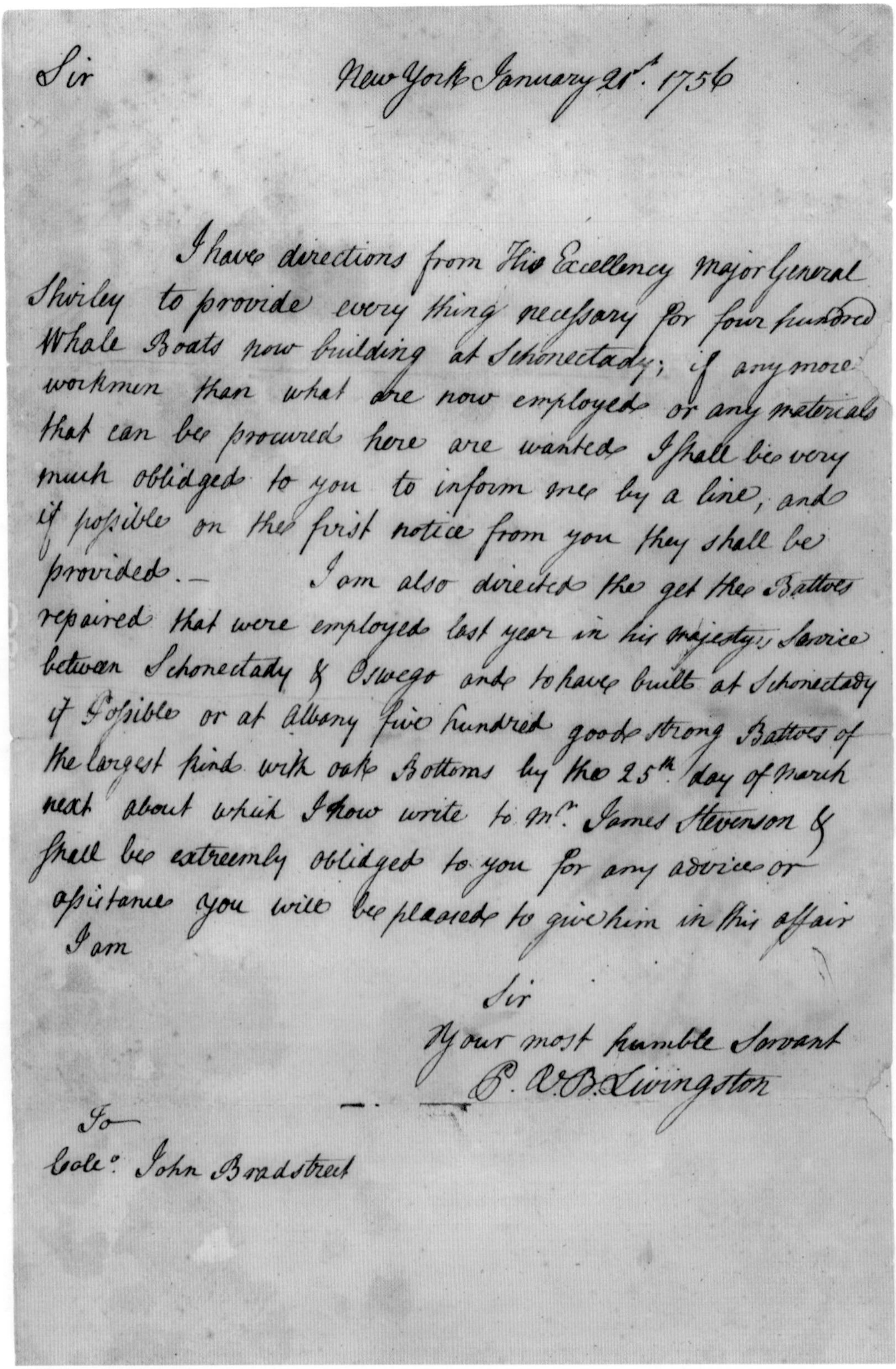

Sir New York January 21st. 1756

I have directions from His Excellency Major General Shirley to provide every thing necessary for four hundred Whale Boats now building at Schonectady; if any more workmen than what are now employed or any materials that can be procured here are wanted I shall be very much obliged to you to inform me by a line, and if possible on the first notice from you they shall be provided.— I am also directed the get the Battoes repaired that were employed last year in his Majestys Service between Schonectady & Oswego and to have built at Schonectady if Possible or at Albany five hundred good strong Battoes of the largest kind with oak Bottoms by the 25th. day of March next about which I now write to Mr. James Stevenson & shall be extreemly obliged to you for any advice or assitance you will be pleased to give him in this affair

I am

Sir

Your most humble Servant

P. V. B. Livingston

To

Coll.o John Bradstreet

Letter, P. B. V. Livingston to Col. John Bradstreet, January 21, 1756. This letter discusses the construction of bateaux and whale boats at Schenectady and Albany to be used between Schenectady and Oswego by the British army during the French and Indian War. *New York State Museum, H-1983.1.1.*

Section of bateau, ca. 1758. Prior to the Erie Canal, the best way to travel shallow waters was by bateau (French for "boat"). This bateau may have been part of British major general James Abercrombie's flotilla, constructed at Albany and Lake George during the French and Indian War. *New York State Museum, H-INV 2626.*

Powder horn, ca. 1760. This French and Indian War powder horn is etched with a map of the colony of New York. The strategic locations of the Hudson and Mohawk Rivers and Lake Champlain are prominently featured, demonstrating the significance of these waterways. *New York State Museum, H-1970.117.1.*

Potash or pot-ash kettle, early nineteenth century. Potash, an important early trading commodity, is a type of salt made by soaking plant ashes and was used primarily as fertilizer. When settlers cleared land for farming, they often used ashes from burning tree stumps to make potash. This commodity was often the only source of income for new settlers until the first crops were harvested. *Collection of The Farmers' Museum, Inc. Gift of Donald Jordan.*

The Hudson River and Mohawk River valleys together formed the most navigable break through the Adirondack Mountains to the north and the Appalachian Mountains to the south, making the passage the best location to construct a canal to connect the Atlantic to the North American interior.

The natural landscape of New York State provided the stage for the dreamers, promoters, speculators, politicians, engineers, and laborers, who all played a part in making the canal a reality. The process was not smooth or quick, but the end result was an engineering marvel and a symbol of the power and resourcefulness of the republican form of government.

IMPROVED WATERWAYS

Concerned over the loss of trade to Canada and a general need for improved inland navigation, the New York State Legislature authorized the exploration, survey, and estimates for improved inland transportation in 1791. Two private companies began work a year later. The Western Inland Lock Navigation Company (WILNC) explored the route from the Hudson River west to Wood Creek (Fort Stanwix/Rome) and north to Lake Ontario (Oswego). The Northern Inland Lock Navigation Company (NILNC) would study the Hudson River from Troy to Lake Champlain at Whitehall.

Both companies struggled, and the NILNC soon ceased operations. The WILNC successfully built three short canals and improved the waterways between Schenectady and Oswego. The company operated until the State purchased it in 1820. Both companies' efforts highlighted the potential for a canal as well as the need for an artificial waterway.

A View of Boats & Manner of Navigating on the Mohawk River, Christian Schultz, engraving, 1810. To improve the Mohawk River for navigation, the WILNC made wing dams that funneled water toward a central point, increasing the depth so boats could pass. *Courtesy of the New York State Library, Manuscripts and Special Collections, N 917.3 S38.*

Philip Schuyler (1733–1804)

Philip Schuyler was a leading political figure in colonial New York, one of the four major generals in the Continental Army and a member of the Continental Congress. His estates shipped goods to New York City, and Schuyler became an advocate for improved inland navigation. From 1791 to 1804, he was president of the Western and Northern Inland Lock Navigation companies (WILNC and NILNC).

Major General Philip Schuyler, John Trumbull (artist), Thomas Kelly (engraver), ca. first half of the nineteenth century. *Courtesy of the New York Public Library.*

WILLIAM WESTON (1763–1833)

As one of the only trained engineers working in America in the 1790s, William Weston was highly sought after both for his opinion and services. The English canal engineer oversaw part of the Western Inland Lock Navigation Company's construction of locks. He served as a mentor for Benjamin Wright, who went on to play a major role in the Erie Canal project. Weston was requested to review the canal commissioner's proposed plans for the Erie Canal and he agreed it was viable, adding professional credibility to the project. The retired engineer was living at home in England when he was offered the position of chief engineer to oversee the construction of the Erie Canal, but he declined, citing his retirement.

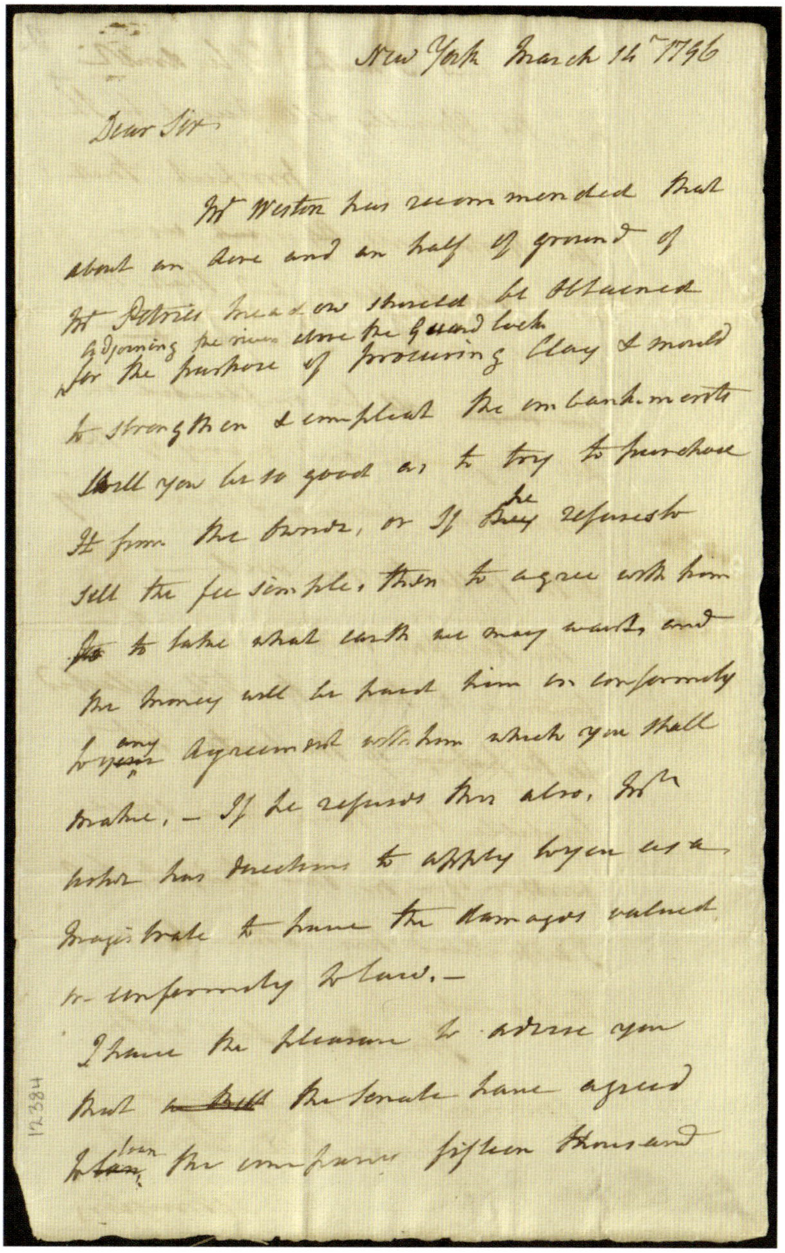

New York March 14th 1796

Dear Sir

Mr Weston has recommended that about an acre and an half of ground of Mr Petries meadow should be obtained adjoining the river above the guard lock for the purpose of procuring Clay & mould to strengthen & compleat the embankments. Will you be so good as to try to purchase it from the owner, or if he refuses to sell the fee simple, then to agree with him to take what earth we may want, and the money will be paid him in conformity to any agreement with him which you shall make. — If he refuses this also, Mr [illegible] who has directions to apply to you as a Magistrate to have the damages valued in conformity to law. —

I have the pleasure to advise you that the Senate have agreed to loan the companies fifteen thousand

Letter, Philip Schuyler to unknown, March 14, 1796. Based on the recommendation of English engineer William Weston, Schuyler requests the recipient try to purchase land for clay to improve an earthen wall near a guard lock and make other improvements to the WILNC works. *Courtesy of the New York State Library, Manuscripts and Special Collections, Schuyler Family Collection, SC19811.*

NEW LINE.

THE subscribers inform the public, that they have established a line of *STAGE BOATS*, to ply between this city and Utica, for the accommodation of passengers from the latter place, and to carry up such valuable articles of merchandize, &c. as require the utmost care and dispatch. One Boat will leave Utica every Monday and Wednesday morning, and Schenectady every Wednesday and Friday morning. For passage at Utica, apply to A. Van Santvoord & Co.

THE OLD LINE CONTINUED,

From Schenectady for Oswego, Cayuga, and Seneca Falls. One Boat will satrt regularly every Saturday, during the season. Goods received between Saturday and Tuesday evening, to be forwarded beyond Utica, will be put on board the *Stage Boat* of Wednesday morning, and will overtake the Saturday's boat, at Utica, where they will be put on board and forwarded as directed.

Wagons will, as heretofore, be kept in constant readiness to transport from the city of Albany to Schenectady, or any part of the United States and Canada. Gentlemen who reside at a distance from the water communication are informed, that their goods will be delivered from the boats at any place they may think proper to designate ; and at the Seneca Falls, to avoid delays, wagons are provided to convey the property, if required, to its place of destination.

The subscribers consider themselves the actual carriers, and responsible for all property passing through their hands, unavoidable accidents excepted.

Eri Lusher & Co.

Schenectady, May 1, 1815.

RIGGS & STEVENS, Printers—Schenectady.

Broadside announcing a "New Line" of "stage boats," Eri Lusher & Co., Schenectady, 1815. This shipping business used the WILNC's improved waterways. The WILNC's canals were plagued by varying water levels, high construction and maintenance costs, and a lack of laborers that resulted in expensive tolls. There were little or no profits for its investors, except for a short period around the end of the War of 1812. *Courtesy of Oneida County History Center, Utica, New York.*

Old Lock from the WILNC Canal at Little Falls, photograph series, 1921. Remnants of the WILNC Canal exist to this day. These photographs from 1921 are of an original lock in Little Falls. *Courtesy of the New York State Archives, 17672-13.*

(page 12–13)
Schenectady Harbor, 1814, L. F. Tantillo, *oil on canvas, 1992.* Schenectady was the eastern terminal for Mohawk River traffic. This depiction of the waterfront illustrates the businesses and warehouses involved in the river trade. The community did not welcome the Erie Canal, since it bypassed the traditional waterfront. *Courtesy of L. F. Tantillo.*

J. MYNDERSE
L.F. TANTILLO '92

Stoneware barrel cooler, Moses Tyler and Charles Dillon (1825–1834), Albany, New York, ca. 1830. This stoneware cooler is incised and decorated with a bateau. Bateaux were generally smaller than the Durham boats used to navigate the Mohawk River after the WILNC improved the route. *New York State Museum, H-2004.46.2.*

Pike point, ca. 1790–1820. Men used pikes on poles to propel bateaux and Durham boats. Recounting his travel on the Mohawk River in 1807, Christian Schultz described the pike poles that the boatmen used to move the boats against the current as follows: ". . . their chief dependence, therefore, is upon their pike poles. These are generally from eighteen to twenty-two feet in length, having a sharp pointed iron with a socket weighing ten or twelve pounds affixed to the lower end . . ."* New York State Museum, H-2000.35.1. *Christian Schultz, *Travels on an Inland Voyage through the States of New-York, Pennsylvania, Virginia, Ohio, Kentucky and Tennessee and through the Territories of Indiana, Louisiana, Mississippi and New-Orleans* Vol. I [microform] (New York: Isaac Riley, 1814), 5.

Model of a Durham boat, Robert E. Hager, ca. 1965. The Durham boat, or Schenectady boat, was larger than a bateau and was used to carry freight once the WILNC made passage possible through to Oswego. *Courtesy of the Canal Society of New York State.*

American Stage Coach, W. H. Lizars after Basil Hall, engraving, ca. 1827. Basil Hall, a British naval officer who documented his experiences traveling in America in 1827 and 1828, made this sketch. Prior to the canal, the stagecoach was the main vehicle for transporting people long distances across the state. Captain Basil Hall, Royal Navy, *Travels in North America in the Years 1827 and 1828* (Philadelphia: Carey, Lea & Carey, 1829). *Courtesy of the New York State Library, Manuscripts and Special Collections, N 917.3 qH168.*

The single-masted Hudson River sloop was the most commonly used vessel for transporting cargo between New York City and Albany during the late 1700s and early 1800s.

Model of a Hudson River sloop, Jack Lowe, 1974. *New York State Museum, H-1976.111.1A.*

Panorama of the Hudson Highlands, mixed media on paper, Montgomery Livingston, ca. 1840. *Courtesy of Clermont State Historic Site, Germantown, New York, New York State Office of Parks, Recreation and Historic Preservation. Photograph © Chris Kendall 2007.*

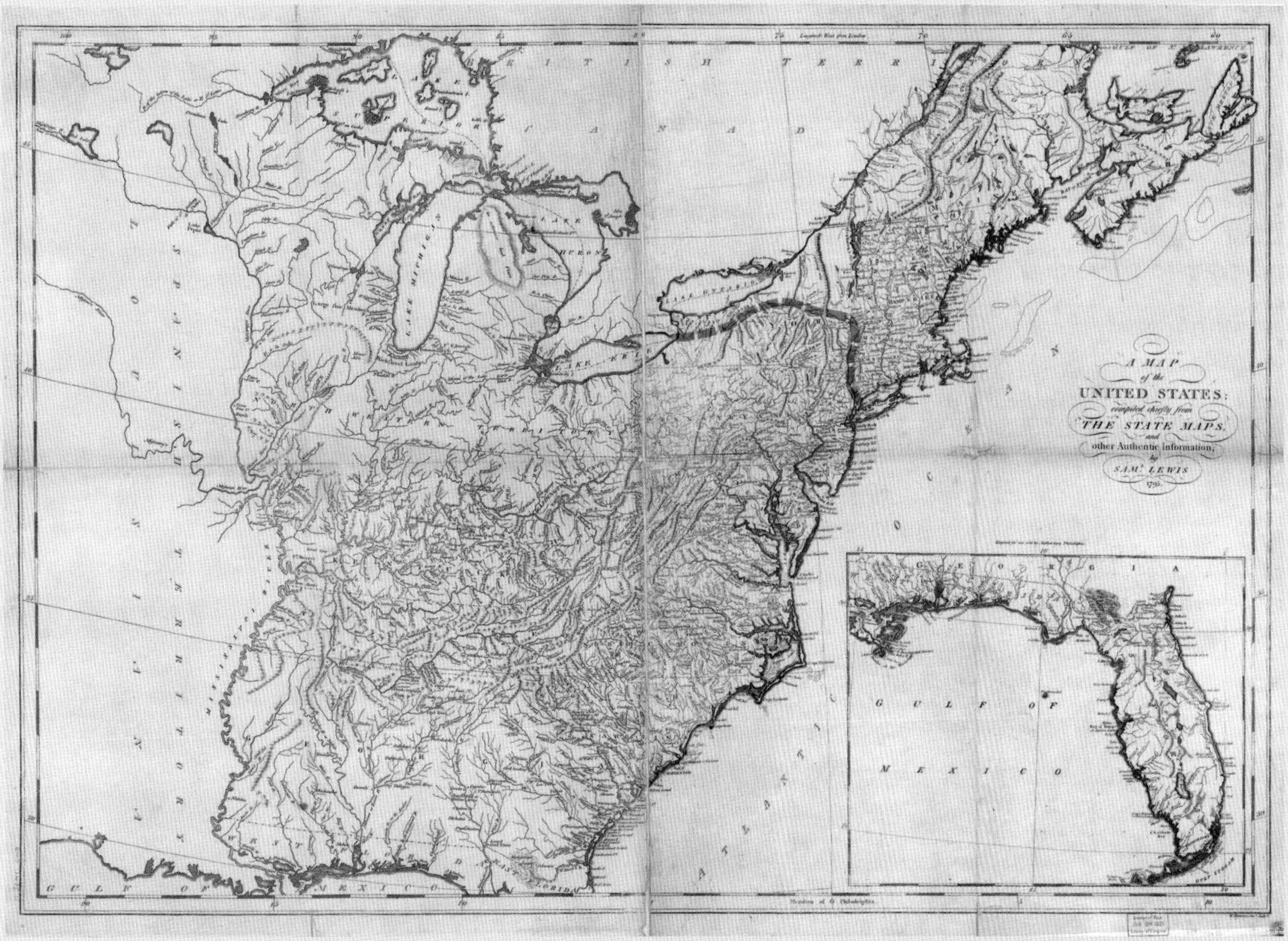

A map of the United States compiled chiefly from the state maps and other authentic information by Sam Lewis, 1795. The blue dotted line denotes the break in the mountain chains and the eventual path of the Erie Canal. *Courtesy of the Library of Congress.*

EARLY SUPPORTERS OF AN INLAND CANAL

> . . . by this, the internal trade will be increased—by this also the foreign trade will be promoted—by this the country will be settled—by this the frontiers will be secured—by this a variety of articles, as masts, yards, and ship timber may be brought to New York, which will not bear the expense of land carriage, . . . by this, in time of war provisions and military stores may be moved with facility in sufficient quantity to answer any emergency, and by this in time of peace all necessaries, conveniences, and if we please luxuries of life, may be distributed to the remotest parts of the GREAT LAKES . . . and to the smallest branches of the numerous rivers which shoot from these lakes upon every point of the compass.
>
> —Christopher Colles, Irish American engineer, 1785[2]

(facing page)
Engraving by John L. Morton based on sketch by Stephen H. Gimber, 1829. Although De Witt Clinton is considered the "Father of the Erie Canal," the concept of a canal was debated for decades before he became involved. The credit goes to many people working over a long period of time, as seen in this pillar from David Hosack's 1829 *Memoir of De Witt Clinton*, celebrating the men whose actions or support helped make the canal a reality. *Courtesy of the New York State Library, Manuscripts and Special Collections, 974.7 Zc6h 1967.*

Gouverneur Morris (1752–1816) was a Founding Father and early canal commissioner who preferred a canal using inclined planes rather than a lift-lock system. Philip Schuyler credited Morris for promoting the canal idea to him during the Revolution.

Cadwallader Colden (1688–1776), surveyor-general of the province of New York, was concerned about losing trade with the Native Americans and implored Governor William Burnet to improve internal navigation.

George Washington (1732–1799) strongly supported internal improvements. He correctly predicted that the success of a canal through New York would help to bind the Union.

Christopher Colles (1739–1816) presented a plan for short canals that would allow larger boats to pass from the Hudson River to the Mohawk River, to Wood Creek (near Rome), and on to Lake Ontario to the state legislature in 1785, but legislators never voted on it.

Jeffrey Smith (1734–1812), a member of the New York State Assembly from Suffolk County, supported Colles's plan in 1785.

Elkanah Watson (1758–1842) helped start and run the Western Inland Lock Navigation Company. In 1820 he wrote *History of the Rise, Progress and Existing Conditions of the Western Canals in the State of New York*, in which he claimed to be the true originator of the Erie Canal idea.

Philip Schuyler (1733–1804), the well-connected Federalist, served as president of the Western Inland Lock Navigation Lock Company and Northern Inland Lock Navigation Company.

George Clinton (1739–1812) was two-time governor of New York (1777–1795, 1801–1804), the vice president of the United States (1805–1812), and uncle to De Witt Clinton. In 1786 Clinton encouraged the state legislature to improve natural waterways.

Jesse Hawley (1773–1842) is credited with being the earliest person to publish a plan for a canal from Lake Erie to the Hudson River. Between 1807 and 1808 Hawley authored of a series of letters published in newspapers and was the first to promote the benefits of a canal to the broader public.

Joshua Forman (1777–1849) was elected to the New York State Assembly from Onondaga County on a "canal ticket" in 1807. In 1808 he and Benjamin Wright introduced a resolution for a survey and to explore the best route for a canal between the Hudson and Lake Erie, to be financed by Congress.

Thomas Eddy (1758–1827) was treasurer of the Western Inland Lock Navigation Company, helped create the 1810 legislation to establish a board of canal commissioners, and served as canal commissioner.

Jonas Platt (1776–1834) also helped to establish the board of canal commissioners in 1810. As a New York State Supreme Court judge, Platt supported the Canal Law of 1817 in the Council of Revision.

Stephen van Rensselaer III (1774–1839) was a long-serving member of the canal commission and elected to posts in state and federal government as a Federalist. He was one of the largest landowners in the United States and a founding patron of Rensselaer Polytechnic Institute.

Cadwallader D. Colden (1769–1834) was a stockholder in Western Inland Lock Navigation Company and the only member of New York City delegation to vote in favor of the canals. In 1825 he authored Memoir, Prepared at the Request of a Committee of the Common Council of the City of New York, and Presented to the Mayor of the City, at the Celebration of the Completion of the New York Canals. He was the grandson of Cadwallader Colden (1688–1776).

De Witt Clinton (1769–1828) served as canal commissioner (1810–1824) and later as governor of New York (1817–1822, 1825–1828). Clinton was the main political force behind the building of the Erie Canal. His detractors called the project "Clinton's Ditch" and "Clinton's Folly" until its success became evident, and then he was heralded as the "Father of the Erie Canal."

Creating an artificial waterway through rugged wilderness required skill, labor, and funds on a scale never before seen in the young republic. George Washington felt that improved inland navigation would help bind the new nation. New immigrants and settlers in the western territories had no more reason to support the United States than Spain or England, but a reliable trade route and the resulting commercial ties could create kinship and loyalty between people on the Atlantic coast and the inland territories. Washington believed that through "the cement of interest alone we can be held together."[3]

Canal promotors argued that New York's geography offered the ideal natural corridor. A canal would allow access to the East, open up the West for settlement, create new markets for commerce, and keep the bulk of western American trade from rival European powers. General George Washington noted in 1784:

> Extend the inland navigation of the eastern waters; communicate them as near as possible with those which run westward; open these to the Ohio towards Lake Erie; and we shall draw the produce of the western settlers, but the peltry and fur trade of the lakes also, to our ports; thus adding immense increase to our exports, and binding these people to us by a chain which can never be broken.[4]

Gouverneur Morris (1752–1816)

As a young man, Gouverneur Morris attended King's College (now Columbia University) and became an attorney in New York City. He served in the Colonial General Assembly, the New York Provincial Assembly, and the Continental Congress, and he helped draft the US Constitution.

De Witt Clinton and others recruited Morris to the cause of the Erie Canal. A devoted Federalist, Morris favored a strong central government and approved of government funding for such public works.

As a Founding Father, Morris provided backing of critical weight and helped convince others to lend their support to the canal. His support for an inclined plane canal from Lake Erie to the Hudson was an obstacle the other commissioners tried to hide because that plan was seen as impossible. Morris felt that one long incline from Albany to Lake Erie could be accomplished with water for the entire route supplied by Lake Erie. Where possible, the canal would be relatively level, but when a major change of elevation was needed, boats would float onto a carriage that would run on tracks to the next level (instead of a lift lock). The carriage would be horse powered. Morris died in November 1816, eight months before the groundbreaking of the Erie Canal. *Courtesy of New York Public Library.*

Jesse Hawley (1773–1842), unknown artist, *oil on canvas, ca. 1825.* Jesse Hawley, a failed Geneva, New York, merchant, is credited with being the first to publish a plan for a canal from Lake Erie to the Hudson River. Between 1807 and 1808, Hawley penned a series of fourteen letters under the name "Hercules" to promote the canal. Although he had no formal engineering training, Hawley accurately predicted the route and cost of the Erie Canal, as well as how the state and New York City would be transformed. *Private Collection of Richard Goodfellow.*

world.

It remains for a free State to create a new era in history, and to erect a work more stupendous, more magnificent, and more beneficial, than has hitherto been achieved by the human race. Character is as important to nations as to individuals — and the glory of a republic, founded on the promotion of the general good, is the common property of all its citizens.

We have thus discharged with frankness and plainness and with every sentiment of respect, a great duty to ourselves, to our fellow citizens, and to posterity, in presenting this subject to the fathers of the commonwealth — and may that Almighty Being, in whose hands are the destinies of States and Nations, enlighten your councils, and invigorate your exertions in favor of the best interests of our beloved Country.

New York February 1816 —

"New York Memorial," petition, 1816. In 1816, De Witt Clinton presented this petition signed by New York City merchants and others to a joint committee of the New York State Senate and Assembly, urging legislators to approve construction of a canal system between the Hudson River and Lake Erie. The petition became known as the "New York Memorial" and it helped mobilize favorable public opinion at a time when prospects were low. The Memorial also inspired more cities and towns along the proposed canal route to submit petitions of their own. This pressure helped to put the canal back on the legislative table. Eventually, a bill authorizing detailed surveys and exploration of funding options was approved. *Courtesy of the New York State Archives, NYSA_A4682-99_B20_F2_s1.*

THE WAR OF 1812

New York's frontier played a major role in the early colonial wars, the Revolutionary War, and the War of 1812. During the wars, it was not only important to protect trade routes but also to ensure that they could not be used as corridors for invading armies. The poor roads and lack of navigable waterways from Albany to the frontier, however, made it more expensive to ship supplies to the war front than the cost to have them manufactured. America's wartime experience in western New York helped to emphasize the need for a canal for national defense.

Battle of Queenston Heights, Thomas Sutherland after James B. Dennis, engraving, 1836. On October 13, 1812, American forces under New York State Militia major general Stephen van Rensselaer launched an attack near the village of Queenston (in present-day Ontario) along the Niagara Frontier in an effort to gain a foothold on the Canadian side of the river for a larger invasion of Canada. The poorly coordinated attack resulted in nine hundred American prisoners and a British victory. *Courtesy of the Library and Archives of Canada.*

War of 1812 storage chest, ca. 1812–1815. This rare War of 1812 ammunition chest originally sat on one or two sets of wheels and housed cannonballs and items used to operate the cannon. The lack of proper roads in the region made the transport of artillery a serious problem for the American army. The design of this type of chest enabled troops to maneuver over obstacles more easily than with a wagon with four fixed wheels. The chest could be lifted off one or both sets of wheels as needed. *Courtesy of Sackets Harbor Battlefield State Historic Site, Sackets Harbor, New York, Office of Parks, Recreation and Historic Preservation.*

Saber, Lemuel Wells & Co., ca. 1800–1810. This saber likely belonged to Solomon van Rensselaer (1774–1852), who served as a lieutenant colonel in the New York Volunteers during the War of 1812. Solomon served alongside his cousin Stephen van Rensselaer at the Battle of Queenston Heights on the Niagara Frontier. After the war, both men were advocates for an inland canal in New York, likely due to their experiences during the War of 1812. *New York State Museum, H-1955.1.1.*

Musket, Smith Cogswell, 1810. New York governor Daniel D. Tompkins contracted production of 750 muskets from Smith Cogswell, who operated an iron works in Albany. In September 1814 the State of New York ordered an additional five hundred firearms at a cost of $13 per musket. After the war, Smith Cogswell continued to manufacture firearms, and many were sent west on the Erie Canal. *New York State Museum, H-1970.22.3.*

Belt plates, British Royal Army, ca. 1800–1810. These belt buckles, or plates, for the Eighth (King's) Regiment of Foot and the One Hundredth (Prince Regent's County of Dublin) Regiment of Foot were excavated along the Niagara Frontier. During the first two years of the War of 1812, much of the conflict centered along New York's border with Canada. *New York State Museum, H-1972.37.5-.6.*

S.E. View of Albany, from Greenbush Ferry, engraving, 1842.
John Warner Barber and Henry Howe, *Historical Collections of the State of New York; Containing a General Collection of the Most Interesting Facts, Traditions, Biographical Sketches, Anecdotes, &c., Relating to Its History and Antiquities, with Geographical Descriptions of Every Township in the State* (New York: S. Tuttle, 1842). *Courtesy of the New York State Library, Manuscripts and Special Collections, 974.7 B23a3.*

PART II

Clinton's Ditch

> No single act—no public measure—except the Declaration of Independence, and the formation of the United States Constitution, has done so much to promote the public prosperity and produce a new era in the history of the country, as the construction of the Erie Canal.
>
> —Jesse Hawley, 1840[1]

De Witt Clinton became one of the strongest proponents of the Erie Canal, and the success or failure of the project weighed heavily on his reputation, hence the moniker Clinton's Ditch. Building the canal would prove challenging, both politically and physically. Once completed, it was an immediate success: shipping costs plummeted, and new services and goods became widely available. Cheap, reliable transportation opened new markets to farmers and businessmen, creating a commercial windfall from New York City to Buffalo. Drawn to new opportunities, settlers moved westward, and forests soon transformed into new communities. "Clinton's Ditch" was no longer used as a derogatory term for the grand Erie Canal.

QUICK FACTS ABOUT THE ORIGINAL CANAL

363 miles long

40 feet wide at the water surface, 28 feet wide at the bottom, 4 feet deep

83 locks, each 90 feet by 15 feet

Overcame a 568-foot change in elevation from the Hudson River to Lake Erie

18 aqueducts

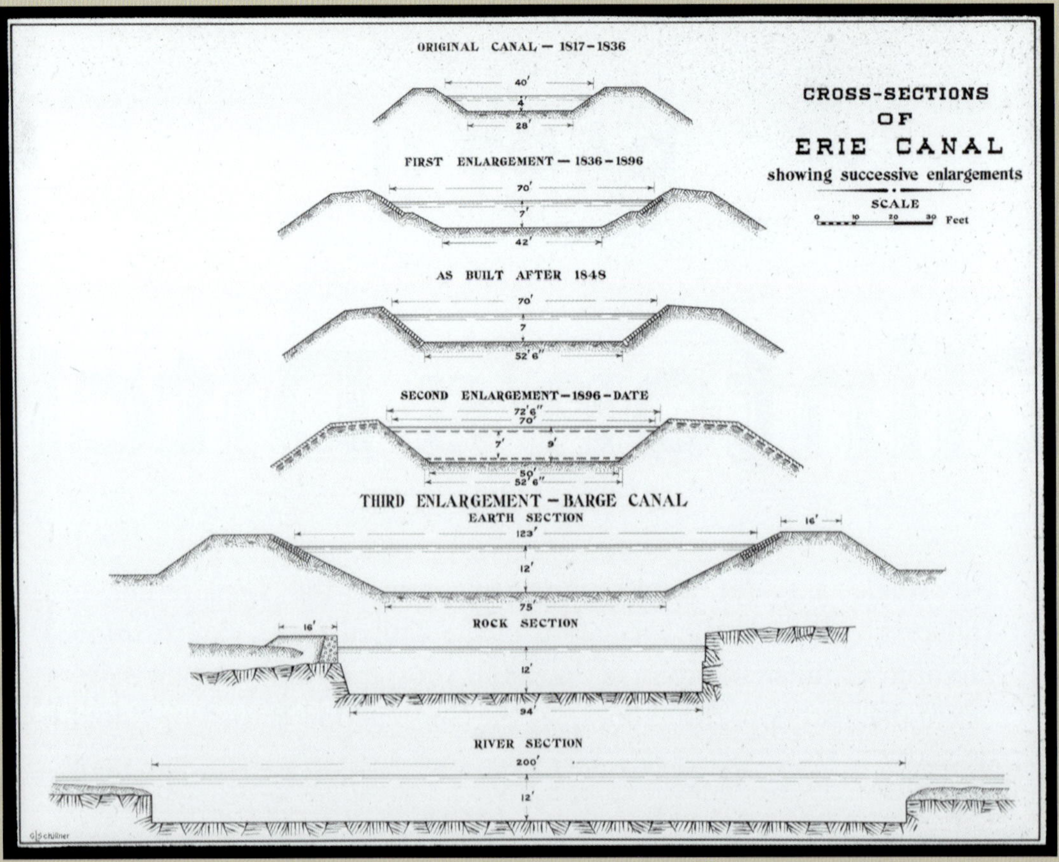
CROSS-SECTIONS
OF
ERIE CANAL
showing successive enlargements
SCALE
Feet
ORIGINAL CANAL — 1817–1836
40′
4′
28′
FIRST ENLARGEMENT — 1836–1896
70′
7′
42′
AS BUILT AFTER 1848
70′
7
52′6″
SECOND ENLARGEMENT—1896—DATE
72′6″
70′
7′
9′
50′
52′6″
THIRD ENLARGEMENT — BARGE CANAL
EARTH SECTION
123′
16′
12′
75′
ROCK SECTION
16′
12′
94′
RIVER SECTION
200′
12′

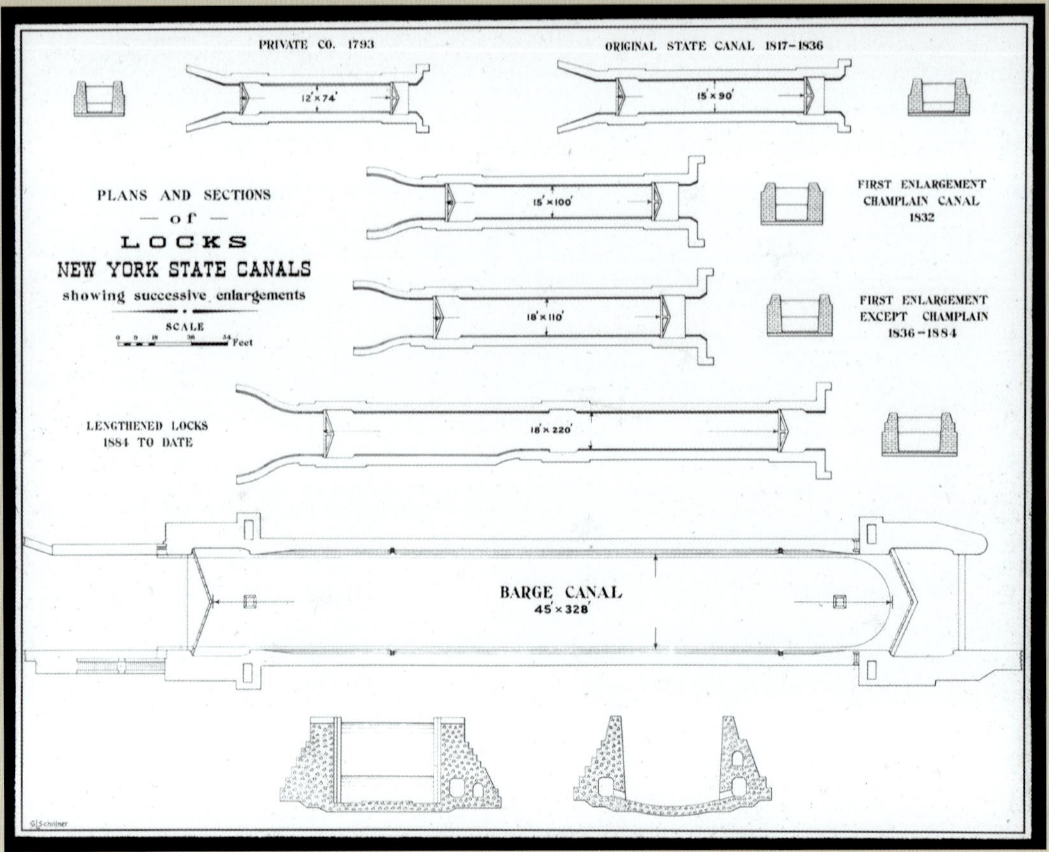
PLANS AND SECTIONS
— of —
LOCKS
NEW YORK STATE CANALS
showing successive enlargements
SCALE
Feet
PRIVATE CO. 1793
12′×74′
ORIGINAL STATE CANAL 1817–1836
15′×90′
15′×100′
FIRST ENLARGEMENT
CHAMPLAIN CANAL
1832
18′×110′
FIRST ENLARGEMENT
EXCEPT CHAMPLAIN
1836–1884
LENGTHENED LOCKS
1884 TO DATE
18′×220′
BARGE CANAL
45′×328′

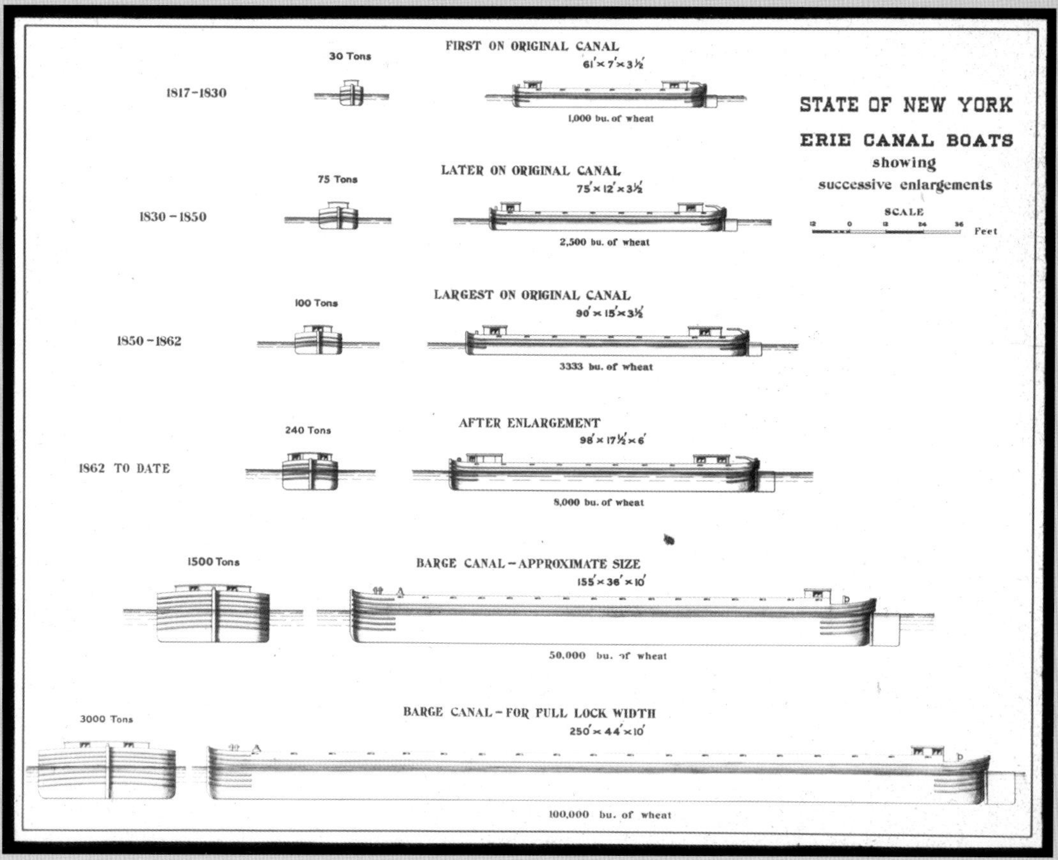

Canal growth diagrams, George Schillner, ca. 1910: *Cross Sections of Erie Canal: Showing Successive Enlargements; Plans and Sections of Locks New York State Canals: Showing Successive Enlargements; Erie Canal Boats: Showing Successive Enlargements.* When the Erie Canal opened on October 26, 1825, it ran from Albany to Buffalo, making it at that time the second-longest artificial waterway in the world (after China's ancient Grand Canal) and the largest public works project in North America. But even then, with its great size and impact, there were calls for improvements and enlargements. As demonstrated by the three sets of diagrams, numerous changes, beginning with the WILNC Canal in the 1790s, allowed for larger boats and the transport of increased tonnage along the way. Once the first enlargement started in 1836, boaters had to deal with different-size locks and varying depths of water (not always at the prescribed minimum). Even though the first enlargement was declared complete in 1862, that was more of a political declaration than a true statement of the condition of the canal. It was not until the Barge Canal was completed in 1918 that each section of the canal met the defined depth. These three charts produced around 1910 by George Schillner, a canal engineering draftsman, outline the growth of the canal from the beginning of construction to the Barge Canal. *Courtesy of the New York State Archives.*

THE POLITICS AND FUNDING OF INTERNAL IMPROVEMENTS

Internal improvements, such as roadways and water-based routes, and their funding were frequent topics of political debate in the early nineteenth century. While many Americans called for improvements, the means to pay for a canal became a divisive issue. A project as ambitious as the proposed canal was deemed too costly for private business to fund and maintain. New Yorkers first sought the help of the federal government and those states who would also benefit from the canal, but no funds were forthcoming. Various plans for federal funding of internal improvements, namely, canals and roads, were not supported by

State Capitol, Albany, N.Y., engraving, ca. 1845. Initially, most political support came from the regions along the proposed canal route, regardless of party. However, few New York City delegates (opponents of De Witt Clinton) supported the Canal Bill of 1817, despite having the most to gain. *New York State Museum, H-1982.76.3.*

Presidents Thomas Jefferson and James Madison. New York, therefore, decided to raise its own funds to build the canal and embarked on the first large-scale public works projects in the country. In 1817 the New York State Legislature established the "Canal Act," which created a board of commissioners to oversee the canal's funding and construction.

The planning and operation of New York's canals became a foremost feature in New York politics. Political careers could be made or broken by one's position on the canals. Political parties jockeyed to take credit for successes and to blame opponents for failures. Once the canal proved successful, party lines were usually drawn regarding policies for the management of the canal.

The White House, Washington, D.C., Benjamin Henry Latrobe, elevation drawing, January 1817. Federal legislation for internal improvements passed in 1817 only to be vetoed by President James Madison, citing constitutional grounds. Many in New York felt that Madison and Thomas Jefferson did not want to see New York get a canal over their home state of Virginia. *Courtesy of the Library of Congress.*

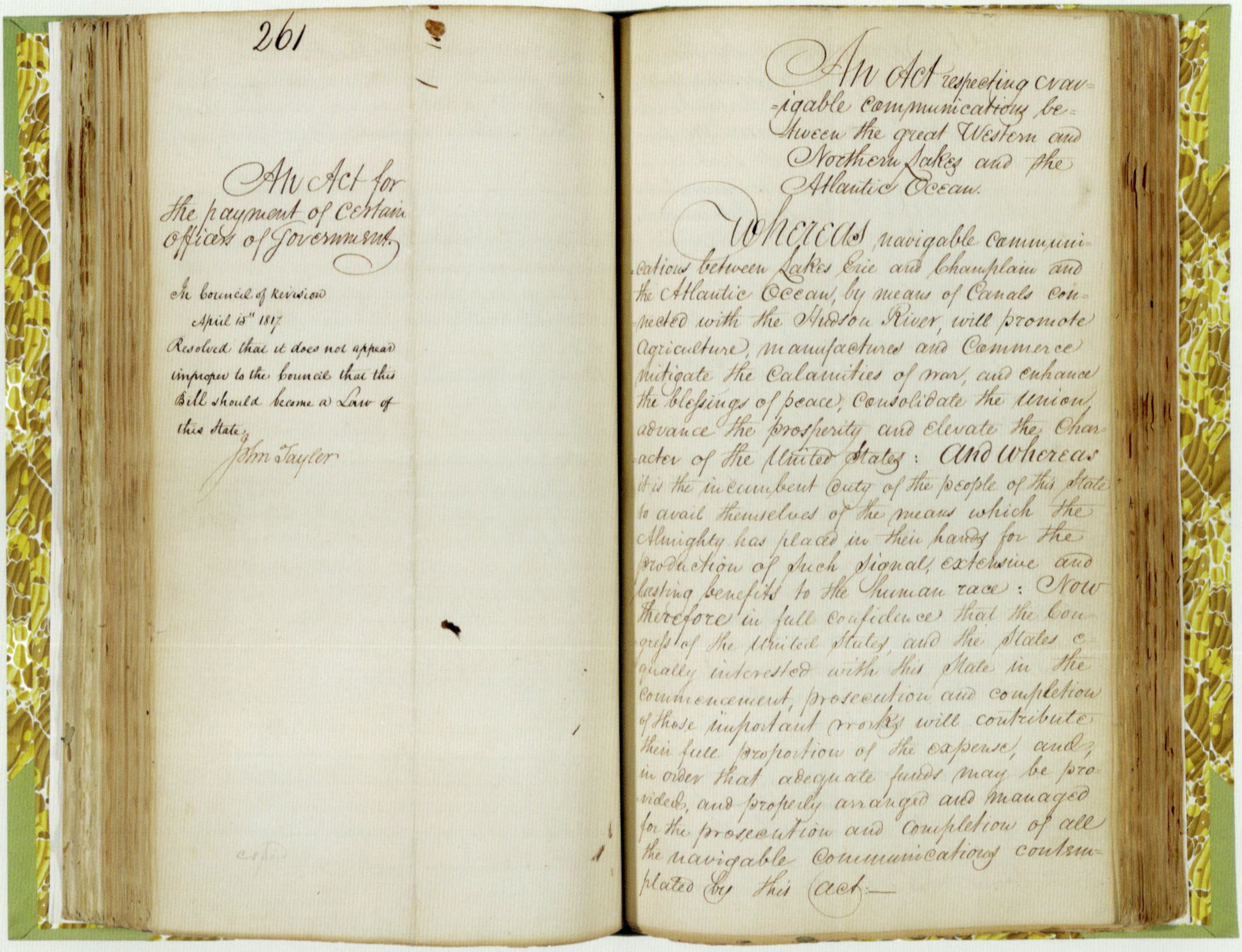

261

An Act for the payment of certain officers of Government.

In Council of Revision
April 15th 1817
Resolved that it does not appear improper to the Council that this Bill should become a Law of this State.
John Tayler

An Act respecting navigable communications between the great Western and Northern Lakes and the Atlantic Ocean.

Whereas navigable communications between Lakes Erie and Champlain and the Atlantic Ocean, by means of Canals connected with the Hudson River, will promote agriculture, manufactures and commerce, mitigate the calamities of war, and enhance the blessings of peace, consolidate the union, advance the prosperity and elevate the character of the United States: And whereas it is the incumbent duty of the people of this State to avail themselves of the means which the Almighty has placed in their hands for the production of such signal, extensive and lasting benefits to the human race: Now therefore in full confidence that the Congress of the United States, and the States equally interested with this State in the commencement, prosecution and completion of those important works will contribute their full proportion of the expense, and in order that adequate funds may be provided, and properly arranged and managed for the prosecution and completion of all the navigable communications contemplated by this act:—

Copy of the Canal Bill of 1817. In 1817 the Canal Bill passed in the New York State Legislature, but it required approval from the State Council of Revision. With the vote tied, Chancellor James Kent would make the final decision. Former governor of New York and then vice president of the United States Daniel Tompkins interrupted the meeting, stating New York should prepare for potential war with Britain. This prompted Kent to declare, "Gentlemen, if we must choose between the canal and a war, I am in favor of the canal."* *Courtesy of the New York State Archives, 13036 Enrolled Acts of the State Legislature, 1778–2010, vol. 88. *David Hosack, M.D., F.R.S., Memoir of De Witt Clinton: With an Appendix, Containing Numerous Documents, Illustrative of the Principal Events of His Life (New York: J. Seymour, 1829), 387–388.*

George Tibbits (1763–1849), Abel Buel Moore, oil on canvas, 1836. Troy's George Tibbits developed a plan to finance the canal project. The Board of Commissioners was authorized to borrow on State credit, selling stocks that were similar to today's bond. Taxes were proposed on the manufacture of salt, steamboat passengers, certain lotteries, auction duties, and on land located within twenty-five miles of the canal route. Sales of State land also added to the pot, including a donation of land from Holland Land Company, which amounted to one hundred thousand acres of rocky and remote land that eventually yielded the State $28,000. Even though the lotteries and land taxes were not used, and the steamboat tax was suspended in 1820, when combined with the revenue from canal tolls and salt taxes, enough funds were raised to cover the initial cost of just over $7 million by 1836. *Collection of the Rensselaer County Historical Society, Troy, New York.*

Canal stock certificate and bundle of stock certificates, 1822. Stock was sold on State credit to raise funds for the canal. This 1822 stock was purchased by John Jacob Astor and was redeemable at 6 percent interest in 1837. Canal stock was viewed by many as a safe investment, especially after sections of the canal opened and revenue from canal tolls came into the State. *Courtesy of the New York State Archives, A1449, New York State Comptroller's Office Cancelled State Stock Certificates, 1815–1920.*

De Witt Clinton (1769–1828)

It remains for a free state to create a new era in history, and erect a work more stupendous, more magnificent, and more beneficial than has hitherto been achieved by the human race.

—De Witt Clinton, "New York Memorial," December 1815

To De Witt Clinton—He has won for his country brilliant victories over time and space.

—Toast to De Witt Clinton at Stewart's Hotel, Pittsburgh, Pennsylvania, August 4, 1825[2]

De Witt Clinton was an ardent supporter of internal improvements. He served as a canal commissioner from 1810 to 1824 and governor of New York from 1817 to 1822 and again from 1825 until 1828, when he died in office. In 1810 he had toured western New York and assessed the canal's economic potential. This trip sparked his enthusiasm for a canal and from then on he spearheaded efforts to get the canal built. His political opponents removed him from the position of canal commissioner on the eve of the canal's completion. This act of political retribution backfired and outraged the public, resulting in a clear victory for Clinton in the election for a third term as governor.

Writing chair, ca. 1825. Referred to as the "Chair of State," this custom-made piece was used by Governor De Witt Clinton during his last term in office. *New York State Museum, H-1901.1.1.*

DeWitt Clinton, attributed to John Wesley Jarvis, oil on canvas, ca. 1816. The sixth governor of New York State, De Witt Clinton's political experience and connections played a large role in making the Erie Canal a reality. *New York State Museum, H-1979.169.2.*

Tumbler, Bakewell, Page, & Bakewell, ca. 1820–1830. Tumblers depicting De Witt Clinton were made to celebrate his visit to Pittsburgh in August of 1825. Clinton was invited to many places around the northern United States to talk about internal improvements or take part in groundbreaking ceremonies for new canals. It is certainly possible that he accepted as many as he could with hopes that it would help him achieve his presidential aspirations. *Collection of the Fenimore Art Museum, Cooperstown, New York. Gift of Mrs. Martin Van Buren Stevens.*

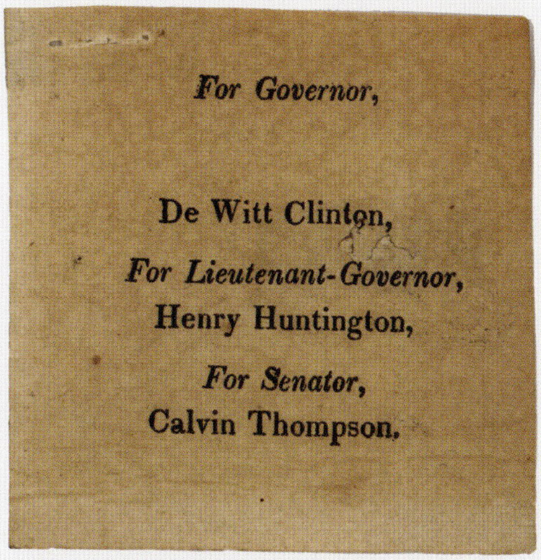

For Governor,

De Witt Clinton,

For Lieutenant-Governor,

Henry Huntington,

For Senator,

Calvin Thompson.

Election ballot, 1826. Incumbent governor De Witt Clinton was elected for the fourth time as governor in the November 1826 election. Clinton's running mate, Henry Huntington, lost to his opponent, Nathaniel Pitcher. Governors and lieutenant governors were elected on separate ballots in New York State until 1950, and terms were extended to four years in 1938. *New York State Museum, H-2006.71.7.*

Bronze bust of De Witt Clinton, after John Henri Isaac Browere, 1825, cast by Roman Bronze Works, 1940. Clinton is depicted in Roman garb, in homage to the virtues of a republican system of government developed in classical Greece and Rome. Contemporary speeches about the canal often credited the republican system for its creation and success. *Collection of the Fenimore Art Museum, Cooperstown, New York. Gift of Stephen C. Clark.*

Man's vest, ca. 1825. This vest, which was made around the time of the canal opening, features the phrase "DeWitt Clinton and the Grand Canal" woven into the fabric. *Collection of the Fenimore Art Museum, Cooperstown, New York. Museum purchase.*

The 1810 Canal Commission report revealed that it was easier and cheaper for western New Yorkers to trade with Canada along existing trade routes than with purveyors in Albany or New York City. However, after fighting the Canadians in the War of 1812, many Americans wanted to promote trade within their own country. When it came time to select the best route, a waterway connecting the Hudson River and Lake Erie (and not Lake Ontario) that bypassed Canada was ultimately accepted.

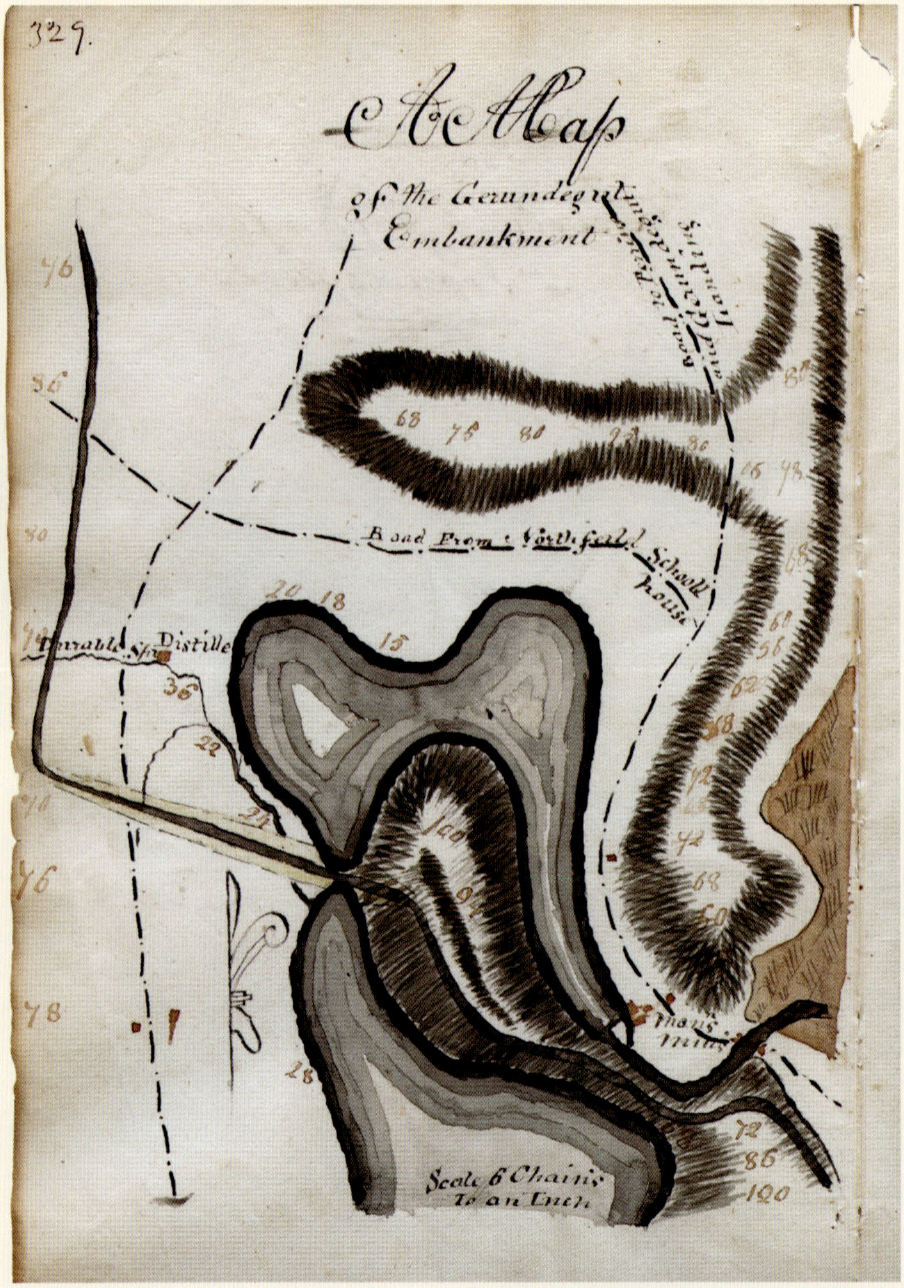

Field book map of Irondequoit Valley, James Geddes, 1808. In 1808 James Geddes (1763–1838) surveyed a potential canal from the Mohawk River to Lake Erie, proving it was possible. This section of his field book reflects the area where Geddes is said to have proclaimed, "Eureka," upon realizing the canal could pass through the Irondequoit Valley at a level that would draw water from Lake Erie to the Seneca River. Geddes would later be appointed chief engineer for the construction of the Champlain Canal. *Courtesy of the New York State Archives, A4019.*

(above) *Buffalo from the Light Houses,* engraving, 1826. *New York State Museum, H-1969.42.4.*
(below) *Buffalo Harbour from the Village*, engraving, 1826. *New York State Museum, H-1969.42.5.*
The small villages of Black Rock and Buffalo competed to be the western terminus of the canal. Both villages built piers and breakwaters, but De Witt Clinton supported Buffalo. Ultimately, the canal went through Black Rock, but it ended in Buffalo.

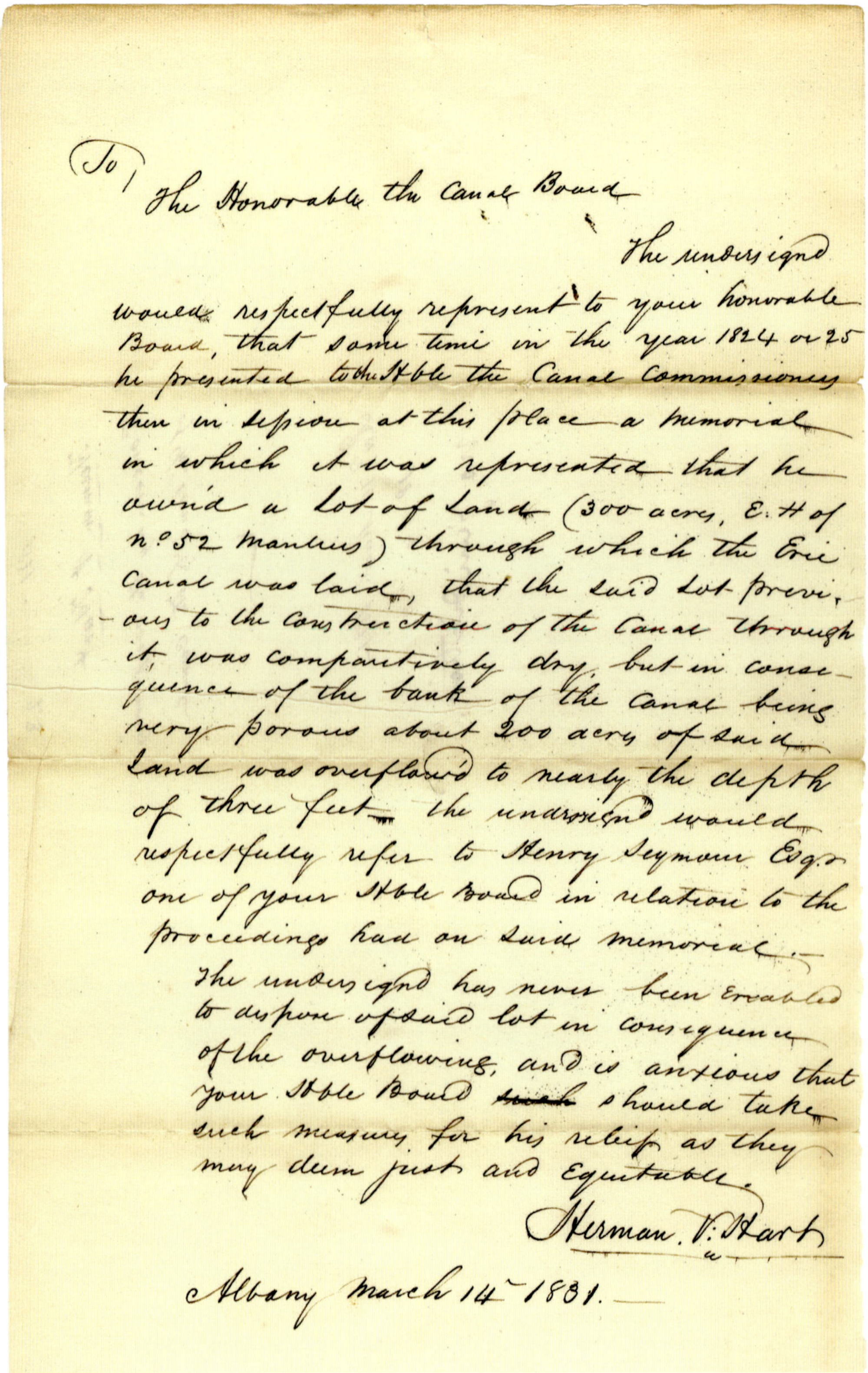

To / The Honorable the Canal Board

The undersignd would respectfully represent to your honorable Board, that some time in the year 1824 or 25 he presented to the Hble the Canal Commissioners then in session at this place a memorial in which it was represented that he ownd a lot of Land (300 acres, E. H of No. 52 Manlius) through which the Erie Canal was laid, that the said lot previous to the construction of the Canal through it, was comparatively dry, but in consequence of the bank of the Canal being very porous about 200 acres of said Land was overflowd to nearly the depth of three feet. the undersignd would respectfully refer to Henry Seymour Esqr one of your Hble Board in relation to the proceedings had on said memorial.

The undersignd has never been enabled to dispose of said lot in consequence of the overflowing, and is anxious that your Hble Board ~~such~~ should take such measures for his relief as they may deem just and equitable.

Herman V. Hart

Albany March 14 1831.

Petition to the Canal Board, 1831. The Canal Board handled a growing number of petitions over the years, especially during the first enlargement of the canal, beginning in 1836. In the petition, a landowner, Herman V. Hart of Manlius, requests compensation for canal water leaking onto his property. *Courtesy of the New York State Archives, NYSA_A1140-78_1831_023_s1.*

A State-Run Enterprise

The Erie Canal was the first major public works project in the nation and defined government's role in funding and overseeing the improvement of transportation routes. Setting many precedents in the process, the state government had to grow and adapt to manage the operation of the canal system.

The Canal Board, which was made up of the canal commissioners and the commissioners of the Canal Fund, was the main government arm of the canal system. Among its many duties, it oversaw a large State workforce, the first in the United States. Most employees were politically appointed and their jobs on the canal were susceptible to political power shifts and corruption.

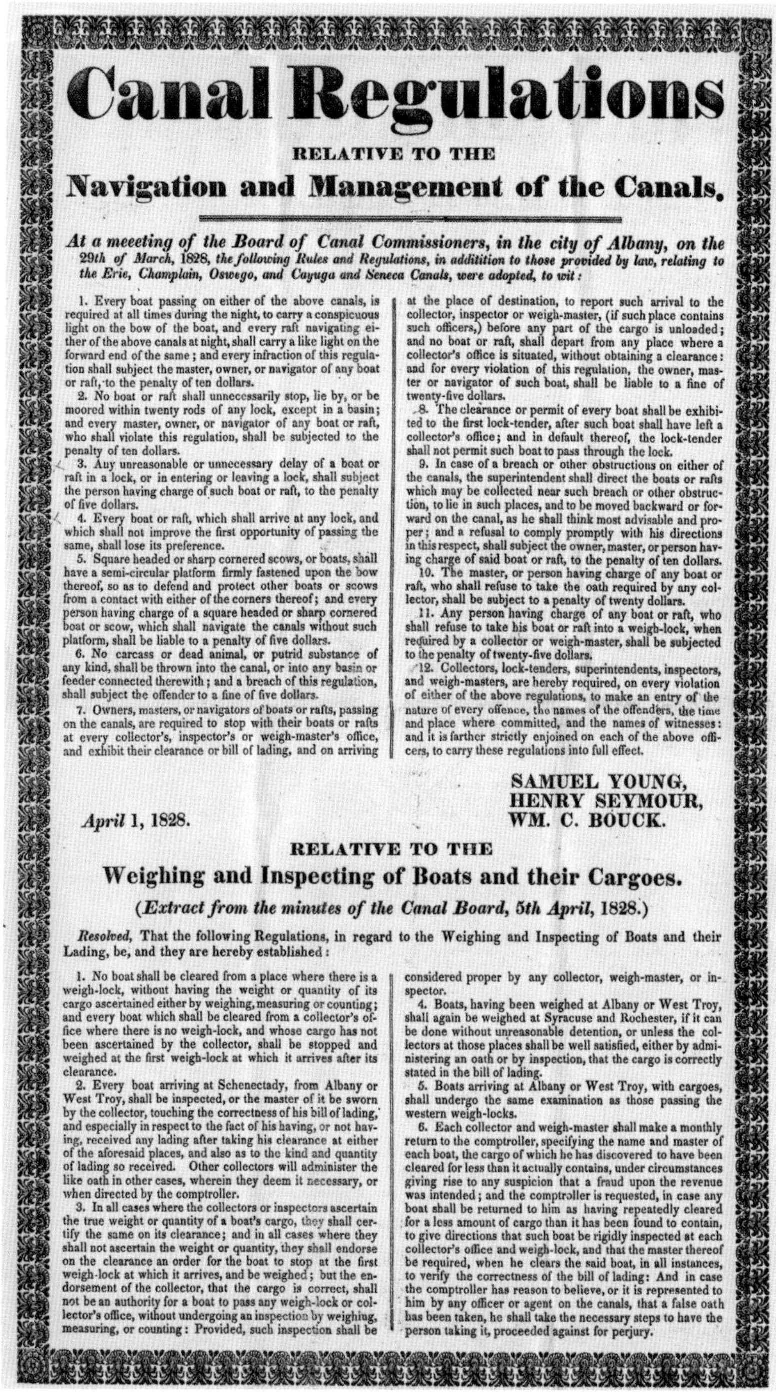

Canal Regulations

RELATIVE TO THE

Navigation and Management of the Canals.

At a meeeting of the Board of Canal Commissioners, in the city of Albany, on the 29th of March, 1828, *the following Rules and Regulations, in addittion to those provided by law, relating to the Erie, Champlain, Oswego, and Cayuga and Seneca Canals, were adopted, to wit:*

1. Every boat passing on either of the above canals, is required at all times during the night, to carry a conspicuous light on the bow of the boat, and every raft navigating either of the above canals at night, shall carry a like light on the forward end of the same; and every infraction of this regulation shall subject the master, owner, or navigator of any boat or raft, to the penalty of ten dollars.

2. No boat or raft shall unnecessarily stop, lie by, or be moored within twenty rods of any lock, except in a basin; and every master, owner, or navigator of any boat or raft, who shall violate this regulation, shall be subjected to the penalty of ten dollars.

3. Any unreasonable or unnecessary delay of a boat or raft in a lock, or in entering or leaving a lock, shall subject the person having charge of such boat or raft, to the penalty of five dollars.

4. Every boat or raft, which shall arrive at any lock, and which shall not improve the first opportunity of passing the same, shall lose its preference.

5. Square headed or sharp cornered scows, or boats, shall have a semi-circular platform firmly fastened upon the bow thereof, so as to defend and protect other boats or scows from a contact with either of the corners thereof; and every person having charge of a square headed or sharp cornered boat or scow, which shall navigate the canals without such platform, shall be liable to a penalty of five dollars.

6. No carcass or dead animal, or putrid substance of any kind, shall be thrown into the canal, or into any basin or feeder connected therewith; and a breach of this regulation, shall subject the offender to a fine of five dollars.

7. Owners, masters, or navigators of boats or rafts, passing on the canals, are required to stop with their boats or rafts at every collector's, inspector's or weigh-master's office, and exhibit their clearance or bill of lading, and on arriving at the place of destination, to report such arrival to the collector, inspector or weigh-master, (if such place contains such officers,) before any part of the cargo is unloaded; and no boat or raft, shall depart from any place where a collector's office is situated, without obtaining a clearance: and for every violation of this regulation, the owner, master or navigator of such boat, shall be liable to a fine of twenty-five dollars.

8. The clearance or permit of every boat shall be exhibited to the first lock-tender, after such boat shall have left a collector's office; and in default thereof, the lock-tender shall not permit such boat to pass through the lock.

9. In case of a breach or other obstructions on either of the canals, the superintendent shall direct the boats or rafts which may be collected near such breach or other obstruction, to lie in such places, and to be moved backward or forward on the canal, as he shall think most advisable and proper; and a refusal to comply promptly with his directions in this respect, shall subject the owner, master, or person having charge of said boat or raft, to the penalty of ten dollars.

10. The master, or person having charge of any boat or raft, who shall refuse to take the oath required by any collector, shall be subject to a penalty of twenty dollars.

11. Any person having charge of any boat or raft, who shall refuse to take his boat or raft into a weigh-lock, when required by a collector or weigh-master, shall be subjected to the penalty of twenty-five dollars.

12. Collectors, lock-tenders, superintendents, inspectors, and weigh-masters, are hereby required, on every violation of either of the above regulations, to make an entry of the nature of every offence, the names of the offenders, the time and place where committed, and the names of witnesses: and it is farther strictly enjoined on each of the above officers, to carry these regulations into full effect.

SAMUEL YOUNG,
HENRY SEYMOUR,
WM. C. BOUCK.

April 1, 1828.

RELATIVE TO THE

Weighing and Inspecting of Boats and their Cargoes.

(*Extract from the minutes of the Canal Board, 5th April,* 1828.)

Resolved, That the following Regulations, in regard to the Weighing and Inspecting of Boats and their Lading, be, and they are hereby established:

1. No boat shall be cleared from a place where there is a weigh-lock, without having the weight or quantity of its cargo ascertained either by weighing, measuring or counting; and every boat which shall be cleared from a collector's office where there is no weigh-lock, and whose cargo has not been ascertained by the collector, shall be stopped and weighed at the first weigh-lock at which it arrives after its clearance.

2. Every boat arriving at Schenectady, from Albany or West Troy, shall be inspected, or the master of it be sworn by the collector, touching the correctness of his bill of lading, and especially in respect to the fact of his having, or not having, received any lading after taking his clearance at either of the aforesaid places, and also as to the kind and quantity of lading so received. Other collectors will administer the like oath in other cases, wherein they deem it necessary, or when directed by the comptroller.

3. In all cases where the collectors or inspectors ascertain the true weight or quantity of a boat's cargo, they shall certify the same on its clearance; and in all cases where they shall not ascertain the weight or quantity, they shall endorse on the clearance an order for the boat to stop at the first weigh-lock at which it arrives, and be weighed; but the endorsement of the collector, that the cargo is correct, shall not be an authority for a boat to pass any weigh-lock or collector's office, without undergoing an inspection by weighing, measuring, or counting: Provided, such inspection shall be considered proper by any collector, weigh-master, or inspector.

4. Boats, having been weighed at Albany or West Troy, shall again be weighed at Syracuse and Rochester, if it can be done without unreasonable detention, or unless the collectors at those places shall be well satisfied, either by administering an oath or by inspection, that the cargo is correctly stated in the bill of lading.

5. Boats arriving at Albany or West Troy, with cargoes, shall undergo the same examination as those passing the western weigh-locks.

6. Each collector and weigh-master shall make a monthly return to the comptroller, specifying the name and master of each boat, the cargo of which he has discovered to have been cleared for less than it actually contains, under circumstances giving rise to any suspicion that a fraud upon the revenue was intended; and the comptroller is requested, in case any boat shall be returned to him as having repeatedly cleared for a less amount of cargo than it has been found to contain, to give directions that such boat be rigidly inspected at each collector's office and weigh-lock, and that the master thereof be required, when he clears the said boat, in all instances, to verify the correctness of the bill of lading: And in case the comptroller has reason to believe, or it is represented to him by any officer or agent on the canals, that a false oath has been taken, he shall take the necessary steps to have the person taking it, proceeded against for perjury.

Canal Regulations, 1828 (facsimile). In addition to the laws enacted by the state legislature, the canal commissioners also enacted a set of rules for boaters to follow, including that every boat that operated at night must have a light on its bow, no throwing dead animals in the canal, and no stopping or blocking a lock when it is your boat's turn to go in. *New York State Museum, Mrs. Arnold B. Barben Canal Collection, H-1988.79.*

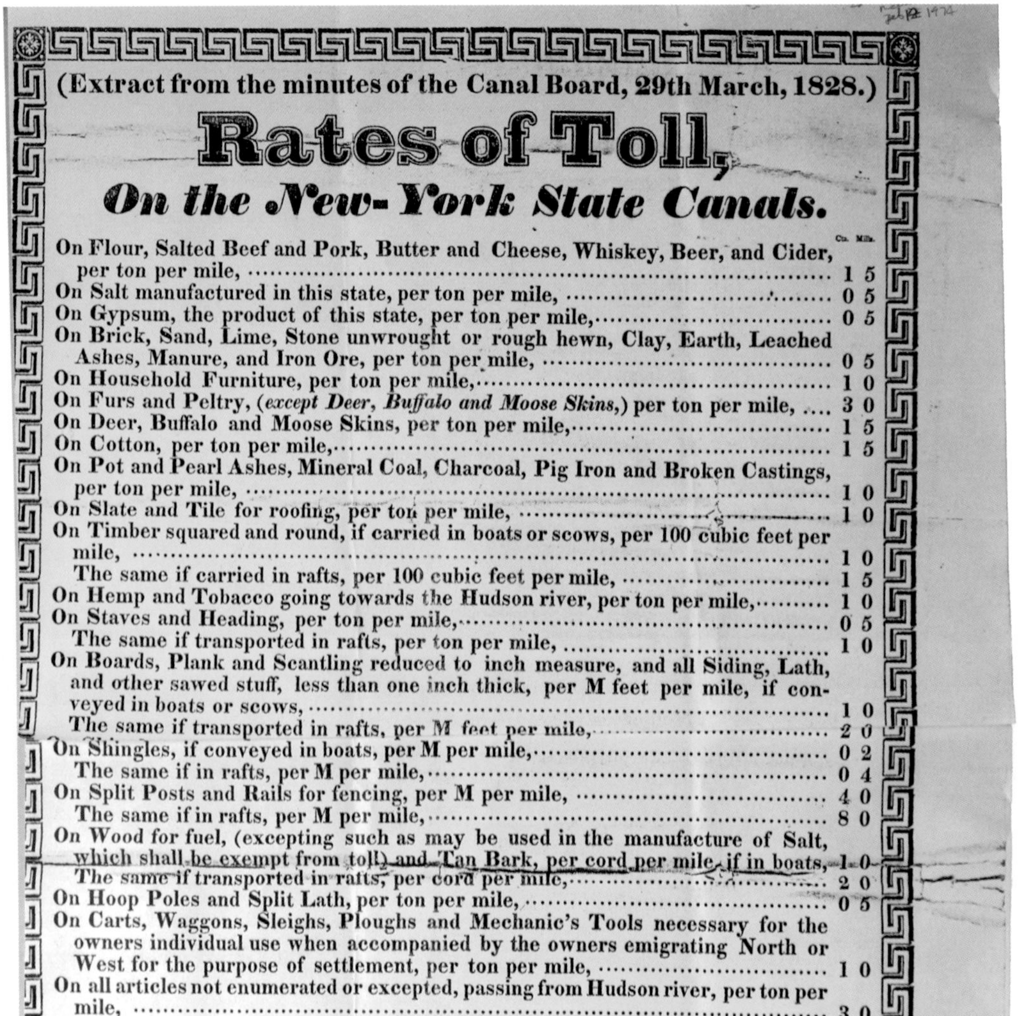

(Extract from the minutes of the Canal Board, 29th March, 1828.)

Rates of Toll,

On the New-York State Canals.

	Cts. Mills.
On Flour, Salted Beef and Pork, Butter and Cheese, Whiskey, Beer, and Cider, per ton per mile,	1 5
On Salt manufactured in this state, per ton per mile,	0 5
On Gypsum, the product of this state, per ton per mile,	0 5
On Brick, Sand, Lime, Stone unwrought or rough hewn, Clay, Earth, Leached Ashes, Manure, and Iron Ore, per ton per mile,	0 5
On Household Furniture, per ton per mile,	1 0
On Furs and Peltry, (*except Deer, Buffalo and Moose Skins,*) per ton per mile,	3 0
On Deer, Buffalo and Moose Skins, per ton per mile,	1 5
On Cotton, per ton per mile,	1 5
On Pot and Pearl Ashes, Mineral Coal, Charcoal, Pig Iron and Broken Castings, per ton per mile,	1 0
On Slate and Tile for roofing, per ton per mile,	1 0
On Timber squared and round, if carried in boats or scows, per 100 cubic feet per mile,	1 0
The same if carried in rafts, per 100 cubic feet per mile,	1 5
On Hemp and Tobacco going towards the Hudson river, per ton per mile,	1 0
On Staves and Heading, per ton per mile,	0 5
The same if transported in rafts, per ton per mile,	1 0
On Boards, Plank and Scantling reduced to inch measure, and all Siding, Lath, and other sawed stuff, less than one inch thick, per M feet per mile, if conveyed in boats or scows,	1 0
The same if transported in rafts, per M feet per mile,	2 0
On Shingles, if conveyed in boats, per M per mile,	0 2
The same if in rafts, per M per mile,	0 4
On Split Posts and Rails for fencing, per M per mile,	4 0
The same if in rafts, per M per mile,	8 0
On Wood for fuel, (excepting such as may be used in the manufacture of Salt, which shall be exempt from toll) and Tan Bark, per cord per mile, if in boats,	1 0
The same if transported in rafts, per cord per mile,	2 0
On Hoop Poles and Split Lath, per ton per mile,	0 5
On Carts, Waggons, Sleighs, Ploughs and Mechanic's Tools necessary for the owners individual use when accompanied by the owners emigrating North or West for the purpose of settlement, per ton per mile,	1 0
On all articles not enumerated or excepted, passing from Hudson river, per ton per mile,	3 0
On all articles not enumerated which are passing towards Hudson river, per ton per mile,	1 5
On all Agricultural productions of the state not particularly specified, per ton per mile,	1 5

EXPLANATION.—*Cattle and Horses, and the Raw Hides of domestic animals, are to be considered as included within the term "Agricultural productions"—and each horse, when not weighed with the boat, is to be estimated at 6 cwt.*

On boats made and used chiefly for the transportation of property, per mile,	2 0
On boats used chiefly for the transportation of persons, west of Utica, 15 cents per mile, and east of Utica, (except those passing on the Junction Canal) 20 cents per mile, or 6 cents per mile on the boat, and 2 mills per mile on each passenger, over 8 years of age, at the election of the proprietors: Providing they render such satisfactory accounts of the number of passengers as may be required, and make such election when their boats commence business for the season.	
On Boats of the above description which pass on the Junction Canal, and which are not connected with regular lines of boats for the transportation of passengers on the Erie or Champlain Canals, per mile,	50 0
On each passenger transported in freight boats, and over twelve years of age, per mile,	0 2

Resolved, That the foregoing Rates of Toll be, and they are hereby established, and that the same be hereafter charged and collected on the several canals of this state.

SAM'L. YOUNG,
WM. C. BOUCK,
HENRY SEYMOUR. } *Canal Comissioners.*

W. L. MARCY,
A. C. FLAGG,
S. DE WITT,
A. KEYSER. } *Commissioners of the Canal Fund.*

COMPTROLLER'S OFFICE,
Albany,

I certify that the above is a correct copy of the Rates of Canal Toll, as established by the Canal Board and filed in this office.

Comptroller.

Printed by Croswell & Van Benthuysen, Albany.

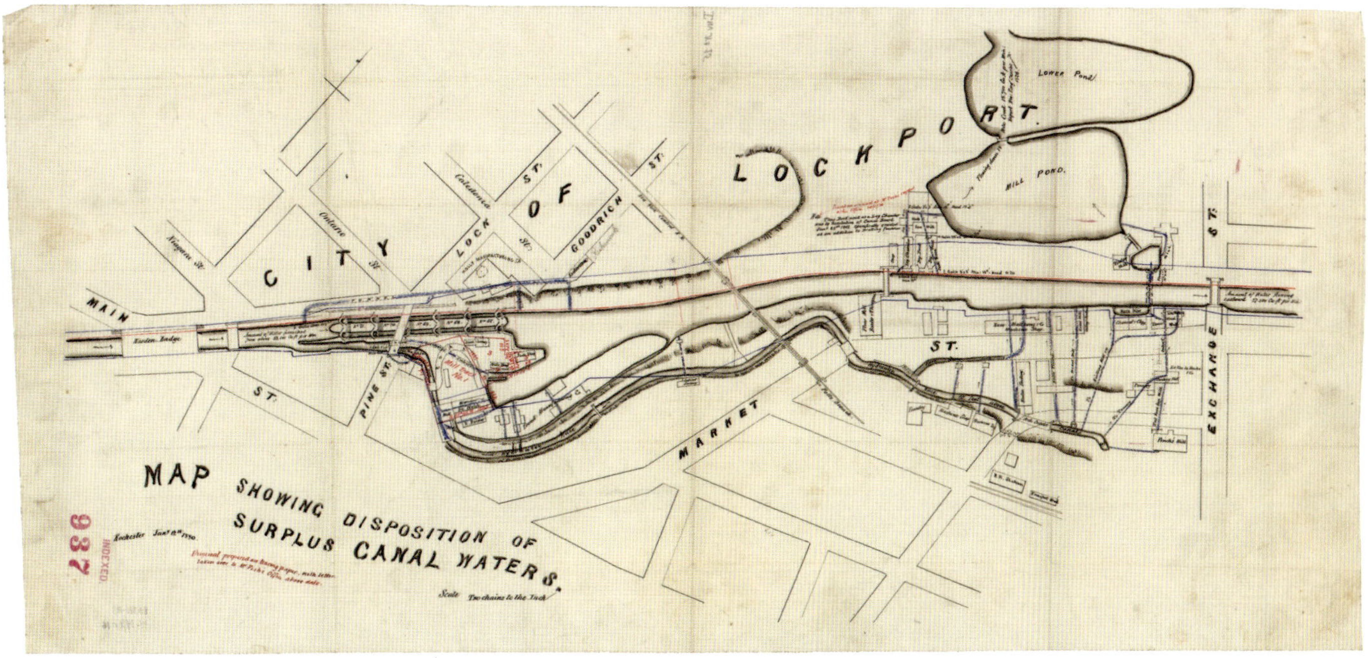

Map Showing Disposition of Surplus Water in Lockport, 1880. To promote business and increase canal revenues, the State leased the rights to use surplus canal water to generate power for businesses. With the use of a water wheel or water turbine, the excess water could power mills or manufacturing plants. *Courtesy of the New York State Archives, 937.*

(facing page)
Rate of Tolls, 1828 (facsimile). Each year the State would determine the rate of tolls that would be charged for cargo shipped on the canal. Tolls were often calculated to advance certain industries. For example, if the commissioners wanted to help New York cheese makers, they could lower the toll on shipping cheese on the canal. *New York State Museum, Mrs. Arnold B. Barben Canal Collection, H-1988.79.*

Myron Holley (1779–1841)

An early canal proponent from Canandaigua, Myron Holley served as a canal commissioner and treasurer from 1816 to 1824. As treasurer, he traveled the canal route during construction to pay and negotiate with contractors. He did not officially charge the State for his own expenses for this travel. In 1824 his political opponents induced the legislature to audit the work of Holley and others, and he could not account for some of the funds used for payment. He resigned his position, admitting that he used some of the public money to purchase land, feeling it was owed to him as compensation for his travel expenses. Holley's property was held by the State in penalty, then returned to him in 1828 when his supporters gained control of the legislature. Holley went on to play major roles in the Anti-Masonic and antislavery movements in New York State. The Village of Holley, Orleans County, is named after him.

Myron Holley (1779–1841), Ezra Ames, oil on canvas, ca. 1820. Collection of the New-York Historical Society. *Gift of Sallie Holley.*

Farmer's Bridge, Augusta Brown, 1895. It was not uncommon for the canal to split a farm in two. There was no guarantee that the State would build a bridge or that it would reimburse the farmer if he built his own. *New York State Museum, Augusta Brown Journal.*

SETTLING THE LAND: ACQUISITION AND DISPOSSESSION

Before construction of the Erie Canal could take place, New York State needed to gain ownership of the land needed to build it. When landowners refused to sell, the State enforced eminent domain—the first large-scale use of the practice in United States history.

The value of the land was determined by the State and then the current owners were paid for the land. Often the State would determine that the benefits of the canal increased the value of the land bordering it, so no money was exchanged. Challenges to land values were voluminous. Established farmers in the Mohawk Valley quickly found that the legal decisions often ruled in favor of commercial interests over their own.[3]

The triumph of the Erie Canal and the nation's drive to the west—for land, natural resources, and nation building—devastated Native peoples, who were forced off their lands in the name of "progress." National defense, land speculation, and growing populations pushed Native peoples off their ancestral lands across the United States.

Through a series of questionable "treaties," former Haudenosaunee (Iroquois) lands became obtainable to European Americans. Land speculators were quick to purchase the rights to those lands and Native Americans were sent to reservations. As settlers flooded western New York, they applied pressure to the government to make more land available, and by 1870 only a few small reservations remained.

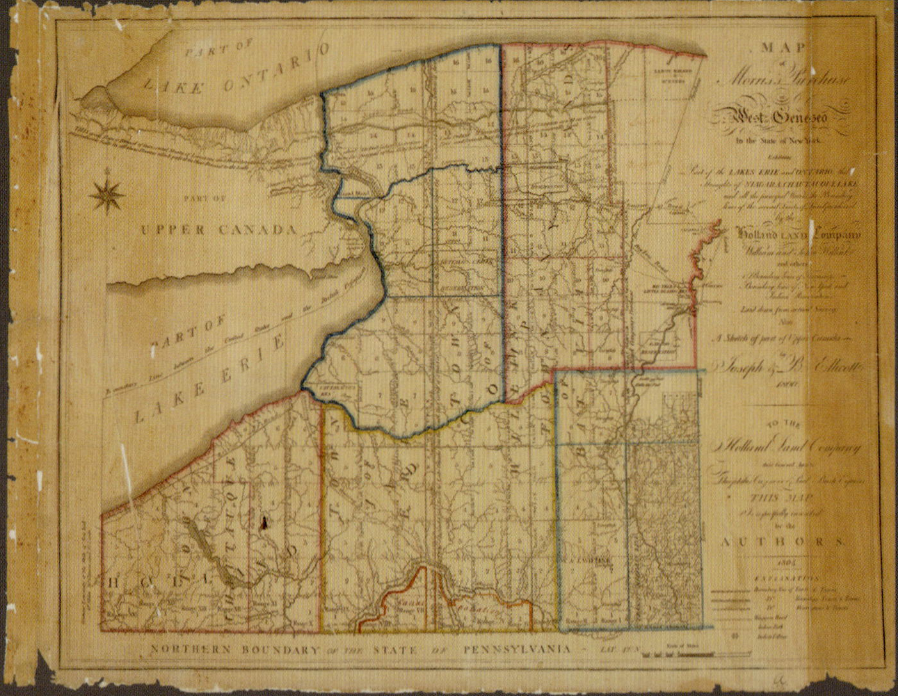

Holland Land Company Map, 1800. As Buffalo's population swelled, the Seneca were eventually removed from their reservation at Buffalo Creek to make room for European Americans. This reservation was home to the Council Fire and considered sacred to the Haudenosaunee. Note the Buffalo Creek Reservation to the east of Buffalo. *Courtesy of the New York State Archives, Series A0273-78 Map #145.*

House of Red Jacket, on the Buffalo Reservation, engraving, ca. 1841. Red Jacket (ca. 1750–January 20, 1830) was a Seneca chief of the Wolf Clan. He negotiated with the United States government on land and war treaties. President George Washington gave him a special "peace medal" for his efforts. Seen as an important orator and representative of the Native Americans, Red Jacket is mentioned, and his home depicted, in an 1842 history of New York State. John Warner Barber and Henry Howe, *Historical Collections of the State of New York; Containing a General Collection of the Most Interesting Facts, Traditions, Biographical Sketches, Anecdotes, &c., Relating to Its History and Antiquities, with Geographical Descriptions of Every Township in the State* (New York: S. Tuttle, 1842). *Courtesy of the New York State Library, Manuscripts and Special Collections, 974.7 B23a3.*

Communion set, pewter, pre-1840. This pre-1840 pewter Communion set is from a Presbyterian mission in "Old Town" near the Allegany Seneca Nation reservation established in the 1830s. The mission intended to convert the Seneca to Christianity and European American culture. *New York State Museum, H-1933.14.1 A-F.*

Beaded purse and watch pocket, Tuscarora Iroquois, ca. 1870–1920. By the 1830s Haudenosaunee (Iroquois) were making and selling to tourists purses decorated with intricate glass seed beads in floral motifs. The purse demonstrates the ingenuity of entrepreneurship and talent from Haudenosaunee peoples and the influence of Victorian aesthetics. *New York State Museum, E-39503 and E-37950.*

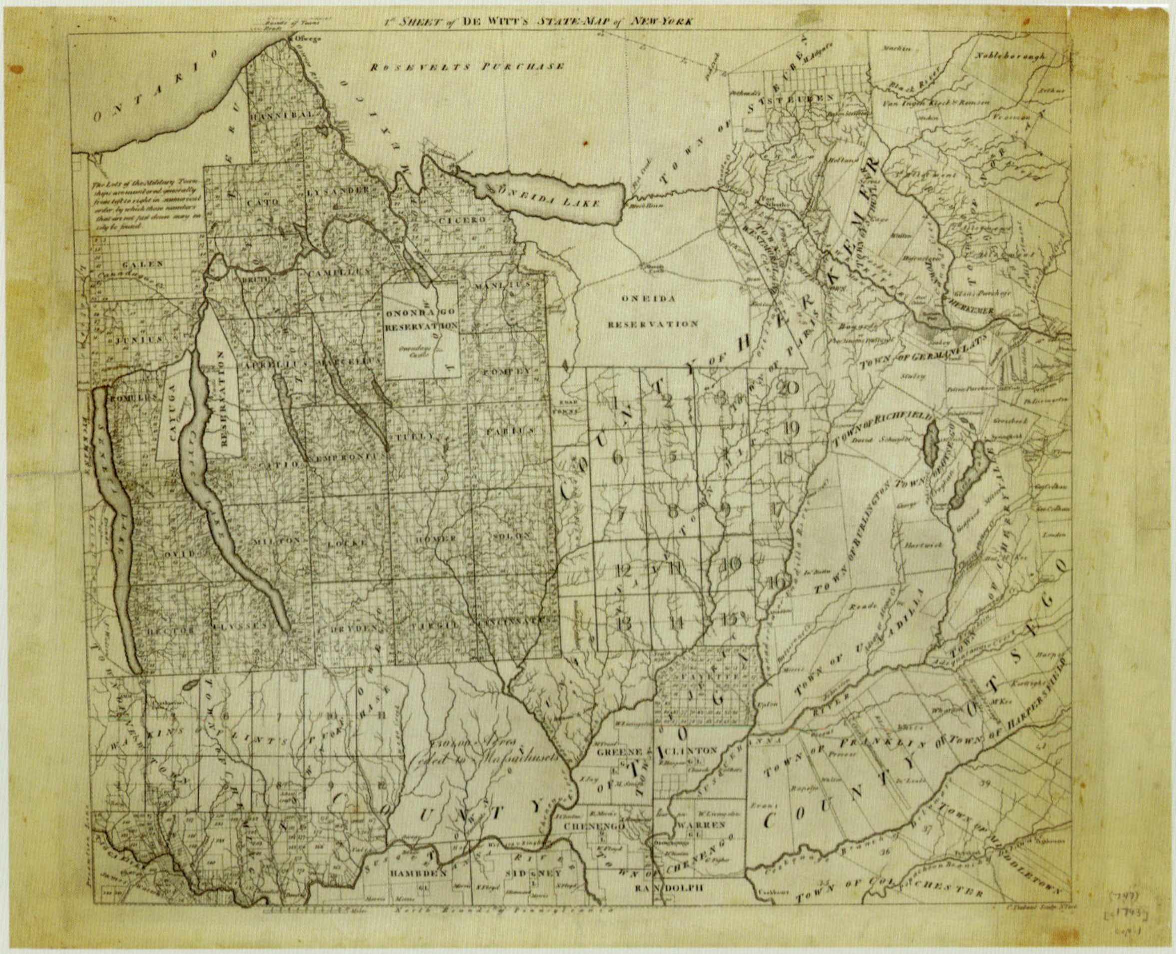

State Surveyor's Map of New York State, Simeon De Witt, ca. 1793. By 1800 various land speculation companies had gained the rights to most of western New York. The Holland Land Company owned most of New York's land west of the Genesee River, so it was in its best interest to promote the canal. The company even gave New York State one hundred thousand acres of land to help raise funds for the project. *Courtesy of the New York State Library, Manuscripts and Special Collections (747) 1793 99-6391.*

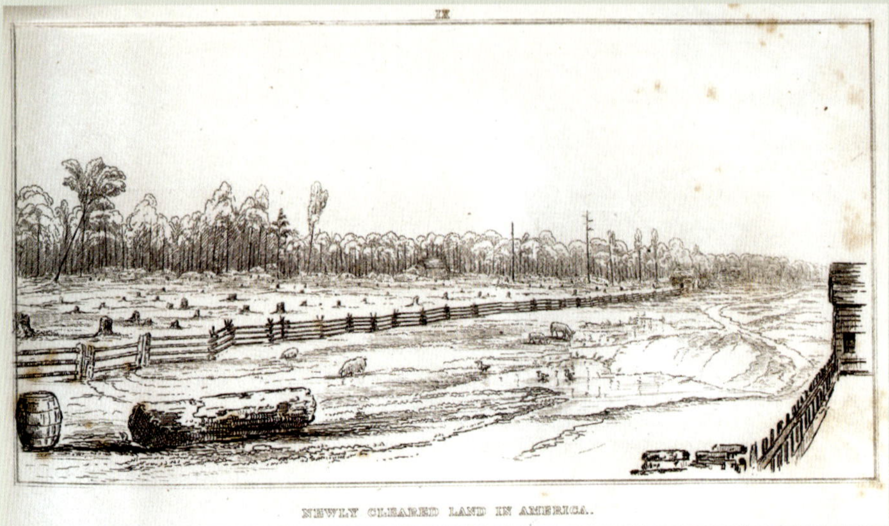

Newly Cleared Land, W. H. Lizars after Basil Hall, engraving, ca. 1827. Newly cleared land in western New York as sketched by Basil Hall in 1827–1828. Captain Basil Hall, Royal Navy, *Travels in North America in the Years 1827 and 1828 (Philadelphia: Carey, Lea & Carey, 1829). Courtesy of the New York State Library, Manuscripts and Special Collections N 917.3 qH168.*

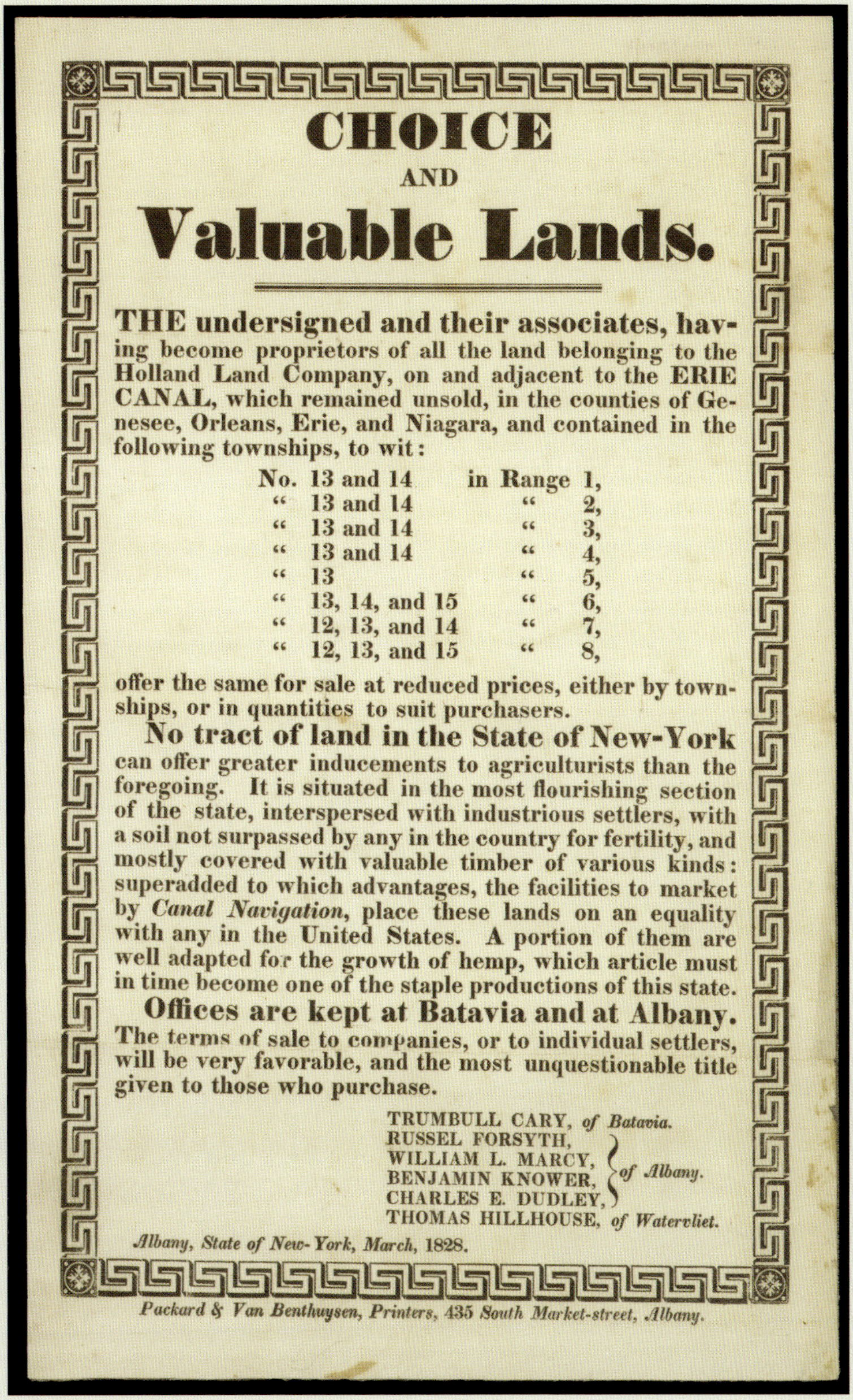

CHOICE
AND
Valuable Lands.

THE undersigned and their associates, having become proprietors of all the land belonging to the Holland Land Company, on and adjacent to the ERIE CANAL, which remained unsold, in the counties of Genesee, Orleans, Erie, and Niagara, and contained in the following townships, to wit:

No.	13 and 14	in Range 1,
"	13 and 14	" 2,
"	13 and 14	" 3,
"	13 and 14	" 4,
"	13	" 5,
"	13, 14, and 15	" 6,
"	12, 13, and 14	" 7,
"	12, 13, and 15	" 8,

offer the same for sale at reduced prices, either by townships, or in quantities to suit purchasers.

No tract of land in the State of New-York can offer greater inducements to agriculturists than the foregoing. It is situated in the most flourishing section of the state, interspersed with industrious settlers, with a soil not surpassed by any in the country for fertility, and mostly covered with valuable timber of various kinds: superadded to which advantages, the facilities to market by *Canal Navigation*, place these lands on an equality with any in the United States. A portion of them are well adapted for the growth of hemp, which article must in time become one of the staple productions of this state.

Offices are kept at Batavia and at Albany. The terms of sale to companies, or to individual settlers, will be very favorable, and the most unquestionable title given to those who purchase.

TRUMBULL CARY, *of Batavia.*
RUSSEL FORSYTH,
WILLIAM L. MARCY,
BENJAMIN KNOWER, } *of Albany.*
CHARLES E. DUDLEY,
THOMAS HILLHOUSE, *of Watervliet.*

Albany, State of New-York, March, 1828.

Packard & Van Benthuysen, Printers, 435 South Market-street, Albany.

"Choice and Valuable Lands" broadside, March 1828. Anyone looking to purchase land in western New York or further west had to use caution. Property value increased with proximity to the canal, but many advertisements for land claimed parcels were close to the canal when they were not. *Courtesy of the New York State Library, Manuscripts and Special Collections 1.28_BRO 0001.*

AN ENGINEERING MARVEL

Indeed, to see a forest tree, which had withstood the elements till it attained maturity, torn up by its roots, and bending itself to the earth, in obedience to the command of man, is a spectacle that must awaken feelings of gratitude to that Being, who has bestowed on his creatures so much power and wisdom.

—Cadwallader D. Colden, American politician, 1825[4]

The first shovel of dirt in excavating for the canal was ceremoniously overturned outside of Rome, New York, on July 4, 1817. Over the next eight years, engineers, surveyors, contractors, and laborers with little or no experience overcame immense obstacles to build the Erie Canal.

Canals, locks, aqueducts, and other canal structures had been used for centuries throughout the world. The wonder of New York's canal lay in the enormous size of the project, the landscape that had to be conquered, the structures used to conquer the obstacles, and the lack of experience of the engineers and laborers.

Little Falls, New York, William Rickarby Miller (American, born England, 1818–1893), watercolor on paper, 1852. Little Falls provided the engineers with one of the most difficult challenges as they traversed a narrow passage through high terrain in the Mohawk Valley. The Erie Canal was a "contour canal" that followed the landscape, hugging the edges of the hills and valleys along the route. *Courtesy of the Albany Institute of History & Art.*

Little Falls, New York, William Rickarby Miller, watercolor on paper, 1853. In this image, Miller avoided any reference to human presence, even though the village of Little Falls is nearby. Instead, from a low vantage point, he emphasized the rugged beauty of the steep, rocky outcroppings and uninhabited woods. *Munson-Williams-Proctor Arts Institute.*

Erie Canal, Risso & Browne (American, active nineteenth century), after unknown artist, hand-colored lithograph, 1832. Among the most popular views of the Erie Canal appearing in books, magazines, and as single prints were images of it curving through the countryside, as seen here in the Mohawk Valley at "the Noses," one of the narrowest points in the valley. *Arkell Museum at Canajoharie. Gift of Bartlett Arkell.*

Ground-Breaking Ceremony, J. Erwin Porter, pastel and watercolor on paper, ca. 1960. Depiction of the July 4, 1817, groundbreaking ceremony in Rome, New York. Though this was the beginning of the most monumental engineering feat the country had seen, the ceremony received surprisingly little press and fanfare outside of Rome. *New York State Museum, H-1984.91.29.*

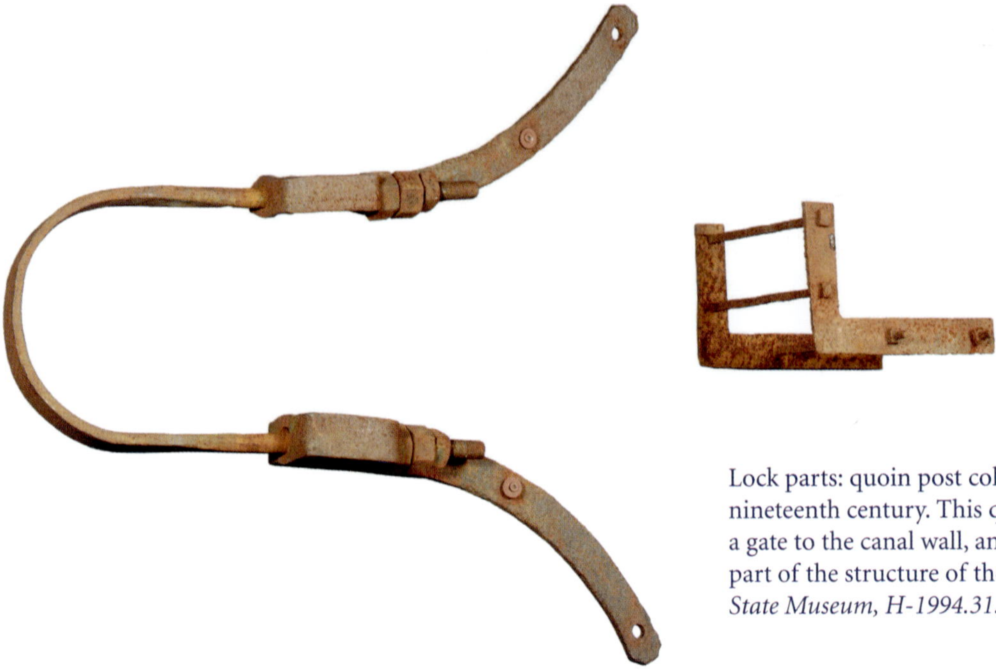

Lock parts: quoin post collar and gate brace, nineteenth century. This quoin post collar held a gate to the canal wall, and the gate brace was part of the structure of the gate itself. *New York State Museum, H-1994.31.1 and H-1994.31.2.*

Model of Erie Canal lock, Marvin R. Clinch and Harvey H. Walle, ca. 1965. The basic function of a canal lock is to raise or lower a boat from one elevation to another, acting as a boat elevator. To go up in the lock, the boat enters the chamber at the lower end of the lock. The lock tender then shuts the gates behind the boat. Next, the lock tender opens the wickets (small doors at the bottom of the lock gate) to let the water from the higher side of the lock into the chamber. The boat slowly rises as the water fills the chamber. Once the water level is the same inside the lock as it is outside on the higher level, the lock tender opens the gates and the boat can exit. To go down, the boat would enter at the high side of the lock and water would be released from the lock chamber by opening the wickets in the lower gates. *Canal Society of New York State.*

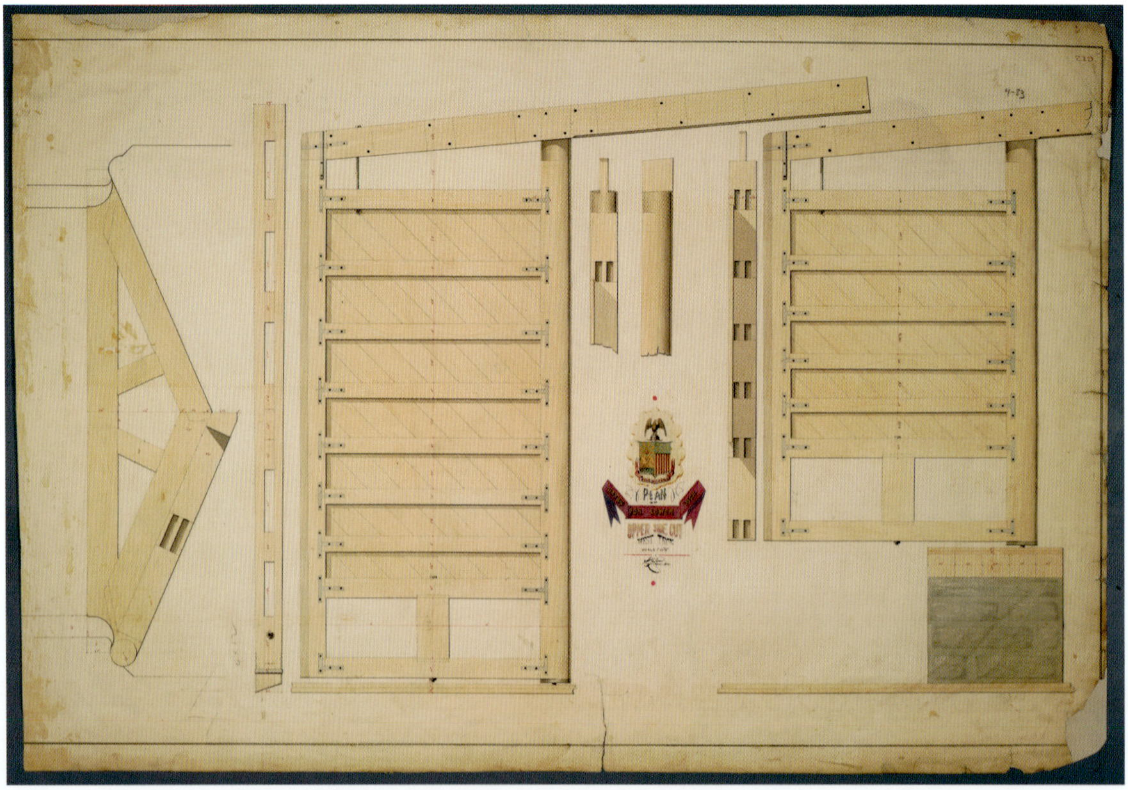

Plan for lock gates at West Troy, ca. 1835–1862. Drawing of gates to be built on a lock of the Erie Canal at "West Troy" (today called Watervliet), Albany County. *Courtesy of the New York State Archives, B0292-85_V004_84.*

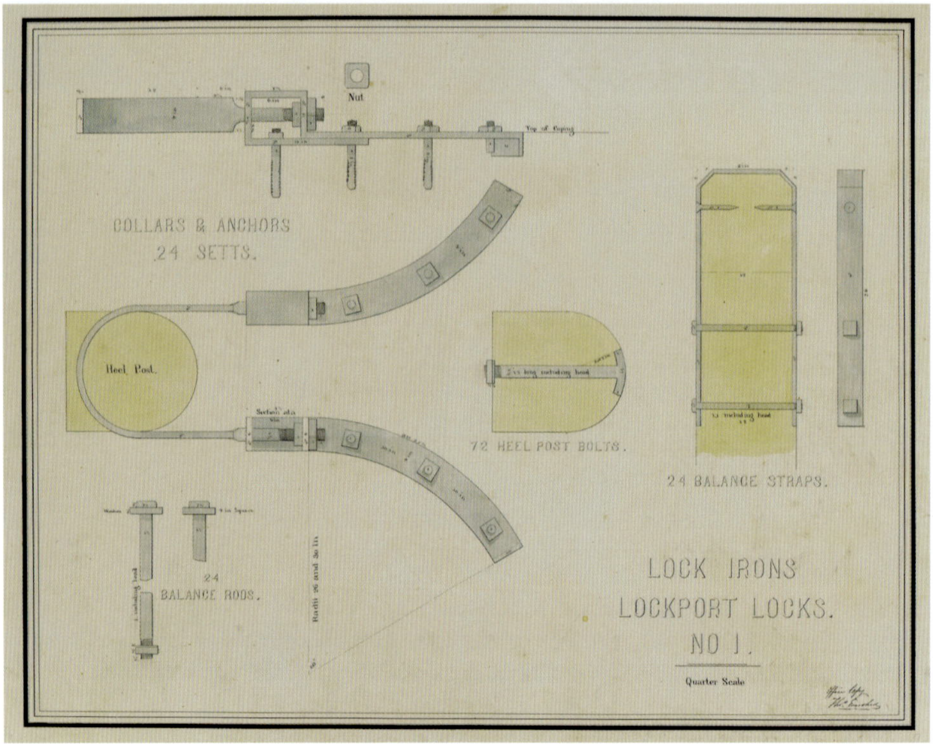

Lock Irons Plan, Thomas Evershed, canal engineer, 1839. This drawing shows the quoin post collar, which held the lock door to the lock wall. Courtesy of the New York State Archives, B0379-85.

Model of an aqueduct, maker unknown, ca. 1965. A total of eighteen aqueducts were used in the initial construction of the Erie Canal. An aqueduct carried the canal over a creek or river. This aqueduct model depicts a wooden trough, which was designed by Asa Waterman Cady. Aqueducts were also built with cement troughs, such as the one in Rochester that crossed the Genesee River. Today, readers can visit a reconstructed aqueduct with a wooden trough at the Camillus Erie Canal Park. *Courtesy of the Canal Society of New York State.*

View of the Lower Aqueduct on the Erie Canal, New York, ca. 1829–1830, John William Hill (American, born England, 1812–1879). Watercolor, white gouache, graphite, and black ink with selective glazing on paper laid on board. Between 1829 and 1831, Hill executed a number of watercolors of the Erie Canal to be published by his father, John Hill, in a portfolio of aquatint engravings devoted solely to canal views. Although several plates were produced, the series was never completed. John William Hill's images often feature charming vignettes of human activity at work or leisure. This view is of the Lower Aqueduct, which crossed over the Mohawk River at Colonie and Halfmoon. *New-York Historical Society*.

View of the Canal, Little Falls, Mohawk River, plate, ca. 1835. Job and John Jackson (English, active 1831–1835), after engraving by T. S. Woodcock, original sketch by W. G. Wall. Earthenware, transfer printed. New York State Museum, H-1970.9.3

Erie Canal Wheelbarrows,

MADE by the subscriber at Rome, N. Y. on a new and much improved plan, and for sale at Rome Utica, Rochester and Palmyra—prices from 5 to 6 dollars. The superior utility of this machine has been proved by actual experiment by numbers the year past. The following recommendations of the Canal Commissioners, the Chief Engineer, and one of Contractors who has used it, are inserted for the information of the public:

JEREMIAH BRAINARD.

Jan. 4, 1820.

WE certify, that we have examined the plan of the wheel-barrow, constructed by Jeremiah Brainard, that we have seen it in use on the Erie Canal in many hands for several months, and that we are of opinion that it is greatly superior to any other wheel-barrow within our knowledge. Its advantages consist chiefly in its being more durable, easier to unload and lighter. We recommend it to general adoption.

Dec. 21st, 1819.

MYRON HOLLEY,
HENRY SEYMOUR,
acting Canal Commissioners.
BENJ. WRIGHT,
principal Engineer.

This may certify that I have made use of Mr. Jeremiah Brainard's newly invented wheel barrow, and find them far superior to any thing of the kind ever used on the Erie Canal

Dec. 21st, 1819. JOHN RICHARDSON, Contractor.

"Erie Canal Wheelbarrow" advertisement, *Patriot* (Utica, New York), February 15, 1820. *America's Historical Newspapers, Newsbank online via New York State Library.*

Wheelbarrow, nineteenth century. Jeremiah Brainard of Rome, a canal contractor, invented a unique wheelbarrow made of a single board bent in a semi-circular shape that was lighter and faster to load and unload than a typical wheelbarrow, which was shaped more like a box. This forerunner to the modern wheelbarrow was widely used for the construction of the canal. The example is a later model inspired by Brainard's design. *New York State Museum, L2017.37.1.*

Scraper, nineteenth century. The blade on this scraper cut through small roots and dug up the ground. This scraper is a later model based on those used during the canal's construction, which had a wooden base with a metal blade attached. *New York State Museum, H-1970.54.1094.*

Model of a stump puller, Tom Rogosta, ca. 2000. Stump pullers like this were used to clear the way for the canal's excavation. It was reported that forty large stumps could be pulled from the earth in one day with a machine like this and a team of seven men and two oxen. *Courtesy of the Watervliet Historical Society.*

Mammoth jaw. Workers found this mammoth jaw around 1820, during the construction of the original Erie Canal. The story passed down with the object is that the workers found an entire jaw and tusks and broke off pieces to keep. When the New York State Museum opened in 1836, the contractor hunted down a few pieces and gave them to the museum. *New York State Museum, VP-26.*

Keeping enough water in the canal was no small feat. To maintain the flow of water, very slight declines over miles had to be calculated into the construction of the canal bed, and small feeder canals were built to help supply enough water. A navigable aqueduct connected the canal with the village of Little Falls and a small feeder canal, a section of the former WILNC Canal, which drew water from the Mohawk River.

James Eights (American, 1798–1882)

Beginning in 1822, James Eights served as draftsman for the geological survey of the Erie Canal. His watercolors and drawings, some of the earliest of the canal, highlighted engineering feats, such as the aqueducts at Little Falls and Rochester, as well as canal landscapes. They were engraved in Albany by Rawdon, Clark & Co. Some were published in 1824 in Amos Eaton's geological and agricultural report summarizing the canal survey and in Cadwallader D. Colden's 1825 memoir chronicling the building and opening of the canal.

Aqueduct Bridge at Little Falls, James Eights, watercolor on paper, 1823. *Courtesy of the Albany Institute of History & Art.*

The Entrance of the Canal into the Hudson at Albany Taken in 1823, pencil, ink, and ink wash on paper, 1823. *Courtesy of the Albany Institute of History & Art*

Entrance of the Erie Canal into the Hudson at Albany, plate, ca. 1825–1830, Enoch Wood & Sons (English, active 1818–1840). Earthenware, transfer printed. *New York State Museum, H-1976.199.1.*

Staffordshire transferware based on the engravings was manufactured in England by Enoch Wood & Sons, one of the major pottery exporters to the United States. The practice of using the original work in different media, including engravings and ceramics, underscored the popularity of canal imagery.

Aqueduct Bridge at Rochester, watercolor on paper, 1823. *Courtesy of the Albany Institute of History & Art.*

Who Built the Canal?

> **When it is considered that the commissioners and engineers could have had no experience in canalling; that the science they acquired must have been in a great measure the result of mental application, while they were constantly employed in the active and anxious duties of their station, they deserve a commendation to which any thing [sic] I could say on this occasion, would be very inadequate.**
>
> **—Cadwallader D. Colden, 1825[5]**

When the famed English canal engineer William Weston turned down the position of chief engineer for the Erie Canal, New York turned to Benjamin Wright, James Geddes, and others who were not formally trained engineers but had previously surveyed for the canal project. They learned by reading trade books, and trial and error, and through experience they became engineers and instructed others on the job. Thereafter, many of the Erie Canal's engineers went on to work on other projects throughout the country, building canals, railroads, bridges, water systems, and roads.

Benjamin Wright (1770–1842)

Benjamin Wright is frequently called the "Father of American Civil Engineering." Wright worked on the Western Inland Lock Navigation Company's (WILNC) works and New York City's expansion, and as chief engineer for the Erie Canal. His leadership and tutelage were crucial to the development of civil engineering in the United States. Wright's early experience on the WILNC and discovery of limestone suitable for stone locks prepared him for his role on the Erie Canal.

Benjamin Wright (1770–1842), unknown artist, oil on canvas, ca. 1825. *Courtesy of Francis Delafield Wright III.*

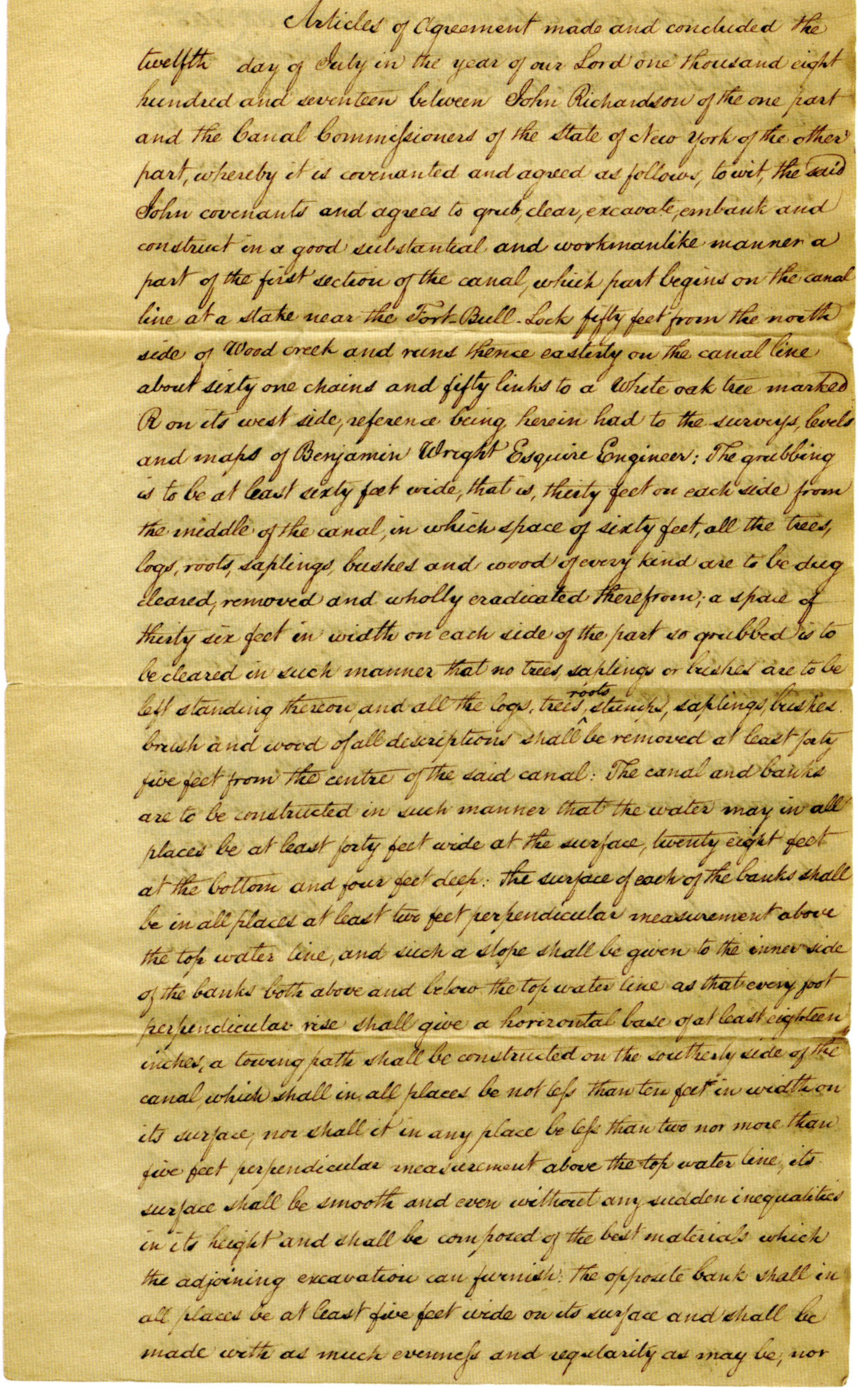

Articles of Agreement made and concluded the twelfth day of July in the year of our Lord one thousand eight hundred and seventeen between John Richardson of the one part and the Canal Commissioners of the State of New York of the other part, whereby it is covenanted and agreed as follows, to wit, the said John covenants and agrees to grub, clear, excavate, embank and construct in a good substantial and workmanlike manner a part of the first section of the canal, which part begins on the canal line at a stake near the Fort Bull Lock fifty feet from the north side of Wood creek and runs thence easterly on the canal line about sixty one chains and fifty links to a White oak tree marked R on its west side, reference being herein had to the surveys, levels and maps of Benjamin Wright Esquire Engineer: The grubbing is to be at least sixty feet wide, that is, thirty feet on each side from the middle of the canal, in which space of sixty feet, all the trees, logs, roots, saplings, bushes and wood of every kind are to be dug cleared, removed and wholly eradicated therefrom; a space of thirty six feet in width on each side of the part so grubbed is to be cleared in such manner that no trees, saplings or bushes are to be left standing thereon, and all the logs, trees, roots, stumps, saplings, bushes brush and wood of all descriptions shall be removed at least forty five feet from the centre of the said canal: The canal and banks are to be constructed in such manner that the water may in all places be at least forty feet wide at the surface, twenty eight feet at the bottom and four feet deep: the surface of each of the banks shall be in all places at least two feet perpendicular measurement above the top water line, and such a slope shall be given to the inner side of the banks both above and below the top water line as that every foot perpendicular rise shall give a horizontal base of at least eighteen inches, a towing path shall be constructed on the southerly side of the canal, which shall in all places be not less than ten feet in width on its surface, nor shall it in any place be less than two nor more than five feet perpendicular measurement above the top water line, its surface shall be smooth and even without any sudden inequalities in its height and shall be composed of the best materials which the adjoining excavation can furnish: The opposite bank shall in all places be at least five feet wide on its surface and shall be made with as much evenness and regularity as may be, nor

Canal contract, 1817 (pages 63–66). This is the first contract awarded for the construction of the canal. Dated July 12, 1817, it describes in meticulous detail the work to be completed by contractor John Richardson. *Courtesy of the New York State Archives, A1125.*

shall either of the banks unless where they contain an extra width at the surface in consequence of a redundance of stuff have a less slope on the outer than on the inner or water side, the extra stuff except where it is used for embankment shall be disposed of with as much evenness and regularity as may be, nor shall it be thrown into detached piles or elevated hillocks to the injury of the adjoining lands, nor shall any part of the earth, trees, logs, stumps, roots, bushes or rubbish of any kind be thrown, felled, removed, placed or left on either of those parts of the canal which are contiguous or adjoining to the part so to be grubbed, cleared, excavated, embanked and constructed by the said John; all the loose and porous materials which are of a perishable nature or permeable to water shall occupy the outer extremities of the banks, and for the distance of at least ten feet measured horizontally from the top water line on each side of the canal the banks shall be wholly made and constructed both above and below the top water line of the most pure solid, compact and water tight earth which the adjoining excavation can supply, nor shall any vegetable mould, leaves, roots, weeds, grass herbage, logs, sticks or any other substance of a vegetable, porous or perishable nature be left, laid, placed or in any way admitted into the said space of ten feet horizontally measured as aforesaid from the top water line or above or below the same: and the said John further agrees that during the progress of the work he will from time to time conform to such deviations from the above designated line and to such alterations in the form, slope and dimensions of the banks, towing path or any other part of the works as either of the said Commissioners or any Engineer by them or either of them appointed for that purpose shall direct. The said John also covenants and agrees to alter and remove the public highway which is twice crossed by the line of the canal near the Fort-Bull-Lock in such manner that the same may run wholly on the northerly side of the canal without crossing the same, and to make and construct the said highway at a proper distance from the canal good passable and convenient for the public travel, causewaying so much of the same as shall be necessary, and covering the said causeway with a sufficient coat of earth, and also that he will make a

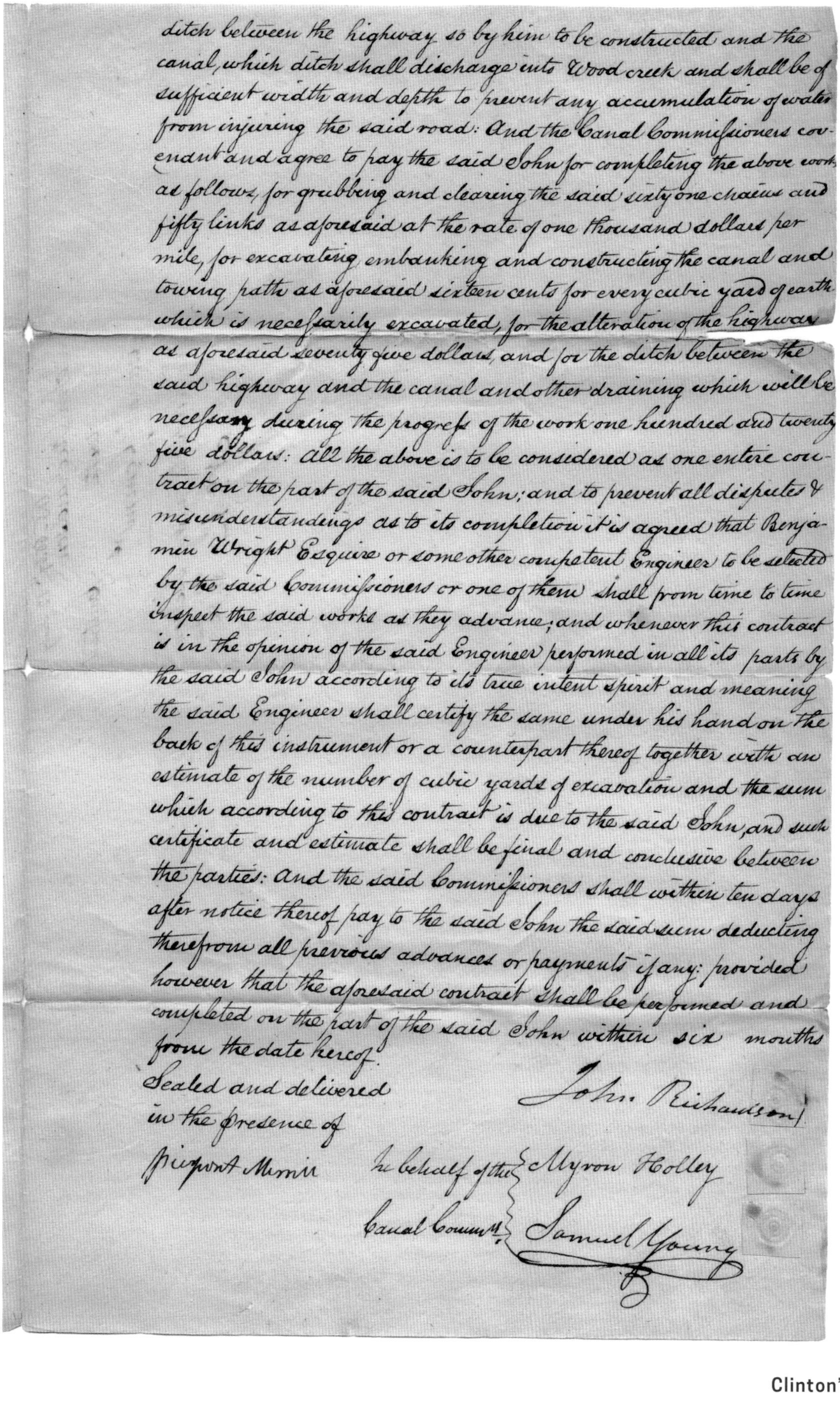

ditch between the highway so by him to be constructed and the canal, which ditch shall discharge into Wood creek and shall be of sufficient width and depth to prevent any accumulation of water from injuring the said road: And the Canal Commissioners covenant and agree to pay the said John for completing the above work as follows, for grubbing and clearing the said sixty one chains and fifty links as aforesaid at the rate of one thousand dollars per mile, for excavating, embanking and constructing the canal and towing path as aforesaid sixteen cents for every cubic yard of earth which is necessarily excavated, for the alteration of the highway as aforesaid seventy five dollars, and for the ditch between the said highway and the canal and other draining which will be necessary during the progress of the work one hundred and twenty five dollars: All the above is to be considered as one entire contract on the part of the said John; and to prevent all disputes & misunderstandings as to its completion it is agreed that Benjamin Wright Esquire or some other competent Engineer to be selected by the said Commissioners or one of them shall from time to time inspect the said works as they advance; and whenever this contract is in the opinion of the said Engineer performed in all its parts by the said John according to its true intent spirit and meaning the said Engineer shall certify the same under his hand on the back of this instrument or a counterpart thereof together with an estimate of the number of cubic yards of excavation and the sum which according to this contract is due to the said John, and such certificate and estimate shall be final and conclusive between the parties: And the said Commissioners shall within ten days after notice thereof pay to the said John the said sum deducting therefrom all previous advances or payments if any: provided however that the aforesaid contract shall be performed and completed on the part of the said John within six months from the date hereof.

Sealed and delivered
in the presence of

John Richardson

Pierpont [illegible]

In behalf of the Canal Commrs. { Myron Holley
Samuel Young

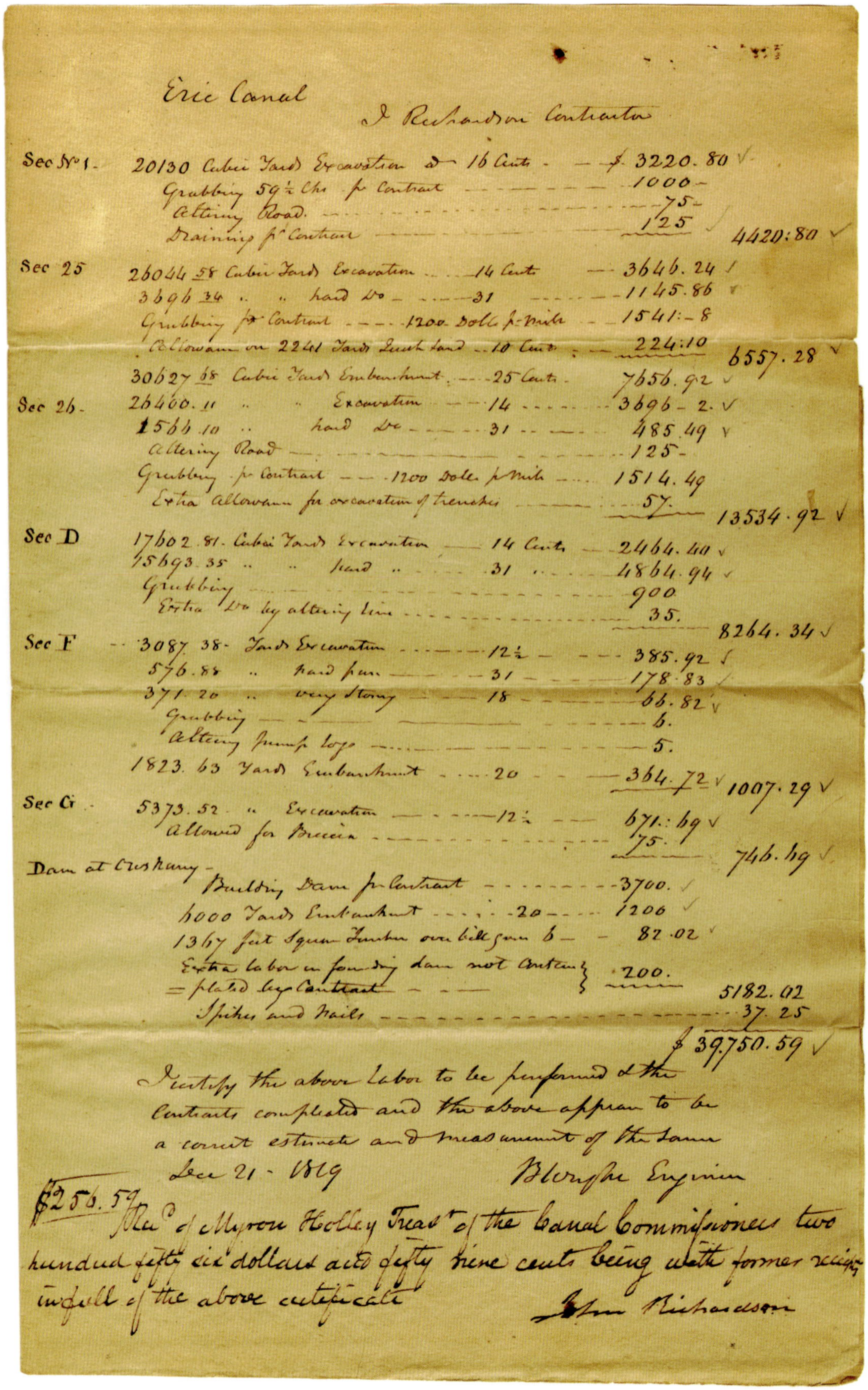

Erie Canal

J Richardson Contractor

Sec No 1	20130 Cubic Yards Excavation at 16 Cents	$ 3220.80	
	Grubbing 59½ Chs pr Contract	1000	
	Altering Road	75	
	Draining pr Contract	125	4420:80
Sec 25	26044 58 Cubic Yards Excavation 14 Cents	3646.24	
	3696 34 " " hard Do 31	1145.86	
	Grubbing pr Contract 1200 Dolls pr Mile	1541:-8	
	Allowance on 2241 Yards Quick Sand 10 Cents	224:10	6557.28
	30627 68 Cubic Yards Embankment 25 Cents	7656.92	
Sec 26	26400.11 " " Excavation 14	3696-2.	
	1566.10 " hard Do 31	485.49	
	Altering Road	125	
	Grubbing pr Contract 1200 Dolls pr Mile	1514.49	
	Extra allowance for excavation of trenches	57.	13534.92
Sec D	17602.81 Cubic Yards Excavation 14 Cents	2464.40	
	15693.35 " " hard " 31	4864.94	
	Grubbing	900	
	Extra Do by altering line	35.	8264.34
Sec F	3087 38 Yards Excavation 12½	385.92	
	576.88 " hard pan 31	178.83	
	371.20 " very Stony 18	66.82	
	Grubbing	6.	
	Altering pump logs	5.	
	1823.63 Yards Embankment 20	364.72	1007.29
Sec G	5373.52 " Excavation 12½	671.69	
	Allowed for Breccia	75.	746.69
Dam at Crusheny	Building Dam pr Contract	3700.	
	6000 Yards Embankment 20	1200	
	1367 feet Square Timber over bill gave 6	82.02	
	Extra labor in founding dam not contemplated by Contract	200.	5182.02
	Spikes and Nails		37.25
			$ 39750.59

I certify the above labor to be performed & the Contracts compleated and the above appear to be a correct estimate and measurement of the same

Dec 21 - 1819 B Wright Engineer

$256.59 Recd of Myron Holley Treasr of the Canal Commissioners two hundred fifty six dollars and fifty nine cents being with former receipts in full of the above certificate

John Richardson

James Geddes (1763–1838)

James Geddes started on the canal project in 1808, conducting some of its early surveys. By 1816 he was appointed the engineer in charge of survey. He later became chief engineer of the Champlain Canal and went on to work on numerous canals.

Canvass White (1790–1834)

Canvass White served as an assistant to Benjamin Wright and eventually became an engineer in his own right. At the request of De Witt Clinton, he spent months in Europe studying canals. Like many of the other engineers who got their training on the Erie Canal project, White went on to serve as chief engineer on other canals and railroads. White's patent for an American version of hydraulic cement, which hardens underwater, was made with New York's natural resources. While he was credited with inventing this version of hydraulic cement, recent scholarship suggests he negotiated with the actual inventor, Andrew Bartow, to hold the patent.

Canvass White, W. G. Jackman, engraving, 1871. Charles B. Stuart, *Lives and Works of Civil and Military Engineers of America* (New York: D. Van Nostrand, 1871). *Courtesy of the New York State Library, 620.92 As.*

Rochester section of the 1817 Geddes Map. In this original plan for the canal, Geddes called for a dam ten feet high to create a pool for boats to cross. A bridge south of the dam would provide a towpath and the crossing point for the boats. It was later decided that an aqueduct would be a better solution for crossing the swift current of the Genesee River. *Courtesy of the New York State Archives, (N-Ar)A0851.*

Chief Engineer of Rome, model, ca. 1820. Canvass White may have brought this model to the United States to serve as an example for boat builders. The first boat used on the Erie Canal, the *Chief Engineer* was based on this model and that name was added to the model after the fact. *Courtesy of The Buffalo History Museum.*

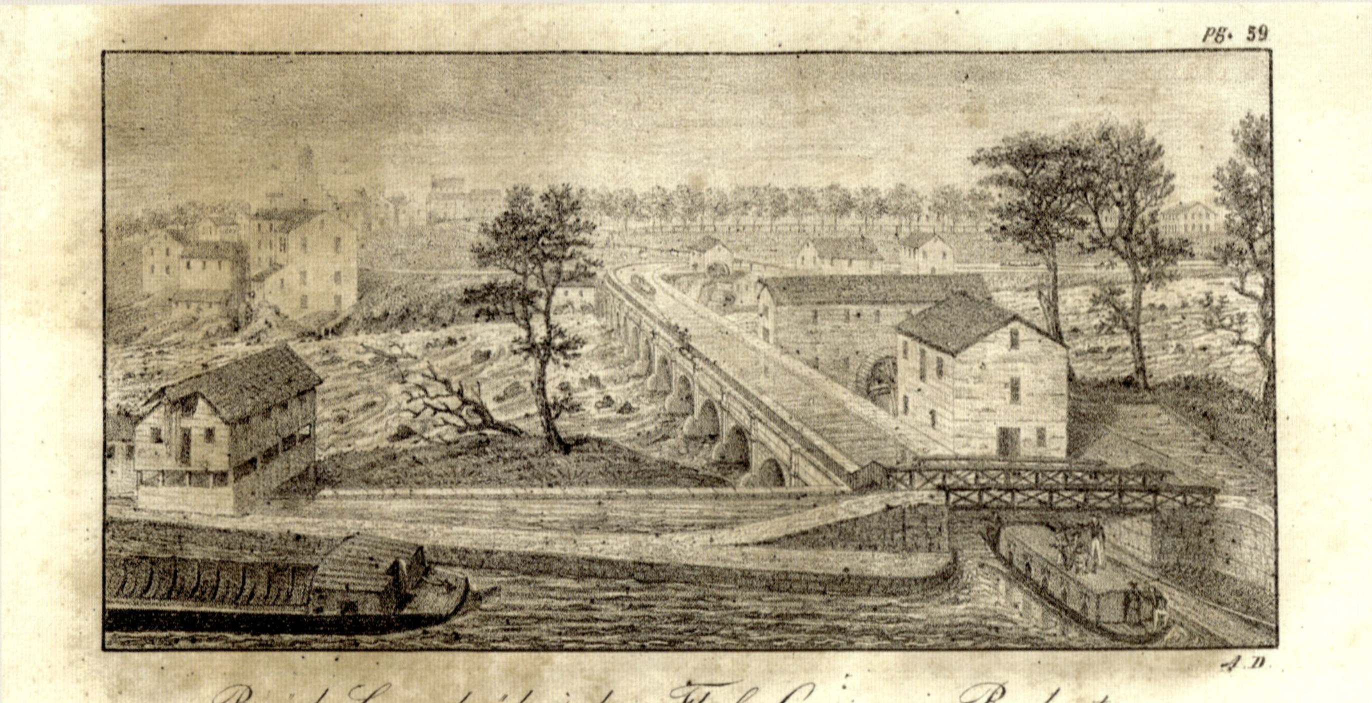

First Aqueduct Over the River at Rochester, 1826, engraving, 1835. Crossing the Genesee River was a major concern for canal engineers. The aqueduct, built under David S. Bates's supervision, was an enormous success, which served as one of the nationally renowned spots on the canal. Courtesy of the New York State Library, Manuscripts and Special Collections, N 917.4 D97.

John B. Jervis (1795–1885)

As a teenager, John B. Jervis left his father's struggling farm to join a canal surveying crew as an axman at Rome. Jervis was a quick study and before long worked his way up to be an engineer. Eventually, he became one of the most successful American engineers of the nineteenth century.

The High Bridge at Harlem, New York, Nathaniel T. Currier, lithograph, 1849. Engineer John B. Jervis is best known for his work on the Croton Aqueduct and the "high bridge" that delivered water to New York City. *New York State Museum, H-1978.150.2.*

Nathan Roberts, Grove S. Gilbert, oil on canvas, ca. 1840. Nathan Roberts (1776–1851) was a former schoolteacher and surveyor-turned-engineer who designed the Lockport "flight of ten locks." He went on to work on other canal projects, including the enlargement of the Erie Canal from 1835 to 1841. *New York State Museum, H-1960.3.1.*

Surveyor's chain, ca. 1800–1850. One of the standard pieces of equipment for surveying, chains measured distances. A standard Gunter's chain was sixty-six feet long and consisted of one hundred links, each measuring 9.92 inches. One chain equals four rods; ten square chains equal one acre; eighty chains equal one mile. *New York State Museum, H-1942.4.2.*

Vernier compass, Horatio Hanks, Auburn, 1818–1826. Horatio Hanks moved from West Troy (Watervliet) to Auburn to make scientific instruments for the growing population in western New York. Surveyors and engineers who worked on the canal would have used this style compass. *New York State Museum, H-1993.8.129.*

Wye level and case, Meneely & Oothout, West Troy (Watervliet), 1836–1841. This later-model level is similar in style and technology to those used by the engineers who worked on the Erie Canal. *Courtesy of the private collection of William Skerritt.*

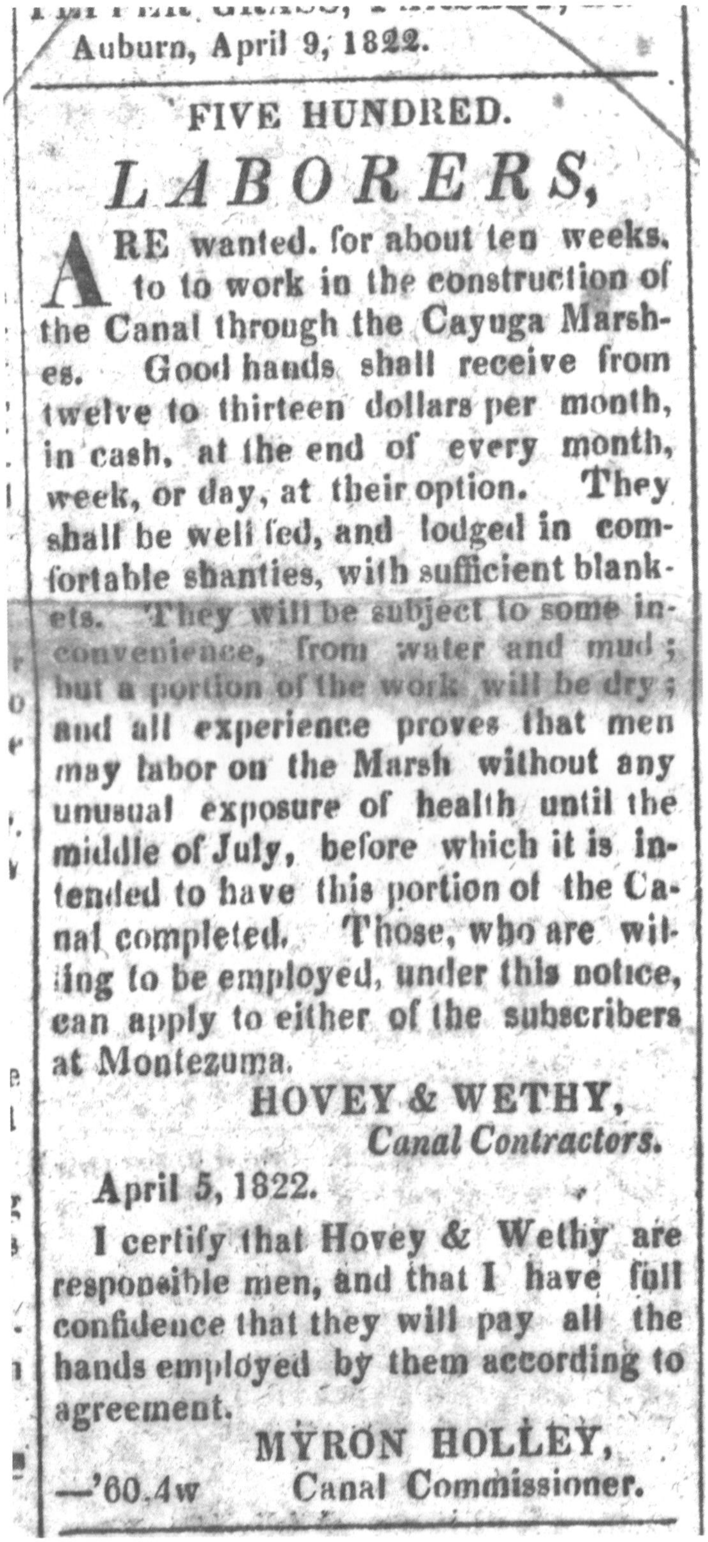

Auburn, April 9, 1822.

FIVE HUNDRED.

LABORERS,

ARE wanted. for about ten weeks, to to work in the construction of the Canal through the Cayuga Marshes. Good hands shall receive from twelve to thirteen dollars per month, in cash, at the end of every month, week, or day, at their option. They shall be well fed, and lodged in comfortable shanties, with sufficient blankets. They will be subject to some inconvenience, from water and mud; but a portion of the work will be dry; and all experience proves that men may labor on the Marsh without any unusual exposure of health until the middle of July, before which it is intended to have this portion of the Canal completed. Those, who are willing to be employed, under this notice, can apply to either of the subscribers at Montezuma.

HOVEY & WETHY,
Canal Contractors.

April 5, 1822.

I certify that Hovey & Wethy are responsible men, and that I have full confidence that they will pay all the hands employed by them according to agreement.

MYRON HOLLEY,
Canal Commissioner.

—'60.4w

Newspaper advertisement calling for Erie Canal laborers, *Cayuga Republican (Auburn, NY), 1822. New York State Museum, Mrs. Arnold B. Barben Canal Collection, H-1988.79.*

The Laborers

The immense scope of the Erie Canal project was split into four main sections: Eastern, Middle, Western, and the Champlain Canal. Each section was divided into smaller parts for contractors to bid on. The contractors in turn hired laborers. The canal commissioners wanted to ensure that the field for bidding was open to all in what was New York's first large-scale use of subcontracting.

During the first few years, construction was completed mostly by local farmers and native-born Americans. In 1819 America experienced its first economic depression. The economic downturn actually helped the canal project; construction costs dropped, and struggling farmers found work as contractors and laborers. As the project grew, it drew laborers from Europe, especially Irish immigrants.

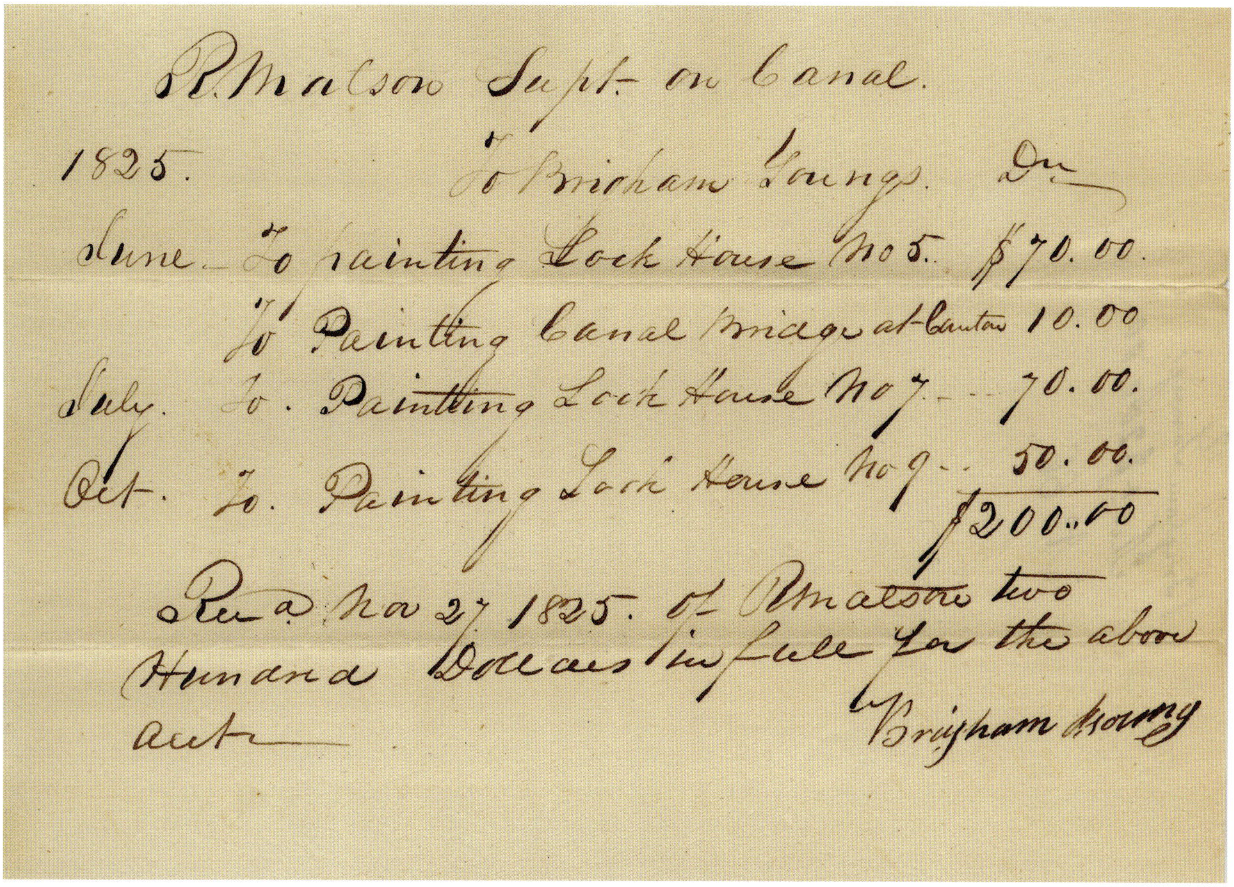

R. Matson Supt. on Canal.

1825. To Brigham Youngs Dr

June — To painting Lock House No 5. $70.00

To Painting Canal bridge at Canton 10.00

July. To. Painting Lock House No 7 — 70.00

Oct. To. Painting Lock House No 9 — 50.00

$200.00

Recd Nov 27 1825. of R Matson two Hundred Dollars in full for the above acct

Brigham Young

Brigham Young receipt, 1825. Invoice from future Mormon leader Brigham Young. He was paid $200 for painting three lock houses and a bridge. *Courtesy of the New York State Archives, A1125-78_B3.*

Copper kettle, ca. 1820. This kettle belonged to Christine Davis Hassett. Family lore indicates that she found work cooking for the laborers and had this special kettle made to prepare larger meals. It is probable that her husband John was a laborer. *Courtesy of the Erie Canal Museum.*

Deep Cutting, Lockport, George Catlin, hand-colored lithograph, 1825. Irish laborers performed the most dangerous work, such as blasting through rock with gunpowder to construct the deep cut of Lockport. They also found work in the swamps of western New York. They wore "Montezuma Necklaces," smoldering leaves in pots hung around their necks to keep mosquitos, and malaria, at bay. It is believed that hundreds of Irish immigrants died in the swamps. *New York State Museum, H-1984.15.1.*

Process of Excavation, Lockport, George Catlin, lithograph, 1825. Orange H. Dibble and Walter Osborn invented the horse-powered crane depicted in this lithograph. Special steel drills were produced and blasting powder used to explode through the rock, sometimes with lethal results. *New York State Museum, H-1984.15.1.*

CONQUERING THE NIAGARA ESCARPMENT

The Niagara Escarpment is a ridge that runs from Wisconsin to western New York. To complete the canal, engineers and laborers had to conquer this great geological formation, and Lockport was chosen as the best place to traverse the sixty-foot obstacle. At the top of the cliff, a seven-mile channel through solid rock was cut to provide a steady flow of water from Lake Erie. A set of five double locks was built to climb the ridge and enter the deep cut—an engineering feat that made Lockport famous across the country.

Entrance to the Harbour, Lockport, George Catlin, lithograph, 1825. *New York State Museum, H-1969.42.2.*

Lockport capstone, 1825. *New York State Museum, H-1950.10.1.*
On August 24, 1825, a grand ceremony was held to honor the completion of the Lockport flight. Over four hundred Freemasons attended the ceremony, along with an estimated three thousand to four thousand citizens. It was common at the time for Freemasons to dedicate cornerstones of new construction. After a blessing and Masonic ceremony, Jesse Hawley, Nathan Roberts, and others made toasts to the magnificent canal. This is one of two capstones ceremoniously placed into the structure of the flight that day. It reads:

The Erie Canal
362 miles in length was
commenced the 4th of July 1817
and completed in the year 1825 at an
expense of about $7,000,000
and was constructed exclusively by the
CITIZENS
of the STATE of
NEW YORK.

Trowel, ca. 1825. This silver trowel was presented to John Maynard of Salina, New York, builder of the first lock at Lockport, as part of the ceremonies when the capstones were dedicated. *Courtesy of the New-York Historical Society, 1952.407.*

Lockport from Prospect Hill, George Catlin, lithograph, 1825. *New York State Museum, 1969.42.3.*

Lockport on the Erie Canal, 1832, Mary Keys (American, active 1830s), watercolor on paper. Likely a student, Keys based her watercolor on a print after a drawing by George Catlin published in Cadwallader D. Colden's 1825 memoir on the building of the Erie Canal and its opening celebrations. Lockport was named after the "flight of five" locks visible at the right. The engineering marvel cut through the rocky ridge known as the Niagara Escarpment, allowing the waters of Lake Erie to supply this section of the canal. *Munson-Williams-Proctor Arts Institute.*

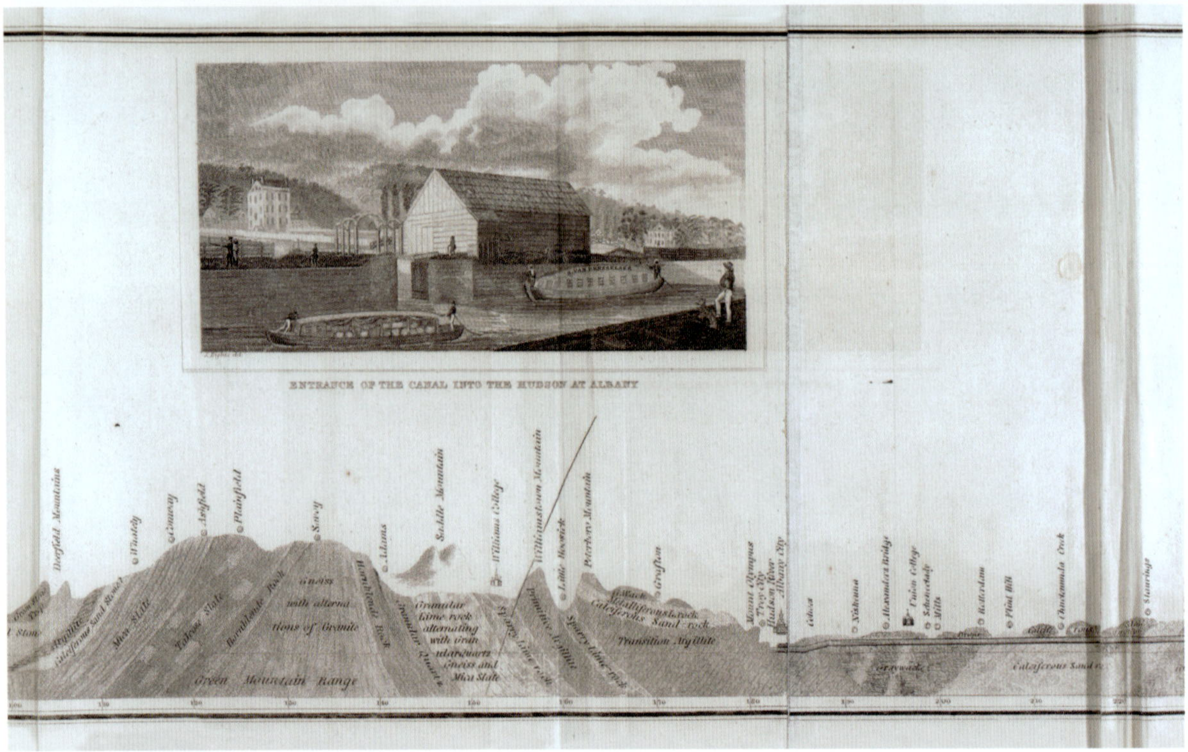

Map, *Geological Profile from the Atlantic Ocean to Lake Erie*, Amos Eaton, 1822–1823 (pages 78–80). Amos Eaton (1776–1842) created this map from his pioneering research on the state's geological, agricultural, and mineralogical resources. A brilliant natural scientist, geologist, popular lecturer, and founding professor of the Rensselaer School (today's RPI), Eaton also used the canal as an innovative mobile classroom. During the summers of 1826–1831, he hired a canal boat, using it as a moving combination laboratory, lecture space, study, dormitory, and living space from which his students explored the natural history of the landscape. *Courtesy of the New York State Library, Manuscripts and Special Collections, N 386.4 qC68 203-5185.*

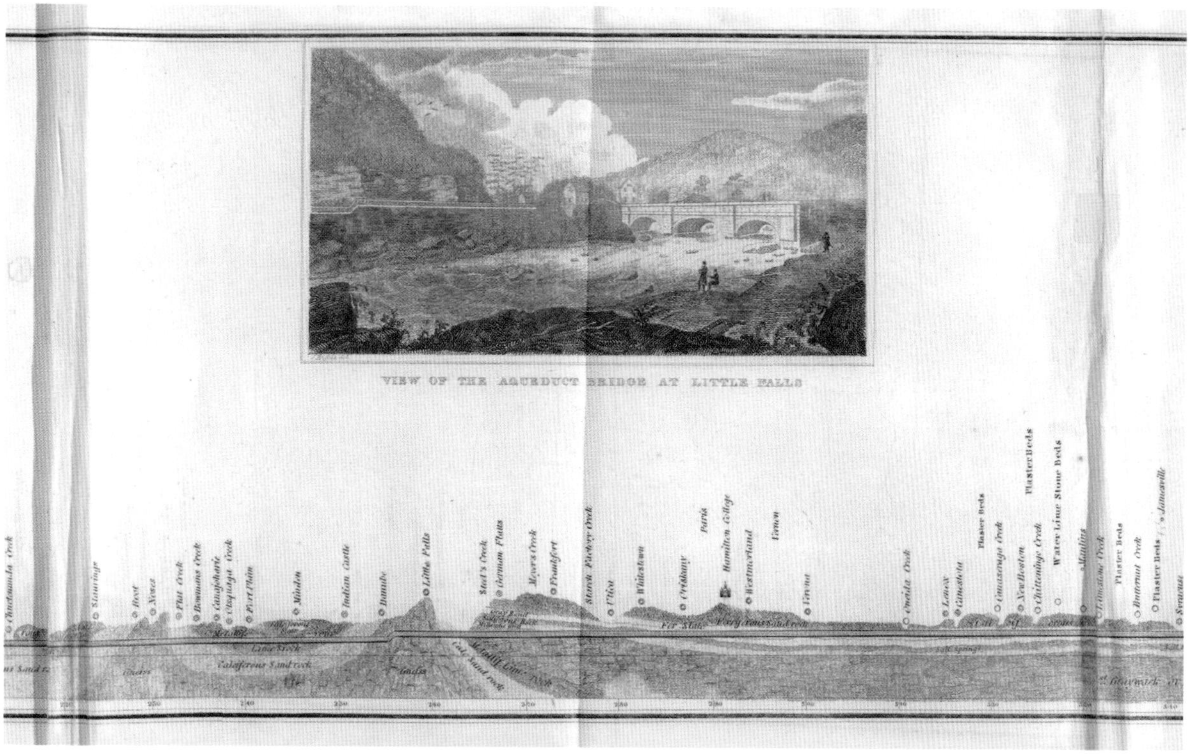
VIEW OF THE AQUEDUCT BRIDGE AT LITTLE FALLS

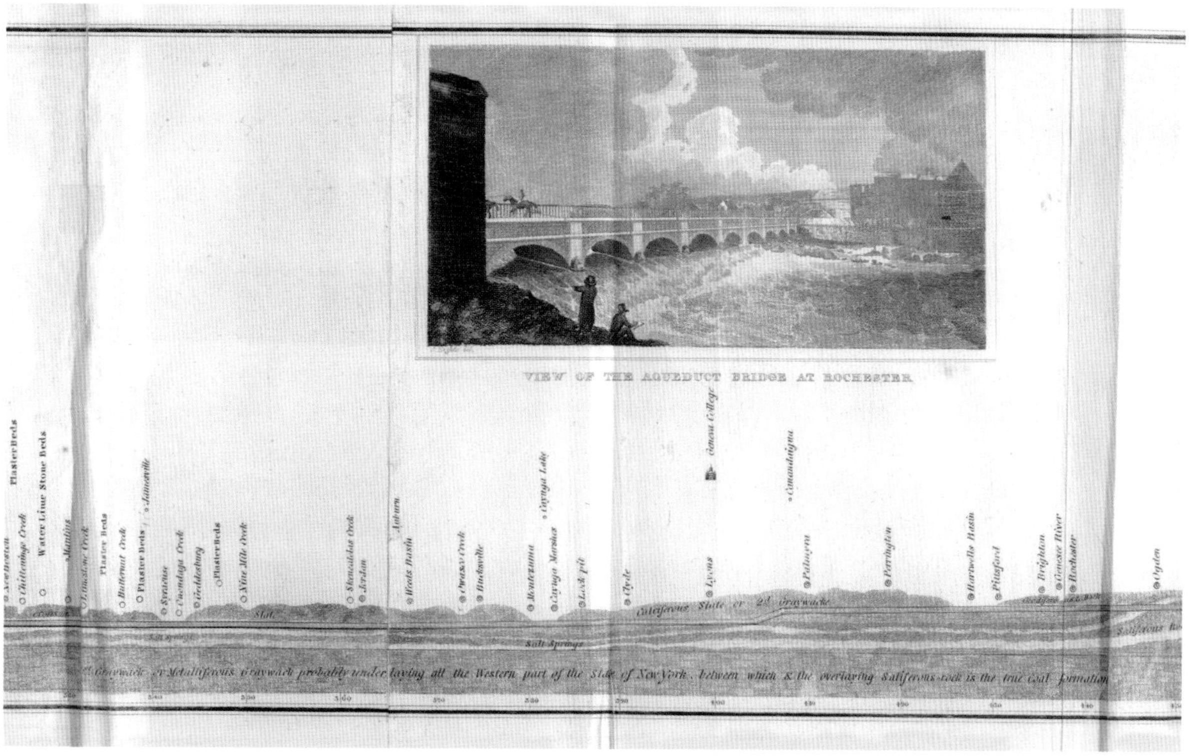
VIEW OF THE AQUEDUCT BRIDGE AT ROCHESTER

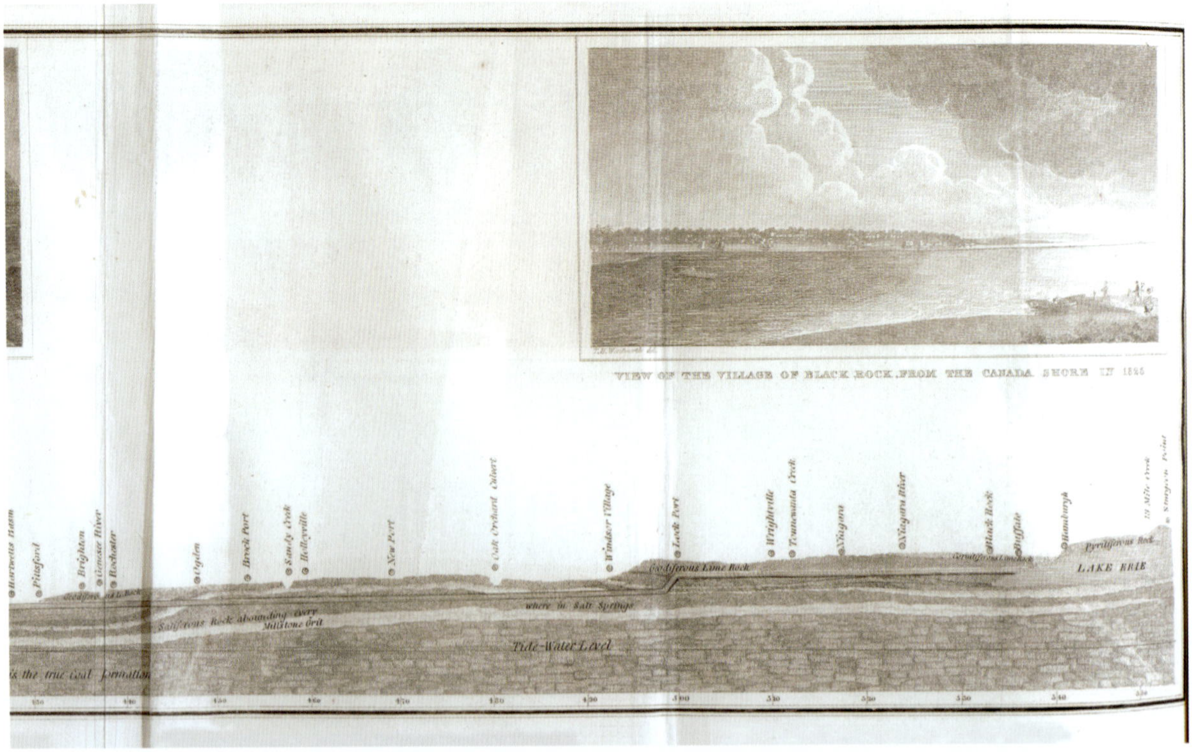

CELEBRATING EARLY ACHIEVEMENTS

On October 23, 1819, Governor De Witt Clinton, canal commissioners, canal engineers, military leaders, religious leaders, and other dignitaries sailed on the *Chief Engineer of Rome* from Utica to Rome on the first celebratory canal boat ride. The water had been let into some sections of the canal just two days before. Laborers were stationed at potential trouble spots along the route, and there was one breach that was quickly patched. The boat was welcomed along the route with cheers as the band on board played patriotic tunes. A large banquet was held at Rome, and the boat returned to Utica. This demonstration of success of the Erie Canal stirred support and enthusiasm for the endeavor and pressure for its completion.

In 1823 a grand celebration was held in Albany for the completion of the Champlain Canal and the Erie Canal from Brockport to the capital. Delegates from around the state joined elected officials, military officers, canal commissioners, engineers, contractors, firefighters, members of various societies, and thousands of onlookers for the festivities. The day included performances by bands, parades—on land and in the water—and speeches, and a capstone was laid at Lock 1. A Masonic ceremony was also held at the entrance of the canal.

Chief Engineer of Rome (depicted in the Hager painting above right), model ca. 1965. Model of the first boat to travel the canal in 1819. The actual *Chief Engineer of Rome* was based on the model that Canvass White brought back from England. However, it was not an exact copy and this model depicts what the boat actually looked like when built. *Courtesy of the Canal Society of New York State.*

First Trip on the Canal, Robert Hager, oil on canvas, 1966. This painting depicts the first official boat ride on the Erie Canal, which took place among much fanfare on October 23, 1819. The trip included Governor Clinton, the canal commissioners, and numerous other elected officials. *Courtesy of the Canal Society of New York State.*

Ewer (pitcher), William Gale, 1823. In 1823 the *Mary and Hannah* was the first boat to travel from Seneca Lake to New York City by canal, carrying a cargo of western wheat, butter, and beans. This ewer was presented to the owners of the vessel, John H. Osborne and Samuel S. Seely, in honor of the trip. *Courtesy of the Albany Institute of History & Art. Gift of William Gorham Rice, grandson of Samuel S. Seely, x1940.435.*

WEDDING OF THE WATERS

> **When we look at a map, and see marked out, the many Lakes and sheets of navigable waters which occupy the centre of our State, and reflect that every place on their shores is, for all purposes of commerce, converted by the Canals into a sea-port, and that the trade of all of them must centre in this metropolis, we may have some idea of the advantages which the city and country will derive from the opening of these water communications.**
>
> **—Cadwallader D. Colden, 1825[6]**

As the deep cut at Lockport neared completion, plans were made for an enormous celebration. The festivities began in Buffalo on October 26, 1825, with speeches and a special cannon "communication" to New York City.

A flotilla left Buffalo on a ten-day voyage to New York City. Aboard the canal boats were elected officials, including Governor De Witt Clinton, as well as dignitaries and products from the western part of the state, including a Native American canoe from Lake Superior, various animals, lumber, potash, flour, and butter, among other things. Communities along the canal welcomed the flotilla with speeches, artillery salutes, and fireworks, celebrating what New York and American democracy had accomplished. Once in New York City, the celebration included the "Wedding of the Waters" ceremony, a large parade, and numerous festivities.

The "Wedding of the Waters" ceremony took place in New York Harbor off Sandy Hook. A choreographed parade of domestic and international vessels formed a circle in the bay while Clinton and others gave speeches and poured water from Lake Erie into the Atlantic.

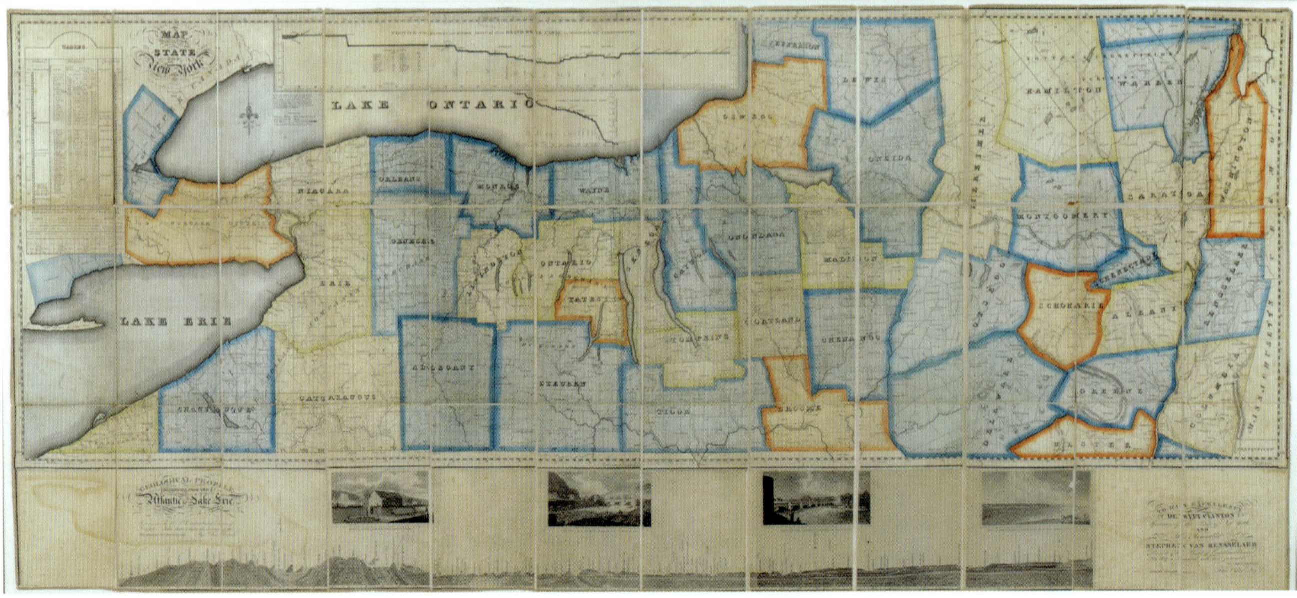

Map of a portion of the state of New York, 1823–1824, engraved by D. H. Vance, published by J. Ogden Dey, and "A Geological Profile Extending from the Atlantic to Lake Erie," 1825, Amos Eaton, engraved by Rawdon, Clark & Co., Albany. This map outlines the final route of the original completed canal across New York State, as well as a profile of the canal route, and geographical information. *Courtesy of the Canal Society of New York State.*

Cannon, model 1819. Celebratory cannon fire alerted communities that the grand flotilla had left Buffalo for New York City. Cannons were placed along the route of the canal and the Hudson River from Buffalo to New York City. Once the first cannon was fired, the next within earshot would fire, and the process continued as cannons were fired successively until reaching New York City, then reversed returning to Buffalo. The first cannon sounded at ten in the morning on October 26, 1825. The progression reached Albany at 10:57 a.m. and New York City at 11:17 a.m. The message went back up the Hudson and returned to Buffalo just before 1:00 p.m. *Courtesy of Sackets Harbor Battlefield State Historic Site, Sackets Harbor, New York, Office of Parks, Recreation, and Historic Preservation, SA.1982.8.a.*

Opening the Erie Canal: Marriage of the Waters, Charles Yardley Turner, mural, 1905. *Courtesy of the Collection of the New York City Department of Education, photograph by Stan Ries.*

WEDDING OF THE LAKES WITH THE OCEAN.

Wedding of the Lakes with the Ocean, engraving, 1888. Benson Lossing, *Our Country: A Household History of the United States for All Readers, from the Discovery of America to the Present Time, 1888. Courtesy of the New York State Library, Manuscripts and Special Collections, 973 qL88o.*

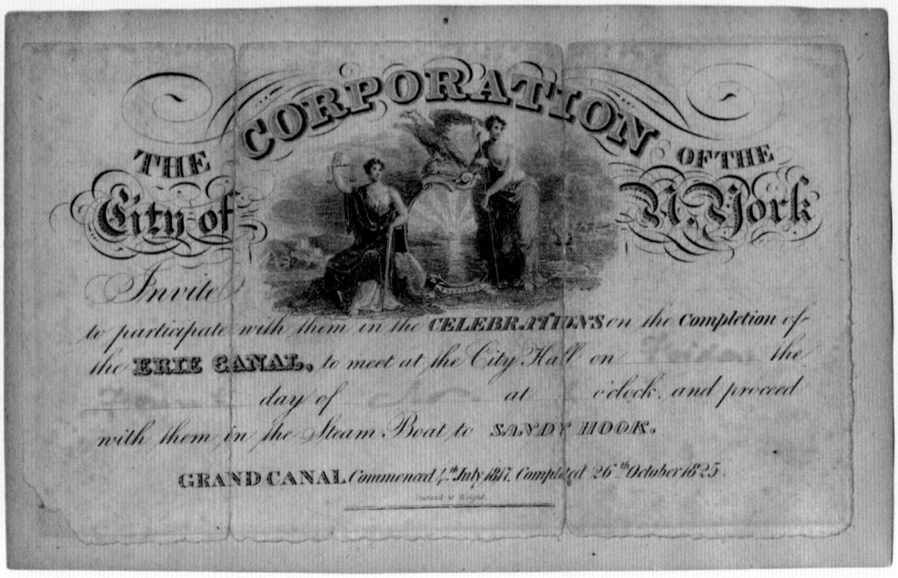

Invitation to Erie Canal Celebration, A. B. Durand, engraving, ca. 1825. *Courtesy of the New-York Historical Society PR.221.12, 1825.*

A View of the Magnificent and Extraordinary Fireworks Exhibited on the N.Y. City Hall, on the Evening of the Celebration of the Grand Canal, November 4, 1825, John F. E. Prud'homme, engraving, 1825. This engraving depicts and describes the fireworks celebration at New York City Hall on November 4, 1825, in honor of the opening of the Erie Canal. *New York State Museum, H-1974.17.15.*

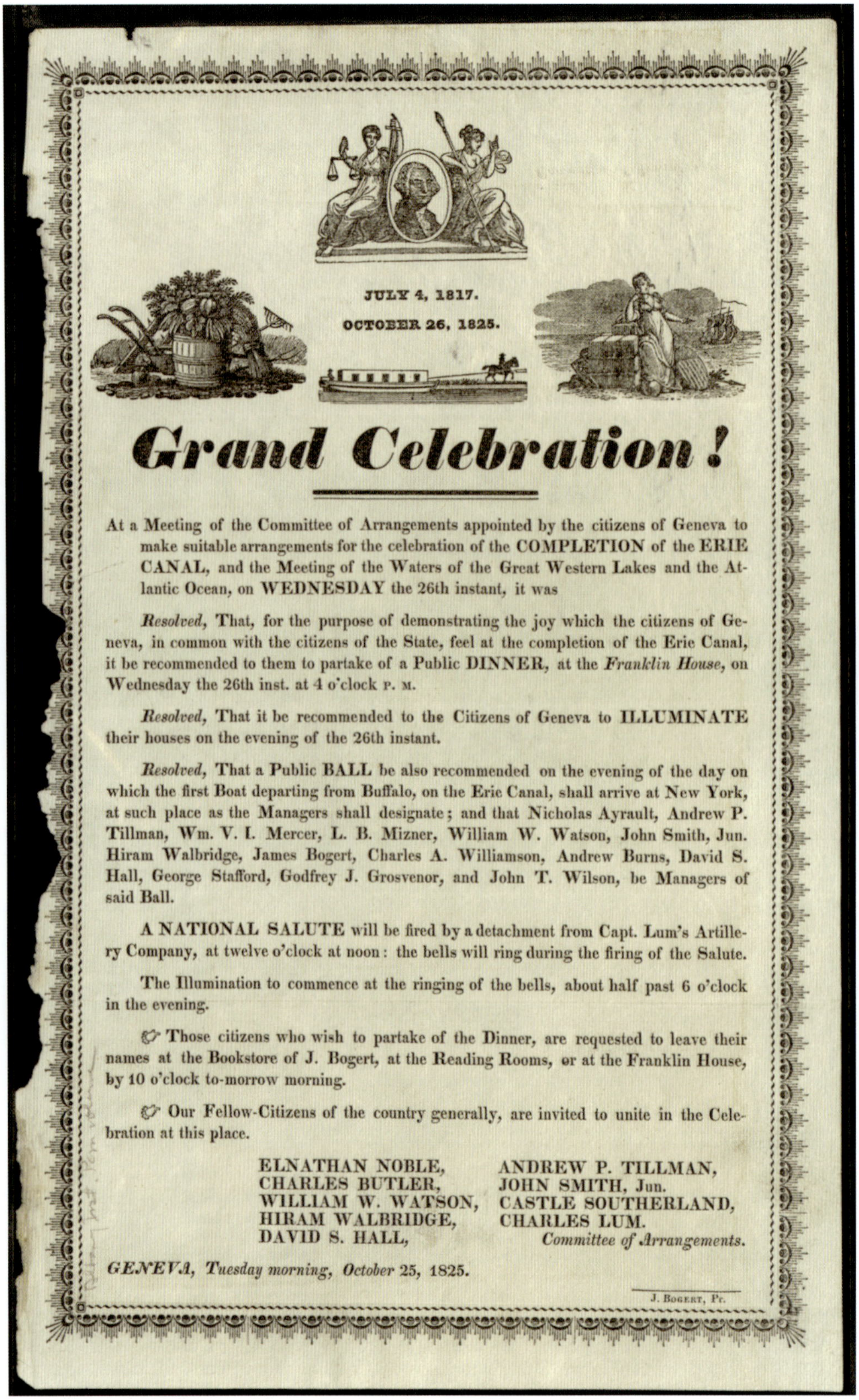

JULY 4, 1817.

OCTOBER 26, 1825.

Grand Celebration!

At a Meeting of the Committee of Arrangements appointed by the citizens of Geneva to make suitable arrangements for the celebration of the COMPLETION of the ERIE CANAL, and the Meeting of the Waters of the Great Western Lakes and the Atlantic Ocean, on WEDNESDAY the 26th instant, it was

Resolved, That, for the purpose of demonstrating the joy which the citizens of Geneva, in common with the citizens of the State, feel at the completion of the Erie Canal, it be recommended to them to partake of a Public DINNER, at the *Franklin House,* on Wednesday the 26th inst. at 4 o'clock P. M.

Resolved, That it be recommended to the Citizens of Geneva to ILLUMINATE their houses on the evening of the 26th instant.

Resolved, That a Public BALL be also recommended on the evening of the day on which the first Boat departing from Buffalo, on the Erie Canal, shall arrive at New York, at such place as the Managers shall designate; and that Nicholas Ayrault, Andrew P. Tillman, Wm. V. I. Mercer, L. B. Mizner, William W. Watson, John Smith, Jun. Hiram Walbridge, James Bogert, Charles A. Williamson, Andrew Burns, David S. Hall, George Stafford, Godfrey J. Grosvenor, and John T. Wilson, be Managers of said Ball.

A NATIONAL SALUTE will be fired by a detachment from Capt. Lum's Artillery Company, at twelve o'clock at noon: the bells will ring during the firing of the Salute.

The Illumination to commence at the ringing of the bells, about half past 6 o'clock in the evening.

☞ Those citizens who wish to partake of the Dinner, are requested to leave their names at the Bookstore of J. Bogert, at the Reading Rooms, or at the Franklin House, by 10 o'clock to-morrow morning.

☞ Our Fellow-Citizens of the country generally, are invited to unite in the Celebration at this place.

ELNATHAN NOBLE,
CHARLES BUTLER,
WILLIAM W. WATSON,
HIRAM WALBRIDGE,
DAVID S. HALL,
ANDREW P. TILLMAN,
JOHN SMITH, Jun.
CASTLE SOUTHERLAND,
CHARLES LUM.
Committee of Arrangements.

GENEVA, Tuesday morning, October 25, 1825.

J. BOGERT, Pr.

"Grand Celebration!" broadside, 1825. This broadside from Geneva called on citizens to join in the grand celebration of the canal. *Courtesy of the New York State Library, Manuscripts and Special Collections, BRO 0705.*

Erie Canal medals, 1826. The canal represented such a boon to the economy of New York City that the Common Council of the City of New York commissioned medals to celebrate the opening. The medals, designed by Asher B. Durand, who would become best known as a Hudson River School painter, feature both real canal elements, such as locks and aqueducts, and mythical figures, including Pan and Neptune. Lumber from the western part of the state, transported aboard the *Seneca Chief* (part of the October 26, 1825, flotilla), were made into presentation boxes for the medals by leading nineteenth-century American cabinetmaker Duncan Phyfe.

Erie Canal completion medal, gold, 1826. Approximately eleven gold medals were made and presented to high-ranking officials, including former presidents, signers of the Declaration of Independence, and the family of Robert Fulton. This one was presented to future US president, then major general Andrew Jackson. *Courtesy of the New-York Historical Society.*

Erie Canal completion medal, silver, 1826. Federal and state officials, as well as other prominent men of the era, received silver medals. This example was presented to author James Fenimore Cooper. *Collection of the Fenimore Art Museum, Cooperstown, New York. Gift of James Fenimore Cooper II. Transferred from Otsego County Historical Society.*

Erie Canal completion medal, white metal, 1826. Medals made of white metal were sent to all invited guests of the grand canal celebration, members of canal committees across the state, and museums. *New York State Museum, H-1949.8.1 A-C.*

Keg from the Erie Canal Celebration, ca. 1825. One of two kegs ceremoniously used by De Witt Clinton to unite the waters of Lake Erie and the Atlantic Ocean. Water brought from Lake Erie in this barrel was ceremoniously poured into the Atlantic Ocean. *Courtesy of the New-York Historical Society.*

Black keg (reproduction). Not everyone welcomed the flotilla. The new canal sometimes bypassed larger, established communities, like Rome and Schenectady. Initially, both communities lost population and commerce because the new canal bypassed the well-established businesses geared around the river trade. To show their dismay of the chosen route, some residents of Rome protested the Wedding of the Waters ceremony with a mock funeral procession. Using a black barrel containing water from the old Western Inland Lock Navigation Canal, they defiantly dumped the water into the Erie in front of the flotilla. Schenectady made no formal celebration plans, and the flotilla's reception was recorded as "rather grave . . ." by William L. Stone, a flotilla participant.* *New York State Museum.* *Cadwallader D. Colden, *Memoir, Prepared at the Request of a Committee of the Common Council of the City of New York, and Presented to the Mayor of the City, at the Celebration of the Completion of the New York Canals (New York: W. A. Davis, 1825), 307.*

Erie Canal pitcher, transfer-printed earthenware, ca. 1825. Staffordshire pottery was popular in early nineteenth century and often decorated to commemorate important events. *New York State Museum, H-1969.38.1.*

View on the Erie Canal, J. W. Hill, watercolor, 1829. *Courtesy of The Miriam and Ira D. Wallach Division of Art, Prints and Photographs: Print Collection, The New York Public Library. "View on the Erie Canal." New York Public Library Digital Collections.*

EARLY COMMERCE AND INDUSTRY

The Erie Canal was an immediate success and surpassed all expectations. Dependable and inexpensive transportation opened new markets to farmers and businessmen, creating a commercial windfall from New York City to Buffalo. Drawn to new opportunities, settlers moved westward, and forests soon gave way to new communities.

Industrial Growth

> **The city of New York, and, indeed, most parts of the State, are now supplied with pails and tubs, and wooden ware of that description, made by turning lathes, and other machinery, moved by water. In our neighboring county of West Chester, there are fields, enclosed by fences . . ., after being transported several hundred miles, were purchased for much less than any other fence, equally good, could be made for, near where they are used.**
>
> **—Cadwallader D. Colden, 1825[7]**

The first half of the nineteenth century saw the rise of both old and new industries that used the canal system for shipping raw materials and large bulk commodities. The Erie Canal opened large regions to commerce and commercial development and opened new markets. Growth in the agriculture, lumber, iron, salt, stoneware, glass-making, furniture, and brewing industries was significant, and New York State

TIME TO TRAVEL BETWEEN ALBANY *and* BUFFALO

CANAL PACKET BOAT	THREE–FOUR DAYS
CANAL FREIGHT BOAT	SIX–SEVEN DAYS
WAGON	TWO WEEKS OR MORE DEPENDING ON ROAD CONDITIONS

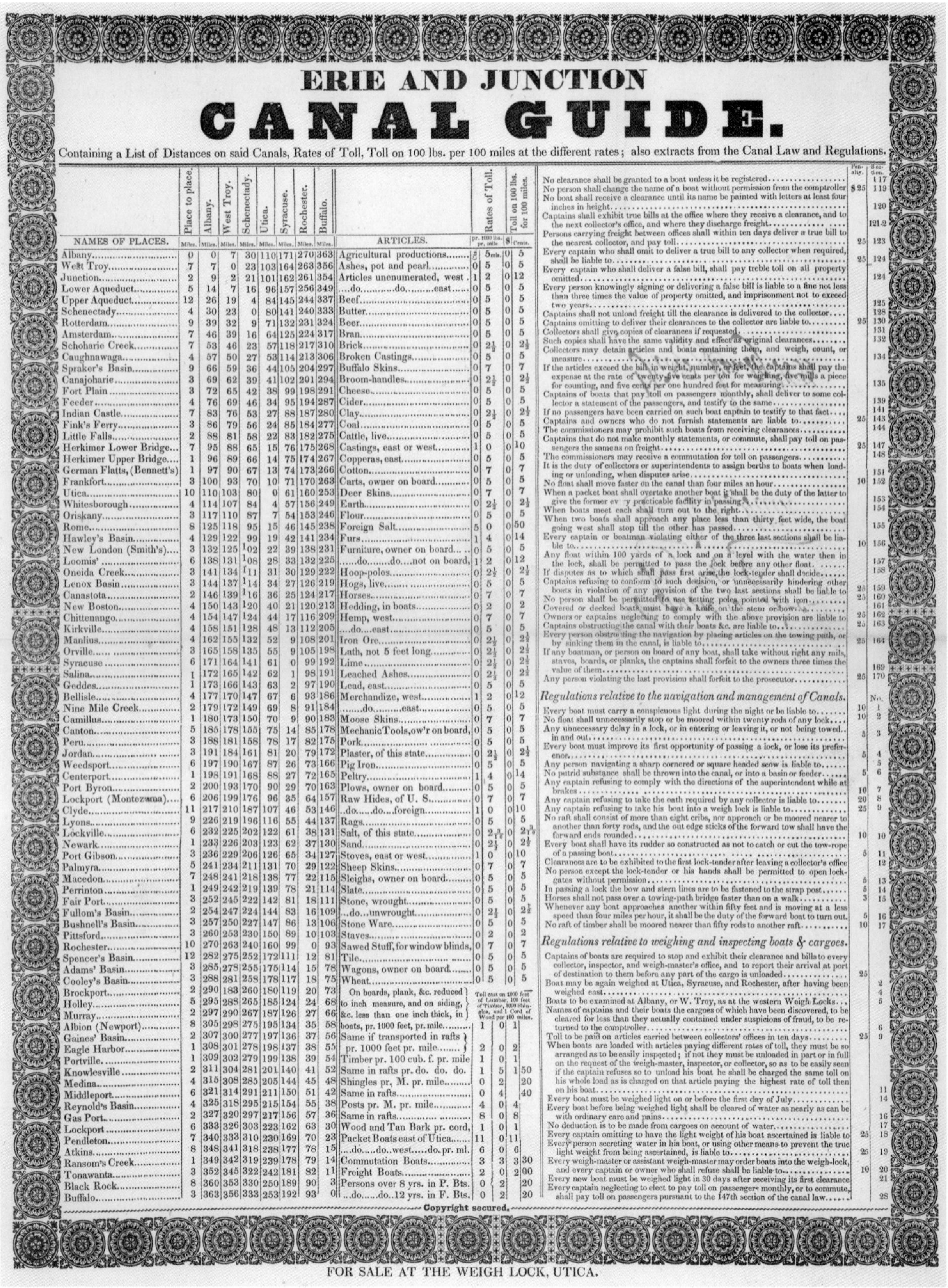

ERIE AND JUNCTION
CANAL GUIDE.

Containing a List of Distances on said Canals, Rates of Toll, Toll on 100 lbs. per 100 miles at the different rates; also extracts from the Canal Law and Regulations.

NAMES OF PLACES.	Place to place. Miles.	Albany. Miles.	West Troy. Miles.	Schenectady. Miles.	Utica. Miles.	Syracuse. Miles.	Rochester. Miles.	Buffalo. Miles.	ARTICLES.	Rates of Toll. pr. 1000 lbs. pr. mile		Toll on 100 lbs. for 100 miles. $	Cents.
Albany	0	0	7	30	110	171	270	363	Agricultural productions	Cts.	5 mls.	0	5
West Troy	7	7	0	23	103	164	263	356	Ashes, pot and pearl	0	5	0	5
Junction	2	9	2	21	101	162	261	354	Articles unenumerated, west	1	2	0	12
Lower Aqueduct	5	14	7	16	96	157	256	349	....do..........do.........east	0	5	0	5
Upper Aqueduct	12	26	19	4	84	145	244	337	Beef	0	5	0	5
Schenectady	4	30	23	0	80	141	240	333	Butter	0	5	0	5
Rotterdam	9	39	32	9	71	132	231	324	Beer	0	5	0	5
Amsterdam	7	46	39	16	64	125	224	317	Bran	0	5	0	5
Schoharie Creek	7	53	46	23	57	118	217	310	Brick	0	2½	0	2½
Caughnawaga	4	57	50	27	53	114	213	306	Broken Castings	0	5	0	5
Spraker's Basin	9	66	59	36	44	105	204	297	Buffalo Skins	0	7	0	7
Canajoharie	3	69	62	39	41	102	201	294	Broom-handles	0	2½	0	2½
Fort Plain	3	72	65	42	38	99	198	291	Cheese	0	5	0	5
Feeder	4	76	69	46	34	95	194	287	Cider	0	5	0	5
Indian Castle	7	83	76	53	27	88	187	280	Clay	0	2½	0	2½
Fink's Ferry	3	86	79	56	24	85	184	277	Coal	0	5	0	5
Little Falls	2	88	81	58	22	83	182	275	Cattle, live	0	5	0	5
Herkimer Lower Bridge	7	95	88	65	15	76	175	268	Castings, east or west	1	0	0	10
Herkimer Upper Bridge	1	96	89	66	14	75	174	267	Copperas, east	0	5	0	5
German Flatts, (Bennett's)	1	97	90	67	13	74	173	266	Cotton	0	7	0	7
Frankfort	3	100	93	70	10	71	170	263	Carts, owner on board	0	5	0	5
Utica	10	110	103	80	0	61	160	253	Deer Skins	0	7	0	7
Whitesborough	4	114	107	84	4	57	156	249	Earth	0	2½	0	2½
Oriskany	3	117	110	87	7	54	153	246	Flour	0	5	0	5
Rome	8	125	118	95	15	46	145	238	Foreign Salt	5	0	0	50
Hawley's Basin	4	129	122	99	19	42	141	234	Furs	1	4	0	14
New London (Smith's)	3	132	125	102	22	39	138	231	Furniture, owner on board	0	5	0	5
Loomis'	6	138	131	108	28	33	132	225	......do........do....not on board,	1	2	0	12
Oneida Creek	3	141	134	111	31	30	129	222	Hoop-poles	0	2½	0	2½
Lenox Basin	3	144	137	114	34	27	126	219	Hogs, live	0	5	0	5
Canastota	2	146	139	116	36	25	124	217	Horses	0	7	0	7
New Boston	4	150	143	120	40	21	120	213	Hedding, in boats	0	2	0	2
Chittenango	4	154	147	124	44	17	116	209	Hemp, west	0	7	0	7
Kirkville	4	158	151	128	48	13	112	205	....do....east	0	5	0	5
Manlius	4	162	155	132	52	9	108	201	Iron Ore	0	2½	0	2½
Orville	3	165	158	135	55	9	105	198	Lath, not 5 feet long	0	2½	0	2½
Syracuse	6	171	164	141	61	0	99	192	Lime	0	2½	0	2½
Salina	1	172	165	142	62	1	98	191	Leached Ashes	0	2½	0	2½
Geddes	1	173	166	143	63	2	97	190	Lead, east	0	5	0	5
Bellisle	4	177	170	147	67	6	93	186	Merchandize, west	1	2	0	12
Nine Mile Creek	2	179	172	149	69	8	91	184	.......do.........east	0	5	0	5
Camillus	1	180	173	150	70	9	90	183	Moose Skins	0	7	0	7
Canton	5	185	178	155	75	14	85	178	Mechanic Tools, ow'r on board,	0	5	0	5
Peru	3	188	181	158	78	17	82	175	Pork	0	5	0	5
Jordan	3	191	184	161	81	20	79	172	Plaster, of this state	0	2½	0	2½
Weedsport	6	197	190	167	87	26	73	166	Pig Iron	0	5	0	5
Centerport	1	198	191	168	88	27	72	165	Peltry	1	4	0	14
Port Byron	2	200	193	170	90	29	70	163	Plows, owner on board	0	5	0	5
Lockport (Montezuma)	6	206	199	176	96	35	64	157	Raw Hides, of U. S.	0	7	0	7
Clyde	11	217	210	187	107	46	53	146	..do......do....foreign	1	0	0	10
Lyons	9	226	219	196	116	55	44	137	Rags	0	5	0	5
Lockville	6	232	225	202	122	61	38	131	Salt, of this state	0	2 3/16	0	2 3/16
Newark	1	233	226	203	123	62	37	130	Sand	0	2½	0	2½
Port Gibson	3	236	229	206	126	65	34	127	Stoves, east or west	1	0	0	10
Palmyra	5	241	234	211	131	70	29	122	Sheep Skins	0	7	0	7
Macedon	7	248	241	218	138	77	22	115	Sleighs, owner on board	0	5	0	5
Perrinton	1	249	242	219	139	78	21	114	Slate	0	5	0	5
Fair Port	3	252	245	222	142	81	18	111	Stone, wrought	0	5	0	5
Fullom's Basin	2	254	247	224	144	83	16	109	...do...unwrought	0	2½	0	2½
Bushnell's Basin	3	257	250	227	147	86	13	106	Stone Ware	0	5	0	5
Pittsford	3	260	253	230	150	89	10	103	Staves	0	2	0	2
Rochester	10	270	263	240	160	99	0	93	Sawed Stuff, for window blinds,	0	7	0	7
Spencer's Basin	12	282	275	252	172	111	12	81	Tile	0	5	0	5
Adams' Basin	3	285	278	255	175	114	15	78	Wagons, owner on board	0	5	0	5
Cooley's Basin	3	288	281	258	178	117	18	75	Wheat	0	5	0	5
Brockport	2	290	183	260	180	119	20	73	On boards, plank, &c. reduced	Toll east on 1000 feet of Lumber, 100 feet of Timber, 1000 Shingles, and 1 Cord of Wood per 100 miles.			
Holley	5	295	288	265	185	124	24	68	to inch measure, and on siding,				
Murray	2	297	290	267	187	126	27	66	&c. less than one inch thick, in				
Albion (Newport)	8	305	298	275	195	134	35	58	boats, pr. 1000 feet, pr. mile	1	0	1	
Gaines' Basin	2	307	300	277	197	136	37	56	Same if transported in rafts				
Eagle Harbor	1	308	301	278	198	137	38	55	pr. 1000 feet pr. mile	2	0	2	
Portville	1	309	302	279	199	138	39	54	Timber pr. 100 cub. f. pr. mile	1	0	1	
Knowlesville	2	311	304	281	201	140	41	52	Same in rafts pr. do. do. do.	1	5	1	50
Medina	4	315	308	285	205	144	45	48	Shingles pr. M. pr. mile	0	2		20
Middleport	6	321	314	291	211	150	51	42	Same in rafts	0	4		40
Reynold's Basin	4	325	318	295	215	154	55	38	Posts pr. M. pr. mile	4	0	4	
Gas Port	2	327	320	297	217	156	57	36	Same in rafts	8	0	8	
Lockport	6	333	326	303	223	162	63	30	Wood and Tan Bark pr. cord,	1	0	1	
Pendleton	7	340	333	310	230	169	70	23	Packet Boats east of Utica	11	0	11	
Atkins	8	348	341	318	238	177	78	15	....do.....do..west.....do. pr. ml.	6	0	6	
Ransom's Creek	1	349	342	319	239	178	79	14	Commutation Boats	3	3	3	30
Tonawanta	3	352	345	322	242	181	82	11	Freight Boats	2	0	2	00
Black Rock	8	360	353	330	250	189	90	3	Persons over 8 yrs. in P. Bts.	0	2		20
Buffalo	3	363	356	333	253	192	93	0	...do......do..12 yrs. in F. Bts.	0	2		20

	Penalty.	Section.
No clearance shall be granted to a boat unless it be registered		117
No person shall change the name of a boat without permission from the comptroller	$25	119
No boat shall receive a clearance until its name be painted with letters at least four inches in height		120
Captains shall exhibit true bills at the office where they receive a clearance, and to the next collector's office, and where they discharge freight		121-2
Persons carrying freight between offices shall within ten days deliver a true bill to the nearest collector, and pay toll	25	123
Every captain who shall omit to deliver a true bill to any collector when required, shall be liable to	25	124
Every captain who shall deliver a false bill, shall pay treble toll on all property omitted		124
Every person knowingly signing or delivering a false bill is liable to a fine not less than three times the value of property omitted, and imprisonment not to exceed two years		125
Captains shall not unload freight till the clearance is delivered to the collector		128
Captains omitting to deliver their clearances to the collector are liable to	25	130
Collectors shall give copies of clearances if requested		131
Such copies shall have the same validity and effect as original clearances		132
Collectors may detain articles and boats containing them, and weigh, count, or measure		134
If the articles exceed the bill in weight, number, or feet, the captains shall pay the expense at the rate of twenty-five cents per ton for weighing, five mills a piece for counting, and five cents per one hundred feet for measuring		135
Captains of boats that pay toll on passengers monthly, shall deliver to some collector a statement of the passengers, and testify to the same		139
If no passengers have been carried on such boat captain to testify to that fact		141
Captains and owners who do not furnish statements are liable to	25	143
The commissioners may prohibit such boats from receiving clearances		144
Captains that do not make monthly statements, or commute, shall pay toll on passengers the same as on freight	25	147
The commissioners may receive a commutation for toll on passengers		148
It is the duty of collectors or superintendents to assign berths to boats when loading or unloading, when disputes arise		151
No float shall move faster on the canal than four miles an hour	10	152
When a packet boat shall overtake another boat it shall be the duty of the latter to give the former every practicable facility in passing		153
When boats meet each shall turn out to the right		154
When two boats shall approach any place less than thirty feet wide, the boat going west shall stop till the other has passed		155
Every captain or boatman violating either of the three last sections shall be liable to	10	156
Any float within 100 yards of a lock and on a level with the water then in the lock, shall be permitted to pass the lock before any other float.		157
If disputes as to which shall pass first arise, the lock-tender shall decide		158
Captains refusing to conform to such decision, or unnecessarily hindering other boats in violation of any provision of the two last sections shall be liable to	25	159
No person shall be permitted to use setting poles pointed with iron	25	160
Covered or decked boats must have a knife on the stem or bow		161
Owners or captains neglecting to comply with the above provision are liable to	25	162
Captains obstructing the canal with their boats &c. are liable to	25	163
Every person obstructing the navigation by placing articles on the towing path, or by sinking them in the canal, is liable to	25	164
If any boatman, or person on board of any boat, shall take without right any rails, staves, boards, or planks, the captains shall forfeit to the owners three times the value of them		169
Any person violating the last provision shall forfeit to the prosecutor	25	170

Regulations relative to the navigation and management of Canals.

	Penalty.	No.
Every boat must carry a conspicuous light during the night or be liable to	10	1
No float shall unnecessarily stop or be moored within twenty rods of any lock	10	2
Any unnecessary delay in a lock, or in entering or leaving it, or not being towed in and out	5	3
Every boat must improve its first opportunity of passing a lock, or lose its preference	5	4
Any person navigating a sharp cornered or square headed scow is liable to		5
No putrid substance shall be thrown into the canal, or into a basin or feeder	5	6
Any captain refusing to comply with the directions of the superintendent while at brakes	10	7
Any captain refusing to take the oath required by any collector is liable to	20	8
Any captain refusing to take his boat into a weigh lock is liable to	25	9
No raft shall consist of more than eight cribs, nor approach or be moored nearer to another than forty rods, and the out edge sticks of the forward tow shall have the forward ends rounded	10	10
Every boat shall have its rudder so constructed as not to catch or cut the tow-rope of a passing boat	5	11
Clearances are to be exhibited to the first lock-tender after leaving a collector's office		12
No person except the lock-tender or his hands shall be permitted to open lock-gates without permission	5	13
In passing a lock the bow and stern lines are to be fastened to the strap post	5	14
Horses shall not pass over a towing-path bridge faster than on a walk	3	15
Whenever any boat approaches another within fifty feet and is moving at a less speed than four miles per hour, it shall be the duty of the forward boat to turn out.	5	16
No raft of timber shall be moored nearer than fifty rods to another raft	10	17

Regulations relative to weighing and inspecting boats & cargoes.

	Penalty.	No.
Captains of boats are required to stop and exhibit their clearance and bills to every collector, inspector, and weigh-master's office, and to report their arrival at port of destination to them before any part of the cargo is unloaded	25	
Boat may be again weighed at Utica, Syracuse, and Rochester, after having been weighed east		2 4
Boats to be examined at Albany, or W. Troy, as at the western Weigh Locks		5
Names of captains and their boats the cargoes of which have been discovered, to be cleared for less than they actually contained under suspicions of fraud, to be returned to the comptroller		6
Toll to be paid on articles carried between collectors' offices in ten days	25	9
When boats are loaded with articles paying different rates of toll, they must be so arranged as to be easily inspected; if not they must be unloaded in part or in full on the request of the weigh-master, inspector, or collector, so as to be easily seen if the captain refuses so to unload his boat he shall be charged the same toll on his whole load as is charged on that article paying the highest rate of toll then on his boat		11
Every boat must be weighed light on or before the first day of July		14
Every boat before being weighed light shall be cleared of water as nearly as can be with ordinary care and pains		16
No deduction is to be made from cargoes on account of water		17
Every captain omitting to have the light weight of his boat ascertained is liable to	25	18
Every person secreting water in his boat, or using other means to prevent the true light weight from being ascertained, is liable to	25	19
Every weigh-master or assistant weigh-master may order boats into the weigh-lock, and every captain or owner who shall refuse shall be liable to	10	20
Every new boat must be weighed light in 30 days after receiving its first clearance		21
Every captain neglecting to elect to pay toll on passengers monthly, or to commute, shall pay toll on passengers pursuant to the 147th section of the canal law		28

Copyright secured.

FOR SALE AT THE WEIGH LOCK, UTICA.

Erie Canal Guide, ca. 1833. Sold at the Utica weighlock, this guide identifies toll rates along the canal. *Courtesy of the Library of Congress.*

grew to become a worldwide industrial and economic leader. Goods of all kinds were shipped on the canal: from live fish to ice to home furnishings, the list of nineteenth-century products that moved along the Erie is almost endless.

Like today, grains formed the base of many of the foods people ate in the nineteenth century. The canal was a cheap and reliable way to transport grains to feed the growing American population. The growing population also needed lumber for fuel and to construct buildings, ships, and wagons. As a result, wheat, flour, and lumber accounted for the most tonnage on the canal for the entire nineteenth century. To demonstrate the boon, between 1815 and 1825 the cost of shipping wheat from Buffalo to New York City dropped from roughly $100 to $10 per ton.

The state's furniture-making industry expanded rapidly in the years following the Erie Canal's opening. Fine-quality furniture was manufactured in cities and towns all along the canal. This likely also indicates an increased local market for luxury items corresponding to a rise in the socioeconomic conditions of residents in these cities.

Elevator & Mills, Fultonville, N.Y. P. Van Antwerp & Son, Prop., colored engraving, ca. 1870–1880. The canal provided communities along the route the ability to import and export products that would have been too costly to ship before the canal opened. Farmers who had already lived in the canal corridor went from subsistence farming to cash-crop farming. The P. Van Antwerp mill could process agricultural products and use the grain elevator and windlass (hoist) to help load and unload busy canal boats. *Courtesy of the Canal Society of New York State.*

Cuba Valley Point Agricultural and Mechanical Society's Fair and Races Held on Smith's Driving Park, Cuba, Allegany County, N.Y., engraving, ca. 1845. Small, formerly remote communities, like Cuba, along the Genesee Valley Canal, received a boost to agriculture-based industries. *New York State Museum, H-1975.120.6.*

Grain cradle or cradle scythe, nineteenth century. A farmer could harvest about two acres of wheat a day with this grain cradle. *New York State Museum, H-1968.36.1.*

Barley fork, nineteenth century. The importance of barley as a crop increased in New York after the opening of the canal. Barley forks, like this one, were used to harvest the grain, which was used as animal feed and as a main ingredient in malt beverages, especially beer, which was a growing industry in New York State. *New York State Museum, H-1919.3.1.*

Model of Joseph Dart grain elevator, ca. 1930. By 1830 Buffalo handled large shipments of Great Lakes grain that needed to be unloaded from the lake boats, stored, and loaded onto canal boats, all by hand. Often there was too much grain coming in and large piles would form on the docks. In 1842, Buffalo resident Joseph Dart invented a steam-powered grain elevator that would load, unload, store, and weigh the grain. This is a model of Joseph Dart's original wooden steam-powered grain elevator. *Courtesy of The Buffalo History Museum.*

Buffalo Harbor, 1847, L. F. Tantillo, oil on canvas, 1990. Joseph Dart's grain elevator figures prominently in this historical depiction of Buffalo Harbor. *Courtesy of L. F. Tantillo.*

The Mill of C. J. Hill, unknown artist, oil on board, ca. 1860. *Courtesy of the Rochester Historical Society.*

In the 1830s Charles J. Hill established a successful flour mill on the Genesee River in Rochester. The proximity of the Erie Canal was critical to his business, helping to ship his products worldwide. Not only does the artist feature the activity outside the mill, but the owner himself is visible in the window under the "C. J. Hill & Son" sign.

Model of a seeder, ca. 1845. New York State manufacturers responded to the increased agricultural industry and produced needed farming equipment. This patent model is believed to have been made by William Seymour of Brockport, New York. The seeder was horse drawn, and the mechanisms turned as the wheels moved, scattering seeds as it went. *New York State Museum, H-1901.1.44.*

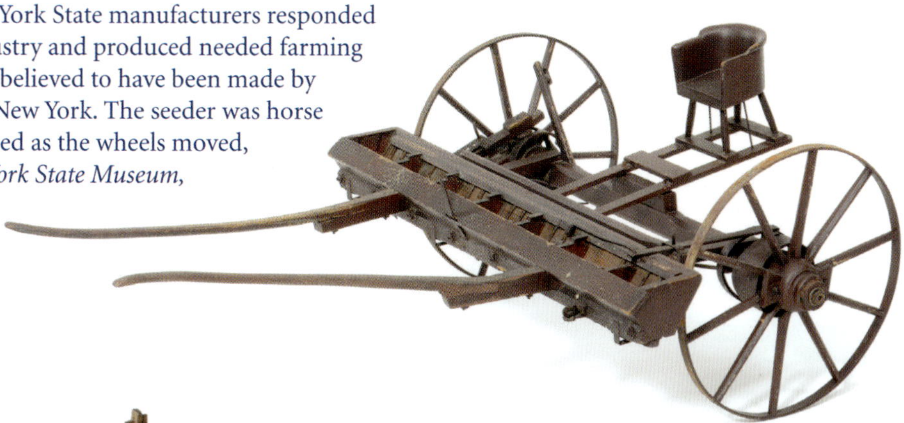

Plow, Peter I. Clute, Schenectady, ca. 1850. The Shakers in Niskayuna used this plow made by Peter I. Clute in Schenectady around 1850. Clute's foundry opened around 1820, one of many sprouting up along the eastern end of the canal. *New York State Museum, H-1927.7.222.*

Felling ax, early nineteenth century. As settlers cleared the land, lumber became a leading raw material shipped on the canal. *New York State Museum, H-XX.362.1.*

Wooden grain shovel, nineteenth–early twentieth century. Wooden shovels were preferred in grain elevators and mills because metal shovels created sparks and posed a fire risk. *New York State Museum, xx.329.1.*

Model of a fanning machine, 1845. The New York Agricultural Society formed in 1832 "to improve the condition of agriculture, horticulture and household arts." It worked to further science in agriculture and promoted new products at its annual fair. This model was used to show a new fanning mill design—a device that removed straw, chaff, stones, dirt, and weed seeds from wheat and other grain crops to help with preservation during storage. *New York State Museum, H-1901.1.45.*

Up-and-down sawmill, photograph, ca. 1933. Lumber was one of the main products shipped on the canal. *Courtesy of the Library of Congress.*

Lumber Boats Locking through on Black River Canal, photograph, ca. 1895. Although this image is from the late-nineteenth century, lumber boats similar to these would have been a common site on the canal from the 1820s through the early twentieth century. *New York State Museum, H-1988.80.1.49.*

Up-and-down saw blade, ca. 1820. Up-and-down sawmills cut logs into planks to be used for building. *New York State Museum, H-7966.NN.*

Cast-iron stove, Ransom & Co., Albany, New York, 1845. *New York State Museum, H-1975.59.1.*

Iron foundries flourished in the Capital District during the mid- to late nineteenth century, aided in large part by the canals. The Champlain Canal provided iron mined from ore deposits in the Adirondacks, and molding sand was abundant locally. Foundries in Waterford, Cohoes, Troy, Watervliet, and Albany produced a wide variety of cast-iron products, including coal-burning stoves like these. Other products included water valves, bells, locomotive wheels, horseshoes, iron plating, fencing, and axes.

Cast-iron stove, Anthony, Davy, & Co., Troy, New York, 1848. *New York State Museum, H-1982.94.1.*

Great Brewery of John Taylor & Sons, Albany, N.Y., engraving, 1858. Seventeenth-century Dutch settlers established a brewing center in Albany that continued to thrive into the nineteenth century. When the Erie Canal opened, Albany brewers accessed new sources of grains and hops to expand their production and outreach. Most of what became known as "Albany Ale" was shipped to New York City and beyond. Brewer John Taylor took full advantage of the benefits of the transportation revolution taking place on his front doorstep. Taylor purchased grains coming in from the west and placed at least one malt house along the canal. His company partnered in steamboats that would ship his brew south. By 1851 John Taylor & Sons had a global distribution and was among the largest producers of beer in America. *Frank Leslie's Illustrated Newspaper 6, no. 152, Saturday, October 30, 1858. Courtesy of the New York State Library, Manuscripts and Special Collections, 071.471 fF828 206-898.*

Glass slag, ca. 1845–ca. 1900. Slag is a by-product from iron production that can be used in the production of glass. This slag is from Durhamville Glassworks. *New York State Museum, H-INV 4409.*

Glass windowpane, ca. 1840. Durhamville Glassworks was operated by the firm Fox and Son for most of its existence. Fox and Son also had a factory in West Sand Lake, where this windowpane was produced. *New York State Museum, H-1972.32.13.*

Durhamville Glassworks, artist unknown, oil on canvas, mid-nineteenth century. The Durhamville Glassworks, specializing in window panes, opened around 1845 and operated until around 1900. This area of Oneida County had several glassworks that used large quantities of sand shipped on the Erie Canal. *New York State Museum, H-1995.69.1.*

Drinking glass and vase, attributed to the Lockport Glass Factory, ca. 1845. These glass pieces are attributed to the Lockport Glass Factory, which operated from 1843 to 1908. *New York State Museum, H-1986.32.2.*

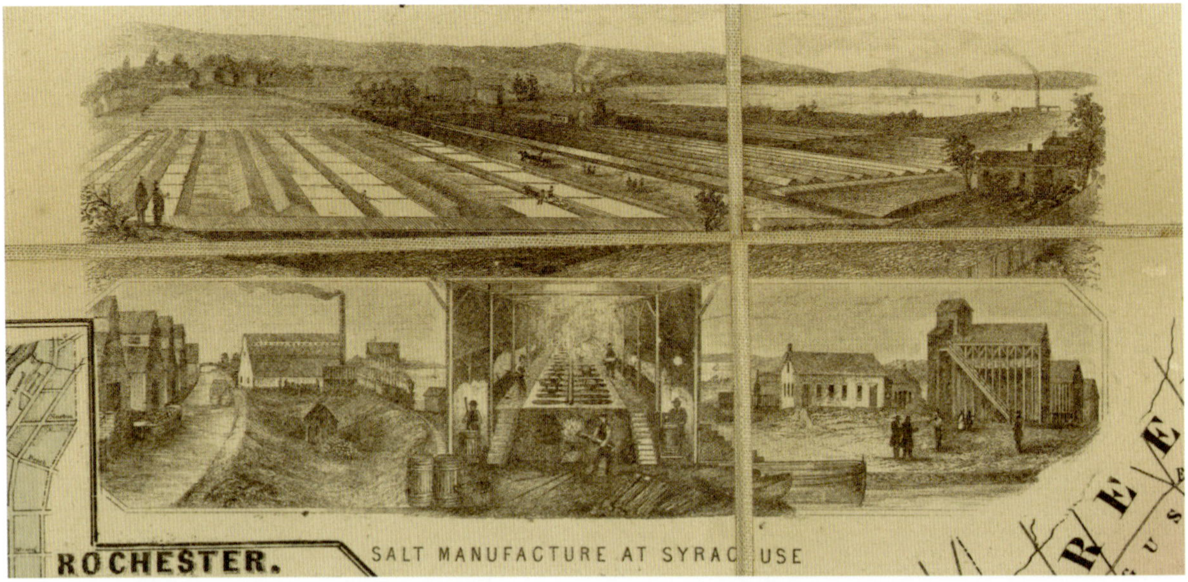

Salt Works, engraving, 1865. J. H. French, *Gazetteer of New York State,* 1865. *New York State Library, Manuscripts and Special Collections, (747) 1865+ 215-1410.*

Syracuse has naturally occurring brine water ideal for making salt. When the canal opened, salt production was already an important business, and large-scale shipping and production enabled tremendous growth in the industry. During the nineteenth century, the Syracuse area produced most of the salt used in the United States.

Salt bag, ca. 1900. Watkins Table Salt, Watkins (Watkins Glen), New York. *New York State Museum Collection, H-1969.80.663.*

SCIENTIFIC AMERICAN

[Entered at the Post Office of New York, N. Y., as Second Class Matter. Copyrighted, 1890, by Munn & Co.]

A WEEKLY JOURNAL OF PRACTICAL INFORMATION, ART, SCIENCE, MECHANICS, CHEMISTRY, AND MANUFACTURES.

Vol. LXIII.—No. 24. Established 1845. | NEW YORK, DECEMBER 13, 1890. | $3.00 A YEAR. Weekly.

1. New York State pumping station and reservoir. 2. Solar evaporation. 3. Settling vats. 4. Salt boiling in kettles. 5. Washing salt. 6. Centrifugal drier.

THE SALT INDUSTRY OF ONONDAGA COUNTY, N. Y.—[See page 373.]

"The Salt Industry of Onondaga, NY," *Scientific American,* December 13, 1890. *New York State Museum Collection, H-1980.96.7.*

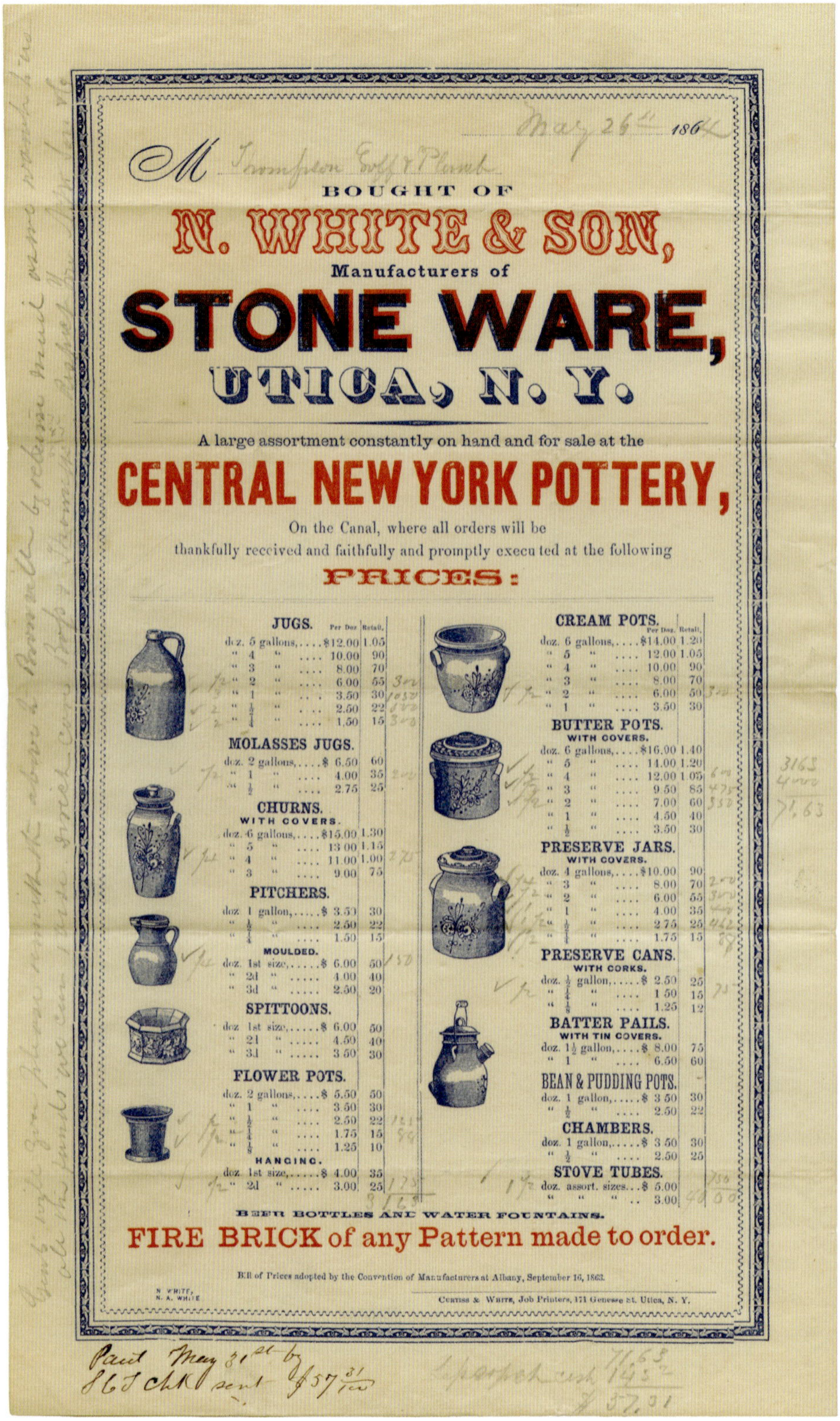

Poster, N. White & Son, 1864. Prior to construction of the canal, many stoneware potteries were clustered in Hudson River towns, where it was easy to get clay from New Jersey and ship finished products to market. Noah White began making pottery in Utica, New York, around 1834, and his pottery's stoneware pieces can be identified by the mark "WHITE'S UTICA." *New York State Museum Collection, H-1998.50.42.*

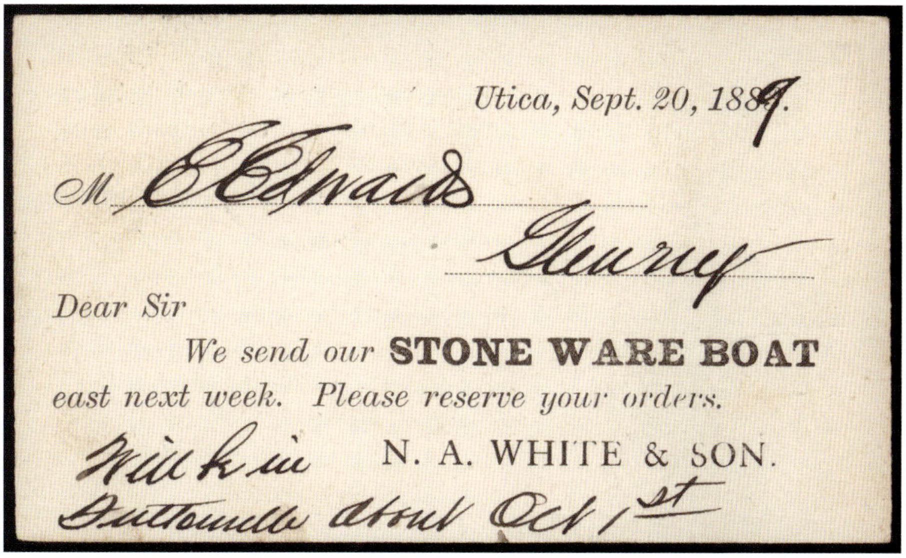

Utica, Sept. 20, 1889.

M E. Edwards

Glen NY

Dear Sir

We send our **STONE WARE BOAT** east next week. Please reserve your orders.

Will be in N. A. WHITE & SON.

Fultonville about Oct 1st

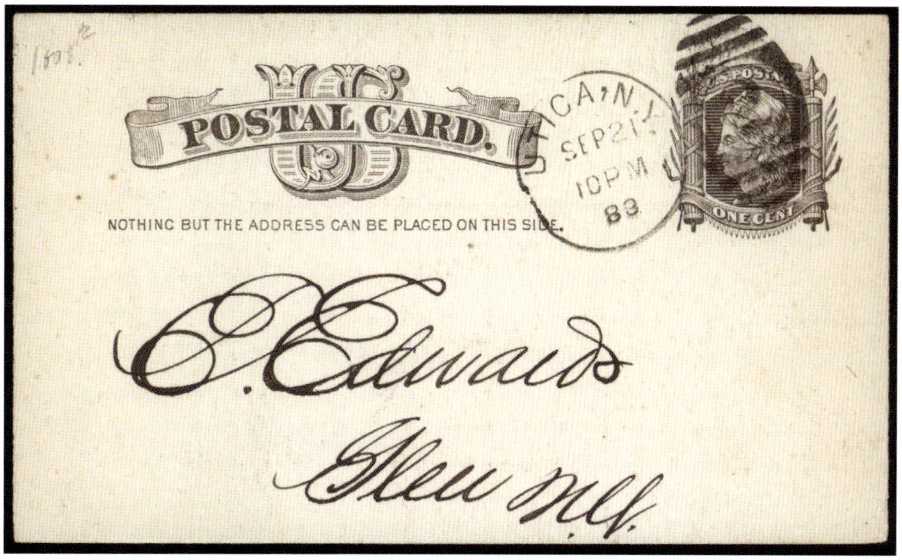

Postcard, N. A. White & Son, Utica, New York, to store owner E. Edwards, Glen, New York, 1889. Both clay and finished stoneware were shipped on the canal. This postcard, from a pottery in Utica to a merchant in Montgomery County, alerted the merchant to a new shipment of finished goods via canal boat. *New York State Museum, H-2006.40.2.*

Fire brick, White's pottery, Utica, ca. 1840–1907. In addition to stoneware vessels, N. White & Son also produced fire bricks that were used to line furnaces, kilns, and fireplaces. *New York State Museum, Archaeology, Cultural Resource Survey Program.*

Stoneware crock, George G. Williams and Company (active 1822–1852), Lyons, New York, ca. 1835. George G. Williams began his career as a potter at the Clark Pottery, in Athens, New York. In 1822 Nathan Clark sent Williams west to establish the pottery in Lyons, in Wayne County, not far from the canal. With the opening of the Erie Canal, owners of existing potteries and other entrepreneurs sent potters west to open new works. *New York State Museum, H-2015.35.22.*

Stoneware churn, John Burger (active 1811–1885), Rochester, New York, ca. 1860. As the population of the state shifted west, pottery owners saw opportunity along the canals, and many expanded their operations to different locations. John Burger of Lyons, Nathan Clark of Athens, Thompson Harrington of Lyons, and George C. Williams were all involved in ownership of potteries in Rochester beginning in 1839. In 1861 John Burger moved his pottery to South Avenue to be closer to the canal. The firm lived on through his son and grandsons, operating until 1890. *New York State Museum, H-2013.12.8.*

Stoneware crock, Albert O. Whittemore (working 1863–1893), Havana, New York, ca. 1870. The village of Havana (now Montour Falls), is located along the Chemung Canal in Schuyler County. The first stoneware manufactory was built there in 1853. The factory of Albert O. Whittemore, established in 1863, was known for crocks featuring buildings and palm trees. Perhaps these decorations are a nod to Havana, Cuba, for which the village was named. *New York State Museum, H-1997.62.1.*

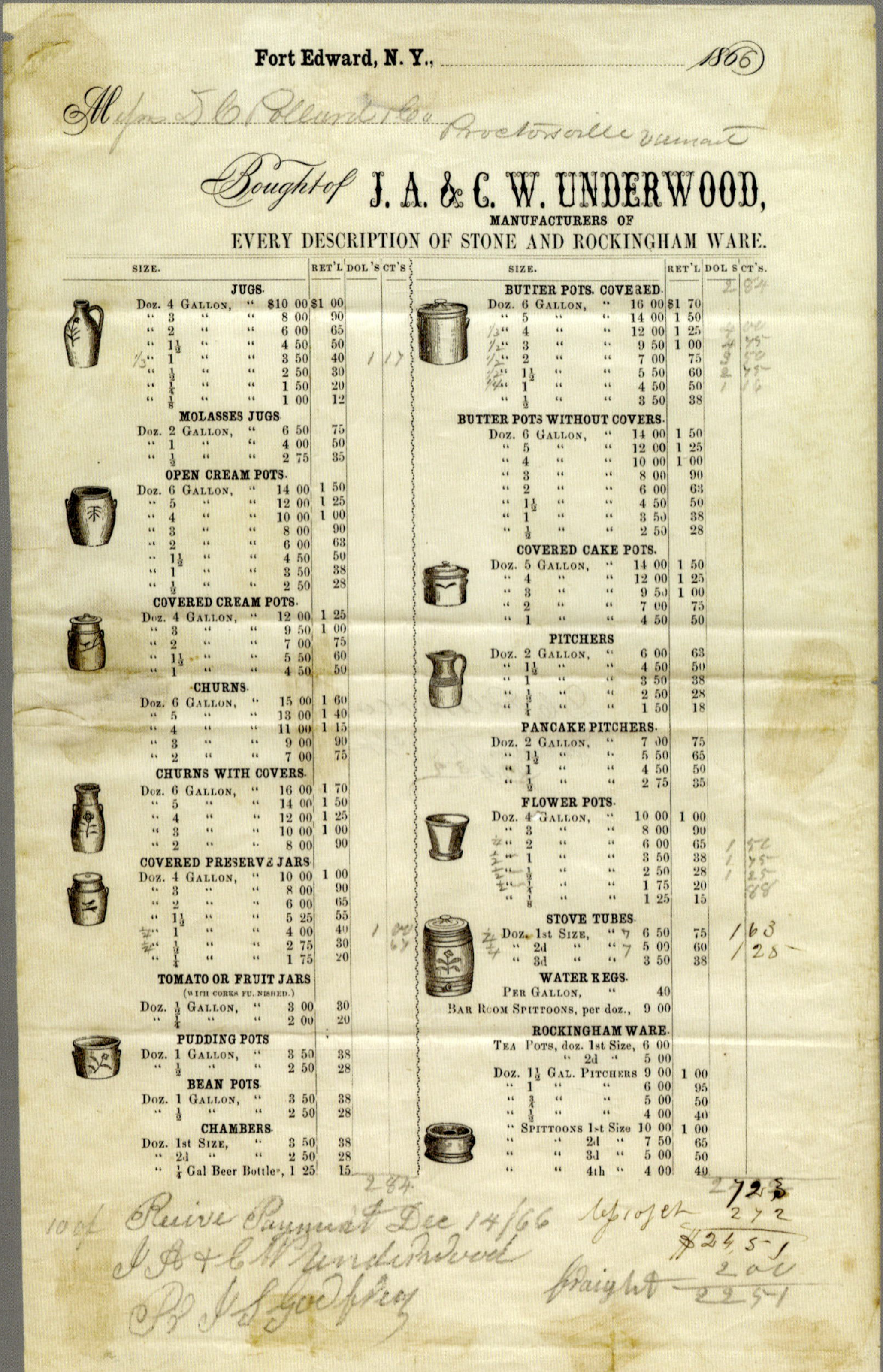

Fort Edward, N. Y., 1866

Bought of J. A. & C. W. UNDERWOOD,

MANUFACTURERS OF

EVERY DESCRIPTION OF STONE AND ROCKINGHAM WARE.

SIZE.		RET'L	DOL'S	CT'S
JUGS.				
Doz. 4 Gallon, "	$10 00	$1 00		
" 3 " "	8 00	90		
" 2 " "	6 00	65		
" 1½ " "	4 50	50		
" 1 " "	3 50	40		
" ½ " "	2 50	30		
" ¼ " "	1 50	20		
" ⅛ " "	1 00	12		
MOLASSES JUGS.				
Doz. 2 Gallon, "	6 50	75		
" 1 " "	4 00	50		
" ½ " "	2 75	35		
OPEN CREAM POTS.				
Doz. 6 Gallon, "	14 00	1 50		
" 5 " "	12 00	1 25		
" 4 " "	10 00	1 00		
" 3 " "	8 00	90		
" 2 " "	6 00	63		
" 1½ " "	4 50	50		
" 1 " "	3 50	38		
" ½ " "	2 50	28		
COVERED CREAM POTS.				
Doz. 4 Gallon, "	12 00	1 25		
" 3 " "	9 50	1 00		
" 2 " "	7 00	75		
" 1½ " "	5 50	60		
" 1 " "	4 50	50		
CHURNS.				
Doz. 6 Gallon, "	15 00	1 60		
" 5 " "	13 00	1 40		
" 4 " "	11 00	1 15		
" 3 " "	9 00	90		
" 2 " "	7 00	75		
CHURNS WITH COVERS.				
Doz. 6 Gallon, "	16 00	1 70		
" 5 " "	14 00	1 50		
" 4 " "	12 00	1 25		
" 3 " "	10 00	1 00		
" 2 " "	8 00	90		
COVERED PRESERVE JARS.				
Doz. 4 Gallon, "	10 00	1 00		
" 3 " "	8 00	90		
" 2 " "	6 00	65		
" 1½ " "	5 25	55		
" 1 " "	4 00	40		
" ½ " "	2 75	30		
" ¼ " "	1 75	20		
TOMATO OR FRUIT JARS (WITH CORKS FURNISHED.)				
Doz. ½ Gallon, "	3 00	30		
" ¼ " "	2 00	20		
PUDDING POTS				
Doz. 1 Gallon, "	3 50	38		
" ½ " "	2 50	28		
BEAN POTS				
Doz. 1 Gallon, "	3 50	38		
" ½ " "	2 50	28		
CHAMBERS.				
Doz. 1st Size, "	3 50	38		
" 2d " "	2 50	28		
" ¼ Gal Beer Bottles,	1 25	15		

SIZE.		RET'L	DOL'S	CT'S.
BUTTER POTS, COVERED.				
Doz. 6 Gallon, "	16 00	$1 70		
" 5 " "	14 00	1 50		
" 4 " "	12 00	1 25		
" 3 " "	9 50	1 00		
" 2 " "	7 00	75		
" 1½ " "	5 50	60		
" 1 " "	4 50	50		
" ½ " "	3 50	38		
BUTTER POTS WITHOUT COVERS.				
Doz. 6 Gallon, "	14 00	1 50		
" 5 " "	12 00	1 25		
" 4 " "	10 00	1 00		
" 3 " "	8 00	90		
" 2 " "	6 00	63		
" 1½ " "	4 50	50		
" 1 " "	3 50	38		
" ½ " "	2 50	28		
COVERED CAKE POTS.				
Doz. 5 Gallon, "	14 00	1 50		
" 4 " "	12 00	1 25		
" 3 " "	9 50	1 00		
" 2 " "	7 00	75		
" 1 " "	4 50	50		
PITCHERS				
Doz. 2 Gallon, "	6 00	63		
" 1½ " "	4 50	50		
" 1 " "	3 50	38		
" ½ " "	2 50	28		
" ¼ " "	1 50	18		
PANCAKE PITCHERS.				
Doz. 2 Gallon, "	7 00	75		
" 1½ " "	5 50	65		
" 1 " "	4 50	50		
" ½ " "	2 75	35		
FLOWER POTS.				
Doz. 4 Gallon, "	10 00	1 00		
" 3 " "	8 00	90		
" 2 " "	6 00	65		
" 1 " "	3 50	38		
" ½ " "	2 50	28		
" ¼ " "	1 75	20		
" ⅛ " "	1 25	15		
STOVE TUBES.				
Doz. 1st Size, "	6 50	75		
" 2d " "	5 00	60		
" 3d " "	3 50	38		
WATER KEGS.				
Per Gallon, "	40			
Bar Room Spittoons, per doz.,	9 00			
ROCKINGHAM WARE.				
Tea Pots, doz. 1st Size,	6 00			
" 2d "	5 00			
Doz. 1½ Gal. Pitchers	9 00	1 00		
" 1 " "	6 00	95		
" ¾ " "	5 00	50		
" ½ " "	4 00	40		
" Spittoons 1st Size	10 00	1 00		
" " 2d "	7 50	65		
" " 3d "	5 00	50		
" " 4th "	4 00	40		

Invoice broadside, J. A. and C. W. Underwood, Fort Edward, New York, 1866. Merchants used invoices to place bulk orders of stoneware directly from potteries. *New York State Museum, H-1998.50.43.*

Button and Blake Hand Fire Engine, 1863. The Button Fire Engine Company was one of many fire-apparatus manufacturers in New York State to take advantage of the extensive canal transportation network. Button was based in Waterford on the Champlain Canal from 1834 to 1891. The company advertised its ready access to canals, railroads, and the Hudson River for quick delivery of orders. The company's name went through different variations until 1891, when Button joined with Silsby Manufacturing Co. of Seneca Falls, Clapp and Jones of Hudson, and Ahrens Manufacturing Co. of Cincinnati, Ohio, to form the American Fire Engine Company, based in Seneca Falls. Subsequent mergers led to the American LaFrance Fire Engine Company, which existed until 2014. The early history of this engine is unclear, but it is known to have served several communities along the canal corridor, including Union Village (now Endicott), Ithaca, and possibly Seneca Falls. The canal system provided a great avenue for shipping engines, and from there New York fire engine manufacturers shipped all over the world. *New York State Museum Collection, H-1971.73.1.*

Mirror, John Thompson Empire Mahogany, Rochester, New York, ca. 1835. *New York State Museum Collection, H-2013.22.23.*

Wall mirror, Wells M. Gaylord, Utica, New York, ca. 1828. *New York State Museum Collection, H-1972.87.1.*

Chair, Elijah Galusha, Troy, New York, ca. 1850. Elijah Galusha relocated to the burgeoning city of Troy from Strattford, Vermont, around 1830. Following the opening of the Erie Canal in 1825, Troy became an attractive destination for skilled craftsmen such as Galusha. *New York State Museum Collection, H-1969.4.2.*

Advertisement, Rochester Coach Factory, 1852. *New York State Museum Collection, H-1976.205.35.*

Rocking chair, Charles Robinson, Rochester, New York, ca. 1850. *New York State Museum Collection, H-1983.82.1.*

Canal Warehouses

Warehouses served a vital commercial purpose that benefited local and regional economies. A forwarding agent managed the warehouse and coordinated with businesses and individuals to ship and store goods. Depending on the merchant's needs, products could be stored for long or short term, or until there was enough on hand to fill a boat going to a particular destination.

7 Dock Street, attributed to Jerome Barhydt, oil on canvas, 1860. A windlass in the top floor of this warehouse hoisted goods in and out of the boats. *Courtesy of the Schenectady County Historical Society.*

STORAGE AND
FORWARDING!

The subscriber having leased the large and commodious STORE HOUSE at

Lowville Landing,

announces to the inhabitants of Lewis County, that he is prepared to Ship Freight to

NEW-YORK

and all points on the line of the Canal, in good Boats and at the most *Reasonable Prices.* I keep constantly on hand and for sale at the Store House,

SALT, WATER-LIME, &c.

Also, at the Old Stand, one door South of the Bank, will also attend to Butter and Cheese as usual.

W. H. GREELEY.

Lowville, June 8th, 1861.

Journal & Republican Cheap Power Press Print, Lowville, N. Y.

Broadside for canal warehouse and forwarding service, 1861. A forwarding agent, merchant, or purchaser was, in the simplest terms, a middleman between the producer and the consumer. He arranged for the shipment and storage of goods. This role was critical to the function and success of the canal and to the local economies along the route. Farmers, merchants, and small-scale manufacturers used forwarding agents and warehouses across the canal system. This broadside is for a forwarding agent and warehouse in Lowville on the Black River Canal. *Courtesy of the New York State Library, Manuscripts and Special Collections 9521.*

THE WINDLASS AND H. G. ROOT & COMPANY

The feature artifact in the *Enterprising Waters* exhibit is the H. G. Root & Company canal warehouse windlass. This giant hoist was used in H. G. Root and Company's warehouse, located on the Erie Canal in the village of Mohawk in Herkimer County. The windlass was most likely built in the 1830s and survived intact until 1971. It was at that time that the highway department for the town of German Flatts decided to raze the warehouse. Luckily, they invited the New York State Museum to inspect the building for artifacts. The curators found a small set of documents, numerous tools, and the fully intact windlass. They were able to remove the windlass and put it in storage, where it sat in pieces waiting for this exhibition.

A windlass is a simple machine using a wheel and axle and pulleys to gain a mechanical advantage. Here is a diagram of our windlass within the Root warehouse. On one side of the building is the canal and on the other side is the road. The windlass was designed to lift freight from the canal side of the building and the road side. Built into the structure of the warehouse on the top floor, the windlass was turned by a rope on the floor below. This mechanism enabled one or two people to lift heavy objects into and out of the warehouse with relative ease. The wheel of the windlass is fourteen feet in diameter, and the axle just over a foot in diameter and about ten feet long. The mechanical advantage is about 20 to 1, meaning that one person can lift an object about twenty times heavier with the windlass than without.

The windlass was built right into the structure of the warehouse attic. To include it in the exhibit, we had to reconstruct a framing system that mirrored the attic framing of the warehouse. A potentially bigger challenge was that the wheel was cut in half to get it out of the original building. There were no guarantees that the wooden machine would go back together after sitting in the warehouse for forty-six years.

Starting with a scale model of the windlass built by curatorial staff, we studied the possibilities for reconstruction, and the staff were confident that we could safely rebuild and exhibit the machine. Given the immense size of the structure, *Enterprising Waters* was designed with the windlass as the anchor artifact, taking center stage in the gallery. It took a little over three months to construct the frame and install the windlass.

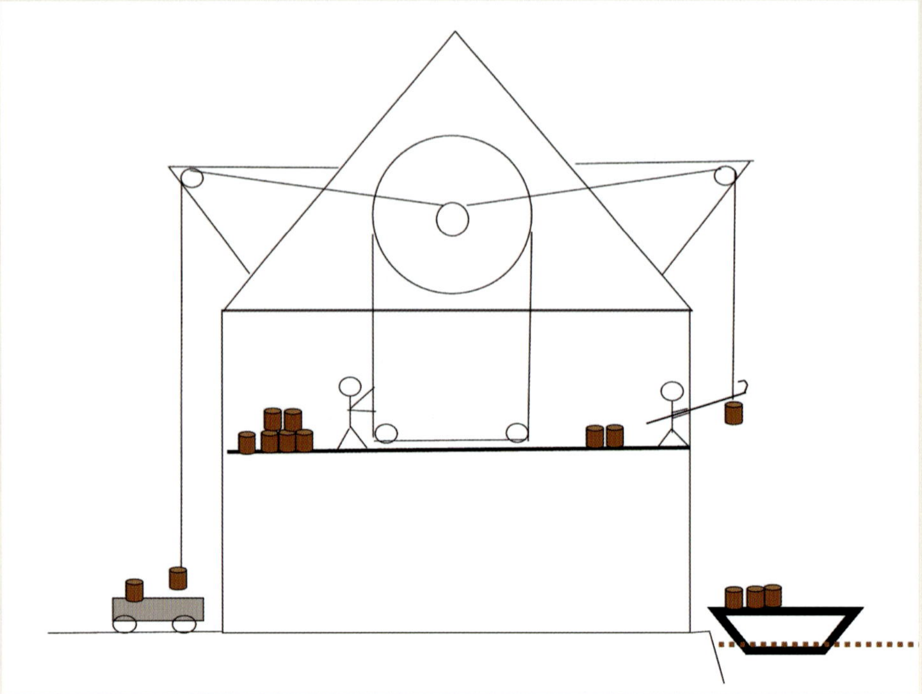

Diagram of windlass in canal warehouse.

Shearman's Store, Crooked Lake Canal, copy photograph after an unlocated original mid-nineteenth-century watercolor, artist unknown. There is a windlass inside this building, lifting the cargo out of the canal boat. Note inside the entryway the two men pulling the rope (attached to a windlass on the top floor) and the gentleman wearing a top hat holding some papers, who is likely the forwarding agent. *New York State Museum, Mrs. Arnold B. Barben Canal Collection, H-1988.79.*

Former H.G. Root & Company warehouse as it appeared in 1971.

Windlass in situ, photographs, 1971. These are record shots that New York State Museum curators took when dismantling the windlass. New York State Museum.

Windlass being reconstructed, 2017. Museum staff carefully laid out the parts of the windlass to make sure the wood had not warped beyond use. We were able to use most of the original pieces the curators salvaged in 1971. The new framing system was devised by using the 1971 photographs and computer software. *New York State Museum.*

The completed windlass.

The completed windlass, with exhibit installed on base.

H. G. Root & Company

Using the documents that the curators found in 1971 and a large collection of similar documents held by the New York State Library, we can get a good overall picture of the business activities that took place in the warehouse and its owners, H. G. Root & Company.

The Root family can be taken as an example of the growing middle to upper middle class during the antebellum period in America. Brothers Humphrey George Root (1809–1892) and Elias Root (1806–1880) were raised in Fort Edward, where their father was a blacksmith. The family included five boys and two girls. Along with their brother Leonard, H. G. and Elias moved to a village in the town of German Flatts, soon to be the village of Mohawk, in 1831. From that point on, they were very involved in the community and owned numerous businesses. In addition to a general store and malt house, the brothers operated as forwarding agents out of the warehouse. Leonard appears to have played a comparatively limited role in the business, and a few years later, younger brother John joined them to learn the trade. H. G. and Elias would eventually help John start a similar business in Michigan.

H. G. Root & Company's forwarding business operated from 1831 until at least 1866, handling a wide variety of items, from agricultural products to shipping an entire household of belongings for someone who was moving. The Roots were partners in at least two canal boats, and they also diversified and partnered in other businesses, such as a maltry, or malt house, and a general store. Both Elias and H. G. were involved in local and statewide politics. Their community involvement helped them gain business, and, in turn, it is also possible that their business ventures helped them in their political dealings. Elias was also involved in the formation of the Mohawk Valley Bank.

Both H. G. and Elias were clearly driven individuals and moved on to other ventures. H. G. went to Washington to work for the federal treasury department. He kept his home in Mohawk and interest in some of the businesses there. Elias moved to Oswego and started a malt house there. Eventually, he became a federal collector at the Port of Oswego and a bank president.

The canal warehouse enabled the men to take advantage of the new waterway and to play a role in the growing economy of the canal corridor. The windlass was the workhorse of the warehouse and today gives us a glimpse into their world.

Barrel, nineteenth century. Barrels of various sizes were used to ship a variety of goods. Using the windlass, barrels could be lifted straight out the canal boat into the warehouse. *New York State Museum, H-1969.66.1942.*

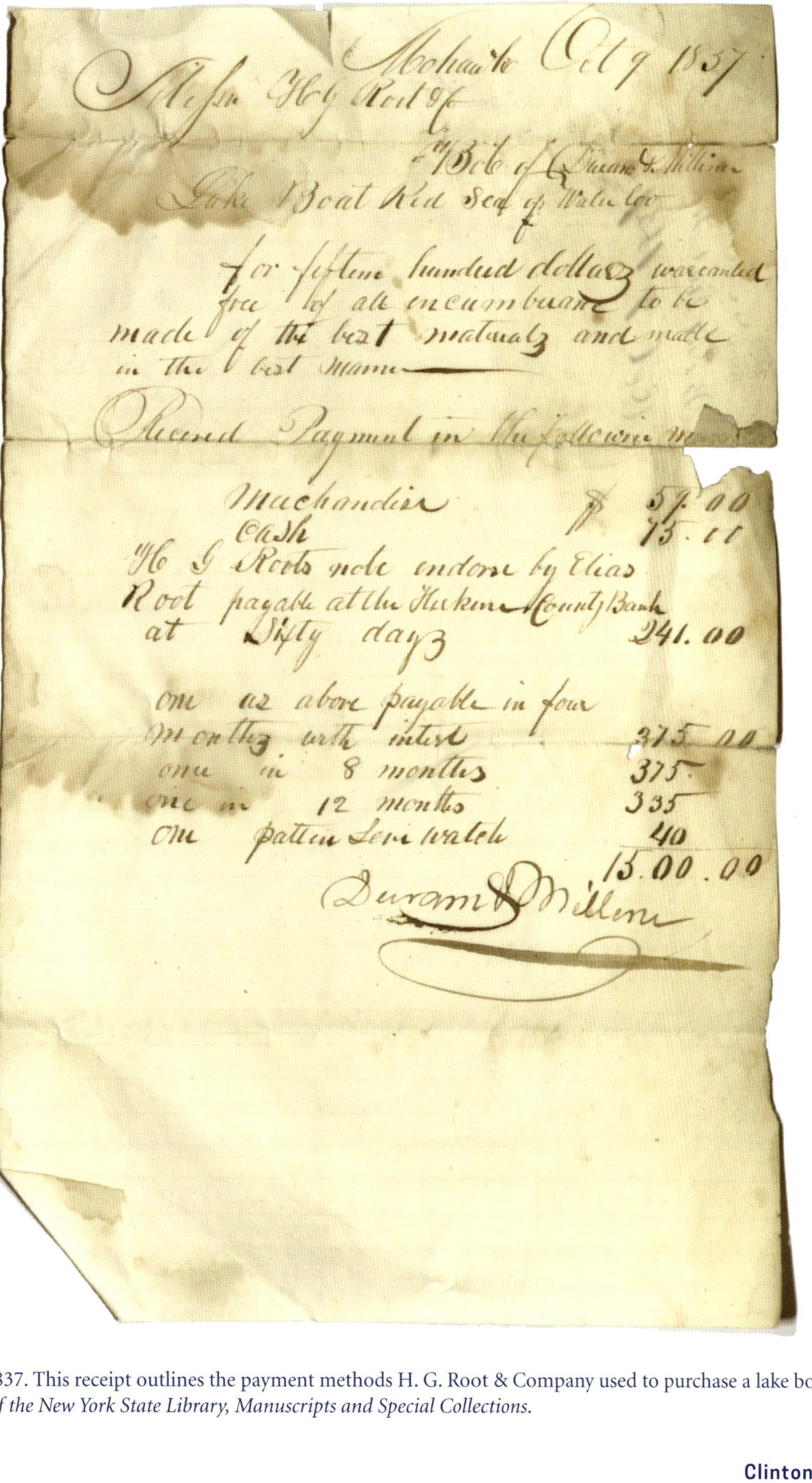

Mohawk Oct 9 1837

Messrs H G Root & Co

Bot of Duram & Millim

Lake Boat Red Sea of Water Cov

for fifteen hundred dollars warranted free of all encumbrance to be made of the best materials and made in the best manner

Received Payment in the following m

Merchandise	$	57.00
Cash	$	75.00
H G Roots note endorse by Elias Root payable at the Herkimer County Bank at Sixty days		241.00
one as above payable in four months with interest		375.00
one in 8 months		375
one in 12 months		335
one patten Lever watch		40
		15.00.00

Duram & Millen

Receipt, 1837. This receipt outlines the payment methods H. G. Root & Company used to purchase a lake boat. *Courtesy of the New York State Library, Manuscripts and Special Collections.*

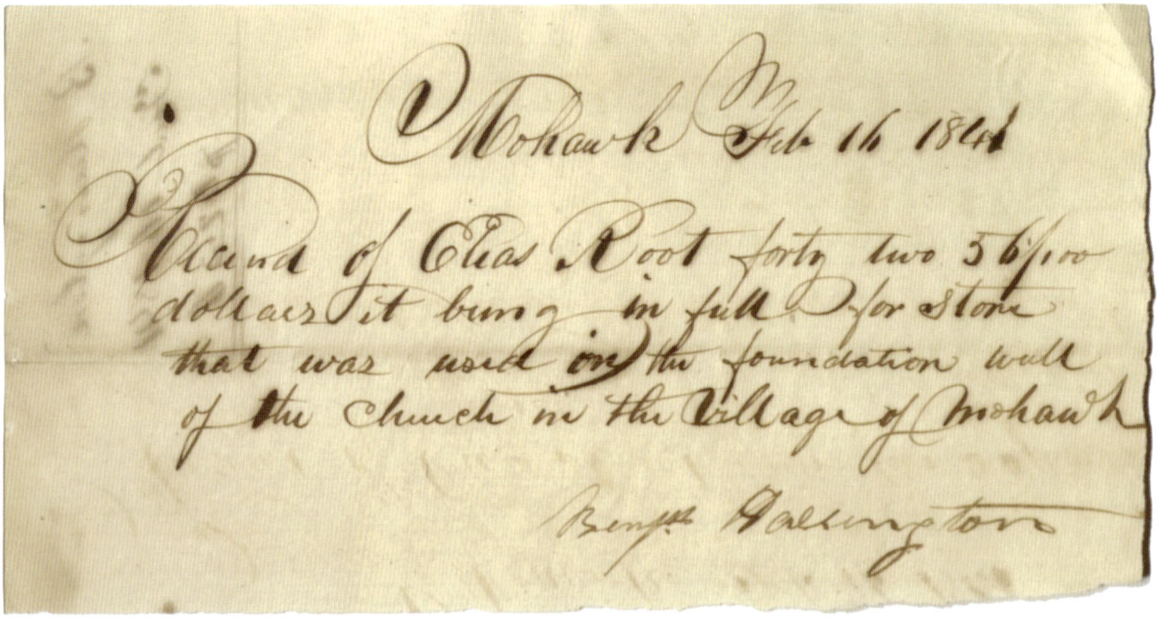

Mohawk Feb 16 1841

Received of Elias Root forty two 56/100 dollars it being in full for stone that was used on the foundation wall of the church in the Village of Mohawk

Benjn Dallington

Receipt, 1841. Elias Root helped pay for the construction for the local Methodist church. This is an 1841 receipt for stone purchased for the church's foundation. *Courtesy of the New York State Library, Manuscripts and Special Collections.*

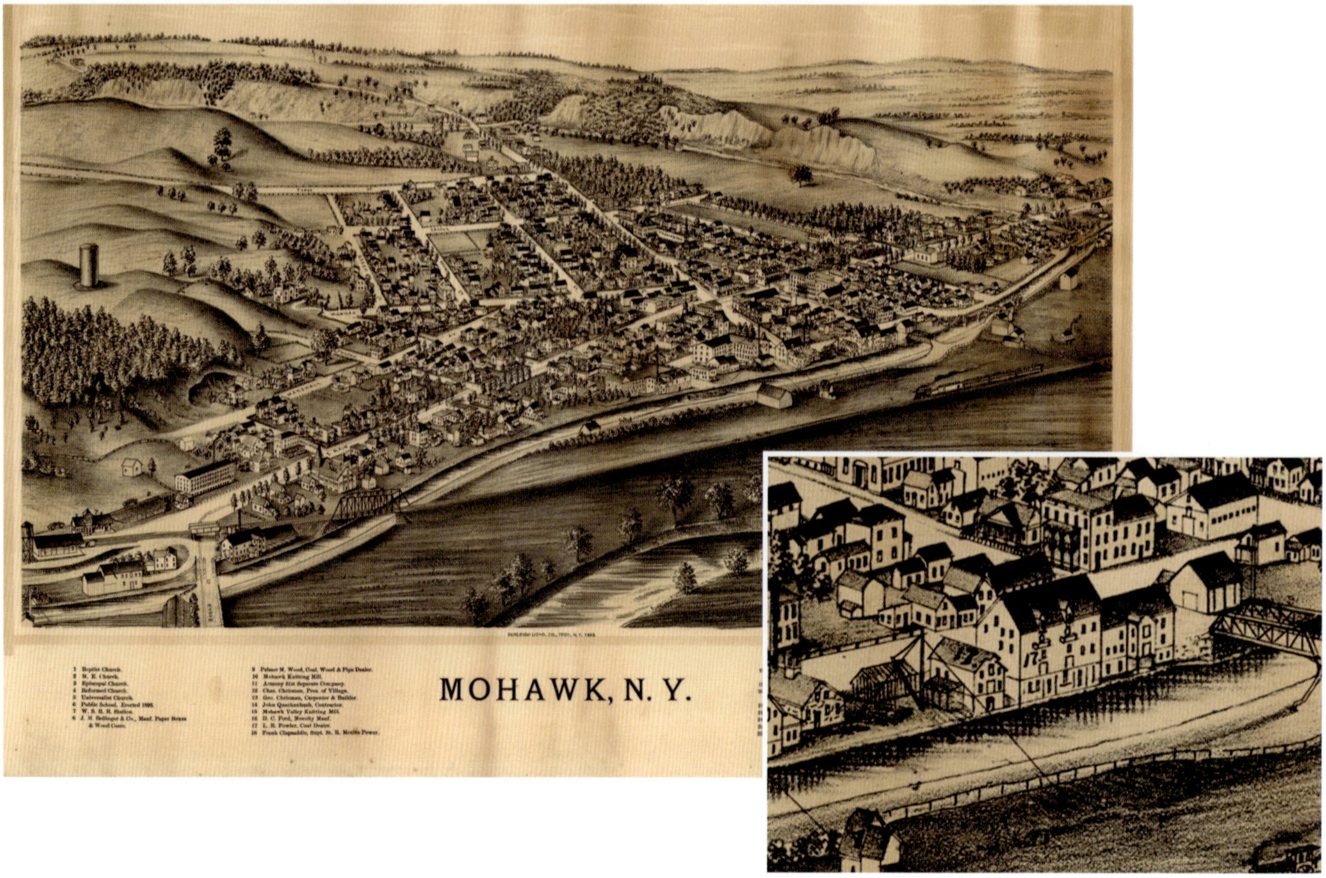

Bird's-Eye View of Mohawk, N.Y., 1893. The H. G. Root & Company warehouse as seen along the Erie Canal in 1893. Note the overhang for boats to pull up under the hoist. Courtesy of the Library of Congress.

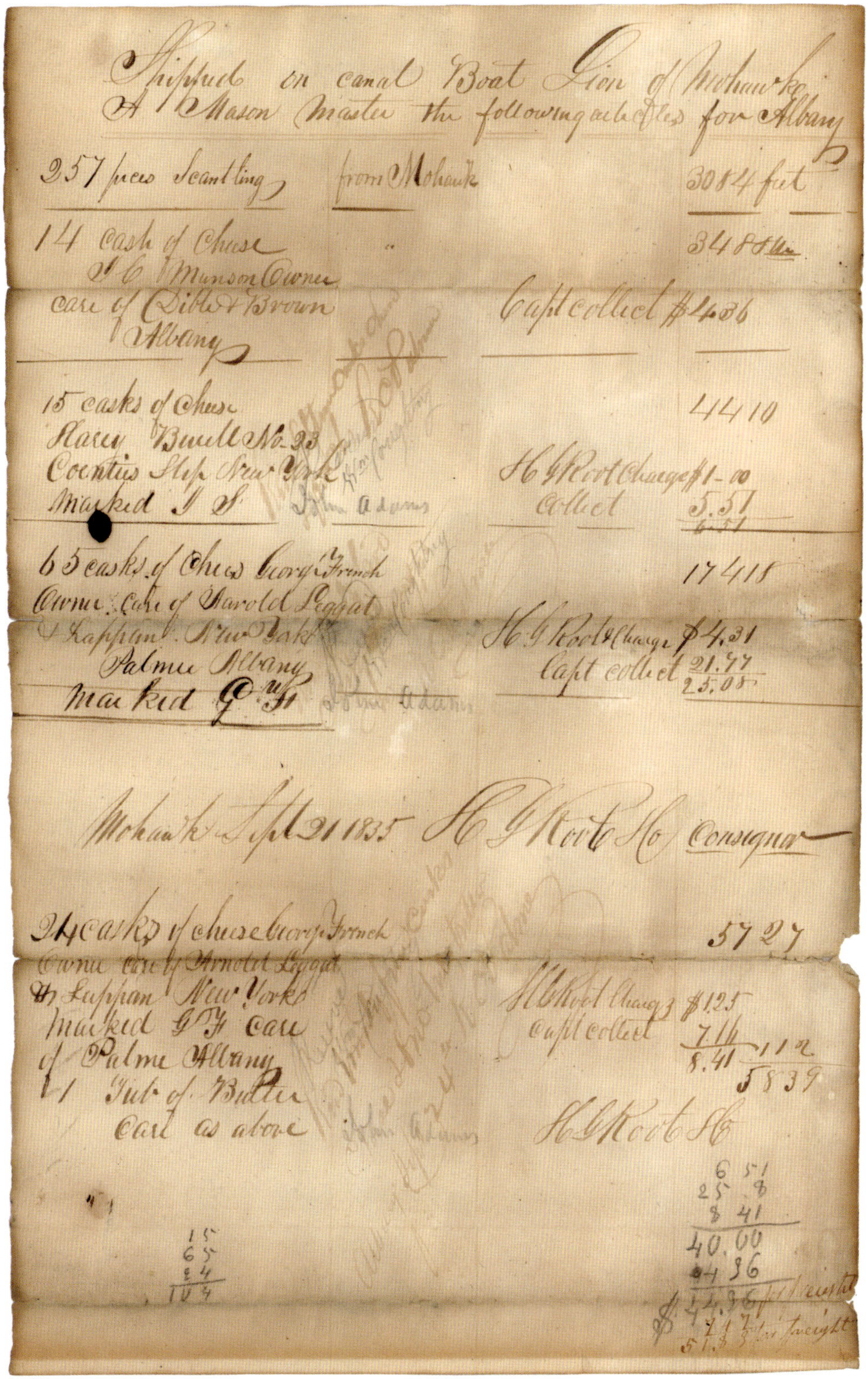

Shipped on canal Boat Lion of Mohawke
A Mason master the following articles for Albany

257 pieces Scantling from Mohawk 3084 feet

14 Cask of Cheese 3488 lbs
S C Munson Owner
care of Dible & Brown Capt collect $4.36
Albany

15 casks of Cheese 4410
Harry Buell No 33
Coenties Slip New York H G Root Charge $1-00
Marked J S Collect 5.51

65 casks of Cheese George French 17418
Owner care of Harold Leggat
& Lappan New York H G Root Charge $4.31
Palmer Albany Capt collect 21.77
Marked G F 25.08

Mohawk Sept 21 1835 H G Root & Co Consignor

24 casks of cheese George French 5727
Owner care of Arnold Leggat
& Lappan New York H G Root Charge $1.25
Marked G F care Capt collect 7.16
of Palmer Albany 8.41
1 Tub of Butter
care as above H G Root & Co

Bill of lading for H. G. Root & Company, September 21, 1835. This is a statement of goods shipped to Albany from Mohawk on the canal boat *Lion of Mohawke*. The statement by H. G. Root & Company, who is listed as a consignor, includes an itemized list of each set of orders on the boat, who owned them, who was purchasing them, H. G. Root & Company's fee, and what the captain collected at each delivery. *New York State Museum, H-1971.55.3.*

Flouring Mill of House & Fulton, Waterford, map, 1856. This image depicts a line boat on the Champlain Canal using a barrel conveyor to load the boat. *Courtesy of the Waterford Historical Museum and Cultural Center. Inset from Map of the Town of Waterford, Saratoga County, New York, 1856, by Richard Clark.*

Barrel conveyor, ca. 1830–1860. This barrel conveyor, recovered from the H. G. Root & Company warehouse, was used to roll barrels into barges or along the ground, or was used to strap down barrels. *New York State Museum, H-1971.59.6.*

Push pole, ca. 1830–1860. Long sturdy poles were multipurpose tools to help maneuver canal boats. This pole is more than thirteen feet long. *New York State Museum, H-9171.59.NN.*

Former H. G. Root Warehouse, photograph, 1897. This image shows the canal side of the warehouse. The windlass was located in the furthest building. *New York State Museum, H-1988.80.1.777.*

MOVING GOODS: THE BOATS THAT MADE IT HAPPEN

> **Our boat, which is of a superior class for freight boats, is about 80 feet long by 20, the bow and stern are 4 feet lower than the middle section, which is divided into three apartments, the two end ones for the accommodation of passengers, the stern to eat in, and the bow to sleep and sit in, each about 23 feet long, and sufficiently high for a six footer to stand erect with his hat on. . . . The centre apartment is appropriated to merchandise.**
>
> **—"The Great Water Highway through New York State, 1829," author unknown[8]**

Various types of boats were used from the early days of the canal's operation. The first boats in use were inspired by European designs and Durham boats. As canallers on the Erie gained experience, a few basic styles evolved to best serve the demands of the New York waterways.

Line boats, lake boats, bullhead boats, and the canal schooners carried freight and were designed with their cargo and route in mind. The line boat had space for both freight and passengers. The canal schooner's mast could be removed while in the canal and raised for sailing on the lakes or rivers.

Scow boats had square ends that sloped up from the bottom of the boat at the front and back. These boats were used by State crews to do repairs on the canal and earned the nickname "hurry-up boats" because they hurried to the spots where repairs were needed. Scows were also used to haul lumber, sand, gravel, and other items that could be exposed to the elements.

Grain-Boat on the Erie Canal.

Grain-Boat on the Erie Canal, engraving, ca. 1883. J. David Williams, ed., *America Illustrated*, ca. 1883. *Courtesy of the New York State Library, 917.3 qW72.*

P. E. Havens, Canal Schooner, postcard, ca. 1900. Canal schooner *P. E. Havens* built in 1865 in Essex, New York, sailing on Lake Champlain.* *New York State Museum, H-1988.80.5253.*
*For additional information on the *P. E. Havens* in Arthur B. Cohn, *Lake Champlain's Sailing Canal Boats: An Illustrated Journey from Burlington Bay to the Hudson River* (Basin Harbor: Lake Champlain Maritime Museum, 2003), 112.

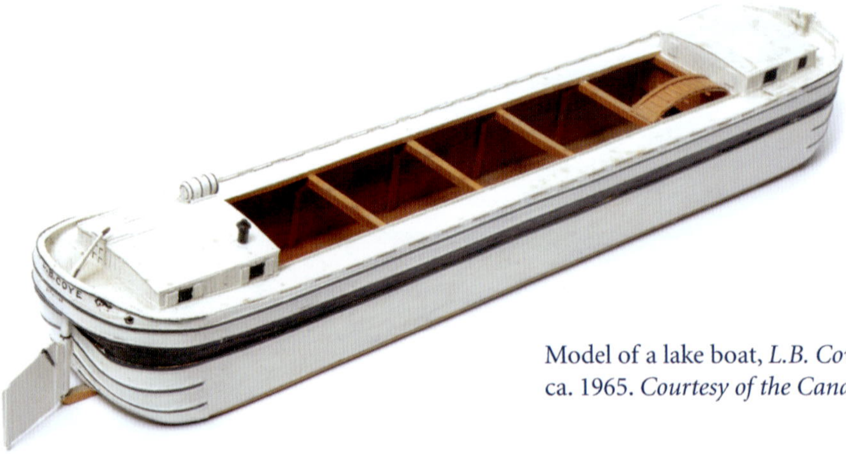

Model of a lake boat, *L.B. Cove*, Robert E. Hager, ca. 1965. *Courtesy of the Canal Society of New York State.*

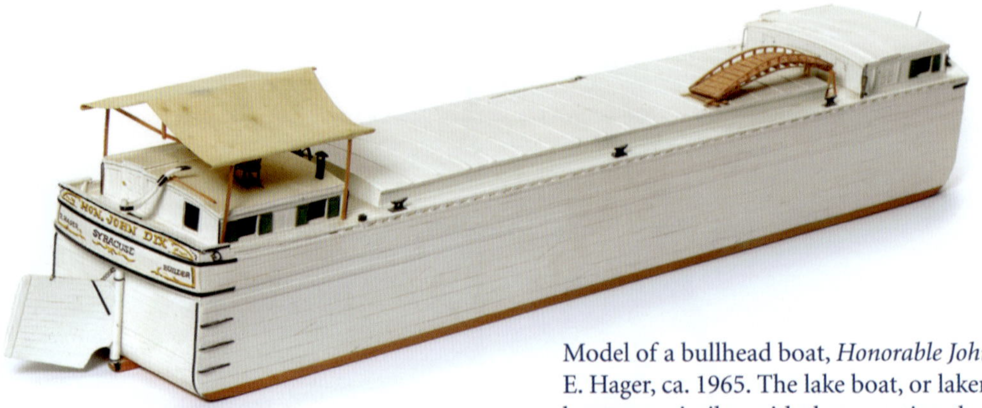

Model of a bullhead boat, *Honorable John W. Dix*, Robert E. Hager, ca. 1965. The lake boat, or laker, and bullhead boat were similar, with the exception that a lake boat had multiple hatches across the top deck and the bullhead had one long cover that looked like a cabin covering the deck. *Courtesy of the Canal Society of New York State.*

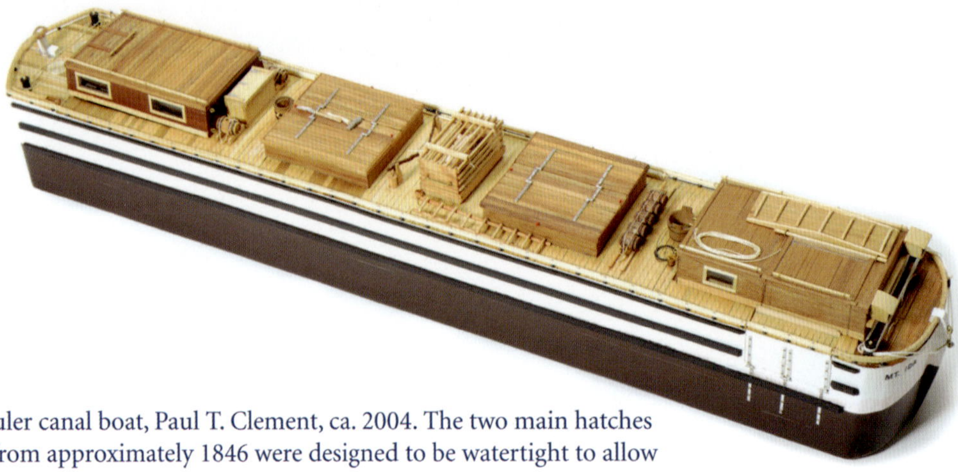

Model of a grain-hauler canal boat, Paul T. Clement, ca. 2004. The two main hatches of this style of boat from approximately 1846 were designed to be watertight to allow loose grain to be stored in the hull. Mules were stabled in the front, or bow, while the crew lived in the rear, or aft. Note the barrel conveyor on the deck, similar to the one from the H. G. Root & Company warehouse, pictured on page 124. *Collection of the Rensselaer County Historical Society, Troy, New York.*

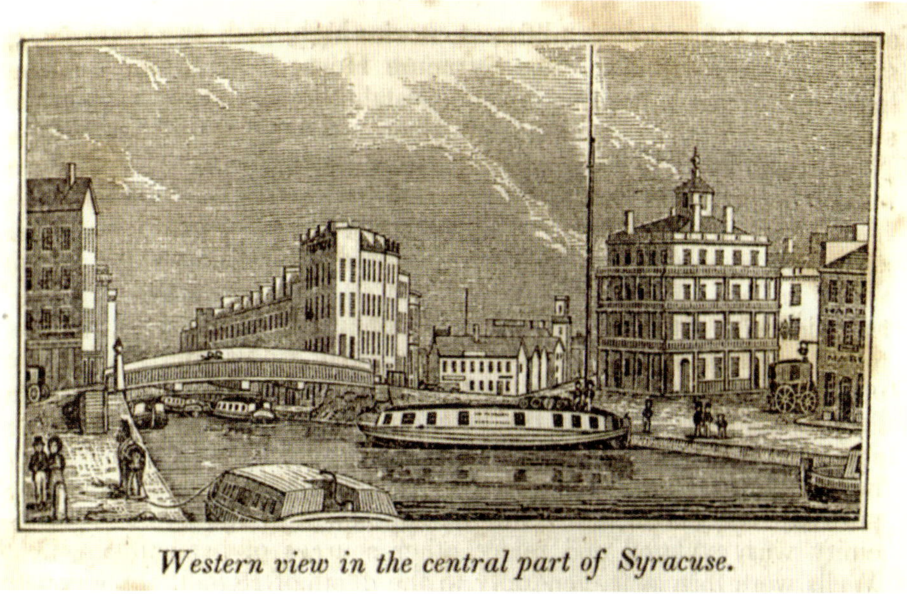

Western view in central part of Syracuse, engraving, 1842. A line boat is featured in the center of this engraving of Syracuse. John Warner Barber and Henry Howe, *Historical Collections of the State of New York; Containing a General Collection of the Most Interesting Facts, Traditions, Biographical Sketches, Anecdotes, &c., Relating to Its History and Antiquities, with Geographical Descriptions of Every Township in the State* (New York: S. Tuttle, 1842). *Courtesy of the New York State Library, Manuscripts and Special Collections, 974.7 B23a3.*

The Line-Boat Cabin, engraving, ca. 1852. Jacob Abbott, *Marco Paul's Voyages & Travels, Erie Canal*, ca. 1852. *Courtesy of the New York State Library, Manuscripts and Special Collections, 813.4 A132 90-245.*

Line boats were operated by freight line companies and hauled both freight and passengers. The fee for passengers aboard a line boat was cheaper than a packet, or passenger-only, boat because of the line boat's limited amenities and comparatively slow progress. This was the preferred method of travel for immigrants because they could save on travel expenses and they could bring furniture and luggage with them.

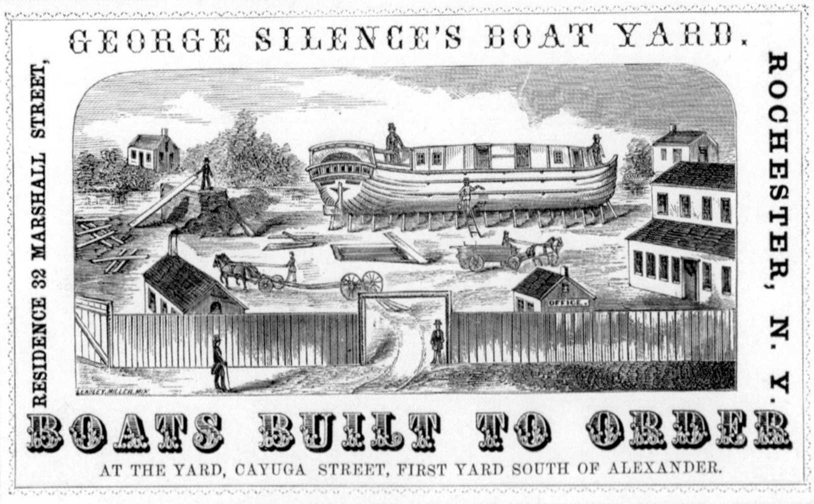

Advertising card for George Silence's Boat Yard, ca. 1850. Even before the canal was completed, the demand for boats was high. Boatyards started to appear along the finished parts of the canal and became big business. This circa-1850s advertisement is from George Silence's boatyard in Rochester. He presumably learned his trade from his father, Frederick, who also built boats. *New York State Museum, Mrs. Arnold B. Barben Canal Collection, H-1988.79.*

Boat Launch, photograph, ca. 1900. Launch of a completed bullhead freight boat. Boats were built adjacent to the canal, in dry docks, or in the canal bed during the winter. Dry docks are enclosed areas used to construct, store, and repair vessels, usually connected to the canal by lock-style doors. *New York State Museum, Mrs. Arnold B. Barben Canal Collection, H-1988.79.*

D. B. Tanner Dry Dock, photograph, late nineteenth to early twentieth century. D. B. Tanner's Dry Dock was located in Port Byron in Cayuga County. A canal dry dock is a small basin or enclosure that can be filled or drained using lock doors connected to the canal. Boats can enter the dry dock when it is full of water, and then, when the water is drained, the boats rest on small piers so they can be worked on or stored. Note the steam vessel resting on piers in the dry dock. *New York State Museum, Mrs. Arnold B. Barben Canal Collection, H-1988.79.*

(above and on page 132)
Boatyards, photographs, late nineteenth to early twentieth century. Views from various boatyards along the Erie Canal. *New York State Museum, H-1988.80.1.1283,1285,1296, 4083.*

DORAN'S DRY DOCK
DURHAMVILLE, N.Y.

Caulking tools, late nineteenth to early twentieth century. A caulker repaired leaky boats by filling the seams in the hull with tarred fiber called oakum. After the seams were caulked—often pronounced "corked"—the boat would be watertight. These tools belonged to Charles A. Pearse (1839–1920), who had a reputation as a master caulker. *Courtesy of the Canal Society of New York State.*

Caulker's folding chair, late nineteenth to early twentieth century. This lightweight folding chair was used by a caulker while repairing lower parts of the boat. *Courtesy of the Erie Canal Museum, PC 2014.85.02.*

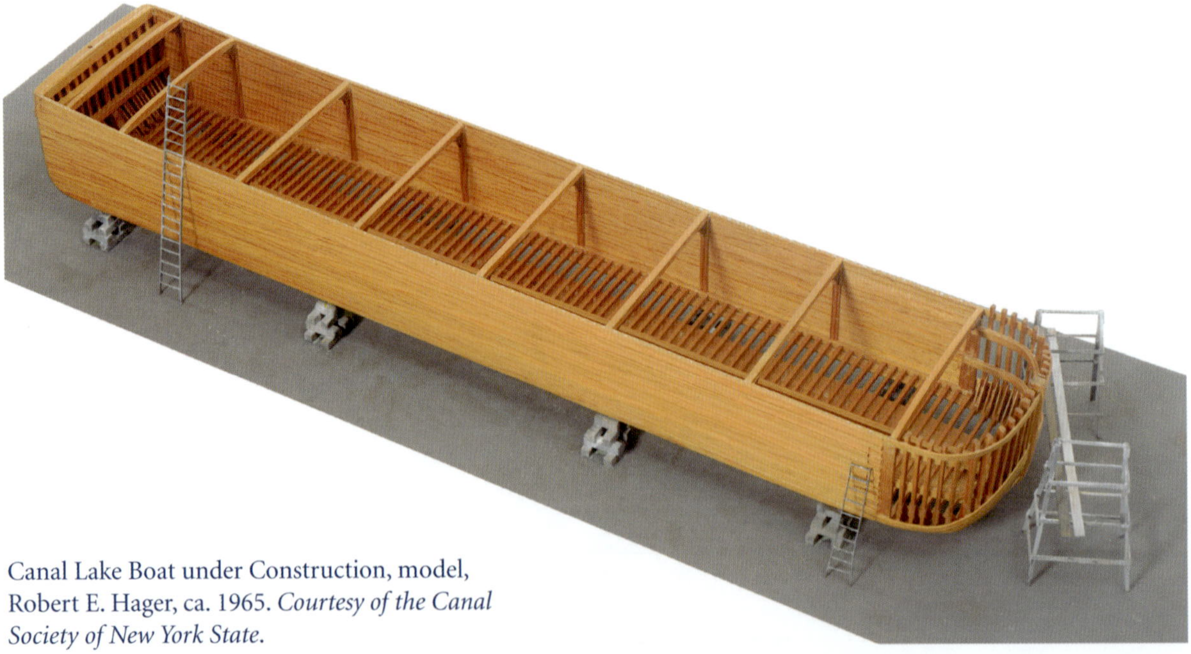

Canal Lake Boat under Construction, model, Robert E. Hager, ca. 1965. *Courtesy of the Canal Society of New York State.*

CANAL STORES

As soon as sections of the canal opened, it was clear that boat crews and patrons needed places to buy supplies. Early on, lock tenders opened general stores next to locks, but that practice became prohibited as some lock tenders proved more eager to make money in their stores than tending to their duties "locking boats through."

Soon, privately owned canal stores opened. As boats waited their turn to lock through, passengers and crewmembers could purchase day-to-day necessities. These general stores also had medicines, tools, general boats supplies—almost anything a boater could need while traveling. The stores also served as a social center for boaters and community members.

Fort Plain Canal Store, photograph, late nineteenth to early twentieth century. Pictured on the left is the Fort Plain Canal Store at Lock 32 on the Erie Canal, in Montgomery County. *New York State Museum, H-1988.80.1.458.*

NEW ASHERY.

THE subscribers are erecting a new ashery in the village of Fort Plain, near the East Guard Lock, which will be ready for reception of good unleached ashes, by or before the 1st day of Feb. next, for which they will pay a fair price in Groceries, Provisions and Liquors, at their store.

NEW GROCERY.

They will at all times keep a choice selection of Groceries, Provisions and Liquors, cheap for Cash.

CASH FOR PORK.

The highest market price paid for Pork, and for first quality Butter.

J. & R. ADAMS.

Fort Plain, January 12, 1847.

Advertisement for Fort Plain Canal Store in the *Montgomery Phoenix and Fort Plain Advertiser newspaper, 1847.* New York State Museum, H-1988.17, Research File.

Fort Plain Canal Store, photograph, ca. 1895. This photograph was taken when the Fort Plain Canal Store was owned and operated by the Fineour family. *New York State Museum, H-1988.17.*

Kearns' Meat Market, Port Byron, photograph, ca. 1895. Meat market alongside a lock on the Erie Canal in Cayuga County. *New York State Museum, Mrs. Arnold B. Barben Canal Collection, H-1988.79.*

Canal store crocks, ca. 1900. These large stoneware crocks are from the Fort Plain Canal Store. They would have been used to make liquid-based foods such as sauerkraut or pickles. *New York State Museum, H-1988.17.*

Grocery Store on the Erie Canal, D. Maitland Armstrong, oil on canvas, 1881. *Courtesy of the Arkell Museum at Canajoharie. Gift of Frank and Bertelle Barbour.*

Erie House, Port Byron, photograph, ca. 1900. This saloon and boardinghouse located in Port Byron was owned and operated by Italian immigrants Pietro Van Detto and Salvatore Van Detto. The building, which is located next to an old lock, has been restored and opened to the public as part of the Old Erie Canal Heritage Park by the Canal Society of New York State. *New York State Museum, Mrs. Arnold B. Barben Canal Collection, H-1988.79.*

Saloon drinking glasses, ca. 1900. These drinking glasses from the Erie House were gifted to the museum by Marie Van Detto, daughter of the original co-owner Pietro Van Detto. Both Marie and her sister Theresa lived in the Erie House for their entire lives. *New York State Museum, H-1988.77.1-2.*

Grocery List from the 1890s

Before starting a trip on the Champlain Canal, Martha Robbins Juckett, a young girl at the beginning of the twentieth century, was responsible for helping to pick up the groceries for her family's boat. In her book, *My Canaling Days, 1897–1907*, she outlines what items they would stock up on before leaving Whitehall for New York City.

> Put me up a half bushel of potatoes, five pounds of lard, four or five pounds of beans. Then you looked in his pork barrel and selected a chunk of four or five pounds as he pulled up several with his hook for your selection. Six cans of tomatoes. No one ever bought small ones then. Oh yes! A dozen cans of Eagle brand condensed milk, a sack of flour, a couple bags of salt, two or three pounds of cheese, a couple of pounds of mixed cookies, a couple dozen of eggs, a package of Magic Yeast, a few cans of corn and peas, a cake of Baker's chocolate. Here's my jug for a gallon of vinegar, and oh! Yes, give me a couple of lemons. For some reason you never bought more than two at a time. A box of matches, coffee. Tea we usually purchased at St. Johns, Canada. Also our butter, usually at St. Ours, Canada. A couple of boxes of tobacco. "Sensation" came in pound tin boxes. And while you are at it, have them take over a towline. That was for canal towing only. When you paid your bill, Brett [the grocer] gave you a cigar.[9]

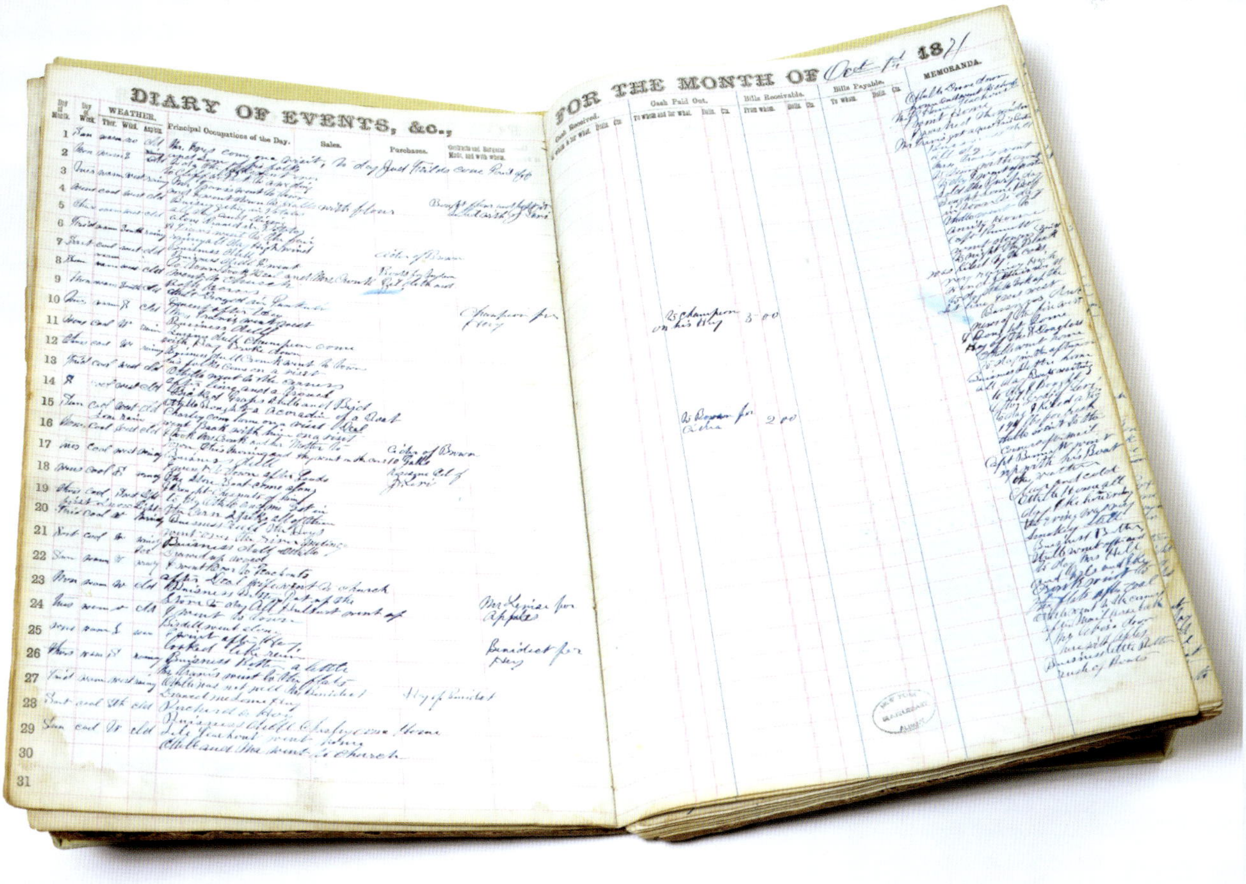

Canal store ledger, Abraham Paris diary, Grooms Corners, New York, 1871–1877. This diary contains a brief summary of daily activities and business transactions of a grocery store located near Lock 22 at Rexford. *Courtesy of the New York State Library, Manuscripts and Special Collections BD22800.*

THE CANAL AND THE HUDSON IN THE AGE OF STEAM

The Hudson River was a vital link in the trade route between the Atlantic Ocean, Lake Champlain, and the Great Lakes. During the 1820s and 1830s, the flat-bottomed canal boats stuck mainly to the canals, while sailing and steam-powered boats cruised the Hudson and the lakes.

By the 1840s canal boats had grown in size, and steam vessels became powerful enough to tow long lines of canal boats and barges between Albany and New York City. By the end of the nineteenth century, as many as 125 boats could make up one long tow. Smaller tugboats were used to help the long tows make turns in the river and to add or remove boats while the tow was moving.

Tow on the Hudson, Augusta Brown, drawing, 1895. For canallers, the two- or three-day tow between Albany and New York allowed time for boat maintenance, laundry, and to socialize with other crews in the tow. Once in New York City, boats and barges were taken off the tow and steered to designated docks. While unloading, the boat captain might search for his next job. It was not unusual for private barge owners to spend many days at the New York docks looking for the next load to haul north. *New York State Museum, Augusta Brown Journal, H-1988.36.1.*

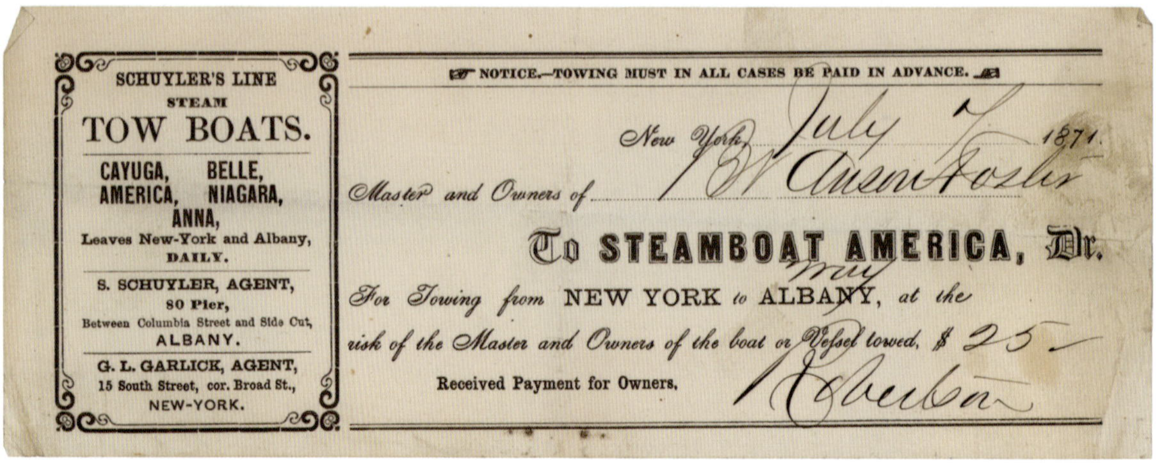

SCHUYLER'S LINE
STEAM
TOW BOATS.
CAYUGA, BELLE,
AMERICA, NIAGARA,
ANNA,
Leaves New-York and Albany,
DAILY.
S. SCHUYLER, AGENT,
80 Pier,
Between Columbia Street and Side Cut,
ALBANY.
G. L. GARLICK, AGENT,
15 South Street, cor. Broad St.,
NEW-YORK.

NOTICE.—TOWING MUST IN ALL CASES BE PAID IN ADVANCE.

New York July 7 1871

Master and Owners of

To STEAMBOAT AMERICA, Dr.

For Towing from NEW YORK to ALBANY, at the risk of the Master and Owners of the boat or Vessel towed, $ 25

Received Payment for Owners,

Receipt for tow on the Hudson River by the Schuyler Line, July 3, 1879. One of Albany's earliest African American businessmen, Captain Samuel Schuyler (1781–1841), founded the Schuyler Line, a lucrative boat-towing service, and the company grew under the leadership of two of his sons. Captain Schuyler also joined with family members in other business ventures, including real estate, a coal yard, and a flour and feed store. *New York State Museum, Mrs. Arnold B. Barben Canal Collection, H-1988.79.*

Portrait of America, ca. 1868, L. F. Tantillo, oil on canvas, 2002. The flagship of the Schuyler Line, the *America*, was capable of towing up to seventy fully loaded barges on the Hudson River. The receipt on page 140 is for a tow from New York to Troy (written in over Albany) by the *America*, the total cost being $25. *Courtesy of L. F. Tantillo.*

The Albany Basin, or Canal Harbor, of the Erie and Champlain Canals, Albany, N.Y., engraving, 1856. New York City was already a bustling port by the 1820s, but Albany was much smaller. A large basin was constructed in Albany to handle the increased boat traffic that came with the opening of the Erie Canal. The four-thousand-foot-long basin included large dock space, piers, and warehouses. The Albany Basin prevented congested traffic on the Hudson River and effectively facilitated the exchange of cargo entering or leaving the Erie Canal. *New York State Museum, H-1982.76.4.*

Robert Fulton (1765–1815)

American inventor and artist Robert Fulton became interested in canals in the 1790s. Traveling in England, he worked on mechanical inventions related to canals, including obtaining a patent for a dredging machine. Fulton envisioned a canal that would use steam-powered tugboats, as well as inclined planes, rather than locks. He befriended social reformer Robert Owen, who offered to finance his designs. Fulton was ultimately awarded a short-lived subcontract with a canal company in England.

From England, Fulton moved to Paris, where he met American minister plenipotentiary to France Robert R. Livingston. Livingston was also an enthusiastic supporter of steam-powered boats, and the two worked together to build a more practical design than earlier vessels created by James Rumsey, John Fitch, and others. The Fulton-Livingston collaboration resulted in the creation of the *North River Steamboat of Clermont*, launched on the Hudson River in 1807. Prior to their having developed, built, and tested their steamboat, Fulton and Livingston were granted a thirty-year monopoly by New York State to operate steamboats on the Hudson. The monopoly was overturned by the Supreme Court in 1824.

Steamboats on the Hudson River greatly enhanced the success of canal-system trade networks. Both Fulton and Livingston were appointed to the Erie Canal Commission.

North River Steamboat of Clermont, model, Fred R. Cron, 1949. Robert Fulton's *North River Steamboat of Clermont*, the first steamboat in public service, was launched in 1807 in New York City, heralding an era of reliable steam travel along the Hudson River. Steamboats transformed the movement of goods and people, allowing for set schedules not reliant on weather and wind conditions, as was the case for sloops and sailboats. New York State Museum, H-1948.7.1 A-B.

Robert Fulton, watercolor on ivory, ca. 1810. Robert Fulton's innovation of steam travel was instrumental to the approval of the Erie Canal construction and the Industrial Revolution in America. Fulton was a man of many talents, including painting—he executed this miniature self-portrait. *New York State Museum, H-1973.100.2.*

View of Albany N.Y. from the East, 1845, Edwin Whitefield (American, born England, 1816–1892), Lewis & Brown, printers (American, active mid-nineteenth century). *New York State Museum, H-1981.108.1.*

View from Mount Ida, 1845, DeWitt Clinton Boutelle (American, 1820–1884), oil on canvas. Private collection.

Both executed in 1845, these views of Albany from the opposite shore of the Hudson River show two distinct approaches to landscape rendering. From a bucolic vantage point in Rensselaer, Whitefield detailed the growth of the city as it spread from the waterfront westward. On the other hand, Boutelle, who was named after Erie Canal mastermind De Witt Clinton, focused on the breathtaking vista from Troy in a classic Hudson River School composition. He emphasized the expansive landscape in which tiny figures hike up the ascent, with Albany visible in the distance.

NEW PORTS AND BOOMTOWNS

New communities with nautical names, like Port Byron, Brockport, Gasport, and Lockport, sprung up along the canal and were rich with opportunities. By the time the Erie Canal was completed, the tiny villages had become prosperous towns, and within a few decades, many became cities.

(pages 144-145)
Pioneer Settlement to Prosperous Farm, engravings, 1849. These images depict the evolution of early settler to farmer in western New York. Orasmus Turner, *Pioneer History of the Holland Land Purchase,* 1849. *Courtesy of the New York State Library, Manuscripts and Special Collections, 974.79 T94.*

Village of Rochester, Captain Basil Hall, engraving, 1827–1828. British naval officer Captain Basil Hall and his wife toured through America in 1827 and 1828. Not only did he write down his observations, he also made sketches. Hall was impressed with the rapid growth of the canal corridor. Here is part of his description of Rochester on June 26, 1827:

> Everything in this bustling place appeared to be in motion. The very streets seemed to be starting up of their own accord, ready-made, and looking fresh and new, as if they had been turned out of the workmen's hands but an hour before. . . . In many buildings the people were at work below stairs, while at top the carpenters were busy nailing on the planks of the roof.
>
> Some dwellings were half painted, while the foundations of others, within five yards' distance, were only beginning. I cannot say how many churches, court-houses, jails, and hotels I counted, all in motion, creeping upwards. Several streets were nearly finished, but had not as yet received their names; and many others were in the reverse predicament, being named, but not commenced,—their local habitation being merely signified by lines of stakes. Here and there we saw great warehouses, without window sashes, but half filled with goods, and furnished with hoisting cranes, ready to fish up the huge pyramids of flour barrels, bales, and boxes lying in the streets. In the centre of the town the spire of a Presbyterian church rose to a great height, and on each side of the supporting tower was to be seen the dial-plate of a clock, of which the machinery, in the hurry-skurry, had been left at New York. I need not say that these half-finished, whole finished, and embryo streets were crowded with people, carts, stages, cattle, pigs, far beyond the reach of numbers;—and as all these were lifting up their voices together, in keeping with the clatter of hammers, the ringing of axes, and the creaking of machinery, there was a fine concert, I assure you!*

Courtesy of the New York State Library, Manuscripts and Special Collections N 917.3 qH168.
*Captain Basil Hall, Royal Navy, *Travels in North America in the Years 1827 and 1828* (Philadelphia: Carey, Lea & Carey, 1829), 87.

New Luxuries

> **Ours is no longer a western settlement, our children are surrounded by comforts, the blessings and the elegances of life, where their fathers found only hardship, privation and want.**
>
> —*Buffalo Commercial Advertiser, November 14, 1848*

As communities grew out of the forests, the people living within the canal corridor had access to goods and services not previously available. From fresh oysters to high-end furniture, the speed and smooth travel of the canal brought the comforts of eastern society to the west.

Walking Dress, 1830. Featured in *The Lady's Book,* vol. 1, this walking dress was one of the "Latest English Fashions." Women along the canal corridor now had access to the latest European fashions and materials shipped from New York City to make them. *Godey's Lady's Book, and Ladies' American Magazine,* vol. 1, 1830. *Courtesy of Princeton University Library via Hathi Trust Digital Library.*

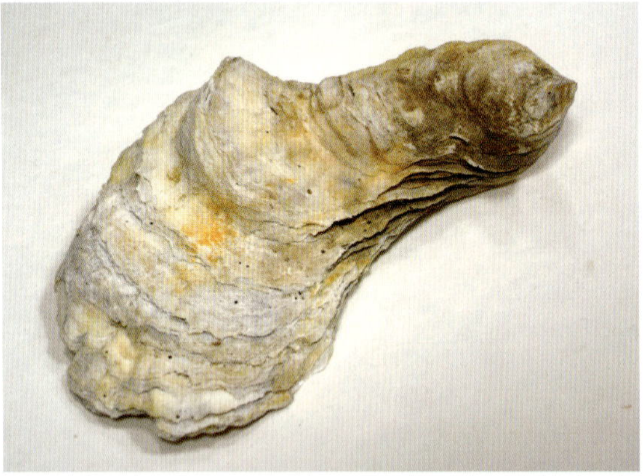

Oyster shell. The canal brought fresh oysters and other seafood safely to communities in western New York for the first time. *New York State Museum.*

Square piano, Robert and William Nunns, New York City, ca. 1825. In 1825 the Wardlaw family of Palmyra, Wayne County, purchased this piano for their house on the banks of the Erie Canal. The ornate piano was a true luxury that would have cost a fortune to ship prior to the canal. *New York State Museum, H-1970.63.1.*

Elizabeth Ann Ferris Preston, ca. 1825–1835, attributed to Sheldon Peck (American, 1797–1868), oil on wood panel. *Fenimore Art Museum, Cooperstown, New York.*

Peck began his career as a portrait painter while living in Vermont. In 1828 he moved to central New York—perhaps to follow opportunities for portrait artists created by the growing wealth along the canal. He lived in Jordan, New York, and later settled in Cato—villages just west of Syracuse. Featured in the portraits are the owners of a Cato general store, Elizabeth Ann Ferris Preston and Andrews Preston. Peck was also active in the reform movements sweeping through what came to be called "the burned-over district" of central New York, which grew with the influx of people along the Erie Canal. Peck was a proponent of abolition, temperance, and free public education.

Andrews Preston, ca. 1825–1835 attributed to Sheldon Peck (American, 1797–1868), oil on wood panel. *Fenimore Art Museum, Cooperstown, New York*

The Itinerant Artist, ca. 1850, Charles Bird King (American, 1785–1863), oil on canvas.
Fenimore Art Museum, Cooperstown, New York

As the Erie Canal gave rise to new villages and cities, and wealth grew, there was new demand for material goods, including portraiture. Just as other businessmen journeyed along the canal seeking opportunity, itinerant artists traveled seeking commissions.

After studying in New York and London, Charles Bird King spent seven years traveling as an itinerant artist, perhaps inspiring this work. He is best known, however, for the portraits of politicians and Native Americans he created in his studio in Washington, DC.

Unidentified Man, 1833, Milton William Hopkins (American, 1789–1844), oil on canvas.
Fenimore Art Museum, Cooperstown, New York. Gift of Bertram K. and Nina Fletcher Little.

Hopkins worked as an itinerant artist and may have provided instruction to other artists. He lived along the canal in Albion, near Rochester, for thirteen years. Despite the booming population of the region, settling into the community and making a living as a portrait painter could be difficult. To help make ends meet, Hopkins also painted houses and signs, made chairs, and even worked as a canal boat captain.

Residence of Mr. & Mrs. Martin Garber, 1898, Fitz G. Vogt (American, born Germany, 1841–1900), crayon and pencil on paper. New York State Museum, H-1985.14.1

Vogt was an itinerant artist focused on agricultural portraiture—rather than drawing people, he recorded family farms and businesses. Using the skills of a trained draftsman, and employing multiple-point perspective, he captured a tremendous amount of detail in his subjects. His views were nostalgic, showing a rural way of life that was in decline.

LIFE ON THE CANAL

It is true the men swore a good deal in their ordinary conversation, but they did it with no air of profanity. It was just an oil to the flow of their remarks.

—Clifton Johnson, 1898[10]

The Erie Canal attracted people from all walks of life. Professional canallers, or "canawlers," had a reputation as rough-and-tough transients who loved to drink and fight, especially when trying to beat another boat into a lock. Although this may have been true of some, there were canallers who did not participate in such activities. In addition to those working on the commercial boats, the State employed workers who kept the canal moving.

Living and working on the canal required the help of many to keep the boats moving and to take care of the needs of the people on board.

The Boat Crew

A typical freight boat crew consisted of a captain, a steersman, two drivers, and a cook. The captain was in charge of the crew and finances. The steersman would pilot the boat, load and unload, and help with the mules. The drivers were responsible for the mules or horses. Steering and driving were done in six-hour shifts called "a trick"—six hours on and six hours off. The cook was often the wife of the captain or steersman.

(above left) *Canal Boat Steersman*, engraving, ca. 1852. Jacob Abbott, *Marco Paul's Voyages & Travels, Erie Canal*, ca. 1852. *Courtesy of the New York State Library, Manuscripts and Special Collections, 813.4 A132 90-245.*

(above right) *Our Steersman*, Augusta Brown, drawing, 1895. *New York State Museum, Augusta Brown Journal, H-1988.36.1.*

Beauty on the Barge Deck, engraving, 1882. Canallers had their own set of social rules that deeply challenged the emerging middle-class sense of what was right and wrong. Single women worked on the canal as cooks or in other roles. These women had greater freedom than those who lived a more traditional lifestyle. *The National Police Gazette, N.Y., N.Y.,* July 22, 1882. *Courtesy of the Canal Society of New York State.*

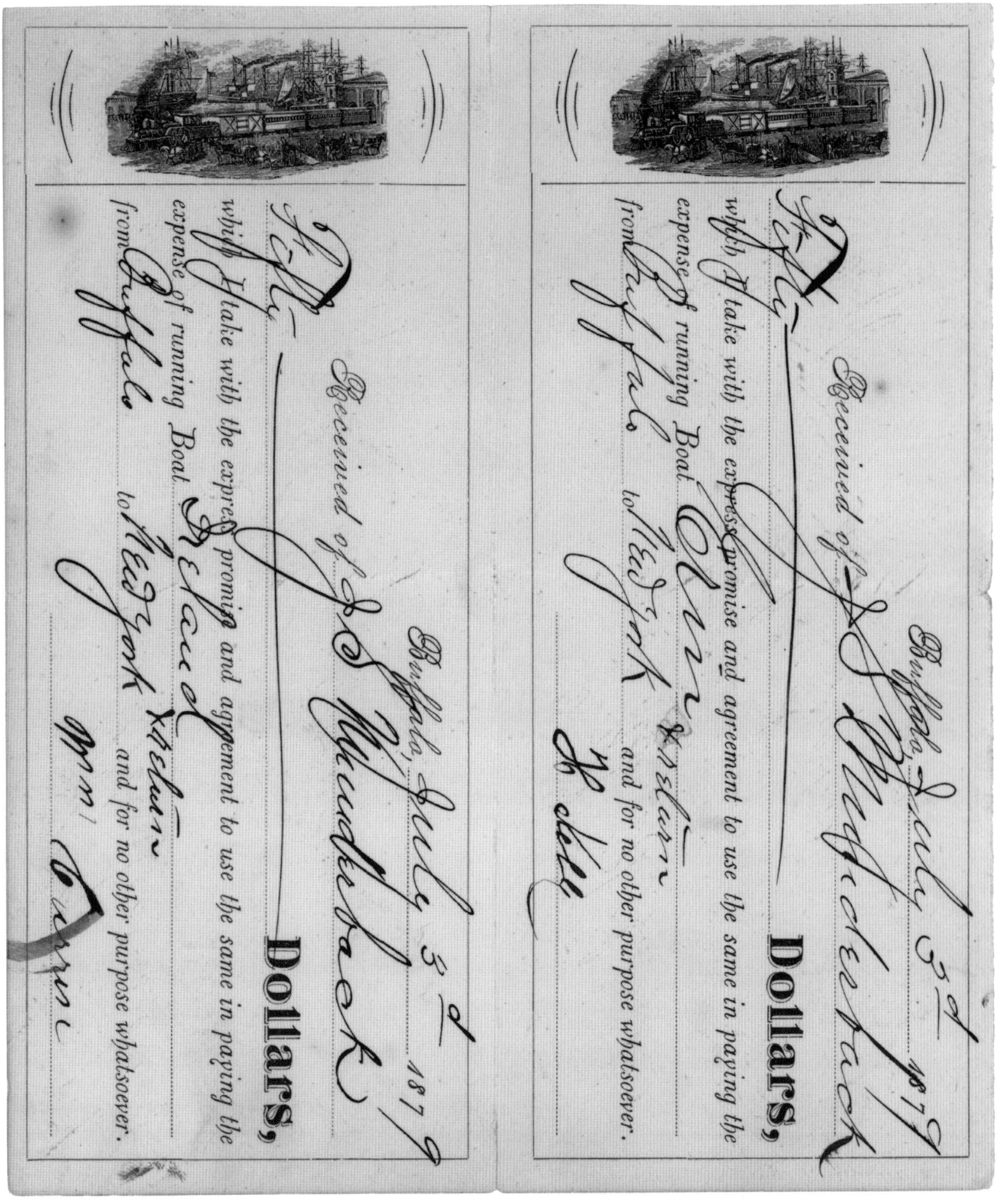

Buffalo, July 3d 1879

Received of [illegible]

Fifty Dollars,

which I take with the express promise and agreement to use the same in paying the expense of running Boat [illegible]

from Buffalo to New York & return and for no other purpose whatsoever.

[illegible]

Buffalo, July 3d 1879

Received of [illegible]

Fifty Dollars,

which I take with the express promise and agreement to use the same in paying the expense of running Boat [illegible]

from Buffalo to New York & return and for no other purpose whatsoever.

[illegible]

Payment to run the boat, July 3, 1879. The boat owner gave the captain an advance of $50 to cover the expenses of taking each boat from Buffalo to New York City and back. *New York State Museum, Mrs. Arnold B. Barben Canal Collection, H-1988.79.*

Boat Crew, photograph, late nineteenth–early twentieth century. The captain, and presumably his wife and children, and crewmembers are seen in this photograph. *New York State Museum, H-1988.80.1.1185.*

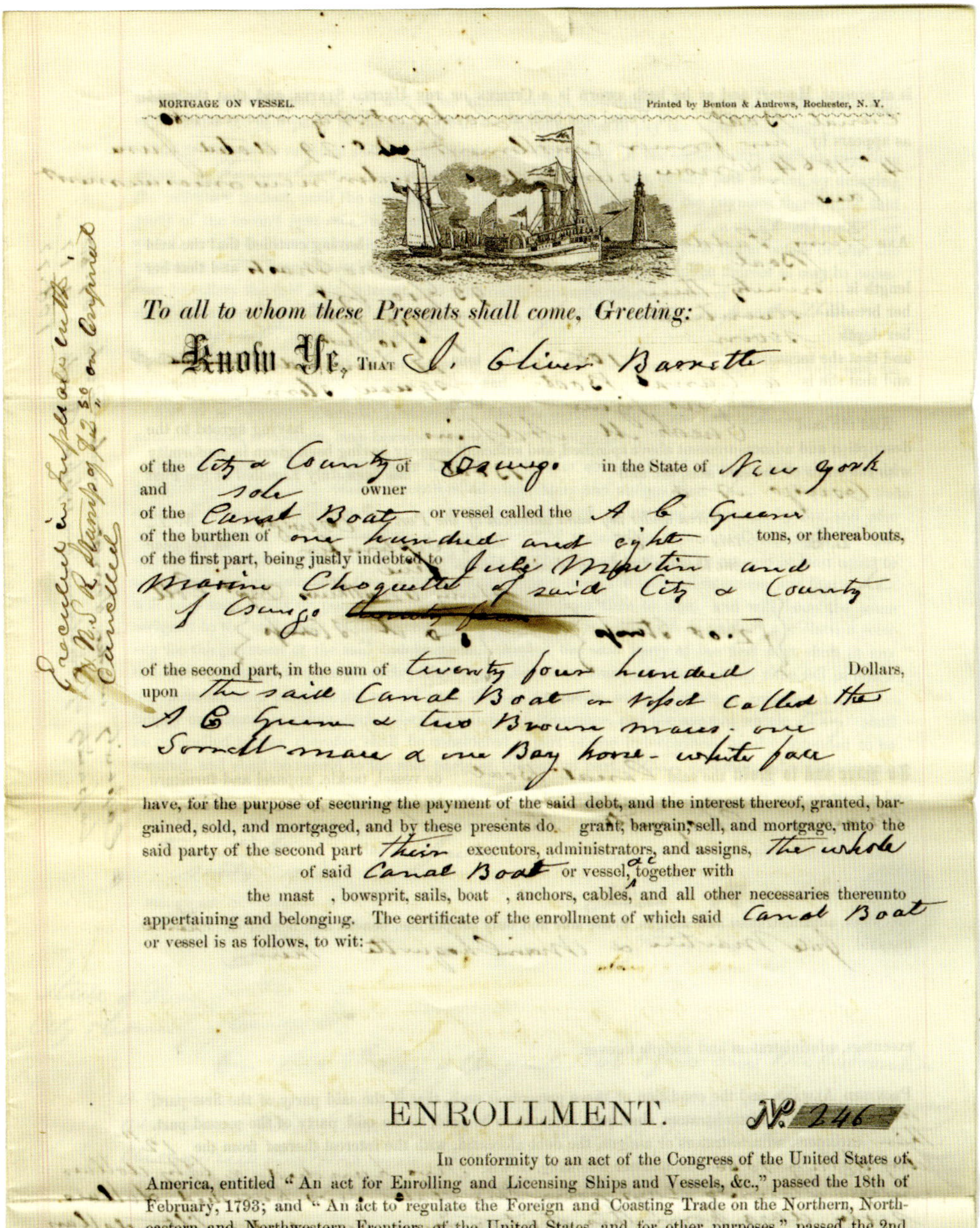
MORTGAGE ON VESSEL. Printed by Benton & Andrews, Rochester, N. Y.

To all to whom these Presents shall come, Greeting:

Know Ye, THAT I. Oliver Barrette

of the City & County of Oswego in the State of New York and sole owner of the Canal Boat or vessel called the A C Green of the burthen of one hundred and eight tons, or thereabouts, of the first part, being justly indebted to Julie Martin and Marine Choquette of said City & County of Oswego

of the second part, in the sum of twenty four hundred Dollars, upon the said Canal Boat or vessel called the A C Green & two Brown mares - one Sorrell mare & one Bay horse - white face

have, for the purpose of securing the payment of the said debt, and the interest thereof, granted, bargained, sold, and mortgaged, and by these presents do grant, bargain, sell, and mortgage, unto the said party of the second part their executors, administrators, and assigns, the whole of said Canal Boat or vessel, together with the mast, bowsprit, sails, boat, anchors, cables, and all other necessaries thereunto appertaining and belonging. The certificate of the enrollment of which said Canal Boat or vessel is as follows, to wit:

ENROLLMENT. No. 246

In conformity to an act of the Congress of the United States of America, entitled "An act for Enrolling and Licensing Ships and Vessels, &c.," passed the 18th of February, 1793; and "An act to regulate the Foreign and Coasting Trade on the Northern, North-eastern and Northwestern Frontiers of the United States, and for other purposes," passed the 2nd March, 1831, and the Acts of the 7th July, 1838; and 29th July, 1850, & June 17 1864 & 6th May 1864

Sarah M Adkins having taken or subscribed the oaths required by the said acts, and having sworn that she is a

CITIZEN OF THE UNITED STATES, sole owner of the Canal Boat or vessel called the A C Green of Oswego N.Y. whereof M J Bough

(pages 157–158) Canal boat mortgage, 1866. Owning a canal boat was a large investment and often required a loan. It was common for multiple people to partner on the purchase of a boat. *New York State Museum, H-1976.46.15.*

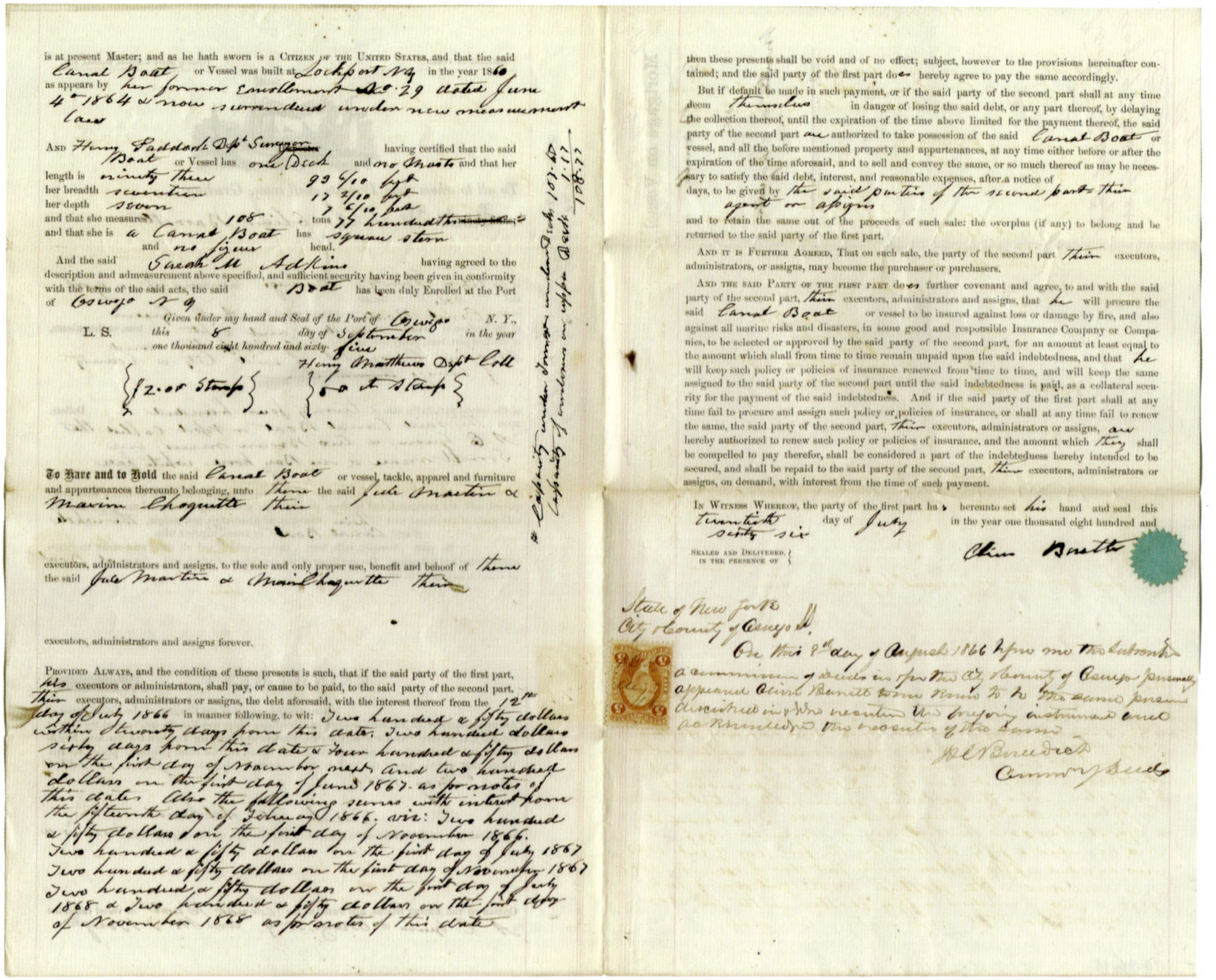

is at present Master; and as he hath sworn is a Citizen of the United States, and that the said Canal Boat, or Vessel was built at Lockport N.Y. in the year 1860 as appears by her former Enrollment No. 29 dated June 4th 1864 & now surrendered under new measurement law

And Henry Paddock Dep't Surveyor having certified that the said Boat or Vessel has one Deck and no Masts and that her length is ninety three 93 6/10 feet, her breadth seventeen 17 3/10 feet, her depth seven 7 6/10 feet and that she measures 108 tons 77 hundredths and that she is a Canal Boat has square stern and no figure head.

And the said Sarah M. Adkins having agreed to the description and admeasurement above specified, and sufficient security having been given in conformity with the terms of the said acts, the said Boat has been duly Enrolled at the Port of Oswego N.Y.

Given under my hand and Seal of the Port of Oswego N.Y., *this* 8 *day of* September *in the year one thousand eight hundred and sixty-* five

L. S. Henry Matthews Dep't Coll

{$2.00 Stamp} {50 ct Stamp}

Capacity under Tonnage under deck 107.60
Capacity of enclosures on upper deck 1.17
108.77

To Have and to Hold the said Canal Boat or vessel, tackle, apparel and furniture and appurtenances thereunto belonging, unto them the said Jule Martin & Marvin Choquette their executors, administrators and assigns, to the sole and only proper use, benefit and behoof of them the said Jule Martin & Marvin Choquette their executors, administrators and assigns forever.

Provided Always, and the condition of these presents is such, that if the said party of the first part, his executors or administrators, shall pay, or cause to be paid, to the said party of the second part, their executors, administrators or assigns, the debt aforesaid, with the interest thereof from the 12th day of July 1866 in manner following, to wit: Two hundred & fifty dollars within twenty days from this date. Two hundred dollars sixty days from this date & four hundred & fifty dollars on the first day of November next and two hundred dollars on the first day of June 1867 as pr notes of this date. Also the following sums with interest from the fifteenth day of February 1866, viz: Two hundred & fifty dollars on the first day of November 1866. Two hundred & fifty dollars on the first day of July 1867. Two hundred & fifty dollars on the first day of November 1867. Two hundred & fifty dollars on the first day of July 1868 & two hundred & fifty dollars on the first day of November 1868 as pr notes of this date

then these presents shall be void and of no effect; subject, however to the provisions hereinafter contained; and the said party of the first part does hereby agree to pay the same accordingly.

But if default be made in such payment, or if the said party of the second part shall at any time deem themselves in danger of losing the said debt, or any part thereof, by delaying the collection thereof, until the expiration of the time above limited for the payment thereof, the said party of the second part are authorized to take possession of the said Canal Boat or vessel, and all the before mentioned property and appurtenances, at any time either before or after the expiration of the time aforesaid, and to sell and convey the same, or so much thereof as may be necessary to satisfy the said debt, interest, and reasonable expenses, after a notice of days, to be given by the said parties of the second part their agent or assigns and to retain the same out of the proceeds of such sale: the overplus (if any) to belong and be returned to the said party of the first part.

And it is Further Agreed, That on such sale, the party of the second part their executors, administrators, or assigns, may become the purchaser or purchasers.

And the said Party of the first part does further covenant and agree, to and with the said party of the second part, their executors, administrators and assigns, that he will procure the said Canal Boat or vessel to be insured against loss or damage by fire, and also against all marine risks and disasters, in some good and responsible Insurance Company or Companies, to be selected or approved by the said party of the second part, for an amount at least equal to the amount which shall from time to time remain unpaid upon the said indebtedness, and that he will keep such policy or policies of insurance renewed from time to time, and will keep the same assigned to the said party of the second part until the said indebtedness is paid, as a collateral security for the payment of the said indebtedness. And if the said party of the first part shall at any time fail to procure and assign such policy or policies of insurance, or shall at any time fail to renew the same, the said party of the second part, their executors, administrators or assigns, are hereby authorized to renew such policy or policies of insurance, and the amount which they shall be compelled to pay therefor, shall be considered a part of the indebtedness hereby intended to be secured, and shall be repaid to the said party of the second part, their executors, administrators or assigns, on demand, with interest from the time of such payment.

In Witness Whereof, the party of the first part has hereunto set his hand and seal this twentieth day of July in the year one thousand eight hundred and sixty six

Sealed and Delivered, in the presence of

Clinton Barrett

State of New York
City & County of Oswego ss.

On this 8th day of August 1866 before me the subscriber a commissioner of deeds in & for the City & County of Oswego personally appeared Clinton Barrett to me known to be the same person described in & who executed the foregoing instrument and acknowledged the execution of the same

H. C. Benedict
Comm'r of Deeds

#7952

Copy

Mortgage on Vessel.

C. Barrett
to
Martin & Choquette

25.
Filed in Canal Dep't
Aug 9 1866 9 a.m.
E. [illegible]
Register

"Canal Boat Sale" broadside, 1857. This broadside advertises the sale of two canal boats that were confiscated by the State for violating canal laws. *New York State Museum, H-1986.76.3.*

Canal boatman's sea chest, mid-nineteenth century. This trunk may have belonged to canal boatman Charles Christian of Lansingburgh in Rensselaer County. "Hoosick," written on the top, may refer to the name of a dock in Lansingburgh. *Courtesy of John Scherer.*

Lantern, nineteenth century. Canal boats ran day and night, and like a headlight, lanterns were placed on the bow to help nighttime navigation. *Courtesy of the Canal Society of New York State.*

Tin horns, nineteenth century. Horns like this were used to alert lock tenders of a boat's approach. *Courtesy of the Canal Society of New York State.*

Bilge pump, nineteenth century. Bilge pumps drew water out of the bottoms of boats. Inside is a pole with a leather basket at the bottom. Suction is created when the pole is pulled, drawing water up and out over the side of the boat. *Courtesy of the Canal Society of New York State.*

Grapple hook and boat hook, nineteenth century. Occassionally, tools, cargo, and crew fell off the boat. Grapple hooks and pike poles were used to snag objects and give the crew a longer reach to retrieve them. *Courtesy of the Canal Society of New York State.*

Mule Drivers

Canal boats glided along the water behind animal power—a horse or a mule or a team of horses or mules. Horses were the most common early on, but mules slowly become the animal of choice. The canal boat "driver" was in charge of leading the mule or horse along the towpath. It was a monotonous task that did not require much skill, yet it was essential to the functioning of the canal. The driver was also in charge of feeding and brushing the mule or horse.

Mule drivers sometimes worked for line companies, which owned several boats and barns, each built at the distance it took to travel in a six-hour shift. At the end of a shift, the animals were replaced with a fresh team. While waiting for work, the drivers would stay in the line barns along the route.

Whether seeking adventure or survival, thousands of children, many of them orphans, worked as drivers. It was not uncommon for them to be cheated out of wages or treated miserably by their employers.

Team and Mule Driver Pulling a Barge, photograph, ca. 1900. *New York State Museum, H-1988.80.1.4561.*

Boat "quick release," nineteenth century. The boat's towrope was attached to a spring-loaded "quick release." If the mule team got into trouble, such as falling into the canal or getting lines tangled with those of another boat, a crewmember would step onto the release and disconnect the rope. *Courtesy of the Canal Society of New York State.*

Team on the Old Champlain Canal in Waterford, photograph, ca. 1910. The towrope connected mule teams using a whippletree or evener, which distributed the force or tension between mules or horses in a team. Note the quick release on the eveners being used on this team in Waterford, New York. *New York State Museum, Michon Collection, H-1990.11.265.*

Team evener, or whippletree, nineteenth–early twentieth century. *Courtesy of the Canal Society of New York State.*

Line company barn wall section, mid- to late nineteenth century. Line barns were owned or rented by line boat companies to house horses and mules along the route, and they were strategically spaced so boat crews could switch out animals and drivers at reasonable intervals. This is a section of wall from the loft area of a line barn in Holley in Orleans County. The loft area was where mule drivers waited for their next job. The initials and graffiti were inscribed by waiting mule drivers. *Courtesy of the Erie Canal Museum.*

(pages 165–166) *Switching the Team,* photographs, late nineteenth–early twentieth century. Teams of horses or mules pulled the boats for about six-hour shifts and then switched out at either a line barn or with another team on the boat. Some boats on the Erie Canal were equiped with a stable on the front of the boat, so the crew could switch teams as needed. *New York State Museum, H-1988.80.1.1528, 4017,4022,4024.*

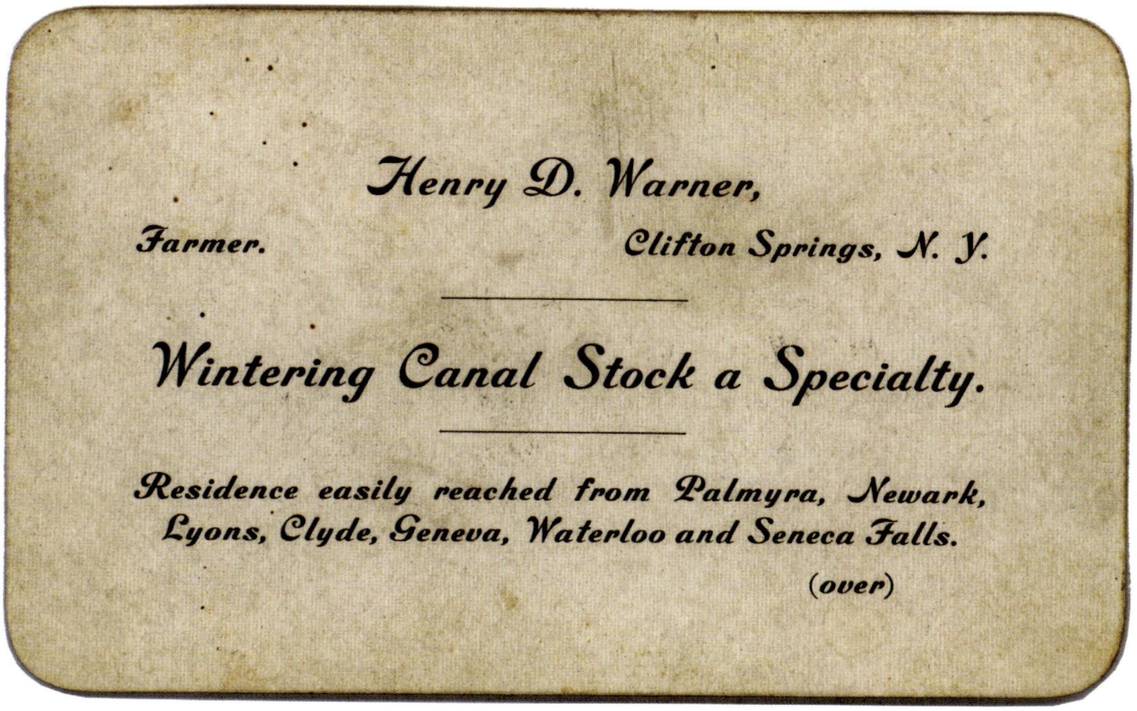

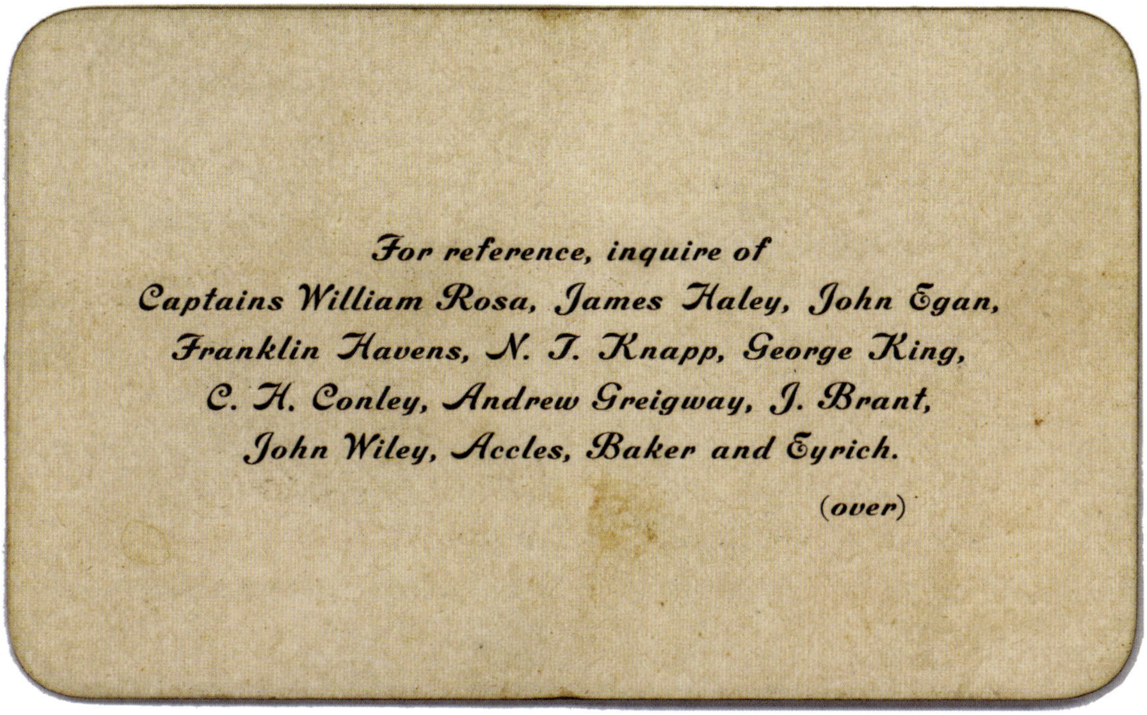

Advertisement card for wintering animals, nineteenth–early twentieth century. The canal closed during the winter months and the mules and horses needed to be cared for. Oftentimes the teams would be sent to live on a farm for the winter. *New York State Museum, Mrs. Arnold B. Barben Canal Collection, H-1988.7.*

Life on the Towpath, 1881, Alfred Wordsworth Thompson (American, 1840–1896), oil on canvas. Arkell Museum at Canajoharie. Gift of Bartlett Arkell, 1943

Alfred Wordsworth Thompson provided illustrations of the Civil War for publications such as *Harper's Weekly* and *Illustrated London News*. In his later career he often featured nostalgic subjects such as this, which avoided any reference to the difficulty of work on the towpath.

Moran Tugs, photographs, ca. 1930–1940. Michael Moran (1833–1906) was an Irish immigrant who settled in Frankfort along the Erie Canal around 1850, where he found work as a mule driver. By 1855 he owned his own canal boat. Five years later, Moran became involved in the steam tugboat business in New York City. His empire grew and became the Moran Towing Company. The business still thrives today in New York City and multiple ports around the country. *New York State Museum, Michon Collection, H-1990.11.138,140.*

Families on the Water

A captain who had his family on the boats lived a fairly comfortable life, as the woman had the meals on time, did the washing and ironing, kept the cabin clean, and made the beds. She also saw that her husband had a bath occasionally so that he did not get lousy as many other bathless canallers did.

—Richard Garrity, canaller[11]

By the mid-nineteenth century, it was common for captains to operate their boats with their families on board. Similar to life on a rural farm, everyone old enough helped with the family business and household chores. Unless the parents gave lessons on board, children had to wait until the winter to attend school, if they went at all. By the mid-nineteenth century, several thousand families transported products across New York State on the Erie Canal and its adjoining waterways.

(above and page 171) Families on the water. *New York State Museum, H-1988.80.1.1259, H-1988.80.1.1271.*

Laid Up for Winter—Canalboat Colony in Coenties Slip, East River, E. J. Meeker, 1884. Many families lived year-round on their boat and spent winters in New York Harbor or another safe port. As travel writer Clifton Johnson observes at the end of the nineteenth century: "Some of the families winter on their boats lying at the wharves in New York City, and they say they do it very comfortably. Mrs. Libbey told of a friend who tried living in a tenement instead. The family paid eighteen dollars a month rent, and it was a crowded, stifling little place, not nearly so good as a canal-boat."* *Harper's Weekly* 28, no. 1417 (1884). *Courtesy of the Canal Society of New York State.* *Clifton Johnson, "A Canal-Boat Voyage on the Hudson," *The Outlook,* October 1, 1898, 318.

Boats Lined Up for the Opening of the Canal in Waterford, photographs, ca. 1920. Living quarters were in the back of the boat. Small children were often tied to the boat to ensure their safety. Note the child anchored to the roof of the cabin on the boat *John B. Shinners* (see insert below). *New York State Museum, H-1990.11.473.*

(pages 174–175) *Canal Boat Interiors,* photographs, late nineteenth–early twentieth century. The family cabin was tight, and every space was utilized to its fullest. The comforts of living in a house were mirrored as much as possible, from decor to dinnerware. *New York State Museum, H-1988.80.1.1262, H-1988.80.1.1266, H-1988.80.1.1267, H-1988.80.1.1268.*

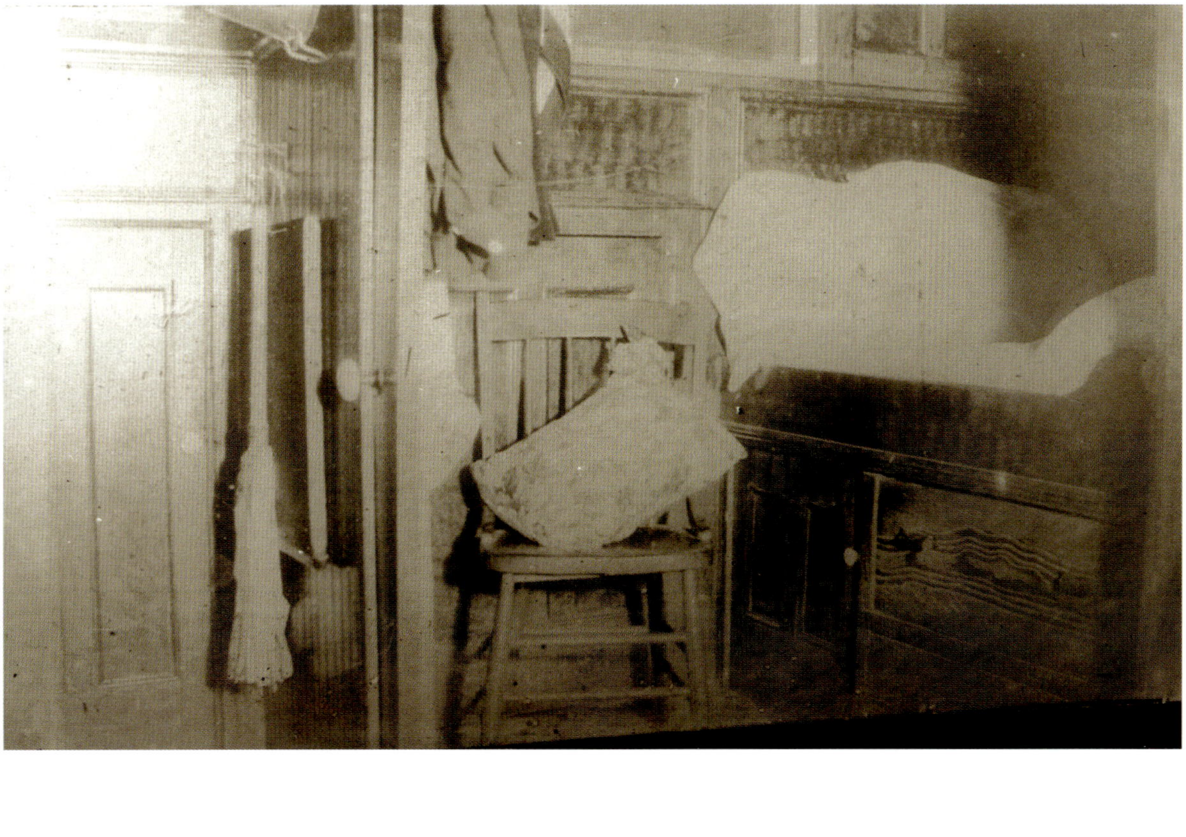

Low-back chair and washstand, ca. 1860 and ca. 1815. This chair and washstand were used on a canal boat. When a family lived on a boat, it was common for the wife to furnish and decorate the living quarters. The circa-1860 chair had a low back so it could be placed under the table to save room. The elegant circa-1815 washstand likely served a high-end packet boat or was old when it saw use on a family boat. *From the collections of the Rochester Museum & Science Center, Rochester, New York.*

Personal items from canal boat wreck on Lake Champlain. These personal items offer a glimpse of family life on the waterways. They were retrieved from a sunken canal boat built sometime after 1873, which likely sank in distress around 1915. Based on an archaeological study conducted 2002–2003, it is believed that at least one man, woman, and child lived on board the boat. Clockwise from top left: storage crock, glass fruit storage jar, glass storage jar (Mason's patent November 30, 1858), glass root beer bottle, glass creamer, glass oil lamp base, wooden saw handle, monkey wrench, iron hair pin, blue transfer-print plate, teaspoons. *Courtesy of the Lake Champlain Maritime Museum, Vermont Division for Historic Preservation.*

Quilt, ca. 1850–1870. According to family tradition, Nancy Snyder Osborn (1823–1909), with help from her mother, made this quilt while traveling with her husband, Chauncey, on a canal boat. The six-foot by eight-foot quilt is made of 21,559 pieces of fabric, likely made on the *J. A. Jarvis* of Ithaca. The *J. A. Jarvis* was first on the canal in 1857, shortly after Nancy and Chauncey married. The 1870 register of canal boats records the vessel as the property of Peter Snyder, Nancy's grandfather, who probably used it to bring wheat and other products to market from his Dryden farm. New York State Museum, H-2004.57.1.

Erie Canal, 1856, S. Georges (American, active mid-nineteenth century), oil on canvas. *Arkell Museum at Canajoharie. Gift of Bartlett Arkell, 1940.*

This image of the Erie Canal is filled with keenly observed details of daily life, focusing on the human element more than the landscape. The canal boat filled with an assortment of goods is pulled through the water by a pair of horses and a rider along the towpath. In the center of the vessel a man, possibly African American, plays a violin; laundry hangs over the bow. Other activity takes place on shore as the boat passes by.

Smooth Operations

New York's canals required an intricate system of state and private workers to keep things running efficiently. The wide variety of jobs included lock tenders, bankwatchers, "hurry-up boats," weighlock masters, and longshoremen.

Here are just some of the jobs needed on the canal:

Lock Tender and Lock Tender House, photographs, late nineteenth–early twentieth century. Lock tenders oversaw each lock. They, and other canal employees, were often the beneficiaries or victims of political patronage. When political power shifted in the legislature, turnover was common in the canal workforce. *New York State Museum, 1988.80.4670, H-1988.80.1.4570.*

Washout in Syracuse, postcard photograph, 1907. A washout or break in the canal bottom or walls could delay traffic for days or even weeks. The breaks could also cause terrible floods in local communities, ruining personal property and crops. Bankwatchers patrolled the canal for signs of damage, such as holes from burrowing animals that could wreak havoc on the canal walls, causing them to weaken and collapse. There are still bankwatchers today, employed in the western section of the Erie Barge Canal. *New York State Museum, H-1984.80.28.*

Hurry-Up Boat Repairing a Bridge, photograph, late nineteenth–early twentieth century. Whenever the canal needed emergency maintenance, the local repair or "hurry-up" boat was called. Like modern emergency responders, the hurry-up boat could bypass traffic. *New York State Museum, H-1988.80.35.*

Hurry-Up Boat, photograph, ca. 1910. State crew working to block up a break in the canal near Brockport, Monroe County. *New York State Museum, H-1988.80.4071.*

Hurry-Up Boat, photograph, ca. 1910. State scow crew working on a canal bank in Durhamville, Oneida County. Scow boats, or repair boats, earned the nickname "hurry-up boats" because of the urgent nature of their service. Scow boats could carry large amounts of materials for repairing breaches. *New York State Museum, H-1988.80.1275.*

Canal Break Repair, photograph, May 11, 1872. Hundreds of men work at a break in the canal on the "Fourteen Mile Level" at Big Nose, near Sprakers, in the Mohawk Valley. *New York State Museum, 1996.58.22.*

Hurry-Up Boat, photograph, late nineteenth–early twentieth century. *New York State Museum, H-1988.80.4919.*

Hurry-Up Boat, photograph, late nineteenth–early twentieth century. This hurry-up boat was part of Section 5 on the canal, based out of Rome, New York. *New York State Museum, H-1988.80.4013.*

Erie Canal, New York, 1831, John William Hill (American, born England, 1812–1879), watercolor, graphite, and white gouache on paper mounted on card. Between 1829 and 1831, Hill executed a number of watercolors of the Erie Canal to be published by his father, John Hill, in a portfolio of aquatint engravings devoted solely to canal views. Although several plates were produced, the series was never completed. John W. Hill's images often feature charming vignettes of human activity at work or leisure. *New-York Historical Society.*

Hurry-up boat tools, nineteenth century. The crews of hurry-up boats used a variety of tools to make repairs. *New York State Museum; wheelbarrow, H-2006.46.1; peavey, H-1970.33, pike pole, H-1971.74.105; cant hook, H-INV 4916 (from the H. G. Root & Company canal warehouse); hoe, H-1982.162.13; mallet/beetle, H-INV 5644; shovel H-2009.20.1; spade, H-1996.16.4; broad axes, H-1957.2.1, H-1928.4.7, 1936.6.1 ("D.R. Barton 1832 Rochester, NY").*

Model of a scow, Robert E. Hager, 1964. State crews used scows to do repairs on the canal, but scows were also used to haul lumber, sand, gravel, and other items that could be exposed to the elements. Canal Society of New York State.

Muskrat. The common muskrat is found in aquatic habitats throughout New York State and, as such, has been no stranger to the Erie Canal. Muskrats often burrowed into the canal walls. If the water entered the burrow, it would eventually undermine the wall and cause it to give way. *New York State Museum.*

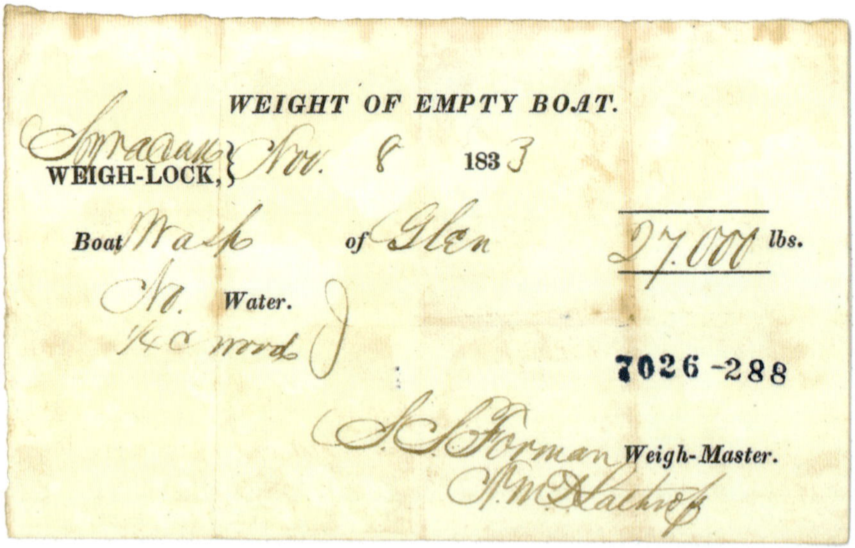

WEIGHT OF EMPTY BOAT.

Syracuse WEIGH-LOCK, Nov. 8 1833

Boat Wash of Glen 27,000 lbs.

No. Water.

¼ c wood

7026-288

S. Forman Weigh-Master.

Base weight receipt, 1833. The weighlock masters weighed empty boats at the beginning of the season. The captain received a receipt showing his boat's base weight. Boats were weighed again when loaded to determine the tolls of each trip. *Courtesy of the New York State Library, Manuscripts and Special Collections, FPO_weighlock_NYSL SC7026-Box2-Folder27-Item288.*

Weighlock in Watervliet, photograph, ca. 1910. Canal tolls were based on the weight of the boat and type of cargo it carried. Weighlock buildings were located at strategic points and equipped with a giant scale and lock to determine the weight of boats and collect tolls. Boats would pull into the lock and the lock drained, leaving the boat sitting on the scale. Once weighed, the lock was refilled, and the boat could float back into the canal. The weighlock master handled this process and paperwork. *Courtesy of the Canal Society of New York State, 1093.1.0045.*

Unloading a Boat, photograph, ca. late nineteenth–early twentieth century. The "along-shore-man," or longshoreman, loaded and unloaded barges at larger ports. *New York State Museum, H-1988.80.1.1027.*

TRAVEL AND ADVENTURE ON THE ERIE CANAL

> I cannot conceive a more beautiful combination of verdue [sic, verdure]; and as the windings of the canal brought us in sight of fresh vistas, new cultivation, new villages, new bridges, new aqueducts, rose at every moment, mingled up with scattered dwellings, mills, churches, all span new. The scene looked really one of enchantment.
>
> —Captain Basil Hall, 1828[12]

Canal Aqueduct Crossing a Stream, ca. 1840s. George Harvey (American, born England, 1801–1878), oil on canvas. Harvey's view is gently centered on the passing of a canal boat on an aqueduct over a small brook in a pastoral landscape. The manmade structure and its cargo seem not to intrude upon the idyllic scene. *New-York Historical Society.*

The Erie Canal captured the world's imagination. With travel to the interior now affordable and accessible, thousands flocked to New York to experience the canal and its natural wonders. Travel guides became widely popular and, in turn, popularized "The Northern Tour" from New York City to Niagara Falls, Saratoga Springs, and Montreal via steamboat, canal, and stage.

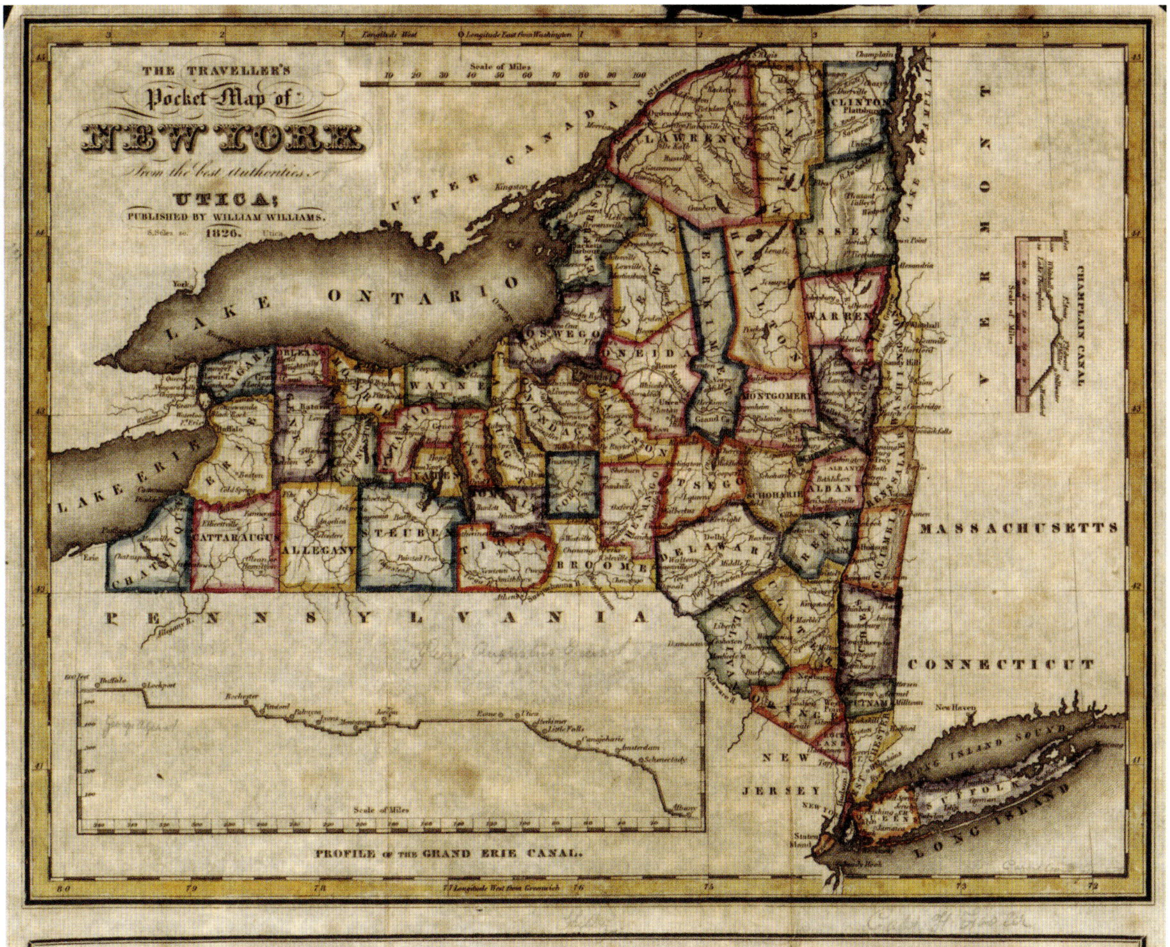

The Traveller's [*sic*] *Pocket Map of New York,* 1826. This map included a "Canal Guide for the Tourist and Traveler." Information on routes, tolls, where to catch packet boats, tourist destinations, and more were listed to help travelers plan their trip. *Courtesy of the Library of Congress.*

Below (Trenton) High Falls, by Ferdinand Richardt, oil on canvas, 1858. Trenton Falls was a fourteen-mile carriage ride north of Utica and was a popular destination for tourists. Visitors tested their nerves by walking down the ravine along the falls while holding on to a chain attached to the rock wall along the trail. In 1827 English writer Frances Milton Trollope observed, "The [Trenton] falls have become within the last few years second in fame to Niagara. The West Canada Creek, which in the map shows but as a paltry stream, has found its way through three miles of rock, which, at points, is 150 feet high. A forest of enormous cedars which droops its branches like the weeping-willow, grow in the clefts of the rock, and in some places almost dip their dark foliage in the torrent."* *Courtesy of the Munson-Williams-Proctor Arts Institute, 72.53.* *Frances Milton Trollope, *Domestic Manners of the Americans (London: Whittaker, Treacher, 1832), 297.*

Horseshoe Falls plate, ca. 1830. Commemorative plates and other keepsakes were sold to tourists at Niagara Falls. *New York State Museum, H-1996.6.6.1.*

Niagara Falls from the American Side, lithogrpahed in Paris by Isidore Laurent Deroy (1797–1886), after a painting by Jacques Milbert (1766–1840), lithograph, 1829. The wedding crock below is believed to have been based on this depiction of the falls. *New York State Museum, H-1968.62.17.*

Stoneware crock, Thomas Harrington and John Burger, Rochester, New York, ca. 1851–1854. Niagara Falls was already a popular honeymoon destination by the 1850s. Family lore has it that this crock was a wedding gift. The decorated view of Niagara Falls was inspired by the 1829 lithograph *Niagara Falls from the American Side*, pictured above. *New York State Museum, H-2014.13.13.*

Niagara Falls was well on the way to becoming a tourist destination by the beginning of the nineteenth century, and the ease of travel on the canal greatly increased this audience. Tourists shopped for both fine and inexpensive souvenirs in stores on both sides of the falls. Objects with images of the falls were popular, as were examples of Native American handwork.

Niagara Falls (Cave of the Winds), ca. 1888, George Barker (American, born Canada, 1844–1894), albumen silver print from glass negative. *Collection of Alexandra C. Anderson.*

Above the Falls, ca. 1888, albumen silver print from glass negative. In 1862 George Barker opened Barker's Stereoscopic View Manufactory and Photograph Rooms in Niagara, New York. He became known for his dramatic views of the falls, which featured sharp contrasts, dramatic skies, churning water, and angular rocks. Barker sold large prints to wealthier tourists and offered an extensive catalog of stereograph cards and smaller souvenirs to travelers on a budget. *Collection of Alexandra C. Anderson.*

Horseshoe Fall—Canada Side, stereograph, ca. 1860–1893. *New York State Museum, H-1993.79.97.*

Niagara Falls—Horseshoe Fall—Moonlight, stereograph, ca. 1860–1893. *New York State Museum, H-1937.5.45.*

Niagara—Prospect Point—Winter, stereograph, ca. 1860–1893. *New York State Museum, H-1941.31.18.*

Stevengraph, ca. 1880, unknown manufacturer, English, woven silk. *Collection of Alexandra C. Anderson.*

A Stevengraph is an image based on a photograph woven in silk. The process was developed by Thomas Stevens in the mid-nineteenth century and became a popular method for making souvenirs, including bookmarks and greeting cards.

Tile, 1875, unknown manufacturer, French, ceramic. This decorative tile, produced in France, shows an idealized view of the falls with just a few picturesque tourists and buildings. By the 1870s, both sides of the falls were built up with hotels, gift shops, and viewing platforms. *Collection of Alexandra C. Anderson.*

Beaded pincushion, ca. 1880–1917, unknown artist, Tuscarora, wool, glass seed beads. *Collection of Alexandra C. Anderson.*

Unknown artists, Tuscarora, fabric, glass seed beads. Needlecase, "Niagara Falls," purple velvet, ca. 1860; decorative bird, "From Niagara Falls" (on tail), ca. 1895; needlecase, "Present from Niagara Falls," brown velvet, ca. 1860; clamshell-shaped needlecase, "From Niagara Falls," early twentieth century; decorative canoe, "From Niagara Falls," early twentieth century. *Collection of Dolores Elliott.*

Tourists frequently visited reservations near the falls and purchased souvenirs of Native American handwork. As Native trade network and landholdings changed, selling to the tourist market became an important income source, and the forms being sold shifted to reflect demand from nonnative patrons. Tuscarora women were noted for their beadwork, which they employed on a variety of objects, including pincushions, purses, and wall hangings.

View on the Erie Canal Near Little Falls, 1839. William H. Bartlett (British, 1809–1854), artist, James T. Willmore (1800–1863), engraver, hand-colored engraving. Bartlett, a London topographical artist, was commissioned by publisher George Virtue to produce views of the United States for the book *American Scenery, or, Land, Lake, and River Illustrations of Transatlantic Nature* (1840), with text by Nathaniel Parker Willis. The engravings from Bartlett's watercolors appeared not only as illustrations in the two-volume work but in subsequent editions, magazines, other books, and as individual prints—such as this romanticized, moonlit image. *Munson-Williams-Proctor Arts Institute.*

The Packet Boat: A Floating Hotel

In the early days of the canal, people traveled by packet boats, which were often crowded and cramped, though they provided board, meals, and sometimes entertainment in the form of small onboard libraries or musical instruments. The boats typically carried forty to sixty people, but larger packets held up to one hundred.

This business thrived until the 1840s, when railroads became competitive in passenger travel. Companies introduced larger, luxurious boats, but by the 1860s they were almost completely gone, superseded by the burgeoning railroads.

Erie Canal Completed, engraving, 1906. Whenever the weather allowed, passengers would ride on top of the boats to avoid the stuffy cabin and to view the scenery. *Courtesy of the New York State Library, Manuscripts and Special Collections, PRI 1937.*

Model of a packet boat, Jim Dixon, 1994. Packet boats carried passengers, with meals and sleeping quarters provided. Pulled by three horses, packets glided four to five miles per hour. The fees varied depending on the time period, ranging from one to four cents per mile for a basic packet boat. *Courtesy of the Erie Canal Museum.*

GOING TO BED.

Going to Bed, engraving, ca. 1852. This image shows packet boat passengers preparing for bed. Bunks were stacked three high along the wall and could be folded up during the day. The men's and women's quarters were separated by a curtain. The space was so tight that it was not uncommon for passengers to choose the floor instead of having someone sleep on the bunk just inches above them. The more luxurious boats had curtains for each bunk, as seen in the depiction. Jacob Abbott, *Marco Paul's Voyages & Travels, Erie Canal, ca. 1852. Courtesy of the New York State Library, Manuscripts and Special Collections, 813.4 A132 90-245.*

Crowd at Schenectady Getting on Packet

THE PACKET BOAT.

The Packet Boat, engraving, ca. 1852. Once travelers arrived in Schenectady by carriage or rail from Albany, they were besieged by the "runners," men or boys trying to get passengers aboard their boat. Canadian traveler Alexander Stewart Scott recorded his experience with the runners in 1826 as follows: ". . . got into Schenectady about 1. P.M. and we were all immediately beset (even before leaving the Carriage) by a set of Canal Boat Captains &c, setting forth the advantages of their several Boats, and with one voice beseeching our Patronage—the opposition very strong; abusive language, and sometimes Blows between the different owners and others interested, not at all uncommon I am told."* Jacob Abbott, *Marco Paul's Voyages & Travels, Erie Canal,* ca. 1852. *Courtesy of the New York State Library, Manuscripts and Special Collections, 813.4 A132 90-245.*

*Alexander Stewart Scott, *"1826 Travel Journal of Alexander Stewart Scott,"* unpublished, 18. *Collection of the New York State Library, Manuscripts and Special Collections, BD13145.*

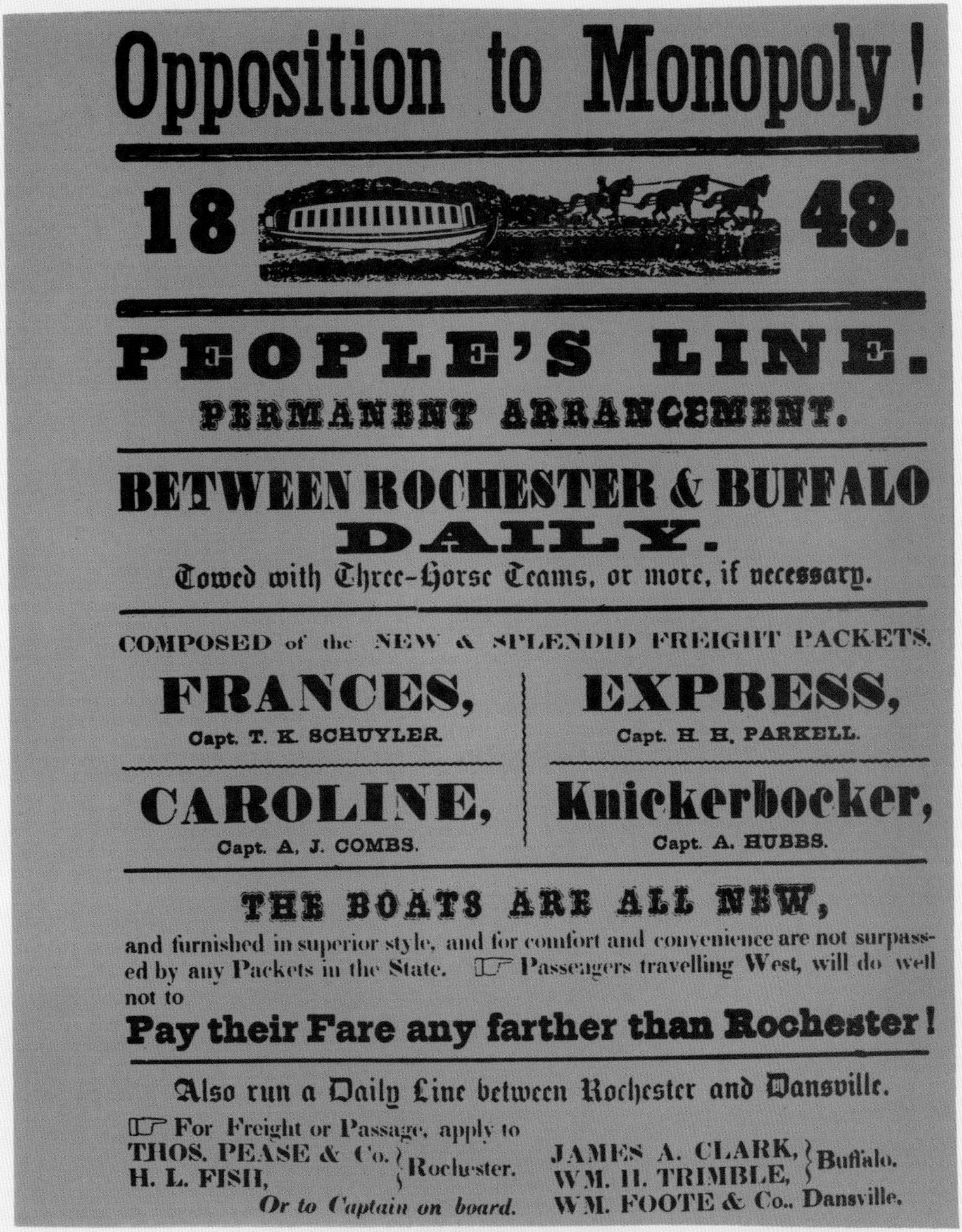

Opposition to Monopoly!

18 48.

PEOPLE'S LINE.

PERMANENT ARRANGEMENT.

BETWEEN ROCHESTER & BUFFALO

DAILY.

Towed with Three-Horse Teams, or more, if necessary.

COMPOSED of the NEW & SPLENDID FREIGHT PACKETS.

FRANCES, Capt. T. K. SCHUYLER.	**EXPRESS,** Capt. H. H. PARKELL.
CAROLINE, Capt. A. J. COMBS.	**Knickerbocker,** Capt. A. HUBBS.

THE BOATS ARE ALL NEW,

and furnished in superior style, and for comfort and convenience are not surpassed by any Packets in the State. ☞ Passengers travelling West, will do well not to

Pay their Fare any farther than Rochester!

Also run a Daily Line between Rochester and Dansville.

☞ For Freight or Passage, apply to

THOS. PEASE & Co.,
H. L. FISH, } Rochester.
Or to Captain on board.

JAMES A. CLARK,
WM. H. TRIMBLE, } Buffalo.
WM. FOOTE & Co., Dansville.

People's Line broadside, ca. 1848. Small packet boat lines, such as the People's Line, had to compete with a few larger ones that carried the bulk of passenger travel. *New York State Museum, Mrs. Arnold B. Barben Canal Collection, H-1988.79.*

. . . even in their Canal Boats [Americans] have generally got a pretty good collection of works of different natures for the use of the Passengers—for the reading of which they are commonly charged at the rate of a cent a volume, and often nothing at all—for those who are fond of Music I have seen some of the Canal Packets provided with a good Hand-Organ &c. . . .

—Alexander Stewart Scott, returning home to Montreal after traveling on the Erie Canal, 1826[13]

Violin, 1840. Musical instruments were sometimes supplied by packet boat owners to improve the voyage for passengers. This Chanot-type violin has a label that reads "D. E. Rago, Late from the City of Paris, Piano, Bass Viol, Violin & Guitar Maker, Old Instruments Restored in a Superior Style, Buffalo 1840." New York State Museum, H-1986.53.1.

Guitar, ca. 1840. This guitar would not have been out of place on an Erie Canal packet boat. *New York State Museum, 1943.1.48.*

Miniature books, ca. 1830–1850. Miniature books were popular for travelers since they did not take up much space. Some packet boats had small libraries for their passengers. *New York State Museum, H-1950.4.90, H-XX.127.35, H-XX.127.37, H-2001.32.76, H-1969.66.485.*

Playing cards, 1881. Card games were also popular recreation to help pass the time while traveling on a boat. *New York State Museum, H-1969.66.3210.*

Travel trunk, ca. 1830, paper lining ca. 1850. Wallpaper honoring the Rochester Aqueduct and the Washington Monument line this travel trunk. The engineering achievement of the aqueduct was a symbol of national pride. *New York State Museum, Mrs. Arnold B. Barben Canal Collection, H-1988.79.12 A.*

Engravings, ca. 1852. Riding on the roof of a packet boat could be dangerous, since the bridges were very low. When approaching a bridge, the steersman would shout "low bridge!" and everyone on top scrambled to get off or lay flat. In 1825 there were almost three hundred bridges between Albany and Utica alone. Jacob Abbott, *Marco Paul's Voyages & Travels*, Erie Canal, ca. 1852. *Courtesy of the New York State Library, Manuscripts and Special Collections, 813.4 A132 90-245.*

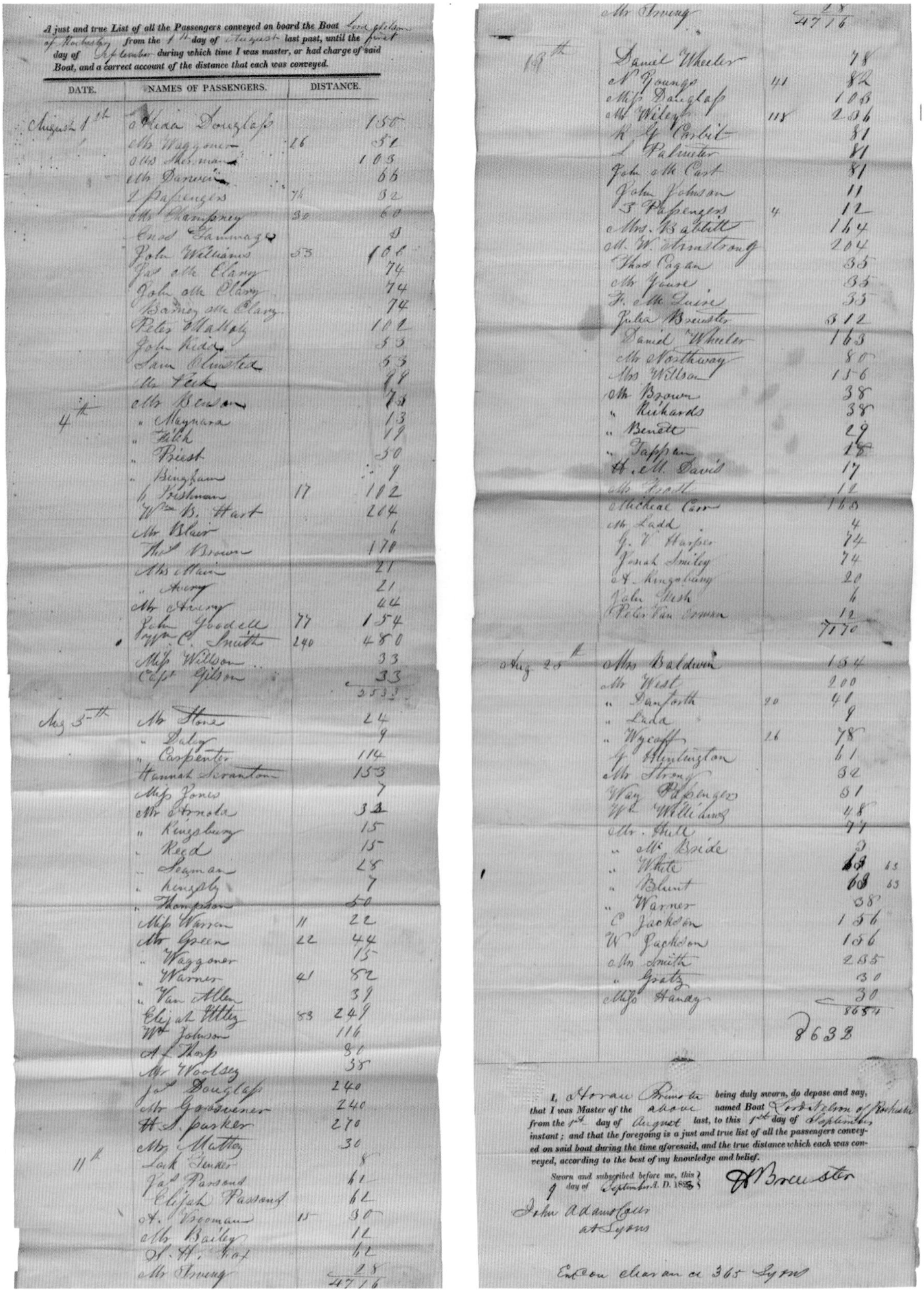

A just and true List of all the Passengers conveyed on board the Boat ________ from the ____ day of ________ last past, until the ____ day of ________ during which time I was master, or had charge of said Boat, and a correct account of the distance that each was conveyed.

DATE.	NAMES OF PASSENGERS.	DISTANCE.

I, ________ being duly sworn, do depose and say, that I was Master of the ________ named Boat ________ from the ____ day of ________ last, to this ____ day of ________ instant; and that the foregoing is a just and true list of all the passengers conveyed on said boat during the time aforesaid, and the true distance which each was conveyed, according to the best of my knowledge and belief.

Sworn and subscribed before me, this ____ day of ________ A. D. 18__

Register of passengers for the canal boat *Lord Nelson of Rochester,* August 1828. The State required canal packets to keep lists of passengers. Sometimes the boatmen keeping the lists were creative with the names, such as "old so and so," "old whats his name," "4 indians," "6 Irishmen," "Scotchman," "Ladies," and so on. *New York State Archives, A1057-78.*

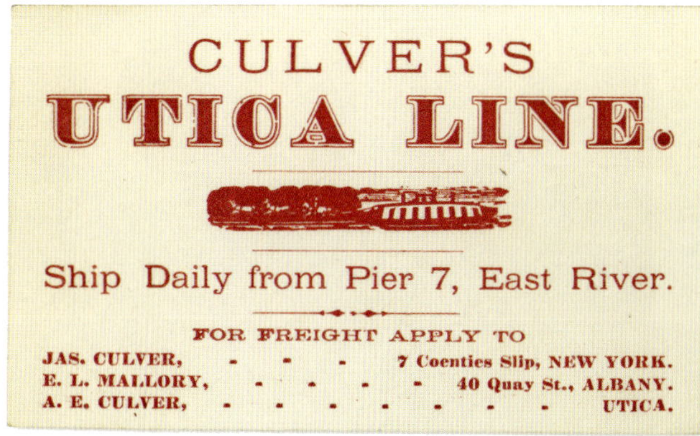

"Culver & Co.'s Utica Line," trade cards, nineteenth century. Like business cards of the twentieth century, trade cards like this were handed out to passengers and merchants as part of advertising efforts by both packet and freight boat operators. *New York State Museum, H-1998.36.1.511, H-1998.36.1.512.*

WINTER ON THE CANAL

During the winter, much of the canal was drained and all traffic came to a standstill. Boats would rush to their port of choice before the canal closed for the season or the onset of an early freeze, sometimes being stuck for the winter before reaching their destination. By the 1840s commercial transportation was year-round with the railroads in operation.

Frozen In for the Winter, photograph, late nineteenth–early twentieth century. If boats did not arrive at their destination before the canal froze over, they could be stuck for the entire winter. *New York State Museum, H-1988.80.*

(pages 208–209) *Harvesting Ice on the Canal,* photographs, late nineteenth–early twentieth century. Some sections of the canal had enough ice for harvesting and skating. *New York State Museum, H-1988.80.1.434, 435, 457.*

Ice plow, ca. 1890. A horse pulled this ice plow to score the ice in a grid pattern. Once the ice was scored a few inches deep, an ice saw could be used to complete the cut. *New York State Museum, H-1977.153.13 A-B.*

Ice-harvesting tools, late nineteenth–early twentieth century. Before refrigerators were common, ice was harvested in the winter and stored in icehouses for use in warmer months. In some stretches of the canal, where the water was left in, ice could be harvested. At one point in the late 1800s, the State declared that ice harvested from the canal could only be used for storing beer. *New York State Museum, Hand plow H-1982.39.22 Ice saw H-1982.39.24 Float hook 1982.39.33 Scoop net 1982.39.8 Sieve shovel 1982.39.9 Splitting fork 1982.39.27 Breaking bar 1982.39.28.*

(page 210–211) *Playing on the Ice,* photographs, ca. 1915. *New York State Museum, H-1988.80.1.1846, H-1988.80.1.4828.*

Pair of ice skates and carrying bag, ca. 1850–1860. Ice skating was a popular pastime in areas of the canal with enough ice. *New York State Museum, H-1949.4.1 A-C.*

> The boat on which we traveled was drawn night and day by two horses, but we did not go forward very rapidly, as the horses had to advance at a walking pace all the time because of the great cargo. The so-called packetboats, however, which likewise pass through this canal—carrying passengers only—have three horses and go more than twice as fast, but the freight charge on the latter boats amounts to four times that paid on the former.
>
> —Peter Testman, Norwegian immigrant, 1838[14]

The canal system directly influenced nineteenth- and early twentieth-century immigration and the settlement of the United States. By connecting the Atlantic Ocean to the Great Lakes, the canal opened access to lands in western New York and the Midwest that were previously hard to reach. Access to western lands and jobs constructing the various canals helped bring immigrants, along with their cultures and religions, shaping and enriching the character of the nation.

While early migrants were from New York and New England, eventually a large influx of settlers came from Europe. It was common that large groups immigrated from a single community and settled together. A majority of these settlers, although not abolitionists, were opposed to the expansion of slavery into the west, a critical factor leading up to the Civil War.

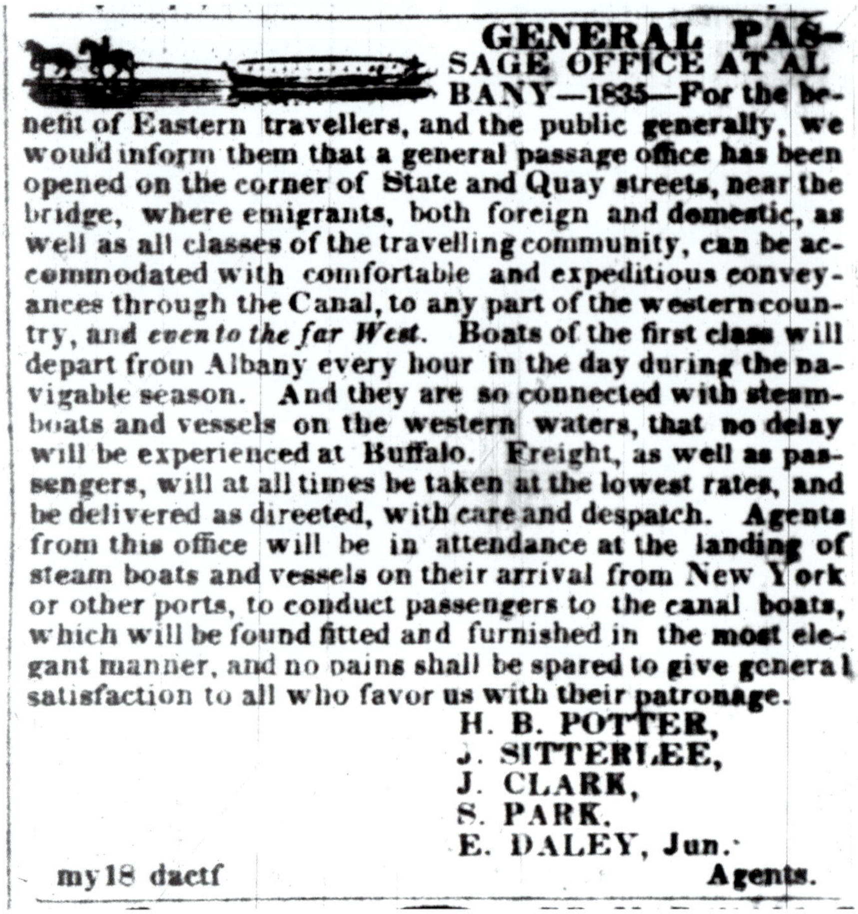

GENERAL PASSAGE OFFICE AT ALBANY—1835—For the benefit of Eastern travellers, and the public generally, we would inform them that a general passage office has been opened on the corner of State and Quay streets, near the bridge, where emigrants, both foreign and domestic, as well as all classes of the travelling community, can be accommodated with comfortable and expeditious conveyances through the Canal, to any part of the western country, and *even to the far West*. Boats of the first class will depart from Albany every hour in the day during the navigable season. And they are so connected with steamboats and vessels on the western waters, that no delay will be experienced at Buffalo. Freight, as well as passengers, will at all times be taken at the lowest rates, and be delivered as directed, with care and despatch. Agents from this office will be in attendance at the landing of steam boats and vessels on their arrival from New York or other ports, to conduct passengers to the canal boats, which will be found fitted and furnished in the most elegant manner, and no pains shall be spared to give general satisfaction to all who favor us with their patronage.

H. B. POTTER,
J. SITTERLEE,
J. CLARK,
S. PARK,
E. DALEY, Jun.
Agents.

my18 daetf

"Travel Agent for People Going West," advertisement, *Albany Evening Journal,* Albany, New York, September 30, 1835. *America's Historical Newspapers, Newsbank online via New York State Library.*

Harnden's Emigrant Passenger Agency.

We learn from Mr. L. S. Littlejohn, Agent of Harnden & Co., that during the season of canal navigation, for 1844, commencing in April and ending in November, Harnden & Co paid $107,775 21, to the Canal Association of Forwarders, for the transportation of Passengers and their extra luggage upon the Erie Canal. The whole number of Passengers for whom Harnden & Co. procured passages were Sixty Thousand, most of whom were Immigrants from Europe, seeking a home in the far West. We are assured, also, that this vast business was conducted in a manner satisfactory to all parties.

The arrangements of this enterprising concern are perfect, not only throughout our own country, but extend to Europe, where Passengers, through their Agents, are enabled to ascertain the expense attending their removal to any of the States, and to protect themselves against the extortions and frauds too often practised. Persons in America who wish to send to Europe for their friends, may do so conveniently through Harnden & Co. While these intelligent and enterprising men conduct their business as they have heretofore, faithfully and honestly, we hope to see them sustained and rewarded.

"Harnden's Emigrant Passenger Agency," advertisement, *Albany Journal,* Albany, New York, May 10, 1845. Companies formed to help immigrants travel west. In some locations, such as Albany, local nonprofit groups formed to help immigrants whom they felt were being taken advantage of by the for-profit companies. *America's Historical Newspapers, Newsbank online via New York State Library.*

Western Guide Book, and Emigrant's Directory, Oliver O. Steele, 1832. Guidebooks were published to help migrants find their way west. *New York State Library, Manuscripts and Special Collections N 917.7 S81.*

Naturalization of Foreigners, Scene in Tammany Hall / Drawn from Life, Engraving in *Frank Leslie's Illustrated Newspaper* 2, no. 48, November 8, 1856. Immigrants and politicians quickly found power in numbers when it came to voting. Immigrant groups were often targeted by politicians to garner votes. *Courtesy of the Library of Congress.*

The Departure, engraving in Frank Leslie's Illustrated Newspaper 2, no. 48, January 12, 1856. Immigrants leaving their homeland are depicted in this 1856 *Frank Leslie's Illustrated Newspaper. Courtesy of the Library of Congress.*

JUNE 26, 1858.] HARPER'S WEEKLY. 405

EMIGRANT WOMEN.

EMIGRANTS.

fully. To protect his wife and daughters, he must unite imposing strength with unusual courage. To resist the brutality of the crew, he must share their pugnacity, and surpass them in shrewdness.

At last the voyage is over, and the emigrant lands on American soil. In olden time his condition at this stage in his fortunes was truly pitiable. Federal, State, and municipal authorities regarded him with as much indifference as if he had been a bale of cheap goods. Scoundrels of the very lowest calibre—emigrant runners—seized him, and made him their own. If he had any money, they robbed him of it. If he had a pretty wife or daughters, they stole them too, if they could. If he had neither money nor daughters, they merely took his luggage. It was well for him if, after having been robbed of all he had, he was not beaten to death, or entrapped into committing crimes which transferred him almost directly from the emigrant vessel to Blackwell's Island or the State Prison. His bewrayers were of his own kith and kin. The easiest emigrants to rob were the Irish; and the majority of emigrant runners belonged to the same race. The brogue was part of their capital in trade.

This is ancient history now. A few years ago, the railways of this State grew jealous of emigrant runners, and proposed to monopolize the business. With the aid of certain politicians, they established an emigrant dépôt at Castle Garden, in the city of New York, where immigrants are now landed, and whence they are forwarded to their destination. Into this dépôt the old class of robbers known as runners are not openly permitted to enter. It is a vast improvement on the old system; though whether it be itself tainted with corruption appears to be matter of debate.

There seems to be some doubt whether European emigration to the United States will continue. Of late years it has greatly fallen off. This year it will not, most probably, amount to one-third what it was a few years since. Germany has thrown off its surplus. Ireland has got rid of its starving thousands, and there is more elbow-room for those who remain behind. Until some convulsion disturb peaceful trade and industry in Europe, there is no reason to suppose that immigrants will flow into the United States at the same rate as formerly; though, so long as we have vacant lands and political privileges to offer, we can hardly fail to levy a large percentage upon the increase of the European people.

LITERARY.

ABOUT a year ago, in noticing a little volume published by Carter & Brothers, entitled THE WAY HOME, a pleasant and touching family story, we remarked upon the fact that an incident was related of a certain Lord N——, whose mother was the author of the well-known lyric, "The Land of the Leal," and we then suggested that an inquiry in the church-yard at Brussels for the grave of Lord N—— would inform us who was the lady referred to, and enable us to ascertain the name of the author of one of the most delightful poems in the language. This casual remark created an amusing excitement among a class of small critics, and a dingy New York street made itself merry over our supposed ignorance. Among the numerous issues which were brought out by our remark, none was more amusing than a letter from a very indignant Scotchman to a Canada paper, which he probably marked and sent to us. He boiled over with indignation, and said, "How very ignorant some would-be literary critics are of their own business, especially among the Americans!"

All these gentlemen were oppressed with the idea that "The Land of the Leal" was by Burns.

No one acquainted with the poetry of Burns had ever attributed it to him. It has not in thought or construction any resemblance to Burns; and although some such persons as we have mentioned might have considered it his, the authorship of this delicious little poem has long been a subject of discussion among literary men.

The matter escaped our attention at the time, but has since been revived, and we are glad to be able to settle the question by authority of private letters from literary friends in Scotland, as well as of a volume of LAYS FROM STRATHEARN, published by Addison & Co., in London. The author of the song so much admired was the Countess of Nairne, a Scotch lady, who died in 1845. The following letter, from a gentleman in Edinburgh, contains some particulars which will be read with interest by all who admire that most exquisite of songs:

"MY DEAR SIR,—In reply to your favor of 20th ult. I beg to state, that there is no doubt whatever that the late Countess of Nairne was the author of the beautiful lyric referred to. In 'The Way Home,' at page 232 you will find it so stated for a fact, and in a work published by Addison & Co., of London, entitled 'Lays from Strathearn,' which contains all the poetical pieces of the gifted Countess, 'The Land of the Leal' appears among them. I will have the pleasure of sending you a copy of this work; and turn to pages 11 and 12, and you will there find it. There is a short biography prefixed to the volume, from which I extract the following sentences:

"'Passing one afternoon through a village where the yearly market was being held, she (the Countess), heard young voices singing to a favorite air words which she disliked. Returning homeward through Strathearn to the old Mansion House of Gask where her childhood and youth were passed, and which is described so touchingly in "The Auld House," the desire arose to remodel some of these old songs and to write new ones. "The occasion of an agricultural dinner," says Dr. Rogers, in his sketch of Lady Nairne, in the "Modern Scottish Minstrel," afforded her a fitting opportunity of making trial of her success in the good work she had begun. To the President of the meeting were sent anonymously her verses entitled, "The Pleughman," and the production being publicly read, was received with much approbation. She was thus encouraged to proceed in her self-imposed task, and to this early period of her life may be ascribed some of her best lyrics. "The Land o' the Leal," at the close of the century, was sung in every district of the kingdom. This song was written for a bereaved friend, and became widely known long before her name was whispered in connection with it. Some years later she added the verse,

"Sae dear's the joy was bought, John,
Sae free the battle fought, John,
That sinfu' man e'er brought
To the Land o' the Leal."

RUNNERS OF THE OLDEN TIME.

EMIGRANT-LANDING IN NEW YORK.

Emigrant-Landing in New York, William John Hennessy, engraving in *Harper's Weekly*, June 26, 1858. *Courtesy of the Library of Congress.*

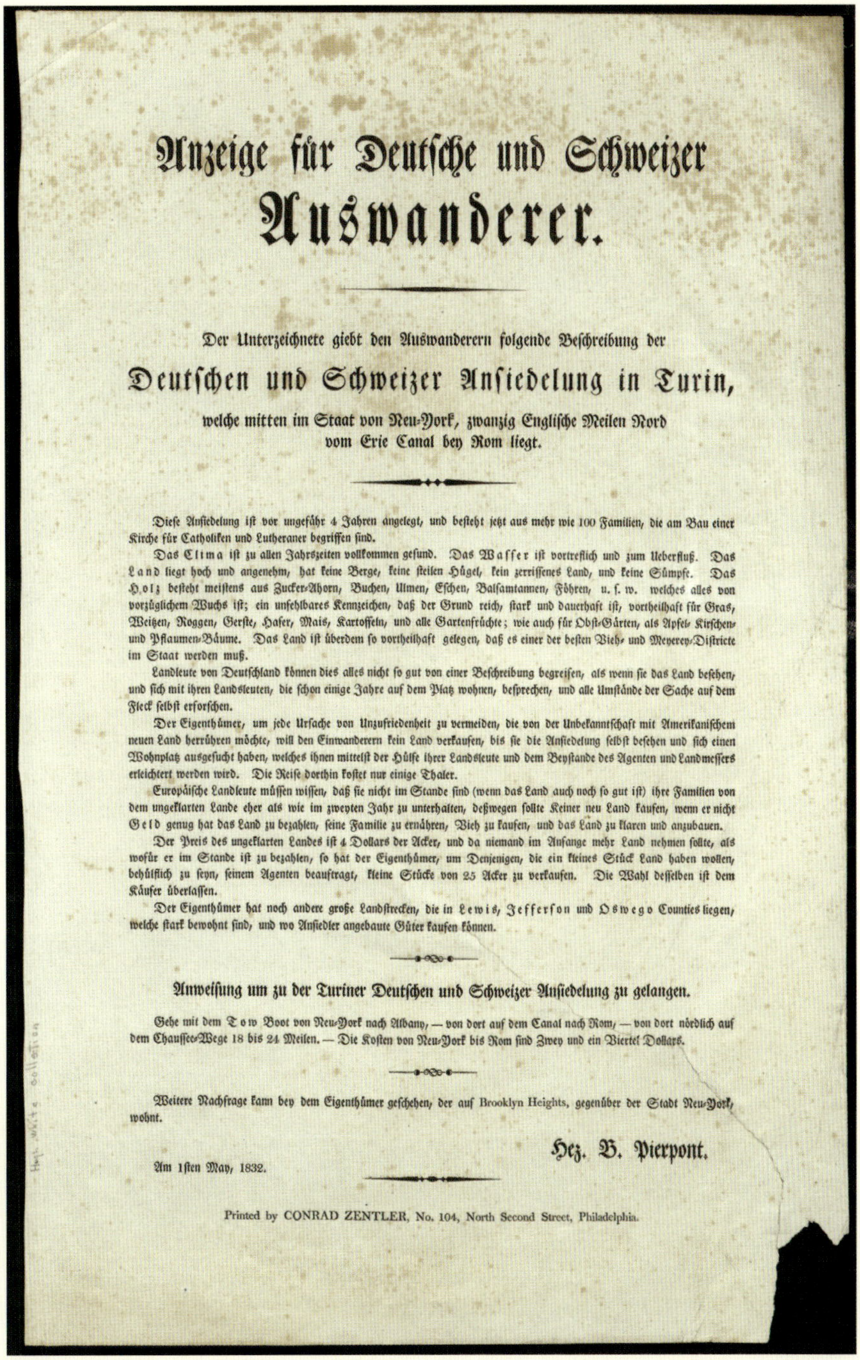

Anzeige für Deutsche und Schweizer Auswanderer.

Der Unterzeichnete giebt den Auswanderern folgende Beschreibung der

Deutschen und Schweizer Ansiedelung in Turin,

welche mitten im Staat von Neu-York, zwanzig Englische Meilen Nord vom Erie Canal bey Rom liegt.

Diese Ansiedelung ist vor ungefähr 4 Jahren angelegt, und besteht jetzt aus mehr wie 100 Familien, die am Bau einer Kirche für Catholiken und Lutheraner begriffen sind.

Das Clima ist zu allen Jahrszeiten vollkommen gesund. Das Wasser ist vortreflich und zum Ueberfluß. Das Land liegt hoch und angenehm, hat keine Berge, keine steilen Hügel, kein zerrissenes Land, und keine Sümpfe. Das Holz besteht meistens aus Zucker-Ahorn, Buchen, Ulmen, Eschen, Balsamtannen, Föhren, u. s. w. welches alles von vorzüglichem Wuchs ist; ein unfehlbares Kennzeichen, daß der Grund reich, stark und dauerhaft ist, vortheilhaft für Gras, Weitzen, Roggen, Gerste, Hafer, Mais, Kartoffeln, und alle Gartenfrüchte; wie auch für Obst-Gärten, als Apfel- Kirschen- und Pflaumen-Bäume. Das Land ist überdem so vortheilhaft gelegen, daß es einer der besten Vieh- und Meyerey-Districte im Staat werden muß.

Landleute von Deutschland können dies alles nicht so gut von einer Beschreibung begreifen, als wenn sie das Land besehen, und sich mit ihren Landsleuten, die schon einige Jahre auf dem Platz wohnen, besprechen, und alle Umstände der Sache auf dem Fleck selbst erforschen.

Der Eigenthümer, um jede Ursache von Unzufriedenheit zu vermeiden, die von der Unbekanntschaft mit Amerikanischem neuen Land herrühren möchte, will den Einwanderern kein Land verkaufen, bis sie die Ansiedelung selbst besehen und sich einen Wohnplatz ausgesucht haben, welches ihnen mittelst der Hülfe ihrer Landsleute und dem Beystande des Agenten und Landmessers erleichtert werden wird. Die Reise dorthin kostet nur einige Thaler.

Europäische Landleute müssen wissen, daß sie nicht im Stande sind (wenn das Land auch noch so gut ist) ihre Familien von dem ungeklarten Lande eher als wie im zweyten Jahr zu unterhalten, deßwegen sollte Keiner neu Land kaufen, wenn er nicht Geld genug hat das Land zu bezahlen, seine Familie zu ernähren, Vieh zu kaufen, und das Land zu klaren und anzubauen.

Der Preis des ungeklarten Landes ist 4 Dollars der Acker, und da niemand im Anfange mehr Land nehmen sollte, als wofür er im Stande ist zu bezahlen, so hat der Eigenthümer, um Denjenigen, die ein kleines Stück Land haben wollen, behülflich zu seyn, seinem Agenten beauftragt, kleine Stücke von 25 Acker zu verkaufen. Die Wahl desselben ist dem Käufer überlassen.

Der Eigenthümer hat noch andere große Landstrecken, die in Lewis, Jefferson und Oswego Counties liegen, welche stark bewohnt sind, und wo Ansiedler angebaute Güter kaufen können.

Anweisung um zu der Turiner Deutschen und Schweizer Ansiedelung zu gelangen.

Gehe mit dem Tow Boot von Neu-York nach Albany, — von dort auf dem Canal nach Rom, — von dort nördlich auf dem Chaussee-Wege 18 bis 24 Meilen. — Die Kosten von Neu-York bis Rom sind Zwey und ein Viertel Dollars.

Weitere Nachfrage kann bey dem Eigenthümer geschehen, der auf Brooklyn Heights, gegenüber der Stadt Neu-York, wohnt.

Hez. B. Pierpont.

Am 1sten May, 1832.

Printed by CONRAD ZENTLER, No. 104, North Second Street, Philadelphia.

Broadside, "Announcement for German and Swiss Emigrants," 1832. This broadside, written in German and signed by H. B. Pierpont, May 1, 1832, was printed and distributed in an effort to entice German and Swiss settlers to Turin in upstate New York. Turin is located near the Black River, about thirty miles north of Rome. Pierpont, a land speculator, stretched the truth somewhat about the climate and the proximity of the land to the canal. He claimed that the new colony for Swiss and Germans already had one hundred families who were constructing "a church for Catholics and Lutherans." He also claimed that it was only twenty miles from the Erie Canal in Rome. "The climate is very healthy the year round. The water is excellent and abundant. The land is high and pleasant, has no mountains, steep knolls, ravines or swamps." The speculator does suggest that no one should buy the land before viewing it and having enough money to last for two years without income from the land. There are instructions on how to travel from New York City to Turin, via the Hudson River, Erie Canal, and then on land at a cost of $2.25. *New York State Library, Manuscripts and Special Collections BRO 0872+.*

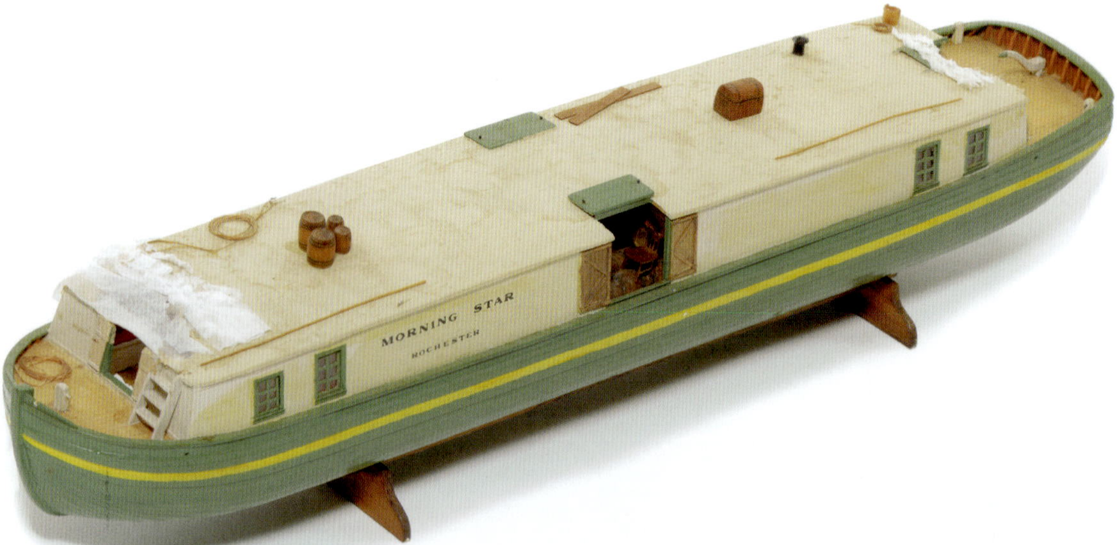

Model of line boat, *Morning Star,* Robert E. Hager, ca. 1965. Line boat companies carried passengers and freight. Fares were less than packet boats because of limited accommodations and slower travel time. Immigrants often journeyed on line boats because it was cheaper and they could bring their larger possessions with them. *Courtesy of the Canal Society of New York State.*

German immigrant's trunk, ca. 1850. The name Dorothea Ammon is painted on the top of this trunk. The mother of Albany inventor Christian Weeber, Ammon emigrated from Colberg Larsen-Meiningen, Germany. *New York State Museum, H-1986.58.1.*

Traditional Swiss shirt, reproduction. Example of traditional Swiss clothing, similar to those described by Hawthorne when he traveled the canal in the 1830s. *New York State Museum.*

Not long after, in the midst of a swamp and beneath a clouded sky, we overtook a vessel that seemed full of mirth and sunshine. It contained a little colony of Swiss, on their way to Michigan, clad in garments of strange fashion and gay colors, scarlet, yellow and bright blue, singing, laughing, and making merry, in odd tones and a babble of outlandish words.

—Nathaniel Hawthorne,
American novelist, 1835[15]

CANAL FEVER

The canals of the United States, links in the great chain which will be the bond of our union.

—Cadwallader D. Colden, 1823[16]

The Erie Canal's overwhelming success led to a national boom in canal building. New York would operate nine more canals to stimulate commerce and settlement and to reach natural resources in the state's interior. Other states followed suit, and this "canal fever" made travel by inland waterway from New York City to New Orleans a reality. Other canals met with varying degrees of success, but none matched the Erie Canal's impact on the nation.

(map pages 220–221) "Profiles of the New York State Canals and Feeders," map, 1881. Of the lateral canals, only the Champlain and Oswego Canals were financially profitable for New York State, but all helped to bring local products to market. Many of the subsequent lateral canals were bypassed by railroads shortly after they were completed. *The New York Public Library Digital Collections.*

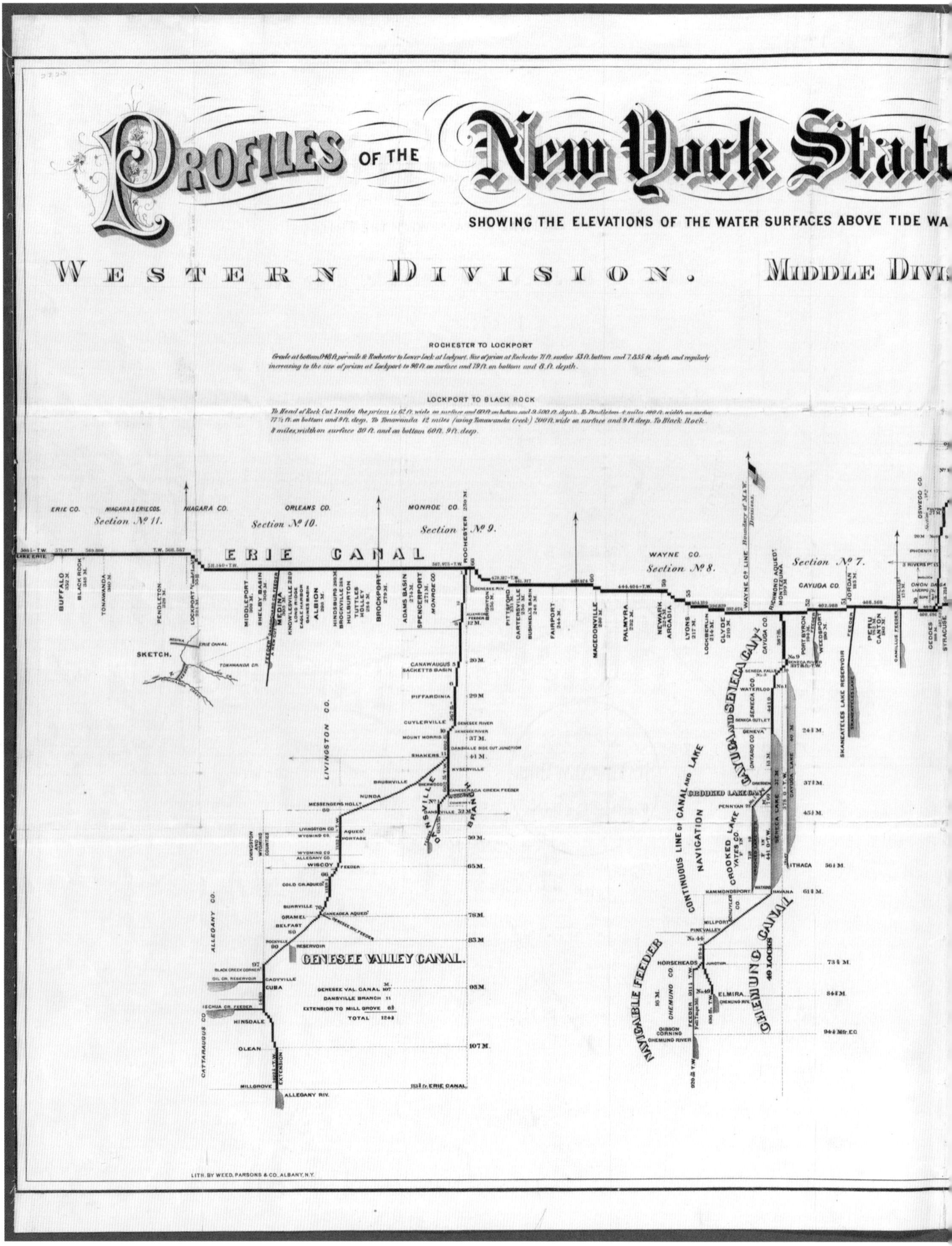
PROFILES OF THE New York State
SHOWING THE ELEVATIONS OF THE WATER SURFACES ABOVE TIDE WA
WESTERN DIVISION.
MIDDLE DIVI
ROCHESTER TO LOCKPORT
LOCKPORT TO BLACK ROCK
ERIE CANAL
Section № 11.
Section № 10.
Section № 9.
Section № 8.
Section № 7.
ERIE CO.
NIAGARA & ERIE COS.
NIAGARA CO.
ORLEANS CO.
MONROE CO.
WAYNE CO.
CAYUGA CO.
LIVINGSTON CO.
ALLEGANY CO.
CATTARAUGUS CO.
BUFFALO
BLACK ROCK
TONAWANDA
PENDLETON
LOCKPORT
MIDDLEPORT
MEDINA
ALBION
BROCKPORT
ROCHESTER
PITTSFORD
FAIRPORT
MACEDONVILLE
PALMYRA
NEWARK
LYONS
CLYDE
JORDAN
SYRACUSE
SKETCH.
GENESEE VALLEY CANAL.
CROOKED LAKE CANAL
CAYUGA AND SENECA CANAL
CHEMUNG CANAL
NAVIGABLE FEEDER
CONTINUOUS LINE OF CANAL AND LAKE NAVIGATION
ITHACA
ELMIRA
OLEAN
HINSDALE
CUBA
MILLGROVE
ALLEGANY RIV.
LITH. BY WEED, PARSONS & CO. ALBANY, N.Y.

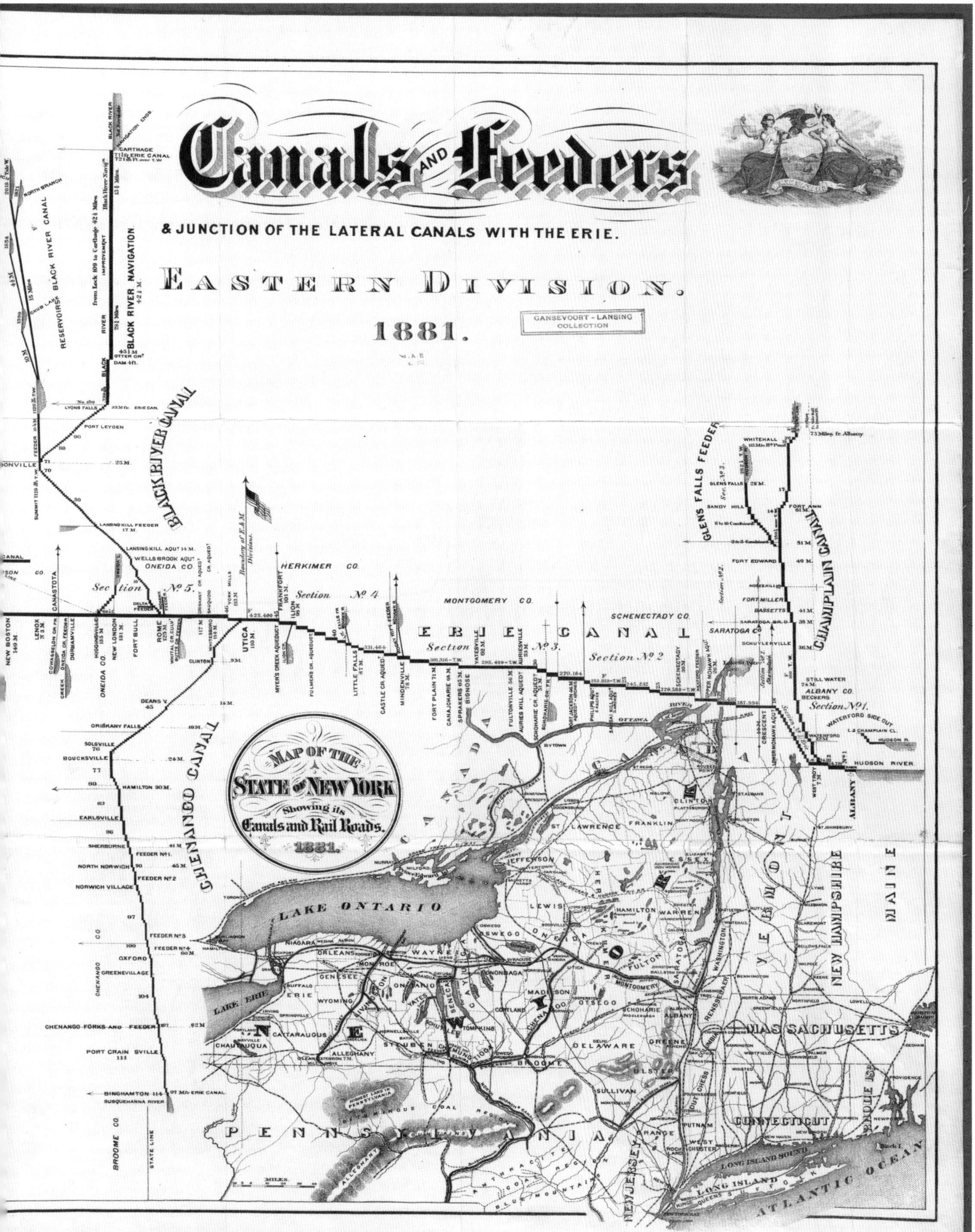
Canals and Feeders
& JUNCTION OF THE LATERAL CANALS WITH THE ERIE.
EASTERN DIVISION.
1881.
GANSEVOORT - LANSING COLLECTION
BLACK RIVER CANAL
BLACK RIVER NAVIGATION
GLENS FALLS FEEDER
CHAMPLAIN CANAL
ERIE CANAL
CHENANGO CANAL
MAP OF THE STATE OF NEW YORK Showing its Canals and Rail Roads. 1881.
LAKE ONTARIO
LAKE ERIE
HUDSON RIVER
ATLANTIC OCEAN
LONG ISLAND SOUND
PENNSYLVANIA
NEW JERSEY
CONNECTICUT
MASSACHUSETTS
VERMONT
NEW HAMPSHIRE
MAINE

Three of the lateral canals—the Champlain, Cayuga and Seneca, and Oswego—were deemed successful enough to warrant upkeep and eventually to be incorporated into the Barge Canal system.

Champlain Canal

Between Cohoes/Waterford and Whitehall, 1822–present

Plans for a Champlain Canal were approved with the original legislation of 1817. This helped bring legislative support from New York's northern counties, enhance national security, and divert trade from Canada. Much of the commerce on Lake Champlain prior to the canal went north to Canada. The canal followed the ancient trade route to Lake Champlain along the Hudson River and north to Whitehall. Adirondack lumber and iron ore were the main products shipped on this canal.

Boats Waiting to Enter the Champlain Canal, Waterford, photograph, ca. 1910. Boats loaded with coal wait to go north on the Champlain Canal. *New York State Museum, Michon Collection, H-1990.11.246.*

Iron ore. Adirondack iron ore shipped on the Champlain Canal led to the growth of large foundry industries in the Capital Region. *New York State Museum.*

Northern View of Whitehall, engraving, 1842. Whitehall was the northern terminus of the Champlain Canal. Canal boats often continued north on Lake Champlain. John Warner Barber and Henry Howe, *Historical Collections of the State of New York; Containing a General Collection of the Most Interesting Facts, Traditions, Biographical Sketches, Anecdotes, &c., Relating to Its History and Antiquities, with Geographical Descriptions of Every Township in the State* (New York: S. Tuttle, 1842). *Courtesy of the New York State Library, Manuscripts and Special Collections, 974.7 B23a3.*

View of the Junction of the Northern and Western Canals [Champlain and Erie] in Cohoes, engraving, ca. 1830. *New York State Museum, H- 1986.101.1.*

Between Montezuma and Geneva, 1828–present

The Finger Lakes were already a link on the water-based trade routes, but to tap into the region's true potential, the lakes needed to connect to the Erie Canal. The Cayuga and Seneca Canal opened in 1828, replacing an older improved waterway, connecting Cayuga and Seneca Lakes to the Erie Canal. Farm products and other manufactured goods contributed to the goods shipped on the canal.

(pages 224–225) Cowing hydraulic ram forcing pump and trade card, Seneca Falls, New York, ca. 1859. Seneca Falls was home to many fire protection–related industries. Cowing started making water pumps in 1840 and operated into the 1870s. *New York State Museum, H-1901.1.47, H-1901.1.47.C-1.*

COWING & Co

SENECA FALLS
4
COWING & Co

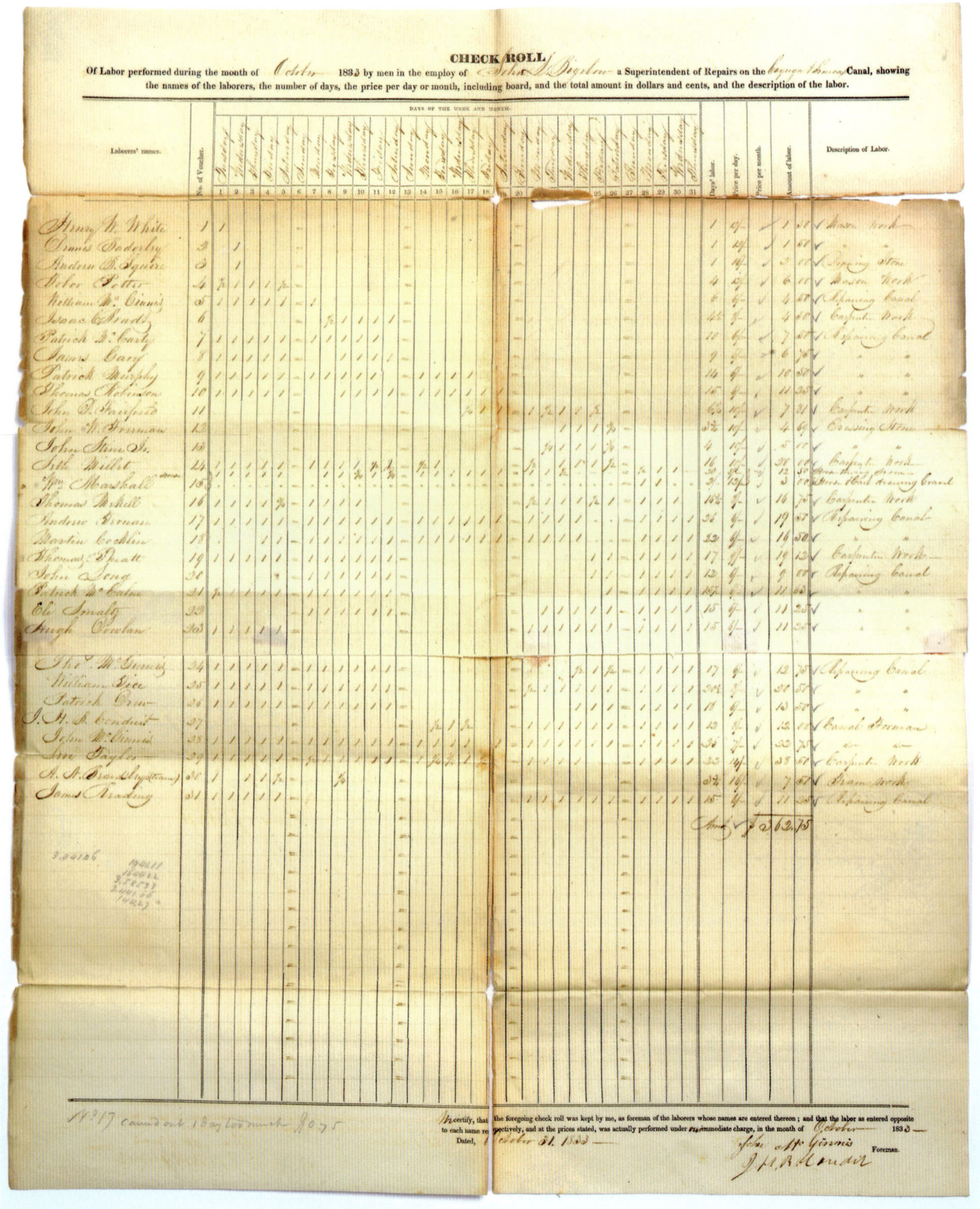

CHECK ROLL

Of Labor performed during the month of October 1833 by men in the employ of John S. Bigelow a Superintendent of Repairs on the Cayuga & Seneca Canal, showing the names of the laborers, the number of days, the price per day or month, including board, and the total amount in dollars and cents, and the description of the labor.

I certify, that the foregoing check roll was kept by me, as foreman of the laborers whose names are entered thereon; and that the labor as entered opposite to each name respectively, and at the prices stated, was actually performed under my immediate charge, in the month of October 1833 —

Dated, October 31. 1833 — Foreman.

“Check Roll” for laborers working for the superintendent of repairs for the Cayuga and Seneca Canal, 1833. Note the many Irish names on the record of employees for work on the Cuyaga and Seneca Canal in 1833. Earlier work on the Erie Canal through the Montazuma Swamp brought Irish immigrants to the area. *New York State Museum, Mrs. Arnold B. Barben Canal Collection, H-1988.79.*

Oswego Canal

Between Syracuse and Oswego, 1829–present

Oswego continued to be a prosperous trading port and strategic military station. Furthermore, the State owned salt works near Syracuse, and a canal connected to Oswego provided access to lumber-rich regions needed for salt manufacturing. The main products shipped on the Oswego Canal were salt, lumber, and grain.

Bird's-Eye View of Oswego, engraving, 1855. *Courtesy of the Library of Congress.*

Harbor View, Port of Oswego, J. Erwin Porter, pastel, ca. 1960. The Port of Oswego, the terminus of the Oswego Canal located on Lake Ontario, bustled with commercial traffic from the opening of the Oswego Canal into the second half of the twentieth century. *New York State Museum, J. Erwin Porter Collection, 1984.91.75.*

Bird's-Eye View of Watkins, NY (later Watkins Glen), Fowler & Bailey, engraving, ca. 1873. The Chemung Canal, which connected Seneca Lake at Watkins Glen to the Chemung River at Elmira, was in use between 1833 and 1878, when it succumbed to the predominance of the railroad. This canal's main cargoes were agricultural products and coal. *Courtesy of the Library of Congress.*

Canal Loading Facilities in Branchport on Kueka Lake, photograph, ca. 1870. Crooked Lake Canal, between Seneca Lake and Kueka Lake, 1833–1877. This canal's main cargoes were lumber and agricultural items. *New York State Museum, Mrs. Arnold B. Barben Canal Collection, H-1988.79.*

Lock No. 4, Sketch of Old Oneida Lake Canal Lock Number 4 by Engineer J. C. Hoadley, ca.1840. Oneida Lake Canal, between Higginsville and Sylvan Beach, operated from 1835 to 1863, when it closed. It reopened in 1877 and operated for one more year. Originally built by a private company and later purchased by the New York State, the canal cut two days' travel from the Erie Canal to Oswego. *Field Book 834 of the Middle Division, Archives Series B0730.*

Genesee Scenery, Thomas Cole, oil on canvas, 1847. Genesee Valley Canal, between Rochester and Olean and later Mill Grove, 1840–1878. In 1839 renowned Hudson River School painter Thomas Cole painted the Genesee Gorge at the request of Canal Commissioner Samuel Ruggles before it was destroyed for the construction of the Genesee Valley Canal. Cole sketched the area and then painted *Portage Falls of the Genesee River*, which was presented to Governor William Seward. Eight years later Cole used the same sketches to paint *Genesee Scenery*.

The main cargoes shipped on the Genesee Valley Canal were lumber, blue sandstone, and grains. The first length of the Genesee Valley Canal opened in 1840 and ran from Rochester southwest to Mount Morris in Livingston County. In 1862 the canal was extended but then abandoned in 1878 due to competition from the railroad, like so many of the lateral canals. *Courtesy of the Jesse Metcalf Fund 38.054, Museum of Art, Rhode Island School of Design, Providence. Photography by Erik Gould, courtesy of the Museum of Art, Rhode Island School of Design, Providence.*

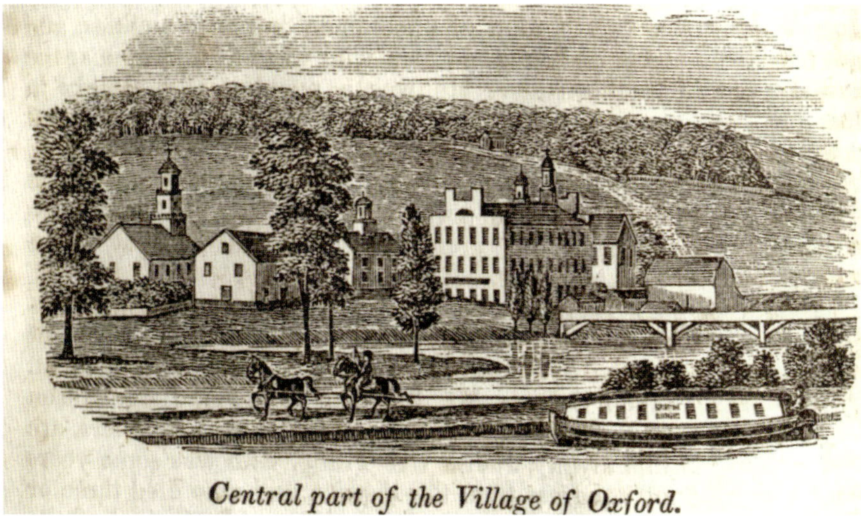

Village of Oxford, engraving, 1842. The Chenango Canal was ninety-seven miles long and ran between Utica and Binghamton from 1837 to 1878. The canal's main cargoes were iron ore, manufactured goods, and agricultural products. John Warner Barber and Henry Howe, *Historical Collections of the State of New York; Containing a General Collection of the Most Interesting Facts, Traditions, Biographical Sketches, Anecdotes, &c., Relating to Its History and Antiquities, with Geographical Descriptions of Every Township in the State* (New York: S. Tuttle, 1842). *Courtesy of the New York State Library, Manuscripts and Special Collections, 974.7 B23a3.*

Lumber Yard on the Black River Canal, photograph, late nineteenth–early twentieth century. Black River Canal linked Rome and Carthage, New York, and was thirty-five miles long. Its main cargoes were agricultural products and lumber, and portions of the canal operated between 1850 and 1924. *New York State Museum, H-1988.80.5012.*

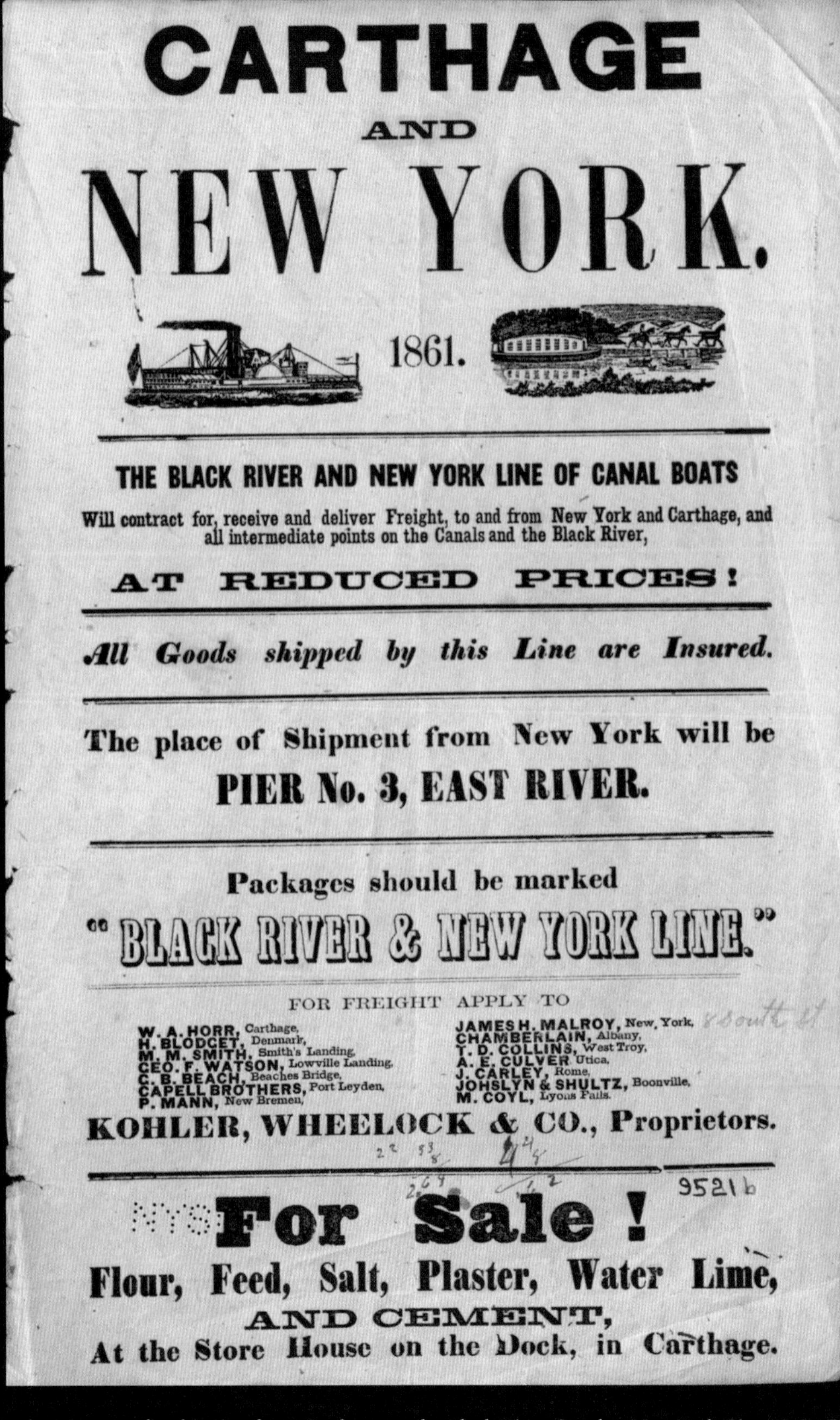

Broadside advertisement for shipping from Carthage on the Black River Canal to New York City, 1861. *Courtesy the New York State Library, Manuscripts and Special Collections 9521.*

Glens Falls Feeder Canal, photograph, 1921. The Glens Falls "Feeder Canal" provided water to the Champlain Canal. It was enlarged in 1832 to make it navigable to the Champlain Canal. There were also numerous smaller navigable feeder canals that served dual puposes: their main function was to bring water to the main canal, and the secondary use was for transport. *Courtesy of the New York State Archives, 17672-92.*

Delaware & Hudson Canal, Rosendale, photograph, nineteenth century. D & H Canal, between Rondout/Kingston in Ulster County and Honesdale, Pennsylvania, operated between 1828 and 1898. This canal was the only successful privately built and operated canal in New York State. It transported coal from Pennsylvannia. *New York State Museum, H-2004.44.2891.*

PART III

The Enlarged Canal

Based on the Erie Canal's success, almost immediately after its opening in 1825 calls were made to increase its capacity. In 1835 the New York State Legislature passed a bill that approved an enlargement of the canal, which began the following year. Politics and engineering were again major factors in the project, as they had been with initial construction (see canal growth diagrams, pages 28–29). That early success also bred competition, and by the 1840s railroads were competing for passengers and cargo, and they would eventually come to dominate New York's transportation systems.

QUICK FACTS ABOUT THE ENLARGED ERIE CANAL

350.5 miles long

70 feet wide at the surface, 56 feet wide at the bottom, 7 feet deep

75 locks (including guard locks), each 110 feet by 18 feet; most locks doubled so traffic could be locked through in each direction at the same time

72 lift locks

32 aqueducts

THE POLITICS OF THE ENLARGEMENT

> **. . .[W]hether New York shall continue to control the vast trade of the Great West; whether or not her commercial supremacy shall be maintained; whether a channel which has rendered her the "Empire State" of the Union, shall assume proportions commensurate with the demands upon it; and whether what has constituted the chief glory of our People shall continue to pour its exhaustless streams of wealth into the coffers of the State . . .**
>
> **—Thurlow Weed, Albany politician and newspaper publisher, in support of the enlargement of the Erie Canal, *Albany Evening Journal*, February 14, 1854**

From the 1810s through the 1850s, the question of canals and internal improvements ruled New York State politics and resulted in a volleying of power and control between political parties. As a State-run entity, the canal system could not escape political ideologies. Each political party had its own position on canals—the operation, the spending, the value, the ownership, and the enlargement.

In 1821 Martin Van Buren, then a US senator and a member of New York State's Democratic-Republican Party, established the nation's first political machine, known as the Albany Regency, in order to facilitate and control political activities across the state. Led by Van Buren, William Marcy, and others, the Regency dominated the state legislature for much of the 1820s through 1854, except for a short time between 1837 and 1841 (in the assembly) and 1839–1841, when the Whigs controlled the legislature. The Albany Regency promoted Jeffersonian-Jacksonian beliefs in small government and no public debt.

Although De Witt Clinton was a Democratic-Republican, he had plenty of detractors within his own party, so many in fact that his supporters gained their own name—the Clintonians. The Clintonian faction favored government-supported internal improvements at the risk of debt, which had become one of the main issues that divided the party. The Whig party in New York formed in the 1830s and saw themselves as the true heir to Clinton's policies in relation to the canals. They favored government-funded public works projects, at the risk of debt. The Whigs also took a more national view in their policies, promoting the canal as an economic stimulus not only New York but the nation.

The subject of enlarging the Erie Canal came to a head in 1835 when a Democratic-led state legislature approved its enlargement. Construction began the following year, but the policy that governed it was vague and the project was underfunded, leading to slow progress.

When it came to the canal, regional affiliation often outweighed party politics. Western New Yorkers overwhelmingly supported a fast enlargement, which helped bring the Whigs to power in 1837. At the same time, the United States fell into an economic depression. The politics of the enlargement of the Erie Canal became a continuous debate between preserving the credit of New York State and delivering the promised economic benefits of an enlarged canal. The Whigs argued that increased revenue from western trade would offset any debt incurred by an expanded canal project and enacted policies to spend more money to speed the project, borrowing on State credit. However, that increase did not materialize quickly enough, and the Whigs were voted out in 1841, when the Democrats swept into the state legislature and put an end to deficit spending.

The "Stop and Tax" bill of 1842 halted further new construction on the canal until the debt was paid. In 1846 the prohibition of deficit spending was codified in the state constitution. The canal enlargement could continue only with the surplus revenue brought in from canal tolls and small appropriations until 1854, when the Whigs regained power in the legislature. They quickly resumed the full-blown construction of the enlargement, and it was declared complete in 1862.

Throughout the Erie Canal's history, the spoils system for contractor awards and canal employees produced frequent accusations of corruption. Various reform efforts were made with short-term successes. In 1875 Governor Samuel Tilden exposed the so-called fraudulent "Canal Ring." Tilden exposed a gross misuse of canal funds when a group of politicians had used a spoils system to award contracts on canal repairs for kickbacks. As a result, the legislature removed the Canal Commission's power and gave control to the superintendent of public works.

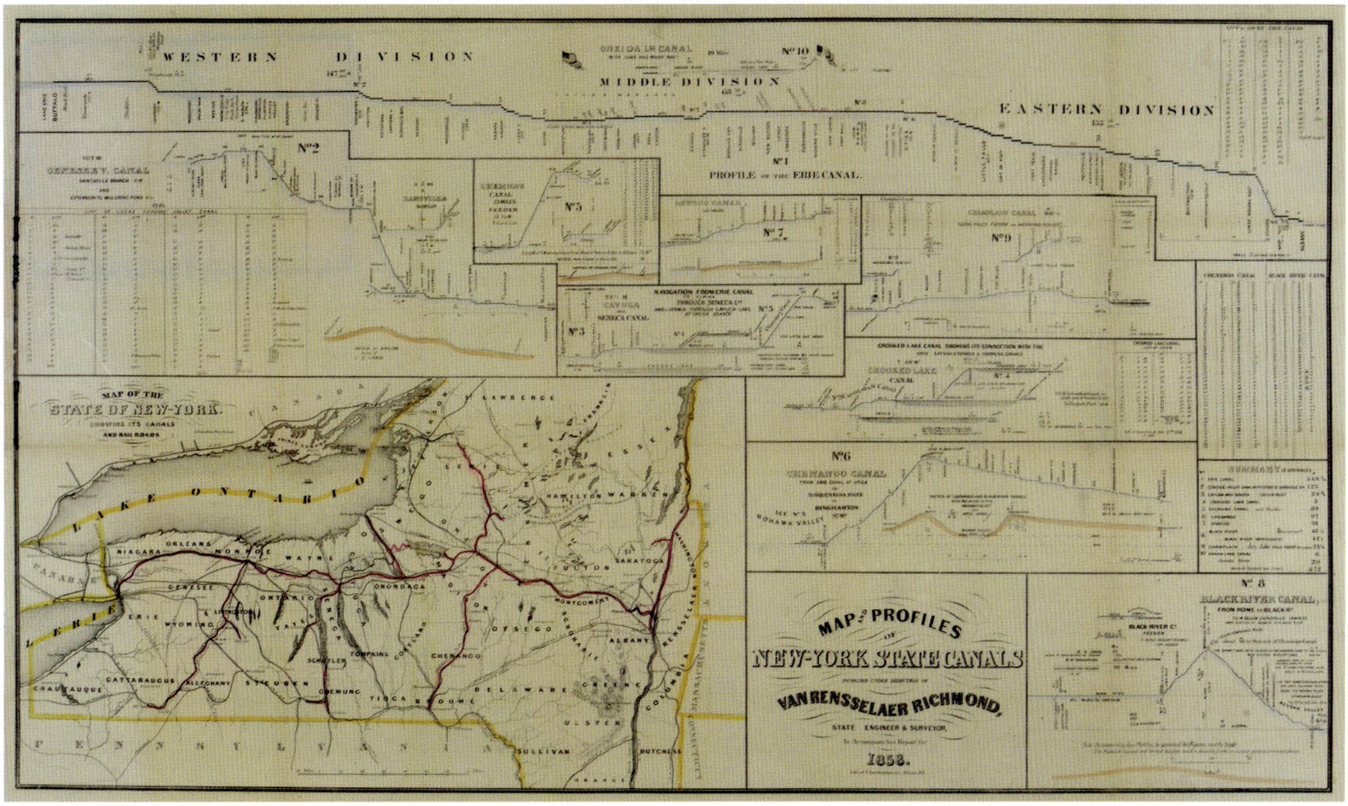

Map and profiles of New York State canals, 1858. By 1858 the canal system had grown to reach much of New York State. *Courtesy of the New York State Library, Manuscripts and Special Collections, (747)1858 200-3314.*

New York State Senate Chamber, ink and watercolor, unknown, 1850. Between 1835 and 1862, the progress of the enlargement depended largely on which political party had control in the state legislature. *Courtesy of the Albany Institute of History & Art.*

Whig political banner, Terrence J. Kennedy, oil on canvas, ca. 1836. Dominating the right side of the banner, the Erie Canal emphasized the Whig philosophy that improved internal transportation and protection of home industries were vital to the commerce and industry of the United States. *Courtesy of the Fenimore Art Museum, Cooperstown, New York, Collection of Elie & Viola Spiess Flannery Nadelman Collection. Gift of Stephen C. Clark.*

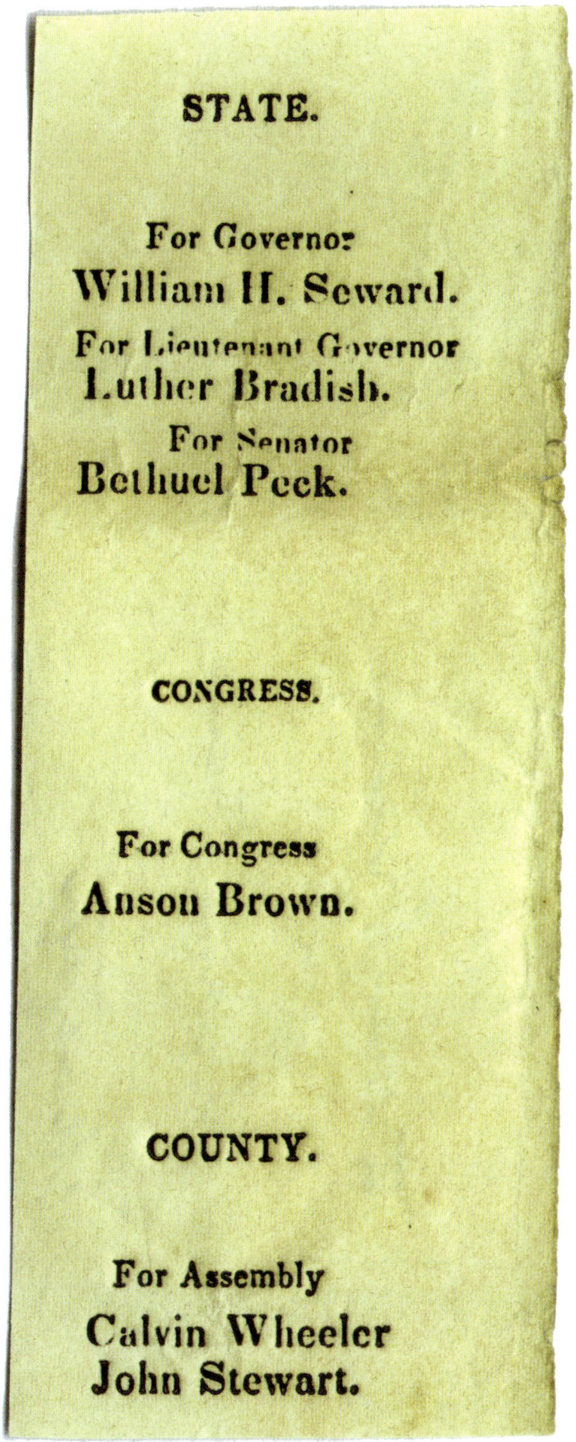
STATE.

For Governor
William H. Seward.
For Lieutenant Governor
Luther Bradish.
For Senator
Bethuel Peck.

CONGRESS.

For Congress
Anson Brown.

COUNTY.

For Assembly
Calvin Wheeler
John Stewart.

Ballot, 1838. Whig Party ballot for the election of 1838. *New York State Museum, H-2006.71.12.*

William H. Seward political pin, 1838. Political pin from the 1838 New York State gubernatorial election, featuring a raised portrait of William Seward. Seward, a Whig, won the election and served as governor from 1839 through 1842. He was a strong proponent of governmental support of internal improvements, railroads, and canals. *New York State Museum, H-2006.71.10.*

"Grand Canal" bandbox, ca. 1850. Due to its popularity, images of the Erie Canal appeared across a range of products, such as this bandbox (used for carrying hats). This popularity with the residents of New York State helped to ensure that politicians pay attention to canal issues. *Courtesy of the Fenimore Art Museum, Cooperstown, New York. Museum Purchase.*

Samuel B. Ruggles, Daniel Huntington, oil on canvas, 1882. Assemblyman Samuel Ruggles (1800–1881) served as a canal commissioner from 1839 to 1842. He developed the Whig-sponsored plan to fund the canal enlargement through deficit spending. Ruggles believed that increased western trade would enable future canal revenue to cover the costs to complete the enlargement. His prediction was ultimately correct but took longer to realize than hoped, and the plan would contribute to the downfall of the Whigs in 1841. *New York State Museum, H-2003.41.18.*

$5,000 canal stock certificate for the enlargement of the Erie Canal, 1838. This loan bond was issued during William Seward's administration. Seward and the Whigs believed that the economic benefits of the canal outweighed any debt accrued. *New York State Museum, Mrs. Arnold B. Barben Canal Collection, H-1988.79.*

WHIG NOMINATIONS.

ALBANY COUNTY.

FOR SENATOR,

Killian Miller.

FOR ASSEMBLY,

AZOR TABER,
MARTIN VAN OLINDA,
ADAM I. SHULTES.

Friends of Internal Improvement rally for your cause! Boatmen stand to your rights! The Locofocos are your enemies! Read the following and judge what hopes you have from the measures of men who adopt the NO IMPROVEMENT doctrines of MICHAEL HOFFMAN. Compare them with those of the Whig party and say which creed YOU will *support* :

Newspaper advertisement, *Albany Evening Journal,* November 2, 1841. Large advertisement for the Whigs of Albany County. This last push before the state election makes the Whigs' case against the LocoFocos, a branch of the Democratic Party, and prominently promotes their record on canals. The Whigs intended "LocoFocos" to be a derogatory term. This last effort to sway the voters was not successful, and the Whigs lost control of the state assembly and senate. Deficit spending for internal improvements quickly came to an end in early 1842 under Democratic leadership. *America's Historical Newspapers, Newsbank online via New York State Library.*

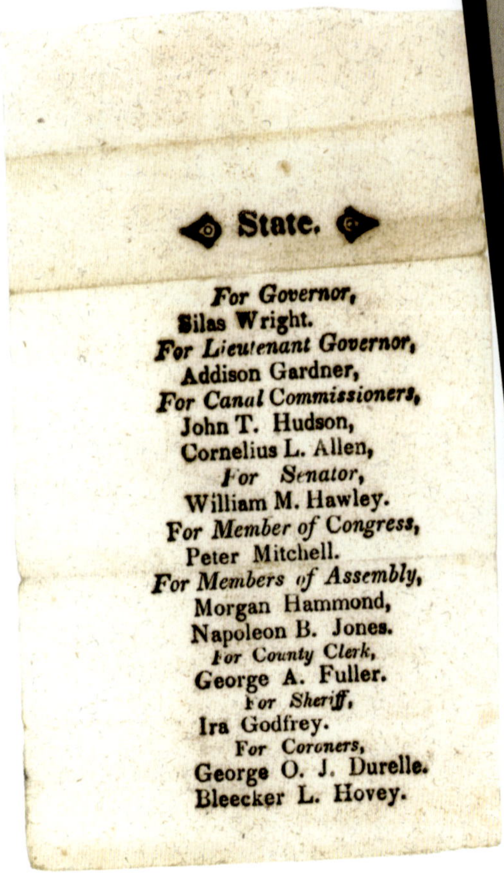

State.

For Governor,
Silas Wright.
For Lieutenant Governor,
Addison Gardner,
For Canal Commissioners,
John T. Hudson,
Cornelius L. Allen,
For Senator,
William M. Hawley.
For Member of Congress,
Peter Mitchell.
For Members of Assembly,
Morgan Hammond,
Napoleon B. Jones.
For County Clerk,
George A. Fuller.
For Sheriff,
Ira Godfrey.
For Coroners,
George O. J. Durelle.
Bleecker L. Hovey.

Ballot, 1844. This New York State ballot for the election of 1844 shows candidates for the Democratic Party. Geographic location complicated party loyalty. The constituents along the canal were likely to reject the Democrats' doctrine and support the enlargement because they would benefit from increased commerce. *New York State Museum, H-2006.71.21.*

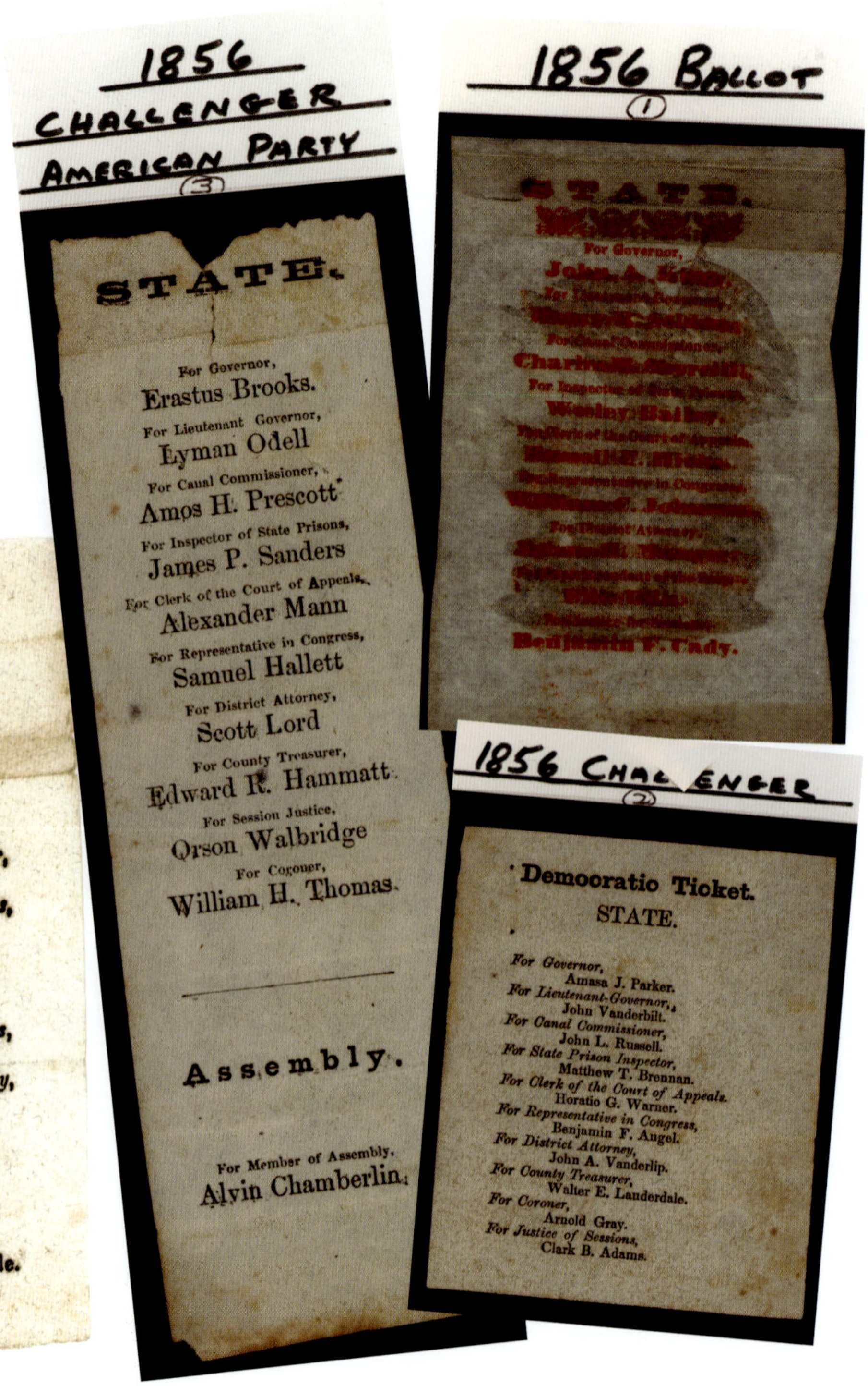

STATE.

For Governor,
Erastus Brooks.
For Lieutenant Governor,
Lyman Odell
For Canal Commissioner,
Amos H. Prescott
For Inspector of State Prisons,
James P. Sanders
For Clerk of the Court of Appeals,
Alexander Mann
For Representative in Congress,
Samuel Hallett
For District Attorney,
Scott Lord
For County Treasurer,
Edward R. Hammatt
For Session Justice,
Orson Walbridge
For Coroner,
William H. Thomas.

Assembly.

For Member of Assembly,
Alvin Chamberlin.

STATE.

For Governor,
...
Benjamin F. Cady.

Democratic Ticket.
STATE.

For Governor,
Amasa J. Parker.
For Lieutenant-Governor,
John Vanderbilt.
For Canal Commissioner,
John L. Russell.
For State Prison Inspector,
Matthew T. Brennan.
For Clerk of the Court of Appeals.
Horatio G. Warner.
For Representative in Congress,
Benjamin F. Angel.
For District Attorney,
John A. Vanderlip.
For County Treasurer,
Walter E. Lauderdale.
For Coroner,
Arnold Gray.
For Justice of Sessions,
Clark B. Adams.

Ballots, 1856. The New York State Constitution of 1846 established that New Yorkers would elect three canal commissioners for three-year terms. These 1856 ballots demonstrate the importance of the commissioner position, with the candidate listed right after the lieutenant governor. *New York State Museum, H-2006.71.33, H-2006.71.34, H-2006.71.33.35.*

Ballot box, mid-nineteenth century. The Whigs' prediction that canal revenues would offset construction debt eventually came true. As a result, in 1854 voters backed another power shift, leading to the removal of the deficit-spending restrictions from the state constitution, and the enlargement fully resumed. *New York State Museum, H-2006.71.1713.*

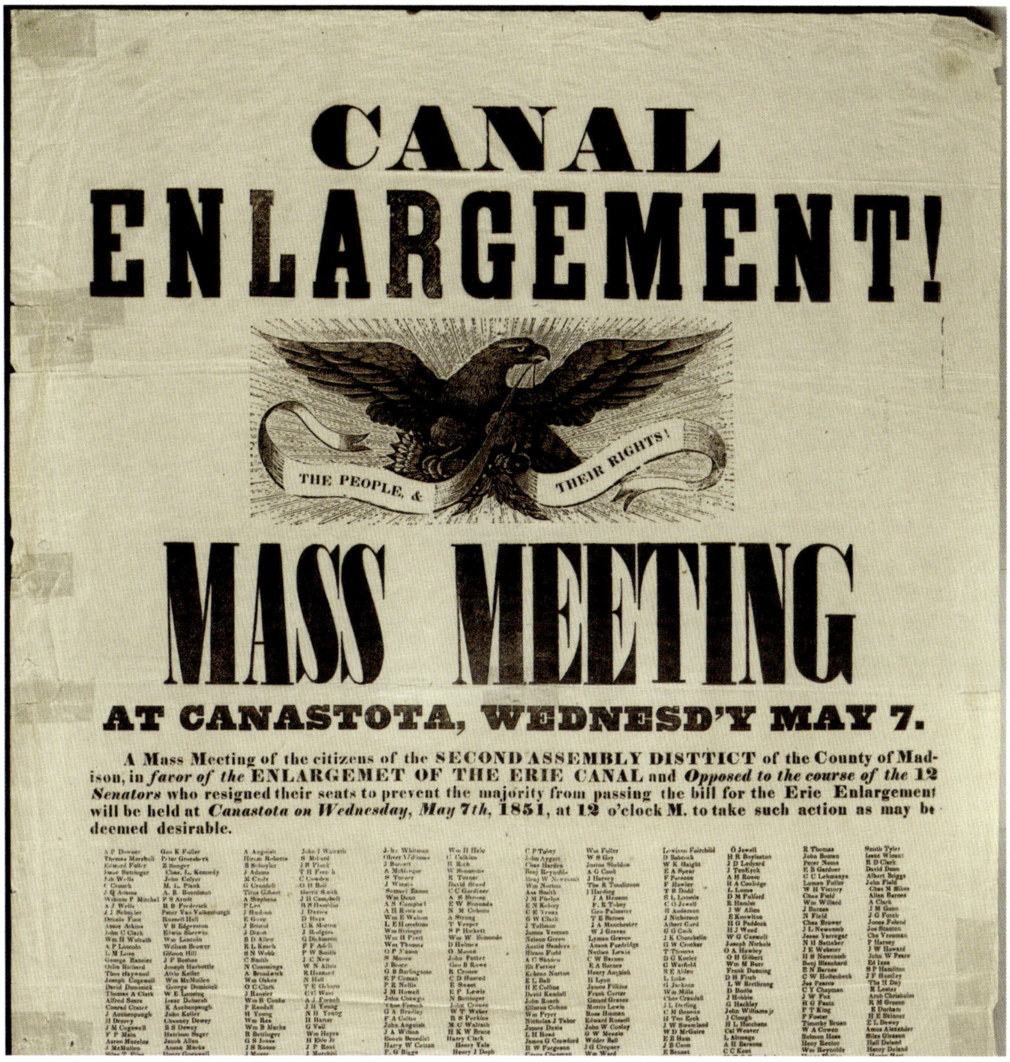

Broadside, 1851. Debates over canal expansion became so heated that twelve (later thirteen) state senators resigned their positions so that there would not be the necessary three-fifths quorum in the senate to vote on a canal bill for funding the enlargement in 1851. *Courtesy of the New York State Library, Manuscripts and Special Collections, BRO 073.*

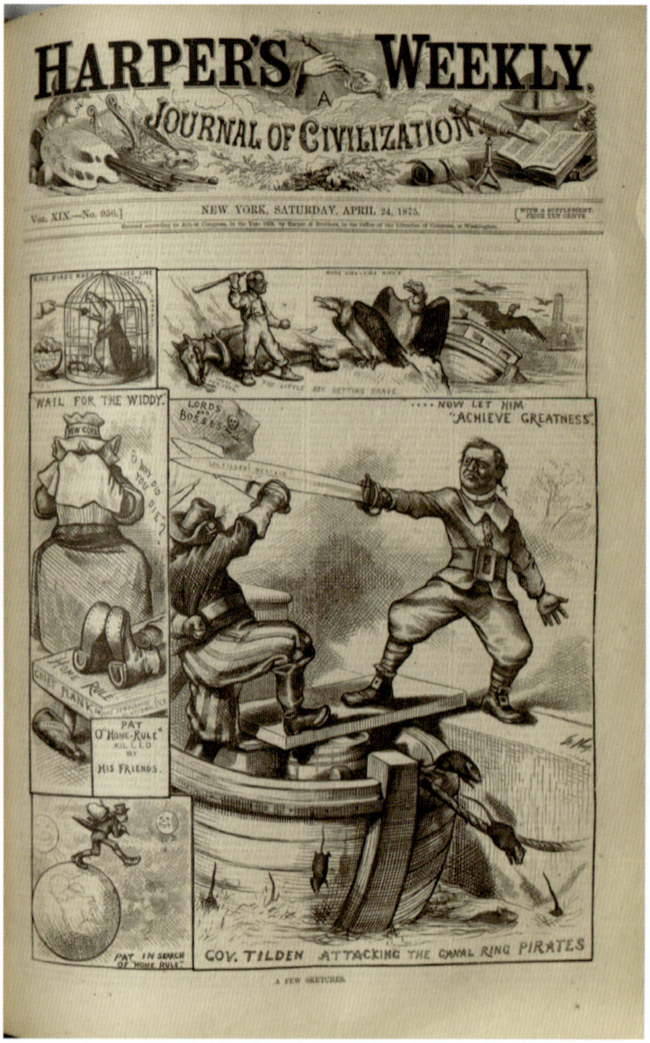

Gov. Tilden Attacking the Canal Ring Pirates, engraving, 1875. This political cartoon depicts Governor Samuel Tilden in his efforts to combat corruption in the canal system. *Harper's Weekly,* April 24, 1875. *Courtesy of the New York State Library, Manuscripts and Special Collections.*

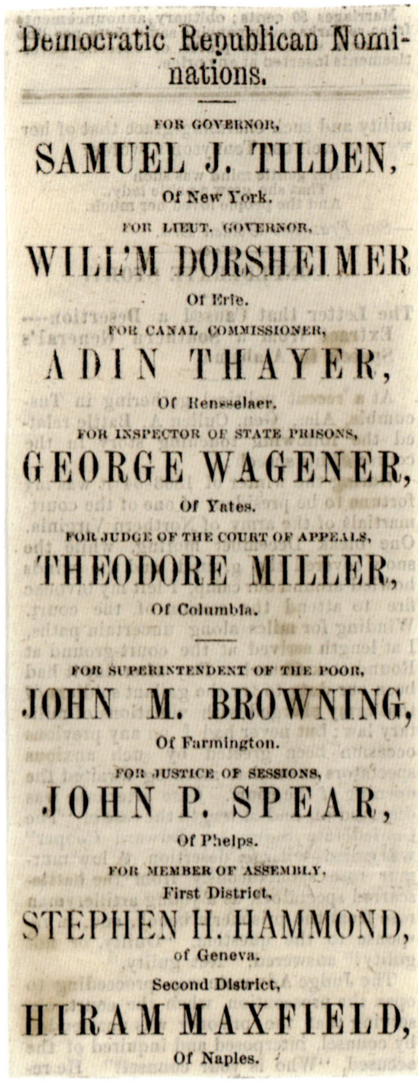

Democratic Republican Nominations.

FOR GOVERNOR,
SAMUEL J. TILDEN,
Of New York.
FOR LIEUT. GOVERNOR,
WILL'M DORSHEIMER
Of Erie.
FOR CANAL COMMISSIONER,
ADIN THAYER,
Of Rensselaer.
FOR INSPECTOR OF STATE PRISONS,
GEORGE WAGENER,
Of Yates.
FOR JUDGE OF THE COURT OF APPEALS,
THEODORE MILLER,
Of Columbia.

FOR SUPERINTENDENT OF THE POOR,
JOHN M. BROWNING,
Of Farmington.
FOR JUSTICE OF SESSIONS,
JOHN P. SPEAR,
Of Phelps.
FOR MEMBER OF ASSEMBLY,
First District,
STEPHEN H. HAMMOND,
of Geneva.
Second District,
HIRAM MAXFIELD,
Of Naples.

Ballot, Samuel Tilden, 1874. A ballot for Samuel Tilden in the 1874 gubernatorial election. *New York State Museum, H-2006.71.65.*

Tilden cane, 1876. This cane was presented to Samuel Tilden in 1876, the same year he won the popular vote for the presidency but lost the election in the Electoral College. The inscription on the top reads "Hon. Samuel J. Tilden from Southern Constituents 1876." It is also inscribed "Be Just and Fear Not," a reference to his battle against government corruption and a well-known Shakespearian quote. *New York State Museum Collection, H-2015.12.1.*

Erie Canal Locks at Little Falls, photograph, late nineteenth–early twentieth century. Boat captains often had to pay bribes to lock tenders to get though the locks quickly and safely. Canal officials made a concerted effort to end the practice in the 1890s, but well into the twentieth century canallers knew it didn't hurt to flip a quarter to or share a beverage with a lock tender. *New York State Museum, H-1988.80.1.582.*

CONSTRUCTION AND ENGINEERING OF THE ENLARGEMENT

The Erie Canal had a direct impact on tremendous growth in population, commerce, and industry in New York State, particularly along the canal corridor. But with an ever-increasing amount of freight coming out of the Midwest, New York's monopoly on western trade was at stake, and the Erie Canal needed to be bigger to handle the volume of trade and maintain its primacy.

The enlargement of Clinton's Ditch started in 1836 and continued into 1862. Engineers were charged with increasing the capacity of the waterway and shortening travel times by enlarging the canal channel to seventy feet wide and seven feet deep. Wherever possible, the canal path was straightened, the number of locks reduced, and double locks—which allowed boats to lock through in each direction at the same time—were added. While boats themselves did not move faster, fewer miles to travel and shorter lines at fewer locks meant it took less time to reach one's destination. Politics and arguments over spending dragged out the enlargement until 1862, when it was declared complete.

Double Locks and Aqueduct in Rexford, photograph, late nineteenth early–twentieth century. Double locks enabled boats to lock through in each direction at the same time. This view of the canal at Rexford, New York, shows a set of double locks and the "Upper Aqueduct" spanning the Mohawk River. *New York State Museum, H-1998.23.955.*

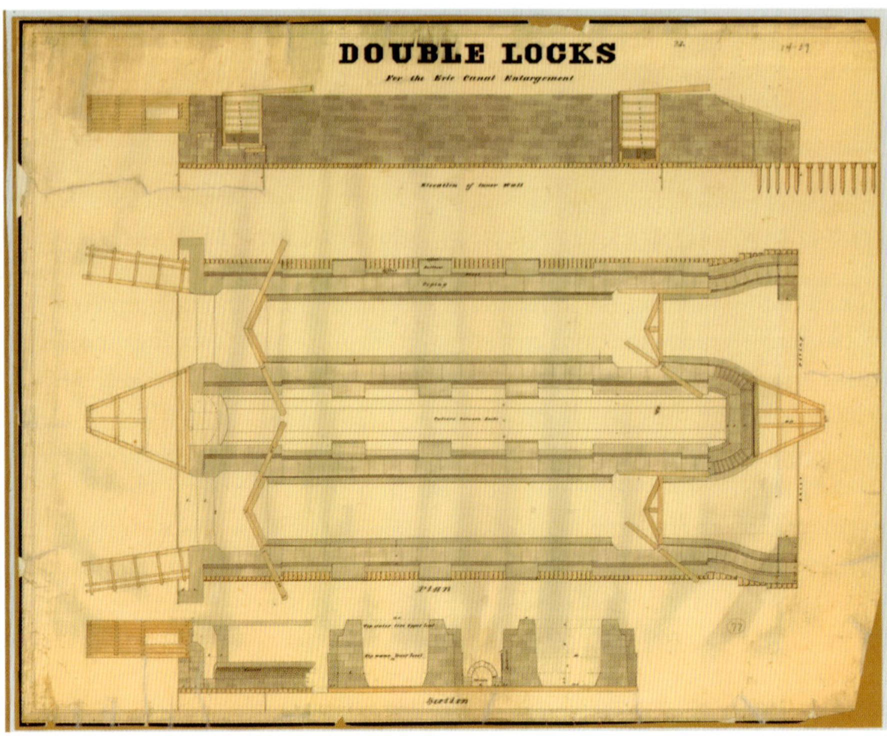

Plans for double locks, ca. 1830s. State engineers and draftsmen produced specific plans for contractors, such as this set of plans for double locks. Courtesy of the New York State Archives, B0292, vol. 14, p. 39.

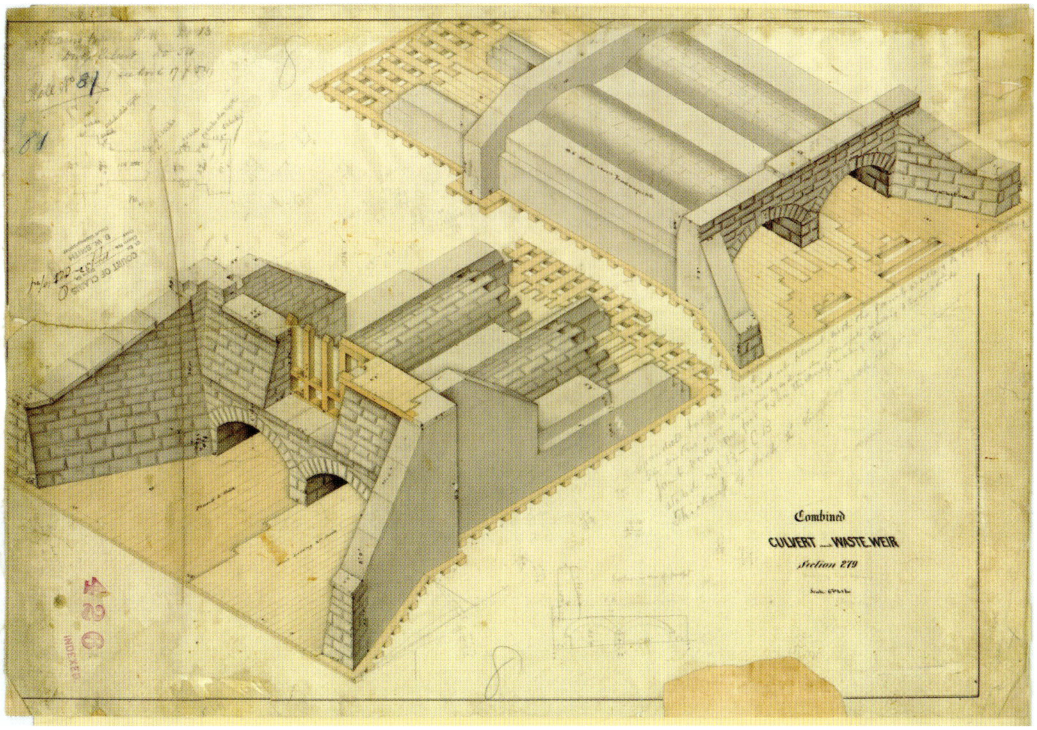

Plans for a waste weir gate, ca. 1855. Waste weirs were designed to allow excess water to flow out of the canal. This helped ensure that water levels did not get too high. *Courtesy of the New York State Archives, Series 706.*

The Erie Canal, 1831, John William Hill (American, born England, 1812–1879), watercolor on paper. This watercolor of the Erie Canal at Profile Rock near Little Falls depicts the original canal, with a single lock. Beginning in 1836, the canal was widened, and the single lock was replaced with double locks. *Union College, Permanent Collection.*

View of Little Falls, New York, 1852, William Rickarby Miller (American, born England, 1818–1893), watercolor on paper. This idyllic view shows the landscape as tamed by the hand of man—both in the settlement of the village in the distance and the building of the canal itself—as passengers take a leisurely ride through the countryside. *Albany Institute of History & Art.*

View Showing the Progress of the Work on the Lock Section, canal engineer Thomas Evershed, drawing, 1839. This drawing was part of a progress report on the enlargement of the Lockport flight of locks. *Courtesy of the New York State Archives, Working Plans of Enlarged Lockport Locks, vol. 17 B569/6.*

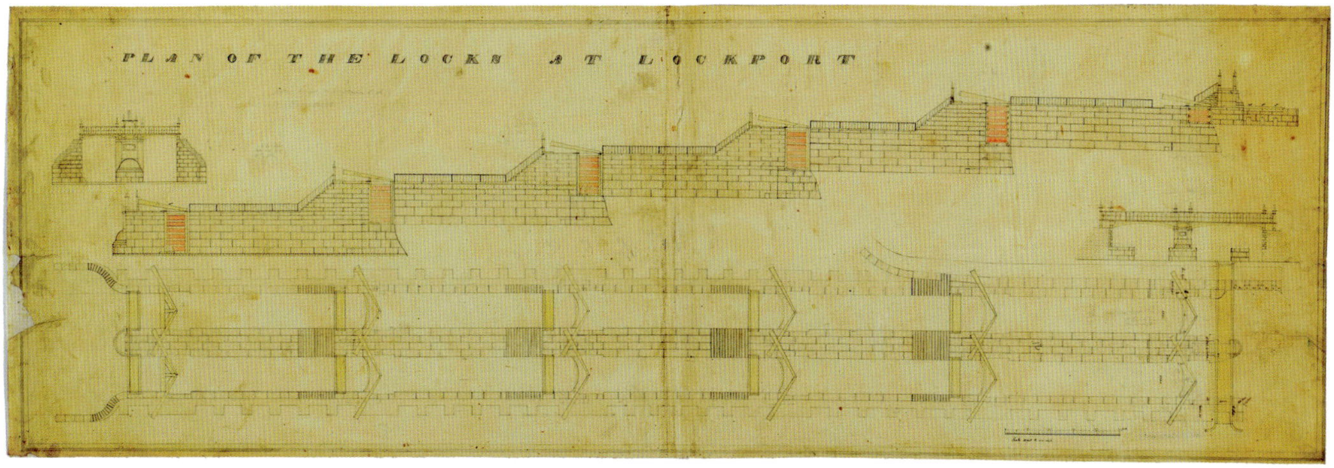

Plans for enlargement of Lockport locks, 1839. Engineer Thomas Evershed drew the plan and oversaw the enlargement of the combined locks at Lockport. *Courtesy of the New York State Archives, Working Plans of Enlarged Lockport Locks, vol. 17 B569/6.*

Who Built the Enlarged Canal?

Throughout the enlargement, Irish immigrants were employed in large numbers as laborers on the canal. The project faced numerous labor shortages, and calls were issued in Europe to encourage additional immigrant laborers to come to New York State. Many of these immigrants made their homes in communities along the canal, adding to the cultural fabric of the corridor.

David Vaughan (ca. 1803–1865), draftsman

Irish immigrant David Vaughan worked as a draftsman for the state engineer and surveyor. In the 1850s and 1860s, Vaughan drafted and illustrated maps and plans for the Erie Canal's enlargement. Vaughan's elaborate illustrations included scenes on the canal, political messages, and, possibly, hints of his homeland in Ireland. In 1864 Vaughan was committed to the New York State Asylum in Utica due to mental health issues. He died shortly thereafter, leaving behind a wonderful legacy in the visual history of the Erie Canal.

Squire Whipple (1804–1888), engineer

Squire Whipple, a trained engineer and Union College graduate, is known for his inventions of various bridges and the mathematical principles that guided bridge designs. His bowstring bridge was patented in 1841, and hundreds were built over New York canals. Made of iron and wood, these bridges provided long-lasting crossings over the enlarged canal. Whipple is frequently referred to as the "Father of Iron Bridge Building" in America.

Holmes Hutchinson (1794–1865), engineer

Holmes Hutchinson was born in Genoa, Cayuga County. He trained as a surveyor, became a canal engineer in 1819, and went on to serve as chief engineer of the Erie Canal from 1835 to 1841. Hutchinson helped to lay out the enlargement of the Erie Canal and oversaw the first clear maps done of the canal system after its completion. The maps established the New York State property line along the canals, known as the "blue line."

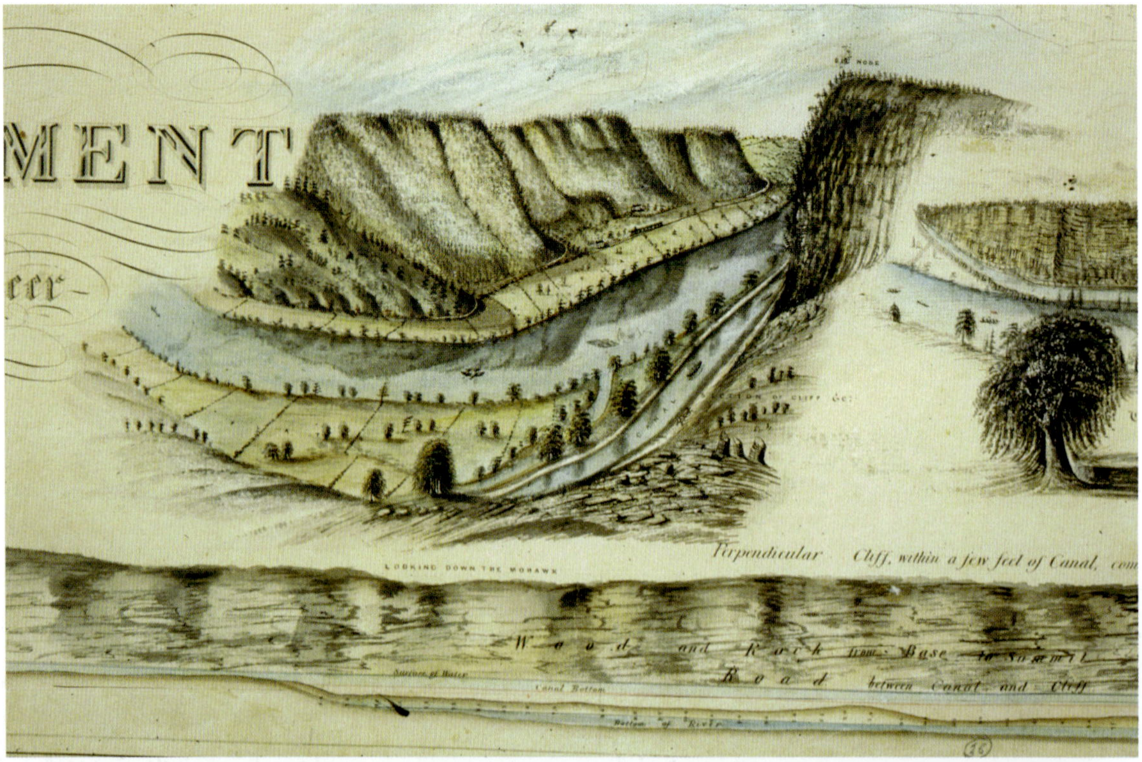

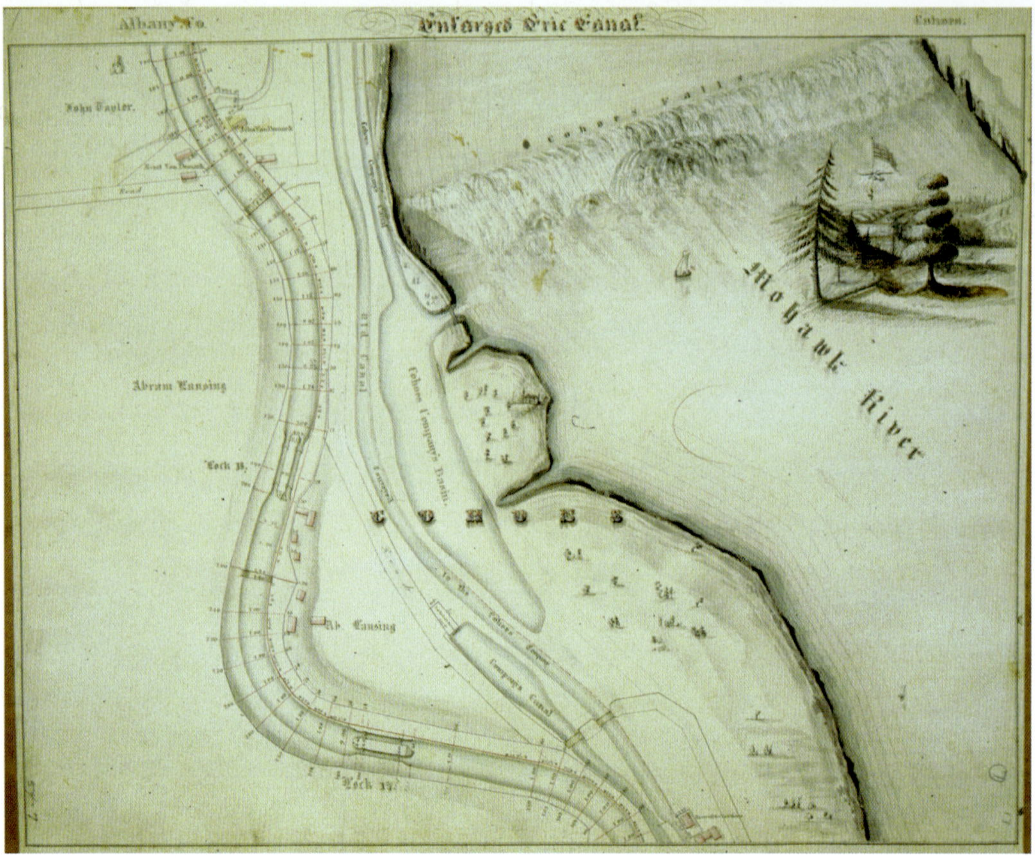

(page 250–251) Map sections, David Vaughan, ca. 1850. *Courtesy of the New York State Archives, B0292, Canal Structure Map and Plan Books, ca. 1827–1905, vol. 35, sheets 20-A/B.*

gement of the Erie Ca
Sec. 54.
contented Farmer
DUTCH
AN UNUSUAL THING
wheat lies ripe
AND THEY WONT cut it
DISCONTENTED WORKMAN

A ROCHESTER MILLER
HOLD ON
HORSE IN THE CANAL

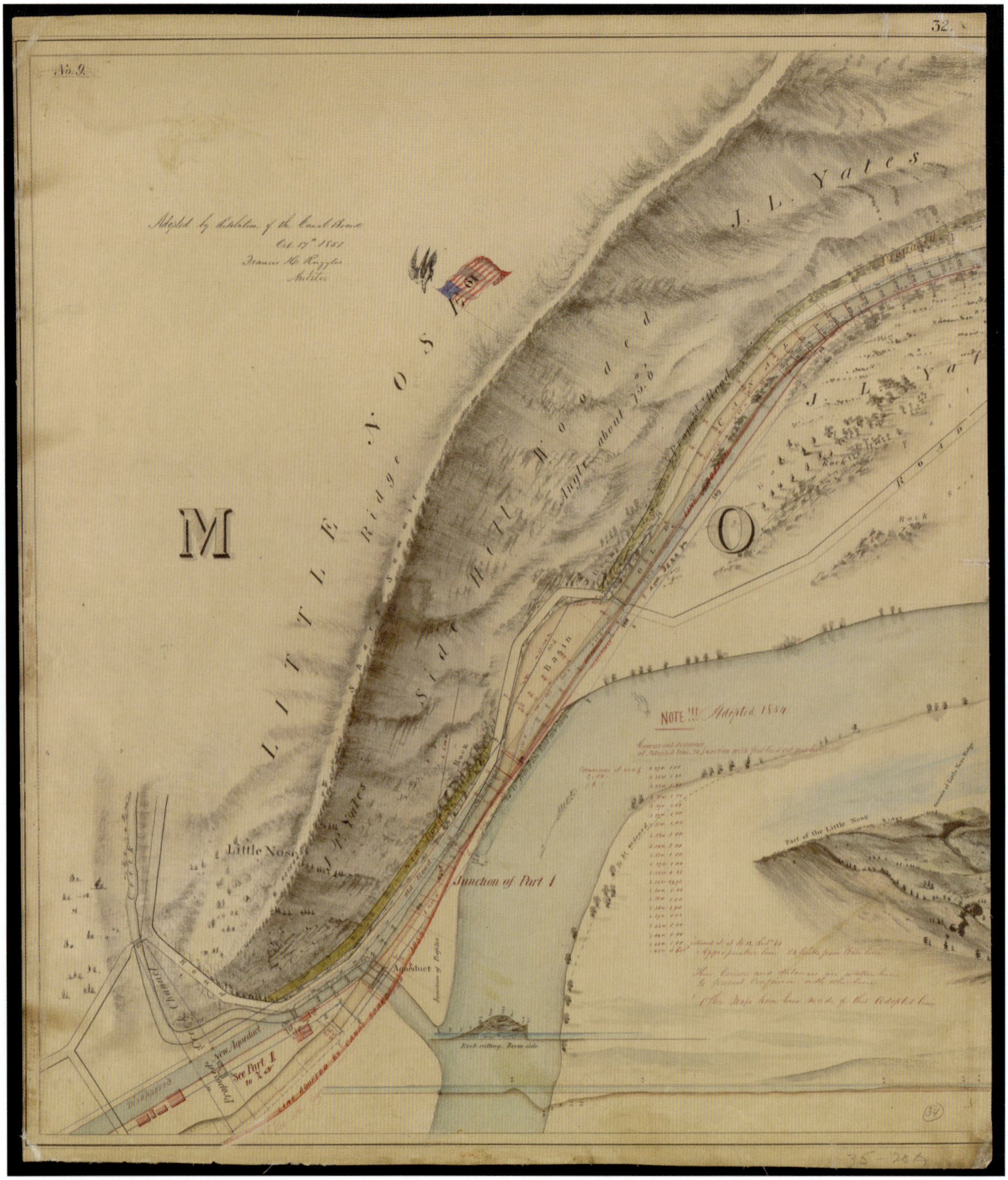

(pages 252–253) Map showing the Erie Canal in Montgomery County, "The Noses," David Vaughan, 1851. "The Noses" are located on the Mohawk River near the hamlet of Sprakers (Town of Root, Montgomery County). The geologic features include the "Big Nose" on the north and the "Little Nose" on the south side of the Mohawk River. Each is a high cliff close to the river, forming a narrow pass. To the east of the Noses the valley is wide, and to the west the valley is narrow with higher and steeper terrain. As you can see in the image, the canal passed right under the cliff of the Little Nose. Today, the New York State Thruway passes over the same spot between the Mohawk and the cliff. *Courtesy of the New York State Archives, B0292-85_V035_20A.*

33.
Proposed Road
Yates
J. L. Yates
G. I. E. Lasher
N O T H A
2
ERIE CANAL ENLA
As Projected by Char.s A. Olmsted Divis
and J. P. Goodsell. Resident.
SURVEYED BY GEORGE E. GRAY, FIRST ASSIST.
1851.
LOOKING UP THE MOHAWK
P R O F I L E.

Whipple Bridge in Fort Hunter, photograph, late nineteenth–early twentieth century. *Courtesy of the Canal Society of New York State.*

Weighlock Building at Utica, photograph, ca. 1900. In 1841 Squire Whipple designed a weighlock that could weigh up to three hundred tons. At the time it was the largest weighing device in America. *Courtesy of the Library of Congress.*

C. Holmes Hutchinson, Utica NY, watercolor on ivory, unknown artist, ca. 1852. *New York State Museum, H-1966.1.1.*

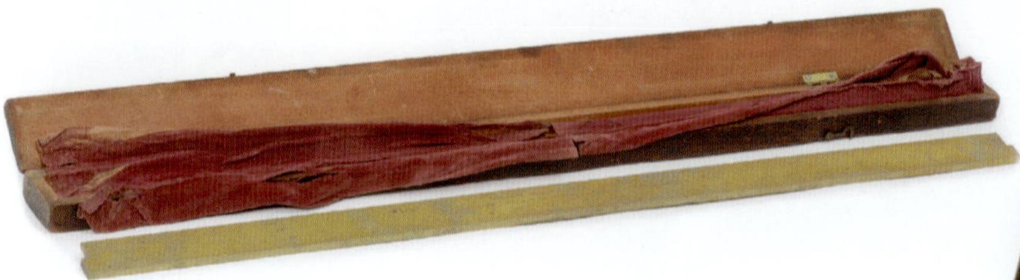

Surveying equipment: level/wye with carrying box, compass, yardstick with case, surveyor's tripod, ca. 1820–1830s. *Holmes Hutchinson's personal surveying equipment. New York State Museum, H-1946.2.1 A-B.*

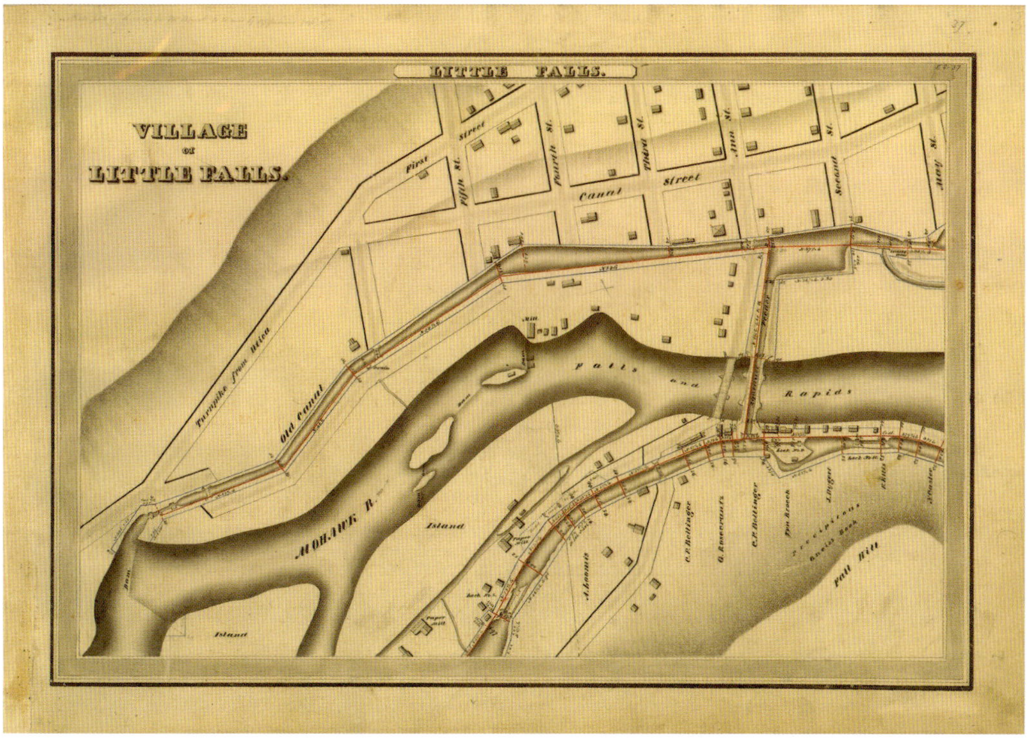

Plans made by Holmes Hutchinson, 1833. Hutchinson's blue line maps were often used in court cases to determine property lines. This map is of the Village of Little Falls. The "Old Canal" on the map is the Western Inland Lock Navigation Company Canal that bypassed the falls. It was maintained as a feeder canal once the Erie opened. *Courtesy of the New York State Archives, Maps and Plans for the Improvement of the Erie Canal, 39-1 A0848.*

Models of bridge types, Sidney Beyland, ca. 1960–1980. A variety of bridge types and styles crossed the Erie Canal. Top left, wood arch bridge, Whipple design; top right, city street bridge, Whipple design; bottom left, lattice wood bridge, Ithiel Town's design; bottom right, iron girder railroad bridge. During the enlargement, more standardized bridges came into use. *Courtesy of the Canal Society of New York State.*

The Mohawk River at Little Falls, New York, 1892, William Rickarby Miller (American, born England, 1818–1893), oil on canvas. *Arkell Museum at Canajoharie. Gift of Bartlett Arkell, 1944.*

Miller painted Erie Canal subjects throughout his life. Many of his watercolors and sketches made in the 1850s and 1860s were engraved and published in popular magazines. He also based later oils on the earlier material. This painting was based on a view by Miller that appeared in the *New York Illustrated News* in 1853.

COMMERCE AND INDUSTRY: INDUSTRIALIZATION AND AGRICULTURE

Gradually, New York transitioned from an agricultural-based economy to an industrial one along the Erie Canal corridor. As large amounts of inexpensive grain came in from the Midwest, many New York farmers turned away from large-scale grain crops to deal in cultivation of fruits and dairy production.

Industries supported by the canal also continued to grow, aided by access to global markets, technological improvements, and growing populations. The canal corridor became home to a new variety of businesses—iron and steel works, clothing processors and manufacturers, food producers, malt houses, boat builders, and sawmills, to name but a few of the types of businesses enabled by the canal's deep and reliable reach into New York and beyond. While some of these enterprises were short lived, others thrived well into the twentieth century.

James Galloway's Res., Malt House, Steam Saw Mill and Ware House Property on Erie Canal, Palmyra, engraving, ca. 1877. *New York State Library, Manuscripts and Special Collections, 974.787, fM15.*

Remington Arms Co., Ilion, photograph, late nineteenth–early twentieth century. *New York State Museum, H-1988.80.1.859.*

Lindley Boat Company, Canastota, three photographs (above and facing page), late nineteenth–early twentieth century. *New York State Museum, 1988.80.1.1323,1339,1351.*

LINDLEY BOA
STRENGTH
PURITY

LINDLEY BOAT CO.

H. A. Deland and Company's Chemical Works, Fairport, engraving, 1876. Published in *Asher and Adams Pictorial Album of American Industry*, 1876. *New York State Museum, History Office Library.*

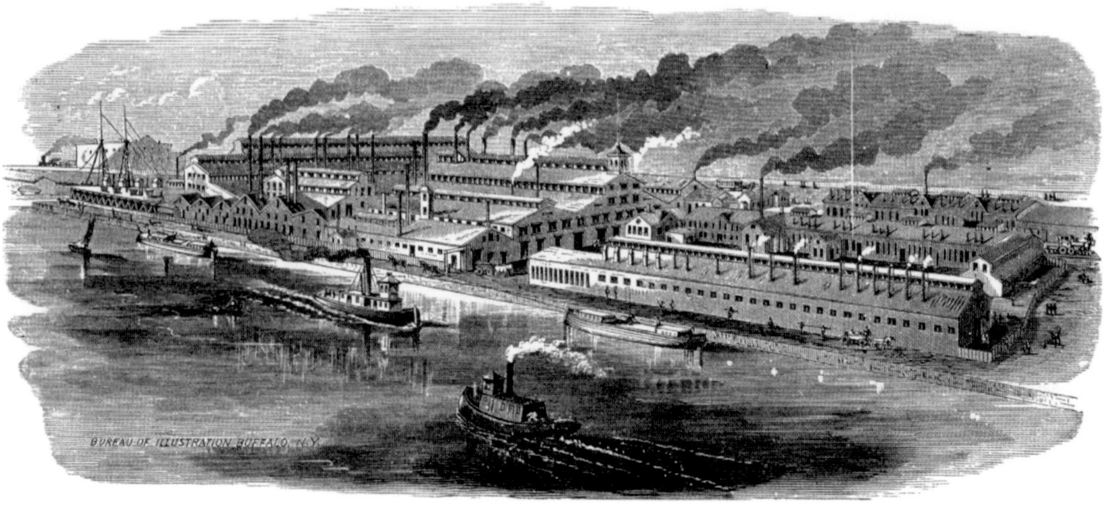

Buffalo Iron & Nail Works, Buffalo, engraving, 1876. Published in *Asher and Adams Pictorial Album of American Industry*, 1876. *New York State Museum, History Office Library.*

VIEW OF HAVEMEYERS & ELDERS SUGAR REFINERY, WILLIAMSBURGH, NEW YORK.

Havemeyers & Elders Sugar Refinery, Williamsburgh (Brooklyn), engraving, 1876. Published in *Asher and Adams Pictorial Album of American Industry*, 1876. *New York State Museum, History Office Library.*

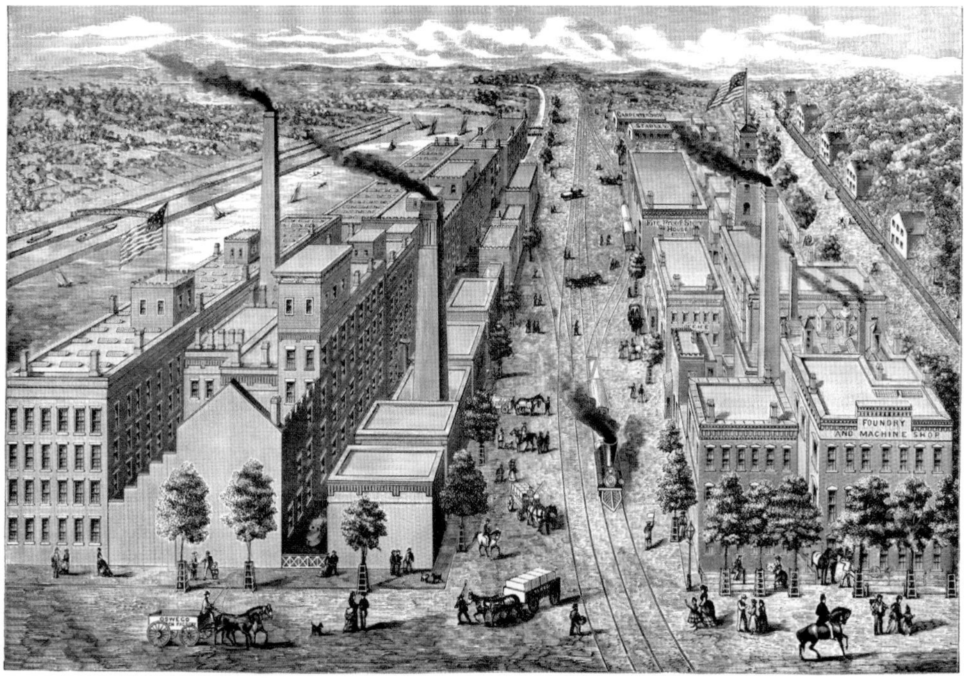

VIEW OF T. KINGSFORD & SON'S OSWEGO STARCH FACTORY, OSWEGO, N. Y.

T. Kingsford & Son's Oswego Starch Factory, Oswego, engraving, 1876. Published in *Asher and Adams Pictorial Album of American Industry*, 1876. *New York State Museum, History Office Library.*

Bird's-Eye View of Cohoes, Cohoes Falls, Erie Canal and Harmony Mills, postcard lithograph, 1853. The Erie Canal is depicted in the foreground, the water power canal is just beyond that, and, beyond that, the Mohawk River. Incorporated in 1836, the Harmony Manufacturing Company, or Harmony Mills, was built along the Erie Canal in Cohoes. Canvass White designed the complex system of waterpower canals that diverted water from the Mohawk River. The knitting company thrived, meeting the demands of the Civil War, but its most successful years came later when it billed itself as the largest complete cotton manufacturer in New York. According the Cohoes Cataract's December 10, 1864, issue, the company had "few rivals in the United States." *New York State Museum, 2006.25.1197.*

Dock Street, Schenectady, postcard, 1907. *New York State Museum, H-2006.25.8777.*

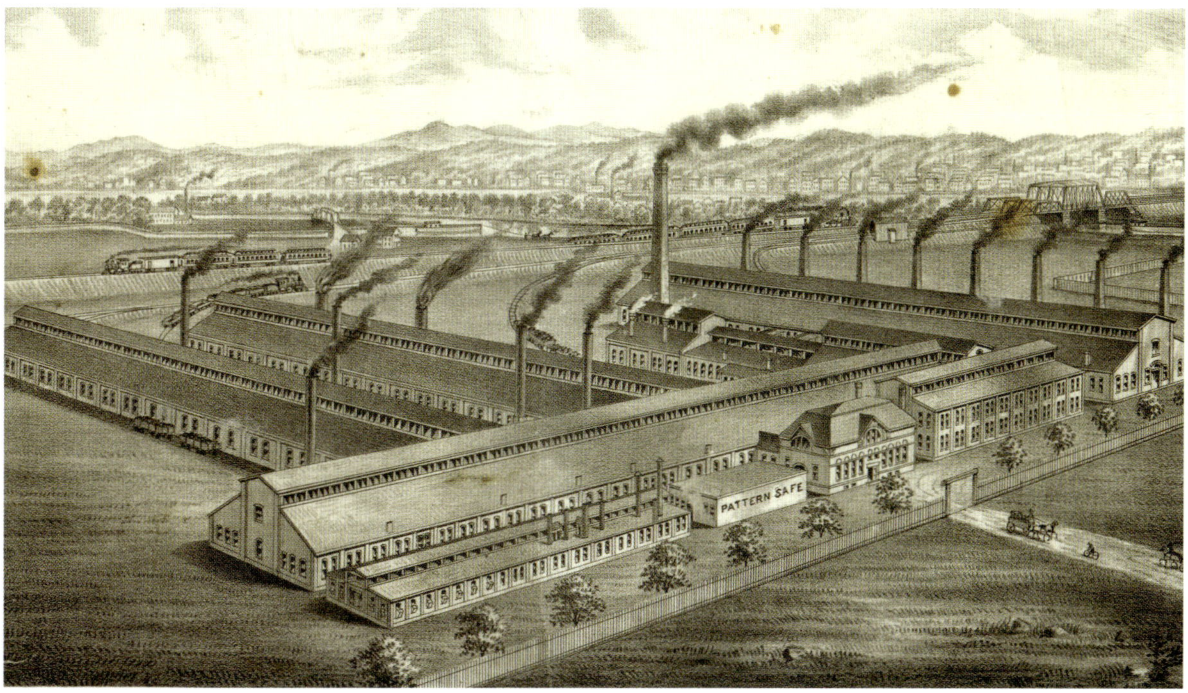

Troy Malleable Iron Co., Troy, N.Y., engraving, ca. 1850–1900. *Courtesy of the New York State Library, Manuscripts and Special Collections, PRI0004+.*

View of J. J. Gilbert's Little Falls Starch Works, Asher & Adams, engraving, ca. 1875. Around the time of the canal's enlargement, newly constructed dykes and a dam on the Mohawk River created waterpower opportunities at Seeley's Island in Little Falls. Joshua J. Gilbert built a cornstarch mill on the island in 1854. To produce power for the mill Gilbert used an eight-foot fall of water created by a dam on the river and two iron water wheels. In 1864 he built the grain elevator shown on the left side of the engraving. The elevator was built directly next to the canal, so canal boats could be loaded and unloaded. A long conveyor connected the elevator with the mill. *New York State Museum, H-1968.62.29.*

Fletcher's Furnace, Hamilton Hamilton (1847–1928), oil on canvas, 1876. Fletcher's Furnace was located between the Erie Canal and the Niagara River in the Black Rock area of Buffalo. In operation between 1864 and 1885, it produced between nine thousand and eighteen thousand tons of pig iron annually. *Courtesy of The Buffalo History Museum.*

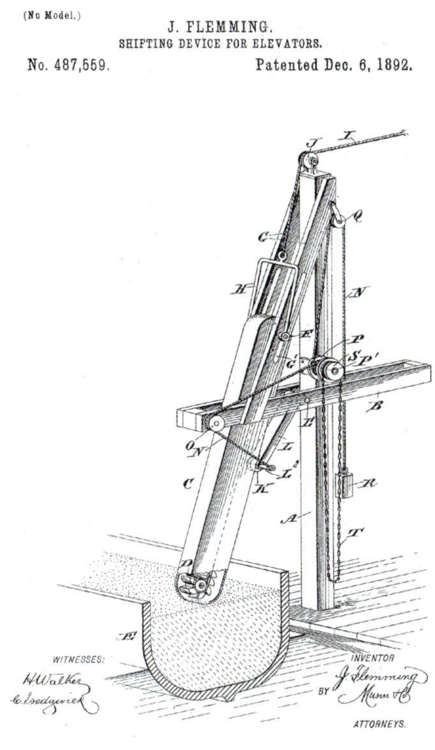

Patent model of grain elevator arm, James Flemming, 1892. With grains of all kinds being among the primary products shipped on the canal, innovations to improve its transport and storage were crucial. This invention, also known as a "marine leg," is for a new and improved shifting device, "especially designed for grain-elevators used to load or unload vessels, and arranged to conveniently shift the elevator-leg to hold the same contact with the grain."* The leg was designed to attach to a floating or land-based grain elevator and had the ability to reach out into a boat to either load or unload the vessel. *Courtesy of The Buffalo History Museum.*
**James Flemming, "Shifting Device of Elevators," Buffalo, New York, United States of America Patent 487,559, December 6, 1892.*

Cheese press, nineteenth century. *New York State Museum, H-INV-5043.*

Cheese rack, nineteenth century. *New York State Museum, H-1923.1.2.*

Butter churn, "Brainard's Churn, Rotary Dash," nineteenth century. *New York State Museum, H-XX.196.1.*

The dairy industry grew in New York as the Erie Canal made access to Midwestern grain easy and cheap, and farmers turned to dairy production. Implements like these are artifacts from the dairy boom.

Fodder cutter, Sanford Wasson & Co., Fulton, ca. 1855. *New York State Museum Collection, H-1901.1.28.*

Feed cutter, M. Gaffey & Co., Buffalo, ca. 1860. *New York State Museum Collection, H-1901.1.50.*

These instruments cut straw or hay, or fodder, into smaller pieces that could be mixed into animal feed. An entire industry emerged along New York's canals focused on the manufacture of machinery and other products that helped to mechanize agriculture across New York and the Midwest.

Model hay bale, Albany Hay Press Works, ca. 1854. This model was used by the Albany Hay Press Works to advertise its services. *New York State Museum Collection, H-1982.34.7.*

Match box and matches, Frankfort, New York, nineteenth century. The match industry began in Frankfort in southern Herkimer County shortly after the Civil War. *New York State Museum, H-1969.66.4010.1.*

Medicine bottle in box, H. H. Warner & Co., Rochester, New York, ca. 1887. Hulbert Harrington Warner (1842–1923) of Rochester built a business empire manufacturing safes and, later, medicines. The prosperity brought to communities by the canal enabled a wide variety of industries to blossom. *New York State Museum, H-1969.66.409 A & B.*

Golden Shield Pure Food Baking Powder tin, Monroe County Chemical Co., Fairport, New York, ca. 1900. *New York State Museum, H-1969.66.1384.*

Wooden box, "Nourishing, Nutritious, Delicate Wheatlet Superior to Oat Meal," Franklin Mills Co., Lockport, New York, ca. 1870–1907. The canal facilitated a ready supply of grains, which fueled a large cereal business in Buffalo and other grain-related food, like Wheatlets made by the Franklin Mills Company in nearby Lockport. *New York State Museum, H-1969.66.1201.*

Hat, Samuel Stocking Company, Utica, New York, ca. 1860. Textile manufacturers, such as Samuel Stocking Company, thrived along the corridor during the second half of the nineteenth century. *New York State Museum, H-1947.4.7.*

Lap robe, Crosby Frisian Fur Co., Rochester, New York, ca. 1900. Lap robes were common, and necessary, accessories in a time when most vehicles exposed travelers to the elements. The Crosby Frisian Fur Company was founded in 1889. With the decline of the American Bison, G. N. Crosby began experimenting with cow, horse, and dog skins to produce bulky robes and coats. The company went on to use seal, gray and red fox, coyote, beaver, otter, raccoon, skunk, mink, ermine, and squirrel. *New York State Museum, H-XX.255.8 or .9.*

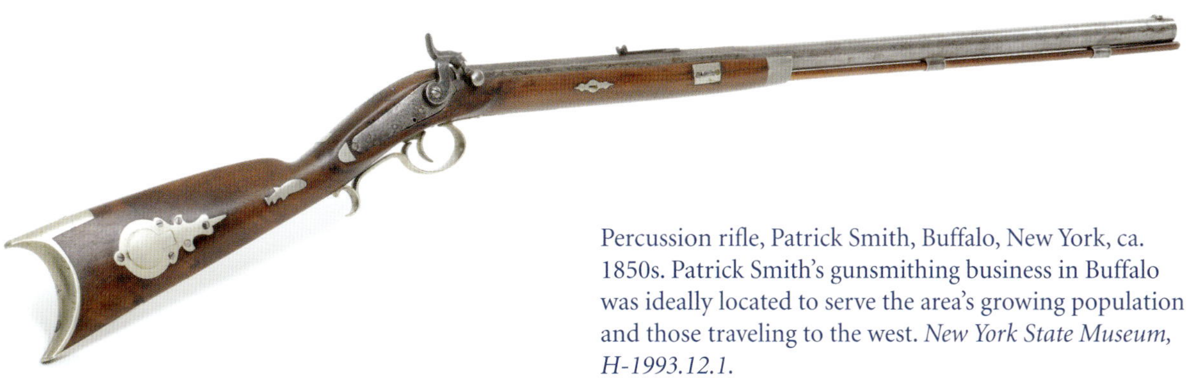

Percussion rifle, Patrick Smith, Buffalo, New York, ca. 1850s. Patrick Smith's gunsmithing business in Buffalo was ideally located to serve the area's growing population and those traveling to the west. *New York State Museum, H-1993.12.1.*

Fort Plain, N.Y., 1879, 1879, H. H. Rowley & Company (American, active 1870s–1880s), artist and publisher; Beck and Pauli (American, active late nineteenth century), printers, lithograph. This view looking south from Nelliston across the Mohawk River shows the growth of Fort Plain. The rise of industry along the Erie Canal spurred development even in small villages. The canal is featured prominently as it stretches diagonally across the composition. *New York State Museum, H-1982.156.2.*

From Flour City to Flower City

The Genesee River provided abundant opportunities for water power and access to Genesee Valley wheat. During the first couple of decades of the canal's operation, Rochester held a monopoly on milling that wheat into flour. However, by the 1850s Rochester no longer held the market on flour manufactory, as large-scale milling had begun in the Midwest prior to shipment and in Buffalo. In response, Rochester transitioned from the "Flour City" to the "Flower City." Led by companies like Ellwanger & Barry Nursery Company, Rochester became internationally known for cultivating seeds for flowers and fruit trees.

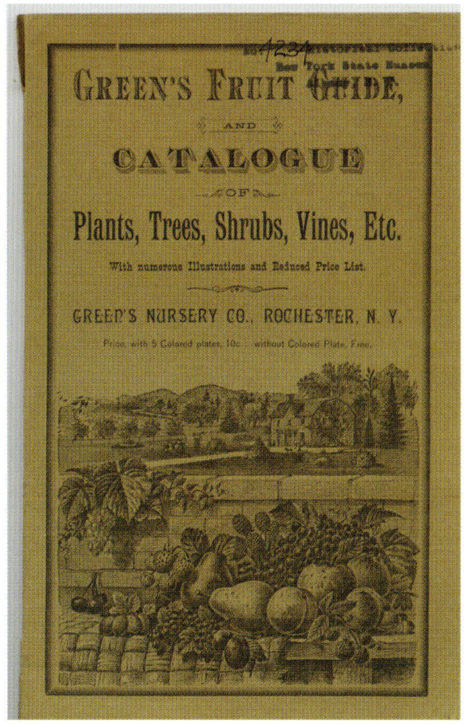

Green's Fruit Guide and Catalogue of Plants, Trees, Shrubs, Vines, Etc., Green's Nursery, Rochester, New York (front cover and back cover), ca. 1850. *New York State Museum, H-1937.10.82.*

Aster Flag on the Flower Seed Farm of James Vick's Sons, Rochester, postcard (front and back), ca. 1910. *New York State Museum, H-1972.85.731.*

Flour bag, J. G. Davis Co., Rochester, late nineteenth–early twentieth century. *New York State Museum Collection, H-1969.66.1201.*

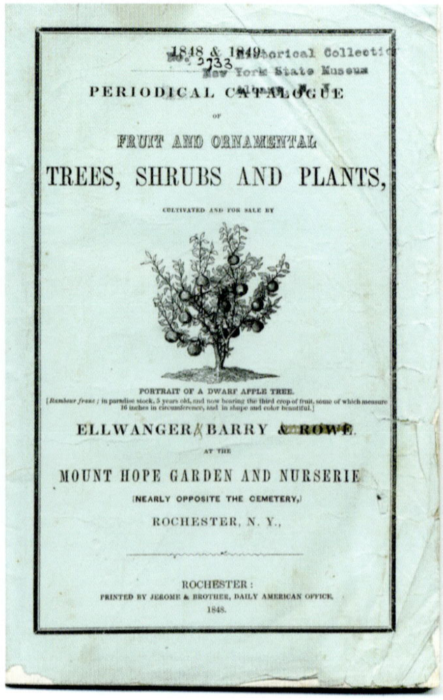

Periodical Catalogue of Fruit and Ornamental Trees, Shrubs and Plants, Ellwanger & Barry at the Mount Hope Garden and Nurseries, Rochester, 1848. *New York State Museum, H-1937.10.73.*

Seed crate, "Crosman Bros., Seeds, Rochester, NY," ca. 1921. *New York State Museum, H-1969.66.1237.*

George Ellwanger (*left*) and Patrick Barry (*right*), oil on canvas, unknown artists, nineteenth century. Proprietors of Ellwanger & Barry Nursery Company in Rochester, New York. The expansion and success of the nursery, from its founding in 1840 through 1865, helped Rochester earn its moniker, "The Flower City." George Ellwanger, a native of Germany, immigrated to the United States in 1835. Patrick Barry emigrated from Belfast, Ireland, the following year. Their company owned five hundred acres of land to cultivate seeds, flowers, and fruit trees, and to house its employees. *Courtesy of the Rochester Historical Society.*

Agricultural medal, awarded to Ellwanger & Barry by the Brooklyn Horticultural Society for best collection of pears, 1858. Agricultural medal, awarded to Ellwanger & Barry by the Allgemein Garten-Ausstellung, Hamburg, 1897. These medals were awarded to Ellwanger & Barry Nursery of Rochester, New York, for their horticultural work. *Courtesy of the Rochester Historical Society, 1000.008.0100, 1000.008.0121.*

Upper Falls of the Genesee River, 1858. J. Jackson (active nineteenth century), oil on canvas. Waterfalls on the rivers near the Erie Canal were popular subjects and appeared in paintings and prints and on ceramics. Their beauty typically appealed to artists as awe-inspiring views associated with the romantic landscape tradition. Interestingly, J. Jackson also emphasized the growing city of Rochester here, rather than solely featuring the natural landmark. *Rochester Historical Society*.

Genesee Falls, Rochester, plate, ca. 1830. Coalport Porcelain Factory (English, active beginning 1792), earthenware, transfer printed. *New York State Museum, H-1996.6.6.3.*

Clinton Square, Syracuse, New York (*Syracuse by Moonlight*), ca. 1871, Johann Mengels Culverhouse (American, born Holland, 1820–ca. 1890s), oil on canvas. *Onondaga Historical Association Museum, Syracuse, New York.*

Culverhouse first arrived in the United States from The Hague in 1849. Following travel and a period of study in Paris, he returned to the United States and established a studio in Syracuse. The Dutch painting tradition, with which he would have been familiar, is rich in canal scenes. *Moonlight* was Culverhouse's specialty, and his talent in the genre is apparent in this painting.

W. H. Farrar & Company: The Beginnings of Syracuse China

William H. Farrar, a native of Vermont, opened a pottery in Geddes (later part of Syracuse), around 1840. Located on West Genesee Street, Farrar's pottery produced gray salt-glazed stoneware crocks and jugs thrown on a wheel. By 1850 the pottery was using 225 tons of clay and 500 cords of wood per year, and it employed six men. The clay was not locally sourced and was brought in on the canal.

In 1857 Farrar sold the West Genesee Street works to a former employee and set up a new pottery on Furnace Street, closer to the Erie Canal. There, he began producing molded stoneware animals with a brown "Rockingham" glaze, in addition to the wheel-thrown salt-glazed stoneware pieces.

Farrar sold his factory to Charles W. Coykendall & Company in 1868, and the name was changed to Empire Pottery. Production then shifted away from utilitarian storage items to finer tableware.

Corner of Decorating Room, Heinrich Ries, photograph, before 1900. In the latter part of the nineteenth century, women were frequently hired to hand-paint decorations on ceramics. Women were believed to be especially suited to the task under the assumption that they had superior fine motor skills and attention to detail. *Clays of New York: Their Properties and Uses*, New York State Museum Bulletin 35 (June 1900). *New York State Museum, H-1990.69.On025.*

Workman Carrying Sagger of Ware into Glost Kiln, Heinrich Ries, photograph, before 1900. In this image, a workman carries on his head a heavy load of greenware, or unfired ceramics, to a kiln. *Clays of New York: Their Properties and Uses, New York State Museum Bulletin 35* (June 1900). *New York State Museum, H-1990.69.On017.*

Pressing White Ware, Onondaga Pottery Co., Syracuse, NY, Heinrich Ries, photograph, before 1900. Plaster molds were used to shape the clay into various forms, including plates. Here, a potter places a flat disk, or a bat, of clay into a mold. *Clays of New York: Their Properties and Uses, New York State Museum Bulletin 35* (June 1900). *New York State Museum, H-1990.69.On018.1-.2.*

Making Cups, Heinrich Ries, photograph, before 1900. Potters in the factory worked on wheels to produce the round bodies for cups, which would then be further formed with the use of plaster molds. *Clays of New York: Their Properties and Uses, New York State Museum Bulletin 35* (June 1900). *New York State Museum, H-1990.69.On021.*

In July of 1871 an expansion of Empire Pottery was announced. Production demands at the factory had exceeded the capacity of the facilities, but the former owners did not have the necessary capital for an expansion, so a group of sixteen businessmen formed to create the Onondaga Pottery Company. The newly expanded pottery focused on white earthenware products, designed for everyday table use.

When it was founded, the Onondaga Pottery Company produced plain, undecorated ceramics. In 1884 Elmer Walter established the Boston China Decorating Works across from the Onondaga workshop. Four years later, in 1886, a fire destroyed the decorating works; the flames had hardly been doused when Onondaga hired Walter and his staff.

In 1885 James Pass became superintendent of the pottery, beginning a period marked by research and innovation in the company. Under Pass's leadership, the pottery developed the first vitreous china body made in America, a glasslike glazing that makes china both shinier and more durable. This ware was presented at the World's Columbian Exposition in 1893 and soon featured the "Syracuse China" back stamp. The durable ware became a popular

W. H. Farrar & Company sign, ca. 1860. This "stoneware pitcher," which is actually made of metal, appeared as a sign above the W. H. Farrar & Company and remained over the Onondaga Pottery Company until the Fayette Street works were razed in 1971. *Courtesy of the Onondaga Historical Association Museum, Syracuse, New York.*

Spaniel figurine, W. H. Farrar & Company, Geddes, New York, ca. 1857–1868. Following W. H. Farrar & Company's move to Furnace Street in Geddes, the pottery began producing molded ware, including figurines like this dog. The company also began using a mottled brown glaze, known as "Rockingham glaze," to mimic the popular Rockingham ware imported from England. *New York State Museum, H-1983.139.9.*

Stoneware jug, W. H. Farrar & Company, Geddes, New York, ca. 1857. Proximity to the canal and salt production in the Geddes-Syracuse area helped the pottery industry thrive. Salt was used to help form the necessary glaze on the pottery. As early as 1824 Amos Russell was producing pottery in the area. W. H. Farrar & Company, makers of this jug, started business around 1840. *New York State Museum, H-2010.21.13.*

Onondaga Pottery Company sign, ca. mid-twentieth century. The Onondaga Pottery Company advertises its "Syracuse China" line, for which the company was best known. *Courtesy of the Onondaga Historical Association Museum, Syracuse, New York.*

Sample plate, Onondaga Pottery Company, 1911. Custom institutional ware made for hotels, restaurants, and railroads made up a large part of the Onondaga Pottery Company's business. Since custom orders required special molds to make the pottery, a sample of the work had to be reviewed by a representative from the company before a custom order went into production. *New York State Museum, H-1997.48.5.*

Clay, ca. 1930. A sample of the clay used by the Onondaga Pottery Company. The clay was brought in from England and North Carolina in the 1930s. *New York State Museum, H-1980.52.1-.9.*

Cup mold, Onondaga Pottery Company, ca. 1930. Plaster molds were used to form the body and handle of a teacup. *New York State Museum, H-1980.52.82.*

Cup and saucer, Onondaga Pottery Company, ca. 1930. This cup and saucer are in the bisque stage of production. They have been fired once in the kiln and would be ready for decoration (either hand-painted, or through the use of decals), glazing, and an additional firing. *New York State Museum, H-1980.52.51 and H-1980.52.53.*

choice for hotels, restaurants, and railroads, for years representing 70 percent of the china used on trains in the United States.

Syracuse China continued its innovation in the production of china, perfecting a way to apply decorative decals under the glaze (a more economical way to produce decorated dinnerware than hand-painting).

In 1971 family ownership of the company ended, and the Syracuse China Corporation was formed, taking its name from the most popular ware produced by the pottery. Subsequent mergers and buyouts have led to new ownership, but ceramics continue to be produced today under the Syracuse China name.

MOTHER OF CITIES

> **This marvelous western metropolis [referring to Chicago] which most of you have made your adopted home is New York's grandchild. New York made possible Chicago's great growth when she opened through her territory the Erie canal . . ."**
>
> **—New York Governor Roswell P. Flower, September 4, 1893[1]**

> **If the canal is to be a shower of gold, it will fall upon New York [City]; if a river of gold, it will flow into her lap.**
>
> **—Elisha Williams, state assemblyman, Columbia County, 1817[2]**

The Erie Canal has many nicknames, including "Mother of Cities." The immigrants and commerce that traveled her waters helped to establish the major cities of western New York, such as Utica, Syracuse, Rochester, and Buffalo, but also those of the Great Lakes region, including Chicago, Duluth, Milwaukee,

New York Harbor, photograph, ca. 1880. View of New York Harbor with Castle Garden in the background. Note the various vessels, including tugboats and barges. *New York State Museum, Stoddard Collection, H-1972.84.366a.*

Cleveland, and Detroit. When the Erie Canal connected New York City to the west, the city's primacy as the capital of commerce and culture was guaranteed. New York would grow to become the nation's largest trading, manufacturing, and financial center.

As the commercial gateway of North America for much of the nineteenth century, New York City enjoyed a monopoly on a majority of western New York and Midwest products that flowed through the canal to New York City, contributing to the growing Atlantic trade.

Shipping Grain at Brooklyn Elevators, photographic reproduction from original by G.W. Peters, 1897. Grains shipped by canal could transfer to oceangoing vessels in New York Harbor, from whence they were shipped anywhere around the world. *New York State Museum, H-1979.154.9.*

The City of New York, lithograph, 1889. *New York State Museum, H-1972.26.1.*

Western Union Telegraph Company stock ticker, ca. 1900. The Erie Canal inaugurated a period of unrivaled prosperity in New York State. New York City emerged as one of the greatest commercial and financial centers in the world. The stock ticker is a printing device that records prices paid for stocks or commodities at exchange markets. Electric stock indicators came into use in New York City in the later 1860s. *New York State Museum, H-1974.55.1.*

SCENE ON THE GREAT FLOUR DOCKS, COENTIES SLIP, EAST RIVER, NEW YORK.

New York Harbor, engraving in *Harper's Weekly*, November 15, 1873. The top scene depicts the active waterfront at Coenties Slip in the East River. The bottom scene shows a floating grain elevator transferring grain from a canal boat to a ship. This invention enabled boats to be loaded and unloaded without docking. Floating grain elevators were used in Buffalo Harbor and New York Harbor and saved time and expense for shippers. *New York State Museum, H-1979.154.8.*

Grain Elevator of New York Central and Hudson River Railroad, W. P. Snyder after Theodore R. Davis (American, 1840–1894), *Harper's Weekly*, December 22, 1877, wood engraving. *Erie Canal Museum.*

The Erie Canal prompted the invention and building of new types of structures, which interested the public and often appeared in the press. A new design for a steam-powered grain elevator was developed in Buffalo by Joseph Dart in 1842, allowing for greater volumes of grain to be moved and stored along the canal. The grain elevator shown in this engraving was erected on the Hudson River at Sixty-Second Street in Manhattan to handle the large shipments of grain coming in from the Midwest via the canal and railroads.

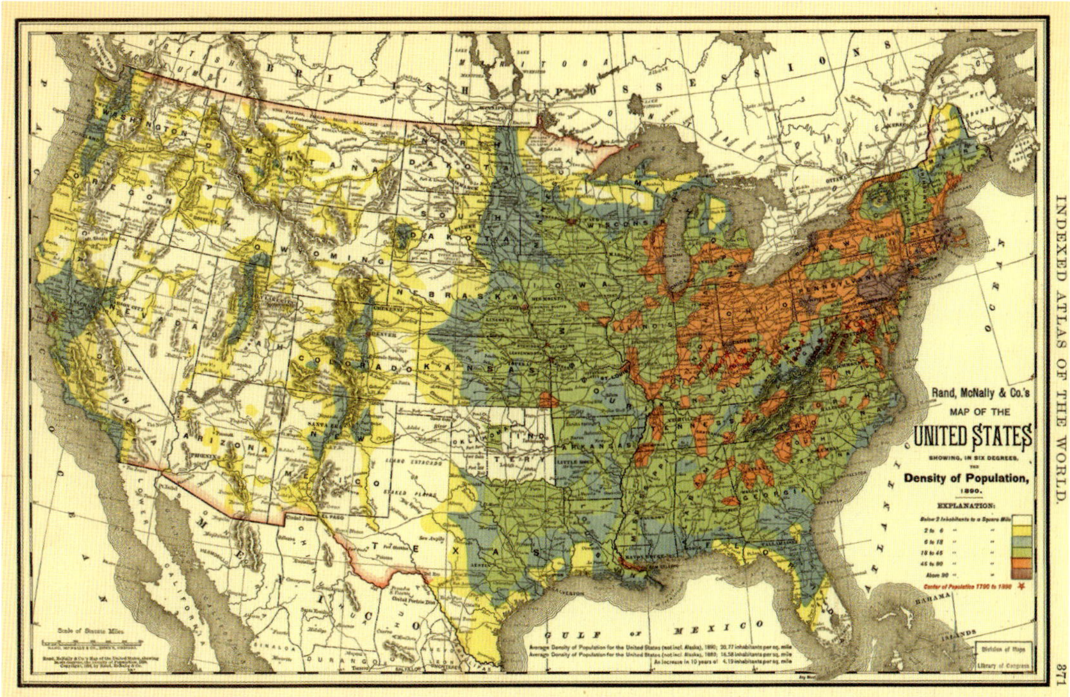

Map of the United States Showing, in Six Degrees, the Density of Population, 1890, Rand, McNally & Co., 1892. *Library of Congress.*

Buffalo and Its Waterfront, Illustrated Buffalo Express, engraving, April 14, 1895. As the western terminus of the Erie Canal, Buffalo grew from a small village to one of the largest cities in America by the mid-nineteenth century. *Courtesy of the New York State Library, Manuscripts and Special Collections, PRI5750.*

City of Buffalo, 1873, Asa Coolidge Warren (American, 1819–1904), artist, engraving, William Wellstood (American, born Scotland, 1819–1900), engraver. Published by D. Appleton & Company. *New York State Museum, H-1969.54.5.*

This engraving originally appeared in *Picturesque America; or The Land We Live In*. Since this publication promoted tourism in the United States, the artist chose to focus on a wealthy, well-kept neighborhood rather than on the more industrial parts of Buffalo.

Buffalo on Lake Erie, vegetable dish, ca. 1835, Enoch Wood & Sons (Staffordshire, England, active 1818–1840). Earthenware, transfer printed. *New York State Museum, H-1969.44.7.*

Erie Canal at Buffalo, plate, ca. 1829. Ralph Stevenson (English, active ca. 1800–1836), after an engraving by W. H. Lizars, original sketch by Captain Basil Hall. Earthenware, transfer printed. *New York State Museum, H-1970.8.5.*

Manufacturers of transfer-printed earthenware did not shy away from scenes of industry. The two pieces shown here (right, and page 288) depict the Erie Canal terminus at Buffalo Harbor, seen from the same vantage point.

Rochester, ca. 1870, unknown artist, G. G. Lange (German, active 1860s–1880s), publisher, Charles Magnus (American, born Germany, 1826–1900), publisher. Hand-colored lithographic transfer from engraved plate. *New York State Museum, H-1969.9.1.*

The impact of the Erie Canal made Rochester a boomtown. In 1815 just over three hundred people lived there; by 1830 the population had increased to almost ten thousand. This bird's-eye view shows the further expansion of the city by the late-nineteenth century with the canal in the foreground winding through the city to the aqueduct over the Genesee River. New York City publisher Charles Magnus recognized there was a market for smaller-sized views to be framed and also used on letterhead.

THE RISE OF RAILROADS

> At Little Falls, while before the depot eating house, we were told that the bridge a little way off had been bored and plugged with powder to blow the bridge and cars up, by the opposing and mob crowd of the Erie Canal men, who fought the cars because they damage the canal interests, and the cars must not run, in injury to the older canal. So the locomotive was detached, and the bridge, a small one just beyond the depot, inspected, and the engine run over it; and backed up and we taken over it, without an accident.
>
> —Samuel Parker, railroad passenger, 1837[3]

The introduction of the passenger railroad to the Erie Canal corridor in 1831 marked a new chapter in the competition for commercial transport. The canallers did not welcome the competition, but actual sabotage as described in the quote was a rare occurrence. Still, canallers had good reason to worry—the railroads were faster, they ran in the wintertime, and they could be built where canals could not. However, they were built peicemeal, with no main line between Albany and Buffalo. This was a big challenge when it came to moving freight across the state, so the railroads of the 1830s and 1840s mainly catered to passenger traffic. The early railroads also provided farmers and merchants without connection to the lateral canals or rivers a way to ship goods. By 1842 railroads connected Buffalo to Albany, along multiple lines that were run by separate companies.

The First Railway Train, Edward L. Henry, 1945 reproduction based on a section of the original painting from 1892–1893. The Mohawk and Hudson Railroad was the first passenger train in the Northeast. It ran from Albany to Schenectady and was built to supplement the canal. The trip between the two locations took thirty-eight minutes. Passengers could board the train in Albany and bypass the sixteen canal locks to Schenectady, which saved an entire day of travel. *Courtesy of the New York State Library, Manuscripts and Special Collections, PRI5249+.*

Another barrier to moving freight in the early years of railroading was that the iron rails could not bear heavy freight. However, by the end of the 1850s the Bessemer steel process made the rails strong and able to support larger locomotives and trains to move vast amounts of goods. By the middle of the nineteenth century, the railroads began to rival the canals in terms of freight. Still, canal promoters believed the Midwest would provide more goods than either canals or railroads alone could carry.

That theory was put to the test throughout the second half of the nineteenth century, starting with the completion of the New York and Erie Railroad in 1851. The new trunk line railroad bypassed the Hudson River–Erie Canal route and linked New York City to Dunkirk, New York, on Lake Erie, more than four hundred miles away, through the Southern Tier of New York. In 1853 several rail lines linking Albany and Buffalo consolidated to form the New York Central Railroad. Up until that point, the state government enacted regulations, imposing taxes and tolls, to keep the railroads from getting too strong an economic advantage over the canals. Even with the regulations lifted, canals helped to hold the railroad shipping prices in check, denying them a true monopoly on freight. This was the most compelling argument for supporters to continue to improve the canal through the Barge Canal era of the early twentieth century.

Model of the DeWitt Clinton train, Fred R. Cron, ca. 1948. The DeWitt Clinton train was a subject of artistic expression for generations after its launch in 1831. Typical of early railroading, the first coaches were literally stagecoaches mounted on railroad "trucks." Built at the West Point Foundry, the DeWitt Clinton was only the third steam locomotive constructed in the United States, and the first passenger train in the Northeast. *New York State Museum, H-1948.7.3 A-H.*

Rail Road Scene in Little Falls, William Henry Bartlett, R. Sands, and George Virtue, engraving, 1838. Passenger service from Schenectady to Utica was available by 1836. Most passenger traffic would soon opt for the quicker railroad over canal packets. *New York State Museum, H-1970.70.14.*

Map of the State of New York: Showing the Locations of Its Canals and Railroads, David Vaughan, 1857. By 1850 more than thirty railroads served the state with over sixteen hundred miles of track and another one thousand miles under construction. Many of the earliest railroad lines followed the trade routes established by the canal system. By 1860 New York had the nation's most extensive railroad system, which eventually would dominate the state's transportation system for both freight and passenger traffic. *Courtesy of the New York State Archives.*

Railroad Crossing Sign, Delaware and Hudson Railroad, twentieth century. *New York State Museum, H-1976.171.1.*

New York Central and Hudson River Railroad lantern, nineteenth century. Rail travel from Albany to Buffalo in the early days required using several different rail lines. In 1853 several lines merged to form the New York Central Railroad (NYCRR). Led by Albany's Erastus Corning, the company continued to grow and played an important role moving freight and influencing product prices well into the twentieth century. *New York State Museum, H-1971.74.8.*

THE AGE OF SOCIAL REFORM

> **We hold these truths to be self-evident: that all men and women are created equal . . .**
>
> **—Declaration of Sentiments, Women's Rights Convention, Seneca Falls, New York, July 1848**

The Erie Canal put the Empire State on the cutting-edge of reform at a time when Americans were searching for their young nation's identity and purpose. The influx of new young people who came to western New York State because of the canals, and the new businesses and ideas that came with them, made the area ripe for reform. Spurred by the Second Great Awakening, New Yorkers felt called upon not just to better their own lives but to perfect society.

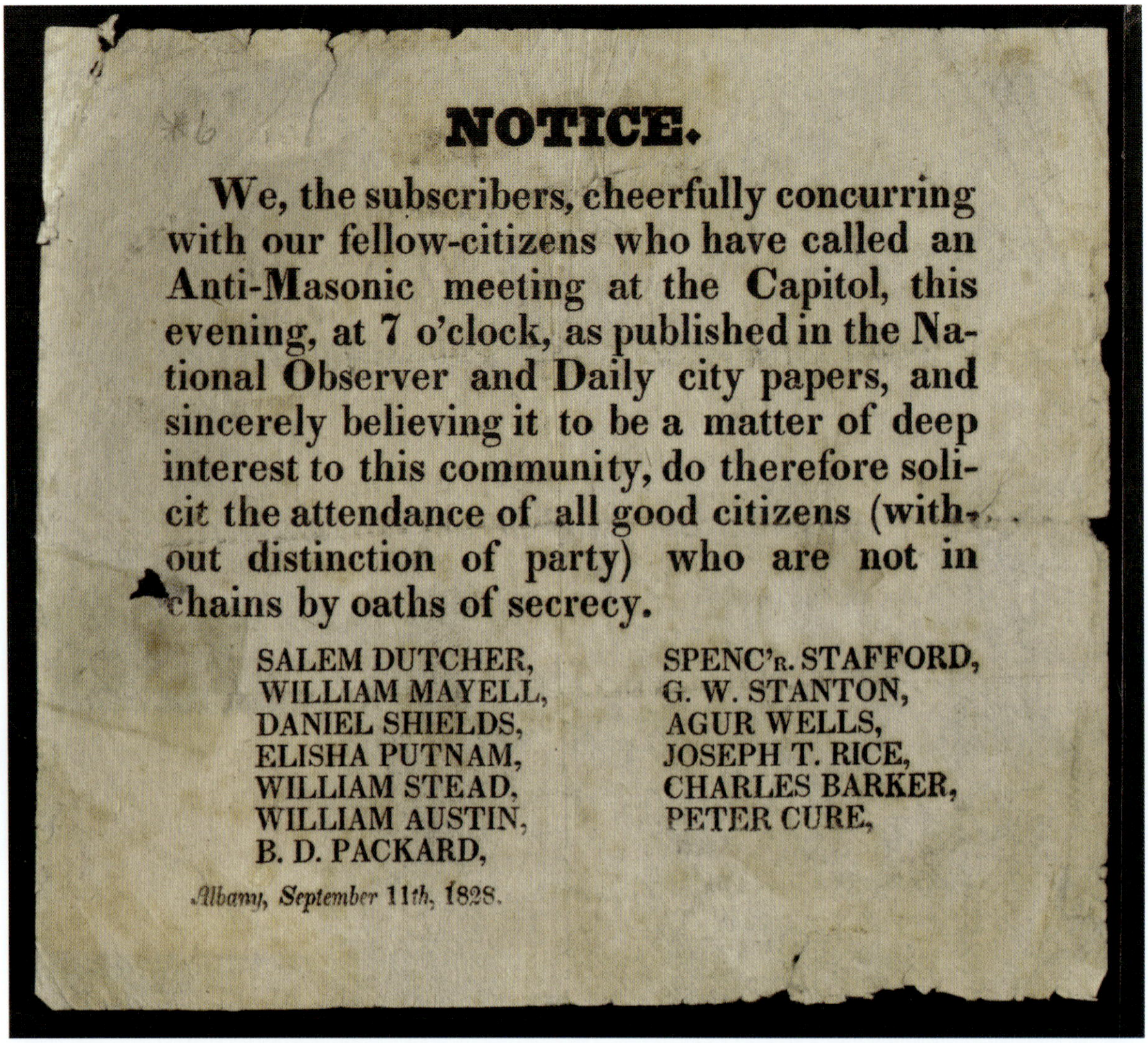

NOTICE.

We, the subscribers, cheerfully concurring with our fellow-citizens who have called an Anti-Masonic meeting at the Capitol, this evening, at 7 o'clock, as published in the National Observer and Daily city papers, and sincerely believing it to be a matter of deep interest to this community, do therefore solicit the attendance of all good citizens (without distinction of party) who are not in chains by oaths of secrecy.

SALEM DUTCHER,
WILLIAM MAYELL,
DANIEL SHIELDS,
ELISHA PUTNAM,
WILLIAM STEAD,
WILLIAM AUSTIN,
B. D. PACKARD,
SPENC'R. STAFFORD,
G. W. STANTON,
AGUR WELLS,
JOSEPH T. RICE,
CHARLES BARKER,
PETER CURE,

Albany, September 11th, 1828.

Anti-Masonic broadside, Albany, 1828. Many historians point to the Anti-Masonic movement of the late 1820s as the start of organized social-improvement efforts in western New York. *Courtesy of the New York State Library, Manuscripts and Special Collections, BRO 3842.*

Some, unsettled by change, sought comfort in religion, while still others became evangelical crusaders determined to cure the country of its social and political ills. The abolition of slavery, mental health reform, women's rights, and temperance were influenced by the people living and working along the Erie Canal.

The Second Great Awakening

The Second Great Awakening was a Christian revival movement in the first half of the nineteenth century. Upstate New York—the Erie Canal corridor, in particular—was a hotbed of religious activity. Disrupted by rapid social and economic change before the Civil War, the area was fertile ground for the spread of evangelical Protestantism, reform movements, and attempts at utopian communities.

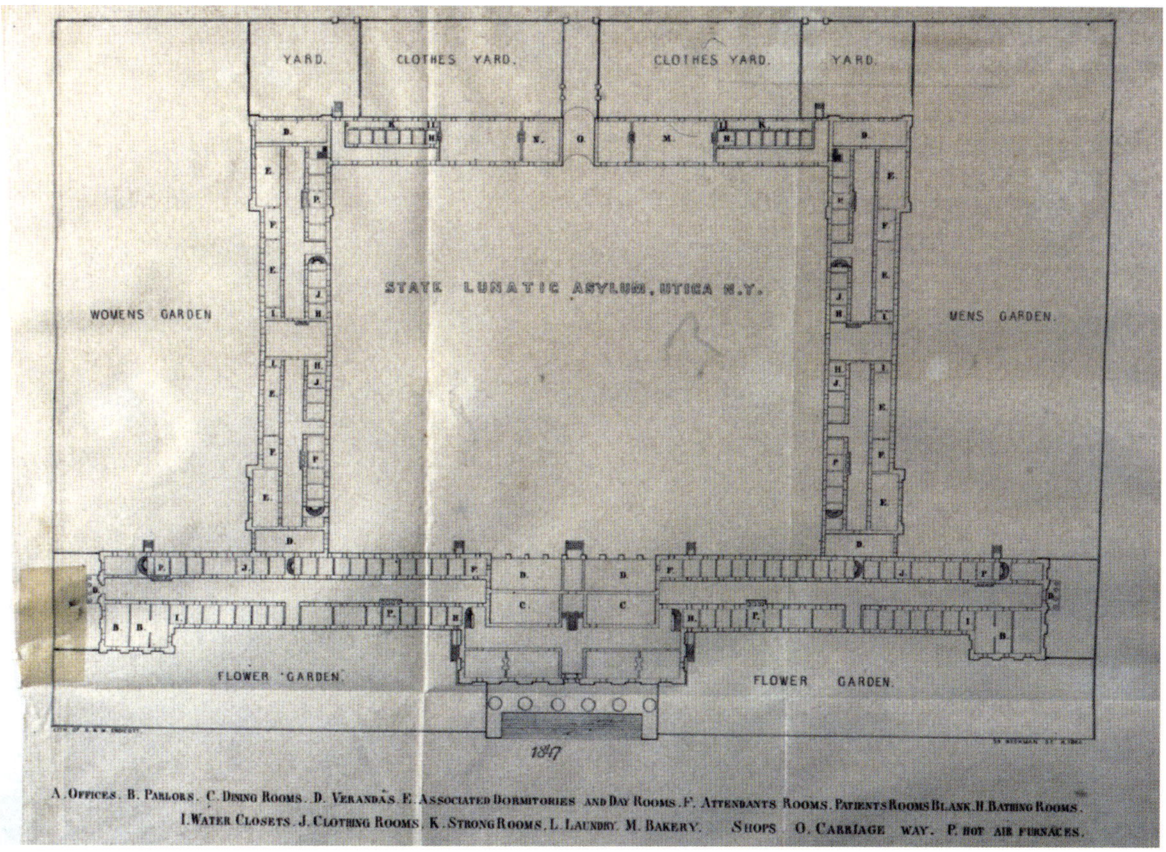

New York State Lunatic Asylum, Utica, engraving, artist unknown, nineteenth century (*above*). Plans for the State Lunatic Asylum, Utica, N.Y., ink on paper, Lewis Bradley and L. M. Taylor, ca. 1839 (*below*). The Utica Asylum was a State-run hospital built next to the canal using canal revenues. The success of the State-run canal system together with the spirit of social and economic improvement inspired public works projects, like the Utica Asylum, and set a precedent for the rest of the nation. *New York State Museum, H-1997.19, H-1997.19.2.*

Canallers, generally, were viewed by middle-class residents as people with no apparent regard for morals and values. Further, the children working on the canal represented a dark future for American society. Inspired by the Second Great Awakening, religious organizations started sending missionaries to ride the boats and save as many souls as possible.

Methodist Camp Meeting, E. W. Clay and H. R. Robinson, engraving, 1836. *New York State Museum, H-1976.26.13.*

"Burned-Over District" Map. In addition to revival in mainstream religions in western New York, new and fringe religions thrived for a time in the canal corridor. The term "Burned-Over District" has a few potential origins; some historians believe that it refers to an "analogy between the fires of the forest and those of the spirit."* *New York State Museum.* *Whitney R. Cross, *The Burned-Over District: The Social and Intellectual History of Enthusiastic Religion in Western New York, 1800–1850* (Ithaca: Cornell University Press, 1950), 3.

Charles Grandison Finney (1792–1875), photograph, ca. 1860–1870. Lawyer-turned-preacher Charles Grandison Finney became one of the most influential evangelists in American history. A Presbyterian minister, he preached against traditional doctrine, which stated that only God would select who would follow the gospel and thus gain salvation. Finney believed that all men and women had the ability to choose to believe in the gospel. He led many revival meetings in western New York in the 1820s and 1830s, inspiring thousands to convert. Preaching with emotion and without prepared text, his energetic style and use of common language connected with thousands. Finney went on to teach and serve as president at Oberlin College in Ohio, and he was involved in the abolition movement. *Courtesy of the New York State Library, Manuscripts and Special Collections, 920 qM57.*

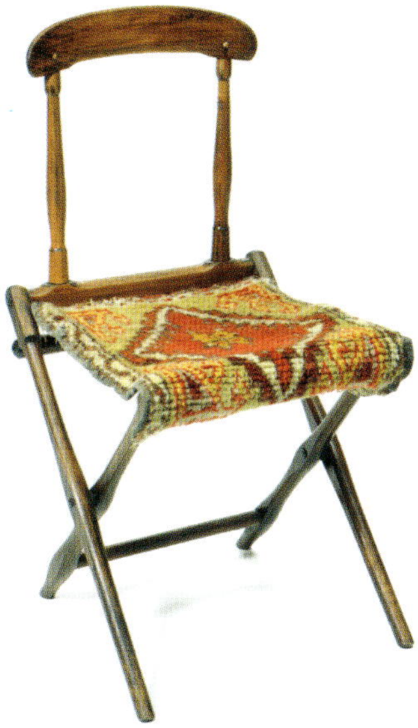

Camp chair, ca. 1860. Camp meetings were widely advertised and drew large crowds. Folding chairs were often used at these revivals since they occurred outdoors in large fields. Some meetings would take place over multiple days. *New York State Museum, H-1982.145.*

Camp meeting of the Methodists in N. America, engraving, ca. 1819. *Courtesy of the Library of Congress.*

Bible, New York Bible Society, 1878. This 1878 Bible was given to the captain of the canal boat *Superior* by the New York Bible Society. "NOT TO BE REMOVED FROM THE BOAT" is stamped on the front cover. A label on the inside front cover reads: "Presented To The Boat Superior By The New York Bible Society, New York, July 14 1878." Bibles were handed out to canal boat crews as part of religious efforts to improve morals on the canal. *New York State Museum, H-2008.61.1.*

Abolition

New York abolished slavery in the state in 1827—and afterward led the movement to remove it from the nation. Religiously motivated abolitionists and many free blacks believed that all men were created equal and that slavery was a moral abomination that could not be tolerated in a free country. However, these groups constituted a minority of New York's population. Many others were indifferent or resistant to the notion of racial equality, but they still opposed slavery. They were opposed to the expansion of slavery into the territories—where they hoped to expand railroads and build Northern-styled businesses and farms.

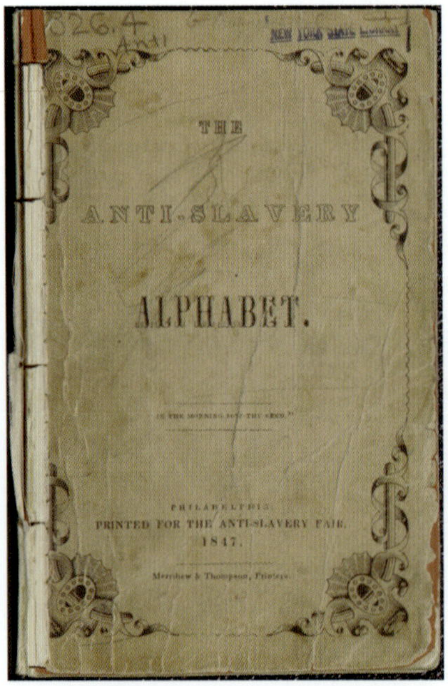
THE
ANTI-SLAVERY
ALPHABET.
PHILADELPHIA:
PRINTED FOR THE ANTI-SLAVERY FAIR.
1847.

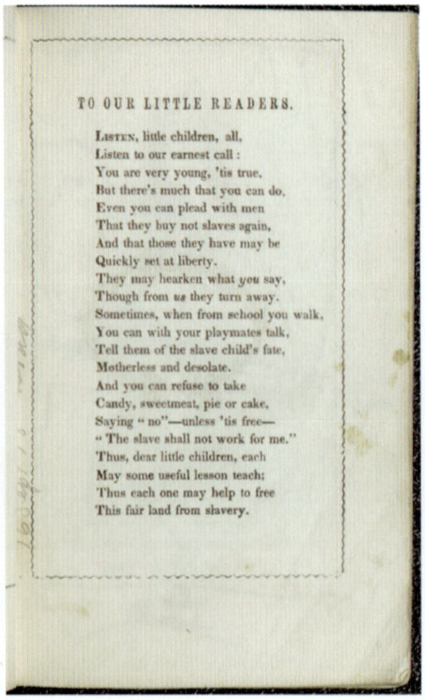
TO OUR LITTLE READERS.

Listen, little children, all,
Listen to our earnest call:
You are very young, 'tis true,
But there's much that you can do.
Even you can plead with men
That they buy not slaves again,
And that those they have may be
Quickly set at liberty.
They may hearken what *you* say,
Though from *us* they turn away.
Sometimes, when from school you walk,
You can with your playmates talk,
Tell them of the slave child's fate,
Motherless and desolate.
And you can refuse to take
Candy, sweetmeat, pie or cake,
Saying "no"—unless 'tis free—
"The slave shall not work for me."
Thus, dear little children, each
May some useful lesson teach;
Thus each one may help to free
This fair land from slavery.

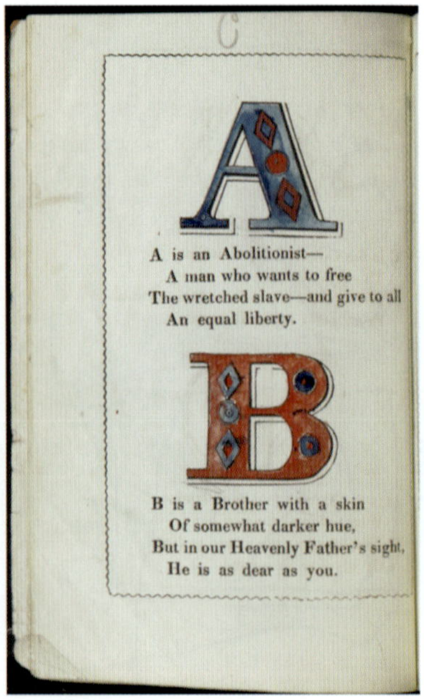
A

A is an Abolitionist—
A man who wants to free
The wretched slave—and give to all
An equal liberty.

B

B is a Brother with a skin
Of somewhat darker hue,
But in our Heavenly Father's sight,
He is as dear as you.

The Anti-Slavery Alphabet, 1847. Abolitionists used various methods to teach children about the horrors of slavery, including this antislavery alphabet. *Courtesy of the New York State Library, Manuscripts and Special Collections, 326.4 A6327.*

Decades before the Civil War and emancipation in 1865, abolitionists organized the Underground Railroad to help slaves escape to freedom. "Conductors," both black and white, often took extraordinary risks by providing fugitives with shelter, transportation, and opportunities to earn income. As many as 1,500 former slaves traveled north each year during the decades before the Civil War.

Routes through New York State were crucial because of the state's shared border with Canada and its well-developed system of canals, rivers, roads, and railroads. While thousands of escaped slaves passed through the state en route to freedom in Canada, many chose to stay in New York.

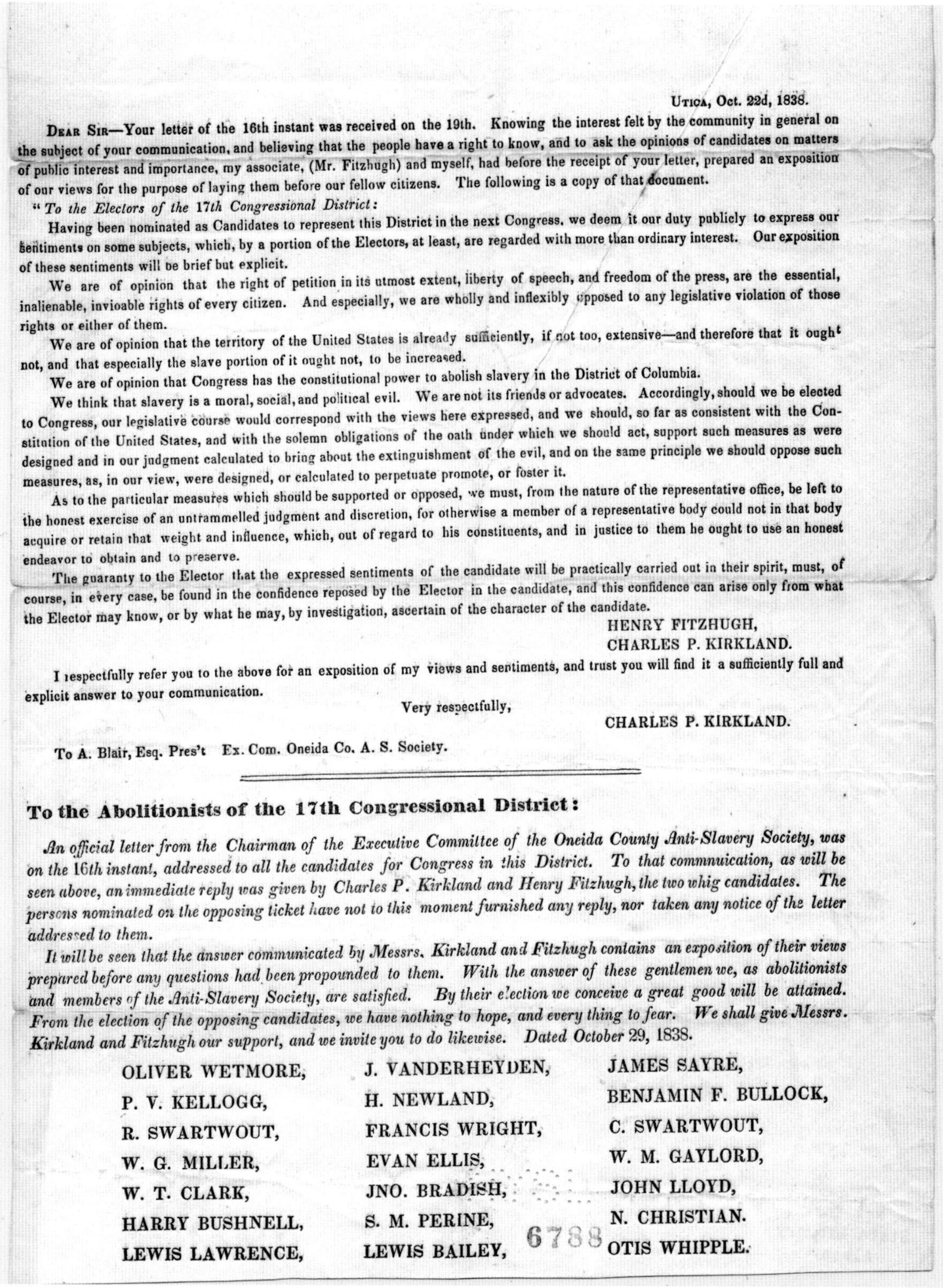

Utica, Oct. 22d, 1838.

Dear Sir—Your letter of the 16th instant was received on the 19th. Knowing the interest felt by the community in general on the subject of your communication, and believing that the people have a right to know, and to ask the opinions of candidates on matters of public interest and importance, my associate, (Mr. Fitzhugh) and myself, had before the receipt of your letter, prepared an exposition of our views for the purpose of laying them before our fellow citizens. The following is a copy of that document.

"*To the Electors of the 17th Congressional District:*

Having been nominated as Candidates to represent this District in the next Congress, we deem it our duty publicly to express our sentiments on some subjects, which, by a portion of the Electors, at least, are regarded with more than ordinary interest. Our exposition of these sentiments will be brief but explicit.

We are of opinion that the right of petition in its utmost extent, liberty of speech, and freedom of the press, are the essential, inalienable, invioable rights of every citizen. And especially, we are wholly and inflexibly opposed to any legislative violation of those rights or either of them.

We are of opinion that the territory of the United States is already sufficiently, if not too, extensive—and therefore that it ought not, and that especially the slave portion of it ought not, to be increased.

We are of opinion that Congress has the constitutional power to abolish slavery in the District of Columbia.

We think that slavery is a moral, social, and political evil. We are not its friends or advocates. Accordingly, should we be elected to Congress, our legislative course would correspond with the views here expressed, and we should, so far as consistent with the Constitution of the United States, and with the solemn obligations of the oath under which we should act, support such measures as were designed and in our judgment calculated to bring about the extinguishment of the evil, and on the same principle we should oppose such measures, as, in our view, were designed, or calculated to perpetuate promote, or foster it.

As to the particular measures which should be supported or opposed, we must, from the nature of the representative office, be left to the honest exercise of an untrammelled judgment and discretion, for otherwise a member of a representative body could not in that body acquire or retain that weight and influence, which, out of regard to his constituents, and in justice to them he ought to use an honest endeavor to obtain and to preserve.

The guaranty to the Elector that the expressed sentiments of the candidate will be practically carried out in their spirit, must, of course, in every case, be found in the confidence reposed by the Elector in the candidate, and this confidence can arise only from what the Elector may know, or by what he may, by investigation, ascertain of the character of the candidate.

HENRY FITZHUGH,
CHARLES P. KIRKLAND.

I respectfully refer you to the above for an exposition of my views and sentiments, and trust you will find it a sufficiently full and explicit answer to your communication.

Very respectfully,
CHARLES P. KIRKLAND.

To A. Blair, Esq. Pres't Ex. Com. Oneida Co. A. S. Society.

To the Abolitionists of the 17th Congressional District:

An official letter from the Chairman of the Executive Committee of the Oneida County Anti-Slavery Society, was on the 16th instant, addressed to all the candidates for Congress in this District. To that communication, as will be seen above, an immediate reply was given by Charles P. Kirkland and Henry Fitzhugh, the two whig candidates. The persons nominated on the opposing ticket have not to this moment furnished any reply, nor taken any notice of the letter addressed to them.

It will be seen that the answer communicated by Messrs. Kirkland and Fitzhugh contains an exposition of their views prepared before any questions had been propounded to them. With the answer of these gentlemen we, as abolitionists and members of the Anti-Slavery Society, are satisfied. By their election we conceive a great good will be attained. From the election of the opposing candidates, we have nothing to hope, and every thing to fear. We shall give Messrs. Kirkland and Fitzhugh our support, and we invite you to do likewise. Dated October 29, 1838.

OLIVER WETMORE,	J. VANDERHEYDEN,	JAMES SAYRE,
P. V. KELLOGG,	H. NEWLAND,	BENJAMIN F. BULLOCK,
R. SWARTWOUT,	FRANCIS WRIGHT,	C. SWARTWOUT,
W. G. MILLER,	EVAN ELLIS,	W. M. GAYLORD,
W. T. CLARK,	JNO. BRADISH,	JOHN LLOYD,
HARRY BUSHNELL,	S. M. PERINE,	N. CHRISTIAN.
LEWIS LAWRENCE,	LEWIS BAILEY,	OTIS WHIPPLE.

6788

Broadside, Oneida County Anti-Slavery Society, 1838. This broadside is in one part a letter from two Whig Party candidates for Congress, Henry Fitzhugh of Oswego and Charles P. Kirkland of Utica, pledging their antislavery views in response to an appeal from the Oneida County Anti-Slavery Society. The second part is an endorsement of the candidates from the society addressed to the "Abolitionists of the 17th Congressional District." Neither of the men won in that election. *Courtesy of the New York State Library, Manuscripts and Special Collections, BRO2675.*

Chair, William "Jerry" Henry, ca. 1853. William "Jerry" Henry was arrested as a fugitive slave in October 1851 in Syracuse, where he was working as a cooper. An estimated crowd of 2,500 people overpowered the federal marshals and rescued Henry. He was successfully escorted to Kingston, Ontario, where he lived the rest of his life. He built this chair as a thank-you to Edward Wheeler, one of his rescuers. *Courtesy of the Onondaga Historical Association, Syracuse, New York.*

Harriet Tubman (1820–1913), Harvey B. Lindsley, photograph, 1895. Harriet Tubman was perhaps the Underground Railroad's most famous "conductor." Born a slave in Maryland, she escaped to Canada in 1849. Tubman returned to Maryland several times, leading slaves through Quaker settlements in Pennsylvania and north to New York. Once in New York, the canal corridor provided multiple avenues to Canada. In 1858 Tubman became a New Yorker when US Senator William Seward sold her a plot of land in Auburn, Cayuga County. Tubman made Auburn her home base for the rest of her life. She went on to serve as a nurse, spy, and military leader during the Civil War and, afterward, as a civil rights and women's suffrage activist. In 2017 her home on that plot of land became the Harriet Tubman National Historic Park. *Courtesy of the Library of Congress.*

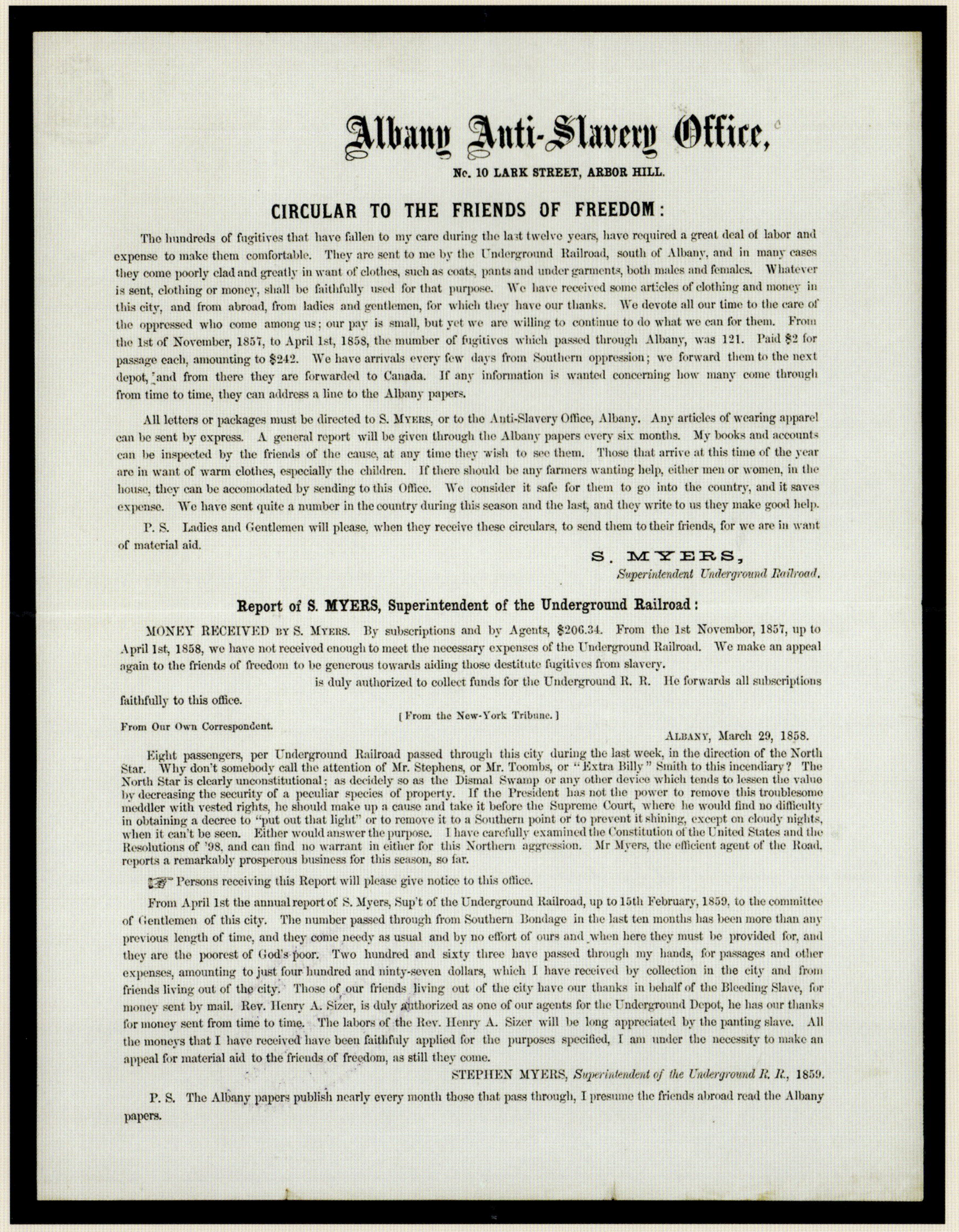

Albany Anti-Slavery Office,

No. 10 LARK STREET, ARBOR HILL.

CIRCULAR TO THE FRIENDS OF FREEDOM:

The hundreds of fugitives that have fallen to my care during the last twelve years, have required a great deal of labor and expense to make them comfortable. They are sent to me by the Underground Railroad, south of Albany, and in many cases they come poorly clad and greatly in want of clothes, such as coats, pants and under garments, both males and females. Whatever is sent, clothing or money, shall be faithfully used for that purpose. We have received some articles of clothing and money in this city, and from abroad, from ladies and gentlemen, for which they have our thanks. We devote all our time to the care of the oppressed who come among us; our pay is small, but yet we are willing to continue to do what we can for them. From the 1st of November, 1857, to April 1st, 1858, the number of fugitives which passed through Albany, was 121. Paid $2 for passage each, amounting to $242. We have arrivals every few days from Southern oppression; we forward them to the next depot, and from there they are forwarded to Canada. If any information is wanted concerning how many come through from time to time, they can address a line to the Albany papers.

All letters or packages must be directed to S. MYERS, or to the Anti-Slavery Office, Albany. Any articles of wearing apparel can be sent by express. A general report will be given through the Albany papers every six months. My books and accounts can be inspected by the friends of the cause, at any time they wish to see them. Those that arrive at this time of the year are in want of warm clothes, especially the children. If there should be any farmers wanting help, either men or women, in the house, they can be accomodated by sending to this Office. We consider it safe for them to go into the country, and it saves expense. We have sent quite a number in the country during this season and the last, and they write to us they make good help.

P. S. Ladies and Gentlemen will please, when they receive these circulars, to send them to their friends, for we are in want of material aid.

S. MYERS,
Superintendent Underground Railroad.

Report of S. MYERS, Superintendent of the Underground Railroad:

MONEY RECEIVED BY S. MYERS. By subscriptions and by Agents, $206.34. From the 1st November, 1857, up to April 1st, 1858, we have not received enough to meet the necessary expenses of the Underground Railroad. We make an appeal again to the friends of freedom to be generous towards aiding those destitute fugitives from slavery.

is duly authorized to collect funds for the Underground R. R. He forwards all subscriptions faithfully to this office.

[From the New-York Tribune.]

From Our Own Correspondent.

ALBANY, March 29, 1858.

Eight passengers, per Underground Railroad passed through this city during the last week, in the direction of the North Star. Why don't somebody call the attention of Mr. Stephens, or Mr. Toombs, or "Extra Billy" Smith to this incendiary? The North Star is clearly unconstitutional; as decidely so as the Dismal Swamp or any other device which tends to lessen the value by decreasing the security of a peculiar species of property. If the President has not the power to remove this troublesome meddler with vested rights, he should make up a cause and take it before the Supreme Court, where he would find no difficulty in obtaining a decree to "put out that light" or to remove it to a Southern point or to prevent it shining, except on cloudy nights, when it can't be seen. Either would answer the purpose. I have carefully examined the Constitution of the United States and the Resolutions of '98, and can find no warrant in either for this Northern aggression. Mr Myers, the efficient agent of the Road, reports a remarkably prosperous business for this season, so far.

☞ Persons receiving this Report will please give notice to this office.

From April 1st the annual report of S. Myers, Sup't of the Underground Railroad, up to 15th February, 1859, to the committee of Gentlemen of this city. The number passed through from Southern Bondage in the last ten months has been more than any previous length of time, and they come needy as usual and by no effort of ours and when here they must be provided for, and they are the poorest of God's poor. Two hundred and sixty three have passed through my hands, for passages and other expenses, amounting to just four hundred and ninty-seven dollars, which I have received by collection in the city and from friends living out of the city. Those of our friends living out of the city have our thanks in behalf of the Bleeding Slave, for money sent by mail. Rev. Henry A. Sizer, is duly authorized as one of our agents for the Underground Depot, he has our thanks for money sent from time to time. The labors of the Rev. Henry A. Sizer will be long appreciated by the panting slave. All the moneys that I have received have been faithfuly applied for the purposes specified, I am under the necessity to make an appeal for material aid to the friends of freedom, as still they come.

STEPHEN MYERS, *Superintendent of the Underground R. R.*, 1859.

P. S. The Albany papers publish nearly every month those that pass through, I presume the friends abroad read the Albany papers.

Broadside, Albany, 1858. In this broadside, Stephen A. Myers requested assistance (money and clothing) to aid escaped slaves traveling through Albany to Canada. Myers signed the broadside as superintendent of the Underground Railroad. The Champlain and Oswego Canals provided direct routes to Canada. *Courtesy of the New York State Library, Manuscripts and Special Collections, SC 7009.*

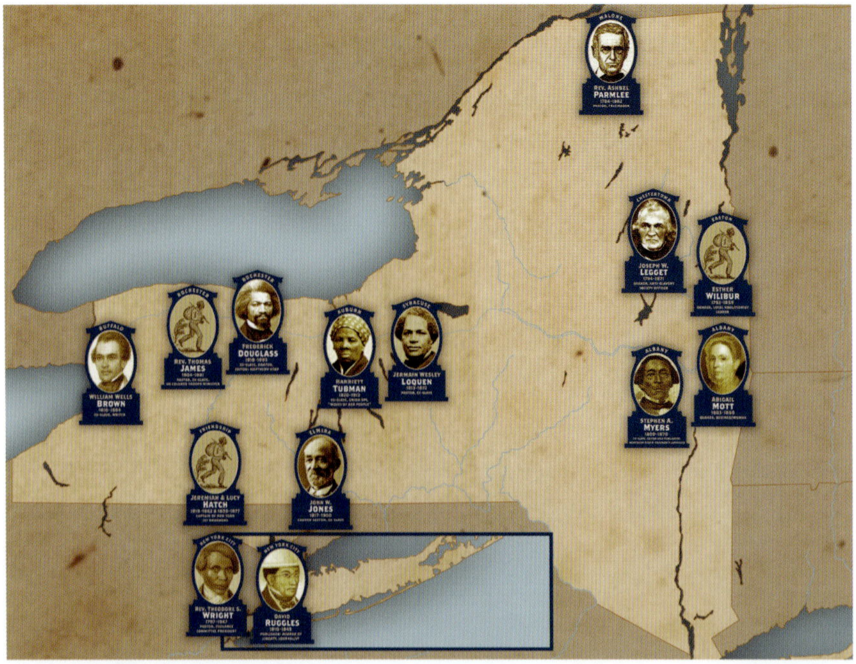

New York's Conductors Map. New York's "conductors" helped thousands of slaves gain their freedom by providing transportation, shelter, or work. Some of the conductors were themselves former slaves, and many were local abolitionist and religious leaders. New York's canals and rivers provided multiple pathways to Canada. *New York State Museum.*

Women's Suffrage

Abolitionism and women's rights were entwined causes for many women who empathized with the plight of slaves. Across New York, women suffragists raised money, clothed and fed fugitives, and organized their own abolition societies.

The women's rights movement gained prominence when abolitionists Elizabeth Cady Stanton and Lucretia Mott organized the 1848 women's rights convention in Seneca Falls, located on the Cayuga–Seneca Canal. The meeting attracted three hundred people and produced the Declaration of Sentiments.

REPORT

OF THE

WOMAN'S RIGHTS

CONVENTION,

Held at SENECA FALLS, N. Y., July 19th and 20th, 1848.

ROCHESTER:

PRINTED BY JOHN DICK,

AT THE NORTH STAR OFFICE.

1848.

"Report on the Woman's Rights Convention, Held at Seneca Falls, N.Y., July 19th and 20th, 1848," printed by John Dick, North Star Office, Rochester, 1848. The report of the women's rights convention in Seneca Falls was published in Frederick Douglass's printing office for the newspaper *The North Star*, located in Rochester. After the Civil War, the report was reprinted as leaders of the early movement sought to interest new recruits in the foundations of the women's rights movement. *Courtesy of the New York State Library, Manuscripts and Special Collections, 323.42 W872 84-20553.*

Amelia Bloomer, engraving in *The Lily*, September 1851. *The Lily*, the first newspaper for women, was started as the journal of the Seneca Falls Ladies Temperance Society, and Amelia Bloomer served as editor. Over time, the paper expanded to a broader focus on women's rights. In 1851 Elizabeth Smith Miller (daughter of abolitionist Gerrit Smith) introduced the reform dress to women's rights reformers, including her cousin, Elizabeth Cady Stanton. Images of it in *The Lily* further helped it spread, and it soon became known as the Bloomer costume. *Courtesy of the New York State Library, Manuscripts and Special Collections, 051 xL731 206-882 1849–1853.*

Lucretia Mott, photograph, 1870. Lucretia Mott was active at the Seneca Falls Convention in 1848 and central to the nineteenth-century women's rights movement in New York State and nationally. Mott and her family were also deeply involved in the antislavery movement. *Courtesy of the Library of Congress, National Woman's Party Records.*

View of Seneca Falls Village, engraving, 1842. This view shows the bustling village of Seneca Falls, full of industry after the opening of the Cayuga–Seneca Canal, which connects the Erie Canal to Cayuga and Seneca Lakes. John Warner Barber and Henry Howe, *Historical Collections of the State of New York; Containing a General Collection of the Most Interesting Facts, Traditions, Biographical Sketches, Anecdotes, &c., Relating to Its History and Antiquities, with Geographical Descriptions of Every Township in the State (New York: S. Tuttle, 1842). Courtesy of the New York State Library, Manuscripts and Special Collections, 974.7 B23a3.*

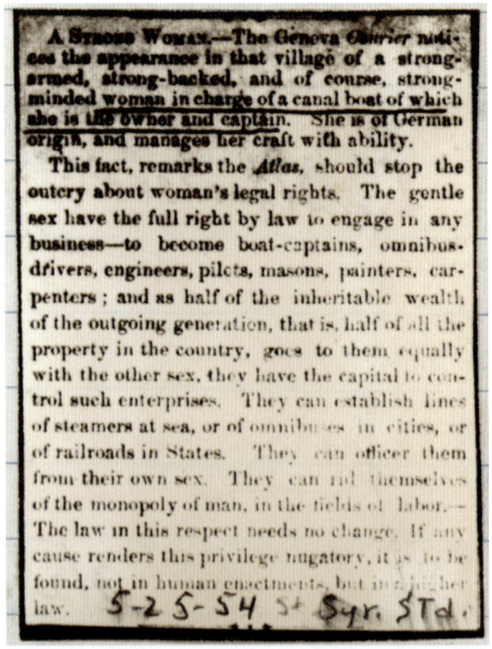

A STRONG WOMAN.—The Geneva *Courier* notices the appearance in that village of a strong-armed, strong-backed, and of course, strong-minded woman in charge of a canal boat of which she is the owner and captain. She is of German origin, and manages her craft with ability.

This fact, remarks the *Atlas*, should stop the outcry about woman's legal rights. The gentle sex have the full right by law to engage in any business—to become boat-captains, omnibus-drivers, engineers, pilots, masons, painters, carpenters; and as half of the inheritable wealth of the outgoing generation, that is, half of all the property in the country, goes to them equally with the other sex, they have the capital to control such enterprises. They can establish lines of steamers at sea, or of omnibuses in cities, or of railroads in States. They can officer them from their own sex. They can rid themselves of the monopoly of man, in the fields of labor.—The law in this respect needs no change. If any cause renders this privilege nugatory, it is to be found, not in human enactments, but in a higher law. 5-25-54 St Syr. STd.

"A Strong Woman," *Syracuse Standard*, 1854. There were women canal boat captains and owners. But as the author of this 1854 newspaper article clearly states, some people thought that women had enough rights. *New York State Museum, Mrs. Arnold B. Barben Canal Collection, H-1988.79.*

Susan B. Anthony (1815–1902) and Elizabeth Cady Stanton (1820–1906), W. Edmonston, photograph, ca. 1891. Elizabeth Cady Stanton and Susan B. Anthony both came from reform-minded families, working for abolition and temperance. In July 1848 Stanton worked with a group of women to plan the women's rights convention in Seneca Falls. The convention passed Stanton's Declaration of Sentiments, which listed the grievances suffered by women. Stanton and Anthony met in Seneca Falls in 1851, and they became lifelong partners in the fight for women's suffrage and women's rights. *Courtesy of the Library of Congress, Records of the National Woman's Party.*

Temperance

As a result of the reforms spreading across the state, many New Yorkers supported temperance, or abstinence from alcohol. In 1829 the New York State Temperance Society was founded with seventy-eight branches across the state. The canal corridor was a hub of temperance activity, although a majority of canallers did not subscribe.

Temperance was also supported by nativists, who viewed Irish and German immigrants as drunkards. It was an important issue that competed with and surpassed antislavery for the voters' attention.

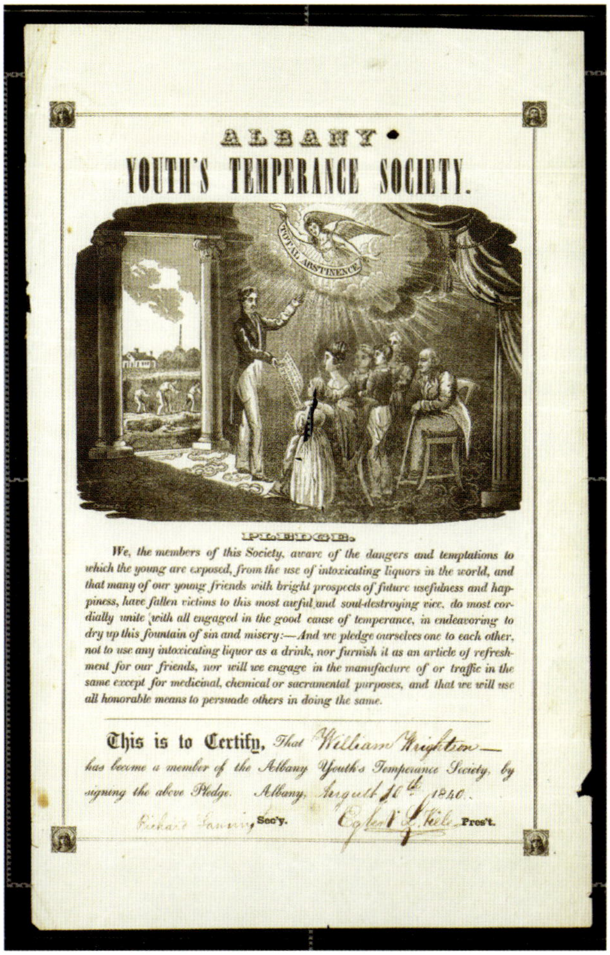

ALBANY

YOUTH'S TEMPERANCE SOCIETY.

TOTAL ABSTINENCE

PLEDGE.

We, the members of this Society, aware of the dangers and temptations to which the young are exposed, from the use of intoxicating liquors in the world, and that many of our young friends with bright prospects of future usefulness and happiness, have fallen victims to this most awful and soul-destroying vice, do most cordially unite with all engaged in the good cause of temperance, in endeavoring to dry up this fountain of sin and misery:—And we pledge ourselves one to each other, not to use any intoxicating liquor as a drink, nor furnish it as an article of refreshment for our friends, nor will we engage in the manufacture of or traffic in the same except for medicinal, chemical or sacramental purposes, and that we will use all honorable means to persuade others in doing the same.

This is to Certify, *That* William Wrighton *has become a member of the Albany Youth's Temperance Society, by signing the above Pledge. Albany,* August 10th *1840.*

Sec'y. Pres't.

Certificate of Membership, Albany Youth Temperance Society, 1840. *Courtesy of the New York State Library, Manuscripts and Special Collections, 17640.*

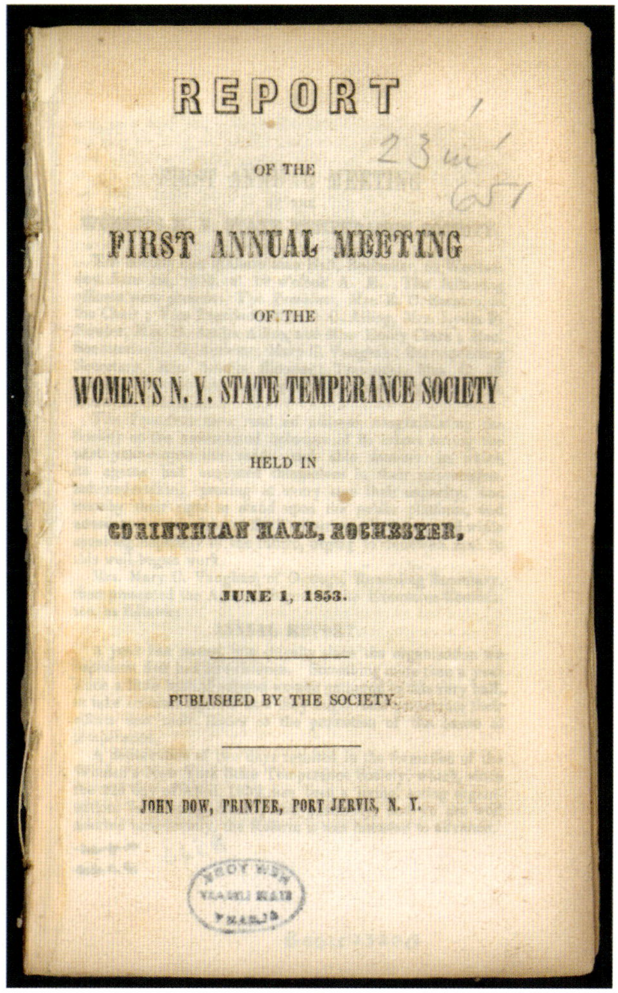

REPORT

OF THE

FIRST ANNUAL MEETING

OF THE

WOMEN'S N. Y. STATE TEMPERANCE SOCIETY

HELD IN

CORINTHIAN HALL, ROCHESTER,

JUNE 1, 1853.

PUBLISHED BY THE SOCIETY.

JOHN DOW, PRINTER, PORT JERVIS, N. Y.

Report of the First Annual Meeting of the Women's N.Y. State Temperance Society, Rochester, 1853. *Courtesy of the New York State Library, Manuscripts and Special Collections, 178.1W872 99-14327.*

Myron H. Clark (1806–1892), photograph, ca. 1840–1860. Myron H. Clark of Canandaigua held many elected offices in Ontario County. He was a fierce supporter of temperance. While serving in the state senate in 1854, he led the effort to pass a prohibition bill, only to see it vetoed by Governor Horatio Seymour on constitutional grounds. That same year Clark was elected governor on a reform ticket. In 1855 he signed a prohibition bill that was declared unconstitutional eight months later by the New York State Court of Appeals. President Abraham Lincoln appointed Clark as the collector of internal revenue in 1862. He continued to promote his temperance views later in life and even accepted the Prohibition Party's nomination for governor in 1874. *Courtesy of the New York State Library, Manuscripts and Special Collections, PRI 3451+.*

Stoneware temperance jug, ca. 1805. This early stoneware jar was probably made in New York City. The incised and cobalt blue–filled decoration depicts a man who appears to be drinking alcohol from a flask. A poem incised on the back of the jar indicates this gentleman was the "Town Drunk."

There is a man in our land,
Upon his feet he cannot stand,
The reason why you all must know,
He drinks too much before he'll go.

New York State Museum, H-2014.13.12.

Centennial snake temperance jug, Anna Pottery, Illinois, 1876. Wallace and Cornwall Kirkpatrick, owners of the Anna Pottery, were both supporters of temperance and often used stoneware as a way to disseminate their political views. The fourteen snakes on the jug represent the evils of alcohol and what can happen if one imbibes too frequently. This stoneware jug was created in honor of the country's centennial celebration in 1876. *New York State Museum, H-2013.12.20.*

The Civil War

The Civil War affirmed New York State's primacy as the industrial and commercial leader of the nation. The Empire State furnished more men, money, and materiel to the Union war effort than any other state. By 1861 the canal enlargement was almost complete, and Mississippi River commerce was blocked by the Confederacy, which directed even more goods through the Erie Canal.

Products shipped on the canal proved vital to the war effort and the Northern economy. Salt from the Syracuse region supplied the Union and helped Chicago become the new meatpacking center of the nation. Remington Arms in Ilion provided vital weaponry. Adirondack iron ore, shipped on the Champlain Canal, was used to produce weapons, ships, railroads, bridges, and horseshoes. The Chenango Canal brought in wool for the knitting mills of the Mohawk and Hudson Valleys. Increased canal revenues helped to pay for the state's war effort. At a time when the railroad was considered the way of the future, the canal handled enough freight to demonstrate that it was still important to the economy.

Gunboat Approaching a Lock, from *Maps, Plans, and Estimates of Enlarged Locks on the Oswego Canal for the Passage of Gun Boats*, 1863. Fears of England supporting the Confederacy fed worries of attacks from Canada. New York State passed legislation to make detailed plans for the enlargement of the canal system to accommodate gunboats, but the canals were not enlarged. Crop failures in Europe led to an increased demand for American grain shipped via the Erie Canal to England. This reliance on American grain may have been a factor in England's failure to support the Confederacy. *Courtesy of the New York State Archives, B0292.*

Map Shewing the Several Routes Proposed for the Passage of Gun-Boats to the Lakes, S. H. Sweet, 1862. *New York State Museum, Mrs. Arnold B. Barben Canal Collection, H-1988.79.*

Ely S. Parker (1828–1895)

Ely S. Parker was born on the Seneca Nation's Tonawanda Reservation and attended a nearby Baptist Mission School. He was a member of a leading Seneca family and would eventually become a prominent leader among Native Americans. In 1844 Parker served as translator, field assistant, and liaison for Lewis Henry Morgan, a New York State anthropologist documenting Haudenosaunee culture. Parker wanted to be a lawyer, but he could not get a license because he was Native American. Morgan turned Parker's attention to engineering and assisted in getting him a job on the Genesee Valley Canal in 1848. In 1850 Morgan helped him secure an engineering position on the Erie Canal enlargement.

During the Civil War, Parker served as Ulysses S. Grant's aide-de-camp. In 1865 Brigadier General Ely S. Parker drafted the terms of surrender of General Robert E. Lee's Army of Northern Virginia at Appomattox Courthouse. After the war, Parker served as commissioner of Indian affairs under President Grant—the first Native American to hold the office.

Ely S. Parker, photograph, ca. 1865. *New York State Museum Ethnology Collections.*

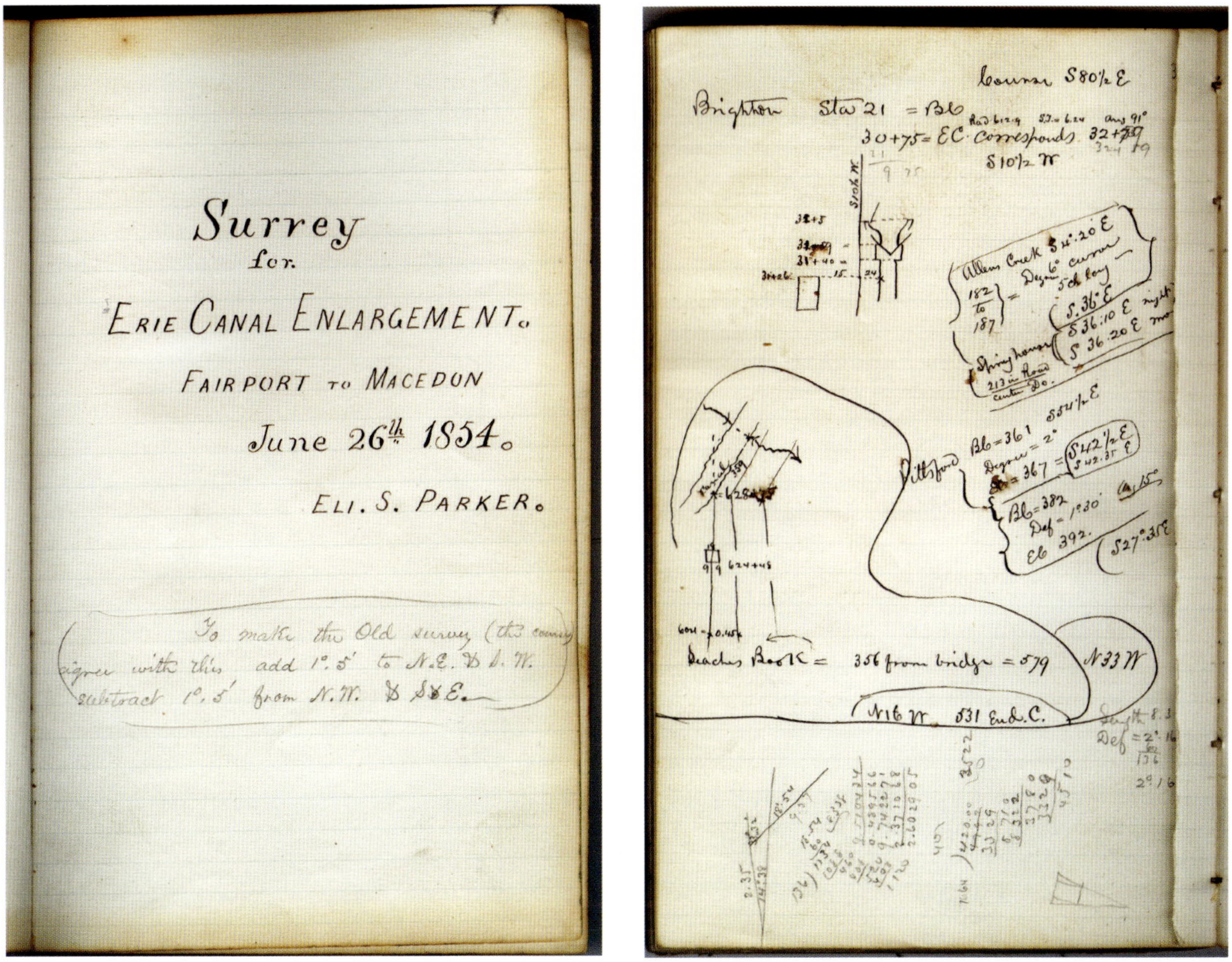

Title page and sketches from Ely Parker's field book, 1854. Engineers used field books to write notes and make calculations as they measured and mapped out the route of the canal. This field book was used by Ely S. Parker during his tenure as a civil engineer for the enlargement of the Erie Canal in the 1850s. *Courtesy of the New York State Archives, B0730-85.*

Revolver, E. Remington & Sons, Ilion, 1861 (patent). During the Civil War, Remington Arms Company became the second largest (after Colt) supplier of revolvers to the Union Army. Located along the Erie Canal, the company constructed a second factory at Utica devoted solely to the manufacture of pistols. By the end of the war, Remington Arms had earned nearly $3 million supplying weapons for the North. *New York State Museum, H-XX.279.1.*

DECLINE OF THE CANAL

The Erie Canal experienced many challenges in the second half of the nineteenth century. Freight tonnage peaked in 1880 and afterward slowly declined. The first enlargement, although declared complete in 1862 for political reasons, was not truly finished, and the work was poorly done. The entire channel had not been maintained at the uniform seven-foot depth, and a lack of water and crumbling infrastructure were constant issues. For a time, the canal's budget was dependent on revenue from now-dwindling tolls, resulting in a lack of funding for needed maintenance. Calls were made for the State to abandon the canal system; however, canal proponents argued that the commercial benefits brought to communities along the canal should outweigh the requirement that it be self-supporting, a debate still taking place today. Corruption and competition from canals in Canada and railroads in the United States led to calls for change. By the 1890s the canal that had made the Empire State was aging and outdated. Its future was unclear.

While it was cheaper to ship goods via the canal, it was often slower when compared to the railroad. The challenge of making the canal more efficient without another enlargement fell to the state's engineers. New York State sponsored contests for inventors to provide viable alternatives to animal power, such as steamboats and electrical "mules." None of the alternatives to animal power proved more economical for boat owners, so they did not gain wide usage on the canal.

Abandoned Section of the Black River Canal, photograph, ca. 1920. *New York State Museum, H-1988.80.4536.*

Watervliet weighlock, out of service, photograph, ca. 1922. Over the years the state legislature used canal tolls to help other industries. For example, lowering the toll on the shipment of glass would help the glass industry. Toward the end of the nineteenth century, it was more efficient to ship goods on railroads or via Canada rather than on the Erie Canal. To help compete, tolls on the canal were removed entirely in 1883. *New York State Archives, 17672-92.*

Abandoned Boat, photograph, ca. 1920. In the late 1890s many of the roughly 2,300 canal boats were in poor condition. With the canal's decline, boat owners did not want to invest in or repair boats, so they would often be abandoned on the side of a wide section of canal or river and sunk on purpose. *New York State Museum, H-1988.80.4562.*

Bridge No. 42 Erie Canal, Berme Abutment, Eastern Division, photograph, ca. 1895. The 1895 State Engineer's Report recommended rebuilding the abutment of multiple bridges because they were liable to fall into the canal. *State Engineer and Surveyor's Annual Report, 1895, New York State Museum.*

The Weighlock Building, ca. 1905–1910, James Cantwell (American, 1856–1926), watercolor on paper. *Erie Canal Museum.*

Weighlock Building, ca. 1960, J. Erwin Porter (American, 1903–1981), pastel and watercolor on paper. *New York State Museum, J. Erwin Porter Collection, H-1984.91.74.*

Cantwell, a Syracuse native, and Porter, from Medina, both included canal subjects in their bodies of work. These two views depict the 1850 Weighlock Building in Syracuse after it no longer served its primary function. Prior to canal tolls being abolished in 1883, boats entered a lock within the building, water was drained, and the boat and cargo were weighed to determine the toll. The scales were removed from the building in 1905 and the upper floor was extended to increase office space—as seen here. A plan in the 1950s to build Interstate 81 through the center of the city included demolition of the building, but it was saved and ultimately preserved as the Erie Canal Museum in 1962.

Double Length Lock, artist unknown, ca. 1960–1970s. In 1884 the State Legislature approved the extension of Lock No. 50 near Syracuse to enable two boats to lock through at once. The double-length lock enabled two boats in a tow to go through without disconnecting, thus saving valuable time. When this proved successful, other locks were enlarged in this manner. With few alternatives, the State settled on doubling the length of the remainder of the locks along the Erie and "bottoming-out" the canal to a uniform depth of seven feet. *Courtesy of the Canal Society of New York State.*

Hoodledasher, photograph, late nineteenth–early twentieth century. When two boats were tied together in a tow it was called a hoodledasher. By the late 1800s it was not uncommon to see a steam-powered canal boat pulling another canal boat, as shown in this picture. *New York State Museum, Mrs. Arnold B. Barben Canal Collection, H-1988.79.*

Fog Gang Working, photograph, 1897. In late winter and early spring the canal had to be cleaned and dredged to the proper levels or "bottomed-out." This task was left to day laborers who were referred to as the "Fog Gang." *New York State Museum, H-1988.80.1.1044.*

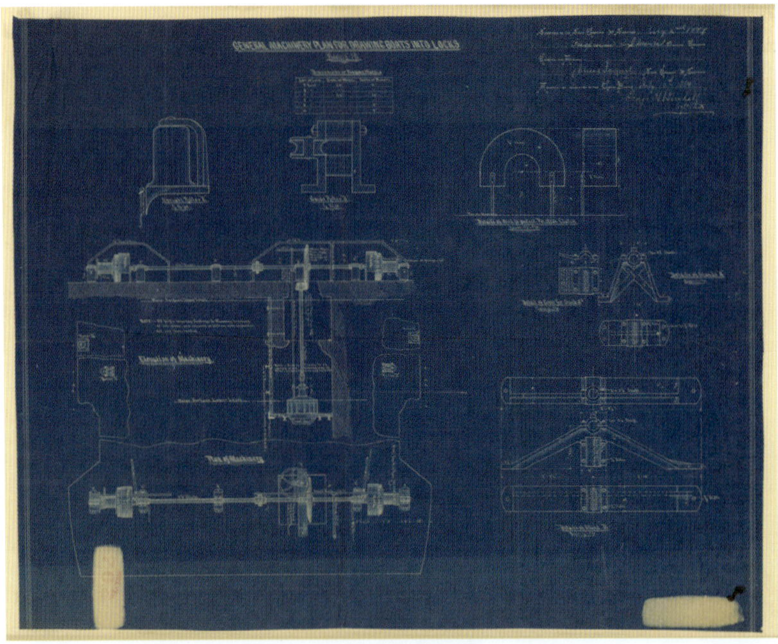

General Machinery Plan for Drawing Boats into Locks, blueprint, 1887–1889. Utilized in double-length locks to pull the "hoddledashers" through, this mechanism used water power to turn a wench that drew the boats into the lock and to work the gates. *New York State Archives.*

SCIENTIFIC AMERICAN

A WEEKLY JOURNAL OF PRACTICAL INFORMATION, ART, SCIENCE, MECHANICS, CHEMISTRY, AND MANUFACTURES.

NEW YORK, SEPTEMBER 6, 1879

THE BELGIAN SYSTEM OF CANAL TOWING.

THE BELGIAN SYSTEM OF CABLE TOWING—THE LOCKS AT LOCKPORT, N. Y.

146 Scientific American. [September 6, 1879.

THE BELGIAN SYSTEM OF CANAL TOWING.

Fig. 2—SIDE ELEVATION OF CABLE TOW BOAT.

CLIP IN DRIVE WHEEL. TAKE-UP SHEAVE.

SCREW DRIVING GEAR.

MISCELLANEOUS INVENTIONS.

The Belgian System of Cable Towing—The Locks at Lockport, N.Y., engraving, 1879. Side Elevation of Cable Tow Boat, engraving, 1879 This towing system relied on cables that ran along the bottom of the canal. Scientific American 61, no. 10 (September 6, 1879), New York State Museum, H-1981.59.7.

The Old Erie Canal, L. F. Tantillo, print after original oil on canvas, 1987. In the 1870s New York held a competition to encourage the design of steam-powered canal boats. The winner of the competition organized the Baxter Steam Canal Boat Company in 1874 and operated seven boats. It was the first operation of this type on New York's canals. The newly designed steamboats, however, did not prove economical. Ship captains refused to invest in upgrading their canal boats to work with the new-style tug, and the steamboat was largely unused. *New York State Museum, H-2009.38.1.*

Trial of Electric Mule in Schenectady, photograph, 1903. The "electric mule" was designed to run along a track system parallel to the Erie Canal to replace the use of animal power. The test of the electric mule was conducted just a few days before the voters of New York went to the polls to decide on the construction of a barge canal to replace the Erie. Barge canal advocates felt the electric mule test was arranged to influence the public; however, the public test did not affect the outcome (a barge canal was approved at the polls), nor was the system ultimately put into full use. *New York State Museum, H-1998.23.481.*

THE $9 MILLION ACT

By the 1890s the Erie Canal was in dire need of upgrades. Routine upkeep was insufficient, and the infrastructure was falling into disrepair. In 1895 the state legislature authorized $9 million to deepen the canal and lengthen the locks, but the amount proved insufficient to undertake the necessary work and repairs.

In 1898 work halted. A special canal commission was formed to investigate the project management but found no laws had been broken. In 1899 Governor Theodore Roosevelt appointed a committee to explore the canal's future.

Near Ilion—Section of Improved Canal, photograph, 1897. The increased depth of the canal was achieved by raising the canal's banks and dredging its bottom. *State Engineer and Surveyor's Annual Report, 1897, New York State Museum.*

CONTRACT NO. 1.—TYPICAL SECTION OF OLD VERTICAL WALL, COMPOSED OF TWO FACE WALLS FILLED IN CENTER WITH SPALLS. NOTE DIFFERENCE IN WIDTH OF BASE OF OLD WALL AND NEW ONE JUST STARTED; ALSO THAT ON REMOVING EARTH BACK OF WALL THE REAR FACE BULGED INWARD, DUE TO ABSENCE OF BOND.

(page 316) *Rebuilding Walls Near Genesee Street, Buffalo*, photograph, 1897. (above) *Typical Section of Old Vertical Wall, Buffalo,* photograph, 1897. After years of neglect, the work done as a result of the legislation popularly called the "$9 million act" included raising the walls of the canal, which exposed the depths of its deteriorated state. State Engineer and Surveyor's Annual Report, 1897, New York State Museum.

(*above*) *Showing Caving In of the Towing-Path at Newport, N.Y.*, photograph, 1897. State Engineer and Surveyor's Annual Report, 1897, New York State Museum.

(*below*) Tool chest, made by John C. Gerding, 1897. *New York State Museum Collection, H-2006.34.2.*

According to family lore, John C. Gerding made this chest while working on the Erie Canal. Census records indicate that he may have worked on the 1895 enlargement as a portable steam engine "fireman." Note the portable steam engine in center of the image.

PART IV

The Barge Canal

> We cannot afford to rest idle while our commerce is taken away from us, and we must act in the broadest and most liberal and most energetic spirit if we wish to retain the State's commercial supremacy.
>
> —New York State Governor Theodore Roosevelt, 1900[1]

To compete with railroads and newer, larger canals and to regain its primacy in western trade, New York needed to act. The answer to this challenge came in the form of the Barge Canal, a third-generation waterway that was yet another engineering marvel that transformed the landscape in its path.

QUICK FACTS ABOUT THE NEW YORK STATE BARGE CANAL SYSTEM

57 lift locks from 6 feet to 40 feet

Locks can pass vessels up to 300 feet long, 44 feet wide, with 12 feet of draft

Erie Canal (Waterford to Tonawanda): 340 miles, 35 locks

Champlain Canal (Waterford to Whitehall): 60 miles, 11 locks

Oswego Canal (Three Rivers/Liverpool to Oswego): 24 miles, 7 locks

Cayuga–Seneca Canal (Montezuma to Cayuga and Seneca Lakes): 17 miles, 4 locks

A new group of immigrants found work building the canal, and many stayed in communities along the route, contributing to shaping the cultural landscape. There was a new breed of canallers and boats who plied the waterways. The new twentieth-century commerce transported on the canal never reached the levels of the Barge Canal planners. Industry came and went along the canal, and today communities are looking back to the canal to bring in tourism dollars and improve the quality of life for their residents. In addition to recreation in and around the waterway, they are tapping into the legacies of the canal, which are vast and still hold a place in New York and American culture today.

THE POLITICS OF THE BARGE CANAL

Like Clinton's Ditch, the evolution of the Barge Canal was a lengthy process. The slow decline of the nineteenth-century canal was met with constant calls for improvements and enlargements. The failure of the $9 million project demonstrated that drastic changes needed to take place and that any change of value would have to be substantial and expensive.

As New York State governor, Theodore Roosevelt believed in the canal system and appointed a special Committee on Canals to explore options and make recommendations for the Erie Canal's future. The committee recommended significant investment in the canal system, a proposition that was debated between 1900 and 1903 before New Yorkers approved the measure. After a hard-fought campaign, the Barge Canal was approved in the general election of November 1903 by referendum.

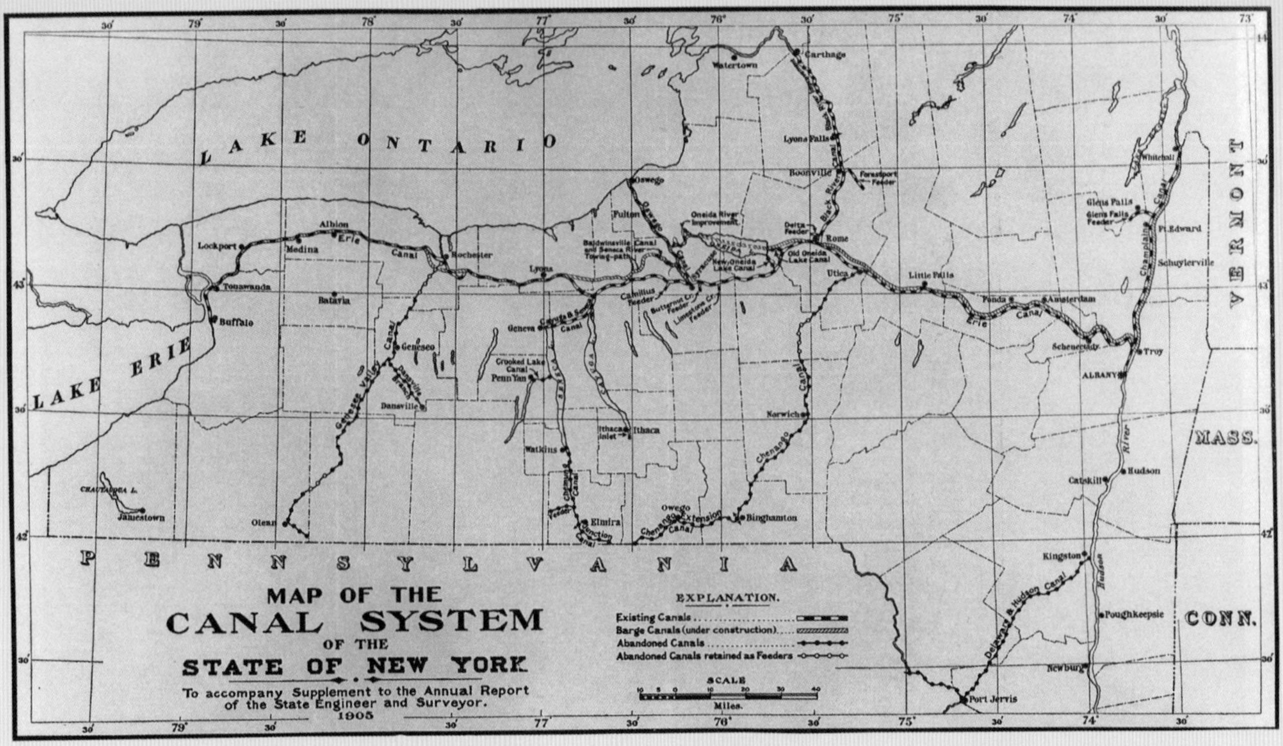

Map of the Canal System of the State of New York, 1905. New York State and the federal government conducted studies on the feasibility of a larger ship canal but ultimately settled on the Barge Canal, which was smaller than a ship canal but much larger than the old canals. This map shows the transition from the old nineteenth-century canal system to the new Barge Canal. The Erie, Champlain, Oswego, and Cayuga and Seneca Canals were to be enlarged as part of the new system. *State Engineer and Surveyor's Annual Report, 1905, New York State Museum.*

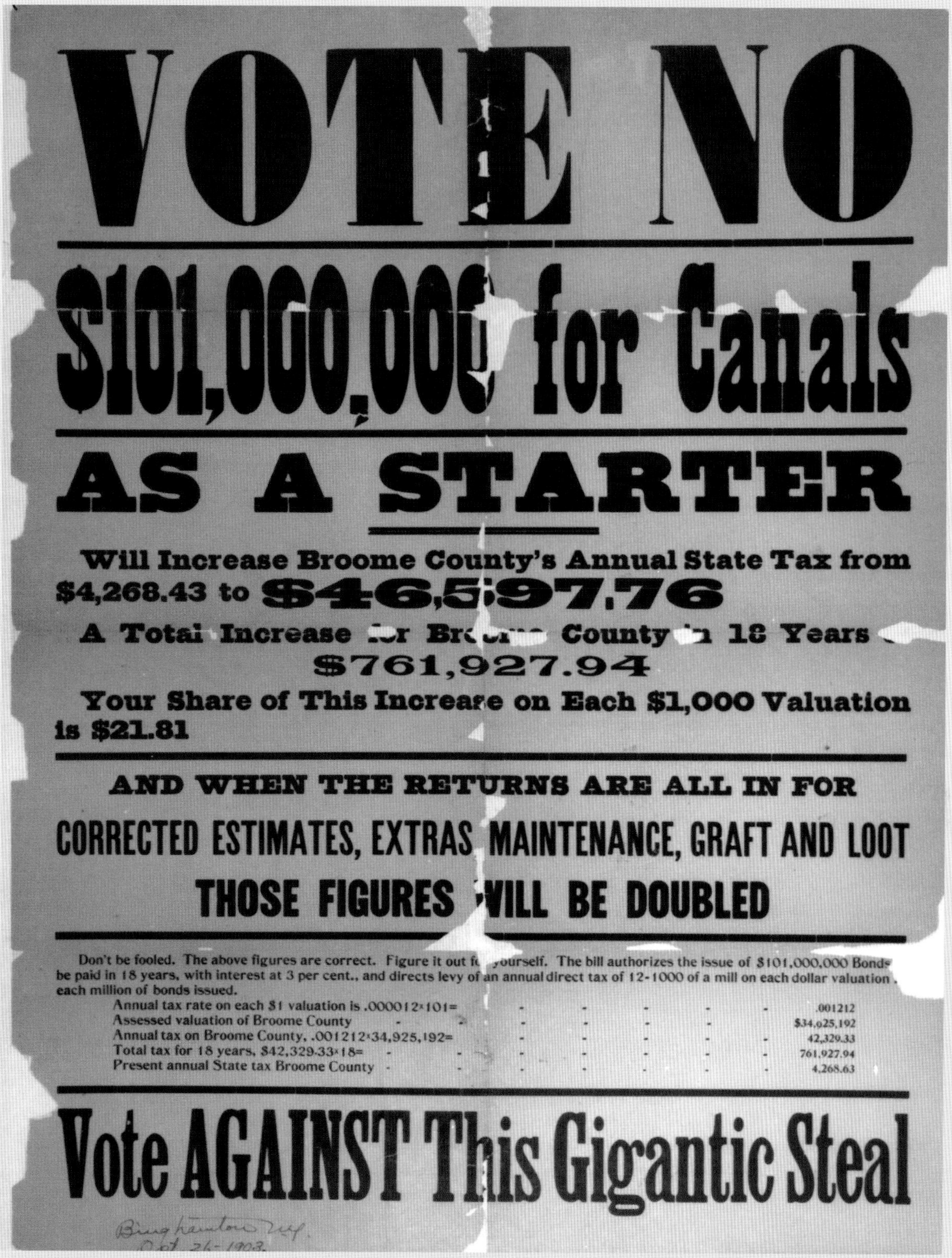

"Vote No" broadside, Binghamton, 1903. Railroad companies financially backed the opposition to the proposed Barge Canal. Regions that would see minimal economic gain were the most vocal opponents of a new canal. *Courtesy of the Broome County Historical Society via the New York State Archives.*

Grain Elevator in Buffalo Harbor, photograph, ca. 1920. *New York State Museum, H-2005.43.71.*

Buffalo wanted the new canal, not only to support the grain trade but also to boost Buffalo's position as an iron and steel center.

Mouth of Erie Canal, Buffalo, New York, stereo view, ca. 1925. *New York State Museum, H-1989.93.3.*

Barge Canal Terminal at Pier 5, E. R. [East River] New York, photograph, 1918. The biggest supporters of the Barge Canal project were from Buffalo and New York City, as the predicted positive economic impact on each was similar to that of the original canal. *State Engineer and Surveyor's Annual Report, 1918, New York State Museum.*

Theodore Roosevelt (1858–1919)

By 1898, concerns about corruption and financial mismanagement led to calls to close the Erie Canal. During that year's election, Republican gubernatorial candidate Theodore Roosevelt vowed to investigate the canal and formed a committee to do so.

Following the committee's report, Roosevelt determined the canal remained an important and commercially viable enterprise. On April 12, 1900, Governor Roosevelt directed the state engineer and surveyor to determine the route for a new Barge Canal system. In 1903 New York voters approved $100 million for the construction of the New York State Barge Canal.

Campaign button, 1898. This campaign button shows Theodore Roosevelt in the Rough Riders uniform he wore in service during the Spanish American War. The button was used as part of his campaign for New York State governor in 1898. *New York State Museum, H-2007.61.173.*

Gov. Theodore Roosevelt, photograph, ca. 1900. In 1901 Theodore Roosevelt became vice president of the United States under President William McKinley. While Roosevelt was longer governor, his early influential support and reputation proved invaluable for the Barge Canal. *Courtesy of the New York State Archives, A3045-78.*

BUILDING THE BARGE CANAL

The Barge Canal plans were ambitious. New technology would harness rivers, large channels were dug through villages and fields, a new modern form of concrete was used, and electrically powered locks were constructed. Tugboats and self-propelled vessels instead of animal power would move the boats. A new style of moveable dam, modeled after some European dams, would increase the depth of the rivers during the boating season and were designed to be raised in winter to help avoid springtime damage. Much of the original equipment is still in use today.

Construction of the Barge Canal radically changed many existing towns and villages, as large trenches appeared across farmland and through the hearts of communities. The new channel bypassed many of the downtowns that grew up along the original canal, including Schenectady, Utica, Syracuse, and Buffalo. New reservoirs were built to supply the Barge Canal with water and in some cases submerged entire communities. For many affected in this way, the new canal was not a welcome development.

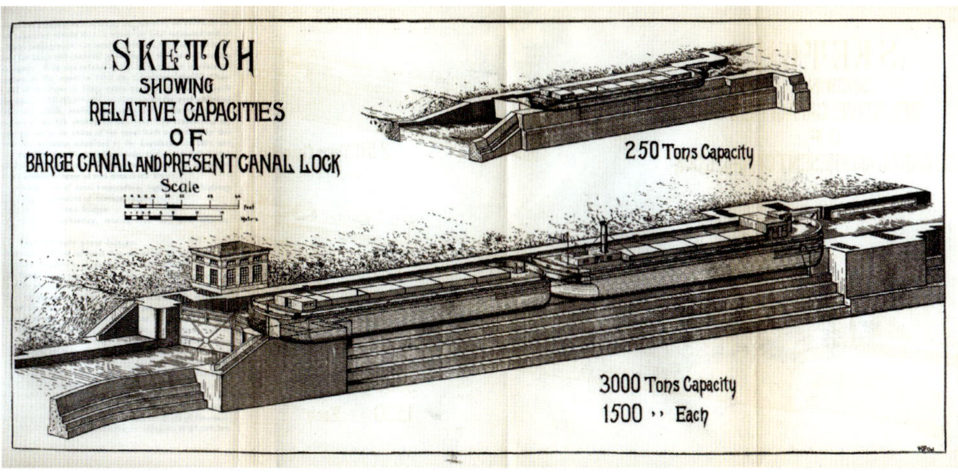

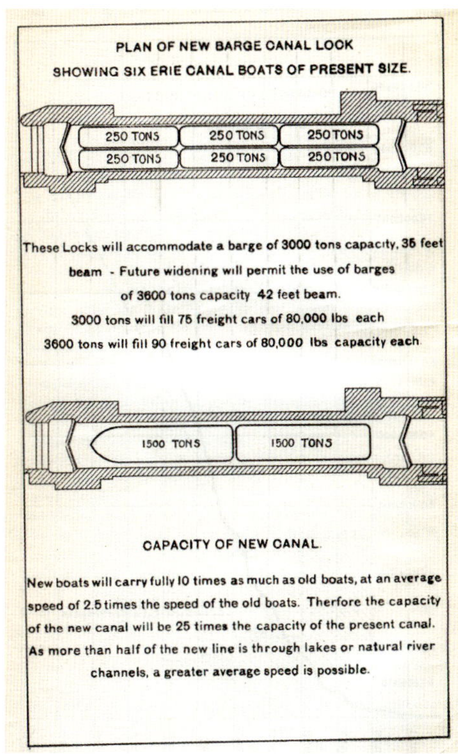

(*above and right*) Sketch Showing Relative Capacities of Barge Canal and Present Canal, 1912. Locks on the Barge Canal were to be 328 feet long by forty-five feet wide with a minimum depth of twelve feet of water. The locks would be deepened later to fourteen feet. *State Engineer and Surveyor's Annual Report, 1912, New York State Museum.*

Lock 17 at Little Falls, photograph, 1921. When built, this guillotine-style lock—at forty feet, six inches—was the highest single-lift lock in the world. It remains the highest single lift on the Barge Canal. *Courtesy of the New York State Archives, 17672-92.*

General View of Bridge, Moveable Dam and Lock, Tribes Hill, Nov. 8–11, photograph, 1910. Moveable dam and lock, in the up position. In the down position, the dam creates a pool of water to enable boats to travel the river. This design was based on one already in use in Europe. The technology enabled engineers to harness the rivers, which the engineers of a century before ultimately could not, leading to the original canal being constructed outside of the rivers. *Barge Canal Contract Book 17, Courtesy of the New York State Archives.*

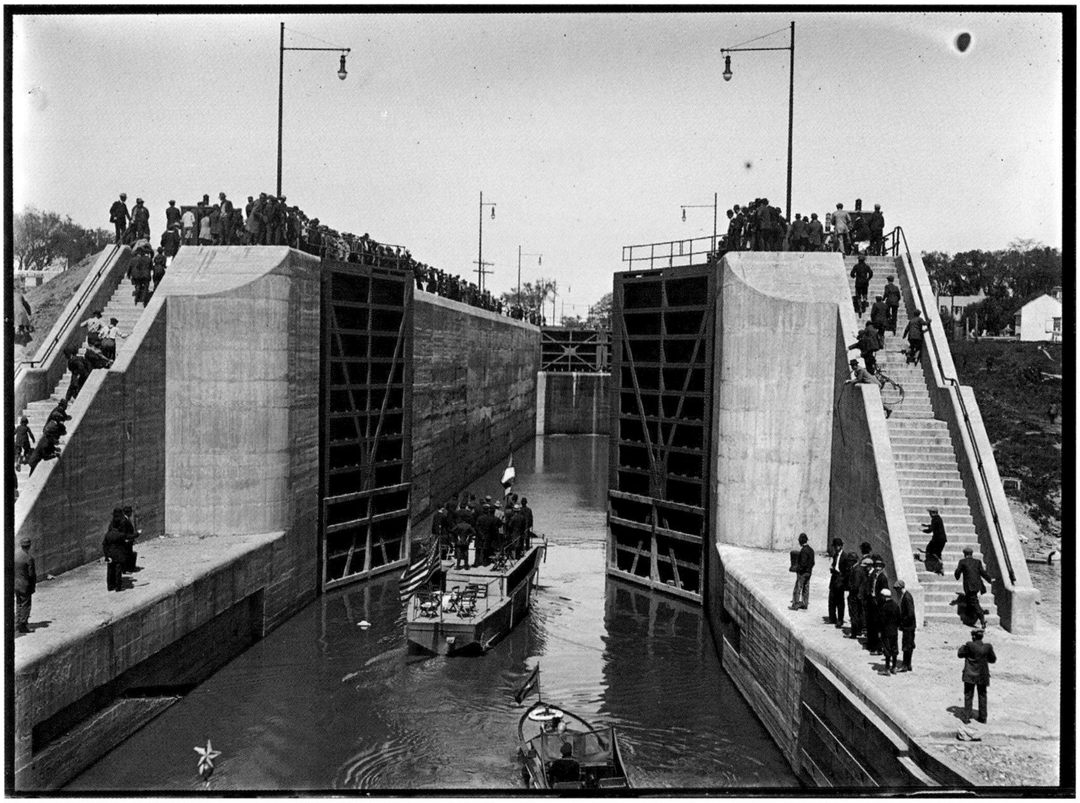

Opening of the Waterford Flight, Lock 2, May 1915. On May 15, 1915, a large celebration took place in Waterford to mark the opening of the Waterford Flight, a set of five lift locks that connects the Hudson River with the Mohawk River, bypassing the Cohoes Falls. Governor Charles Whitman was escorted through the village in a parade that ended at the waterfront, where he and other dignitaries motored through the flight. *New York State Museum, Michon Collection, H-1990.11.C46.*

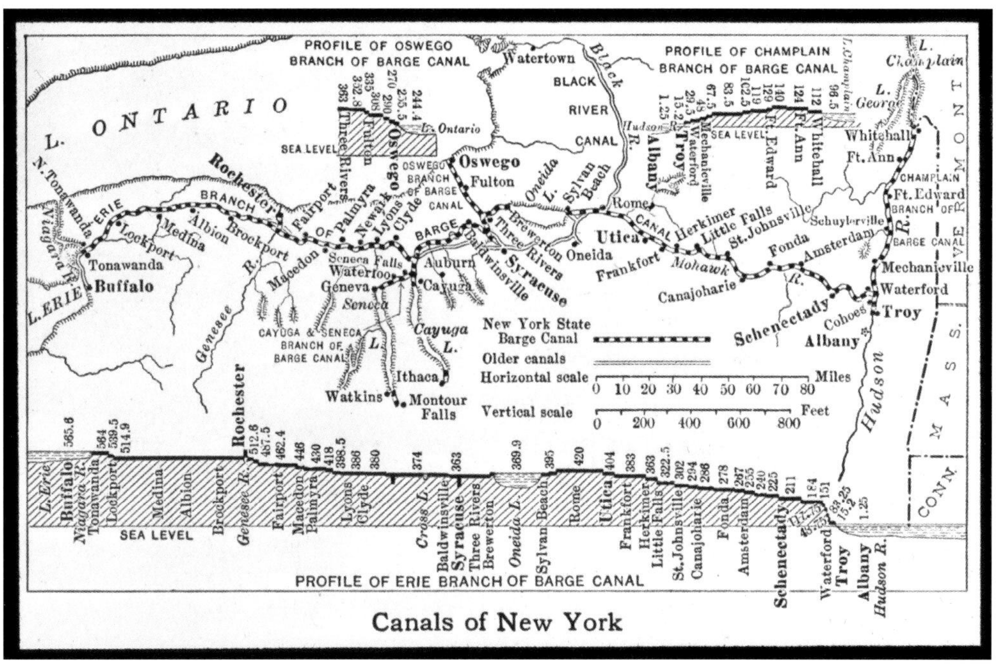

Map of Completed Barge Canal System, 1922. *Courtesy of the New York State Archives, A3045-78_Dn_Bc12.*

Panorama of Waterford Flight of Locks Erie Canal, photograph, ca. 1915. The village and town of Waterford in Saratoga County were split by the construction of the Waterford Flight. The flight is a set of five lift locks that serves as the entrance to the Erie Canal and connects the Hudson River with the Mohawk River. When built, it was the highest lift in the shortest distance of any set of lift locks in the world. *Barge Canal Contract Book, 92,93,94 Mac Arthur Bros. Co.-Lord Electric Co., J.T. Mc Mahon. Courtesy of the Waterford Historical Museum and Cultural Center.*

(pages 329–330) Various views of Seneca Falls Barge Canal Construction, photographs, ca. 1917. There are no longer waterfalls at Seneca Falls due to the large lake created when the Seneca River was dammed for the Barge Canal. The old canal is still at the bottom of the lake, and locks can be seen when the lake is drained. Numerous factories were torn down to make way for the new canal. *Barge Canal Contract Book C. Courtesy of the New York State Archives and State Engineer and Surveyor's Annual Report, 1917, New York State Museum.*

BARGE CANAL, CONTRACT C

Pool above the locks and dam at Seneca Falls. On most of the properties submerged the buildings were razed. The basement of the church seen in the view was filled in and the property was protected by a wall.

Delta Reservoir, photograph, May 12, 1909. The construction of the Delta Dam caused the village of Delta, Oneida County, to disappear beneath the reservoir. The buildings in the community were moved or razed to make way for the new reservoir. *Barge Canal Contract Book 55. Courtesy of the New York State Archives.*

Steam Equipment at Work in Baldwinsville, photograph, October 1, 1908. Unlike the original Erie Canal, which was dug with hand tools, the Barge Canal was built with steam power equipment to do the heavy lifting. This image shows three of the main steam workhorses of the Barge Canal construction: a steam crane, a dinky steam locomotive (small gauge train), and a steam shovel. *Barge Canal Contract Book 45. Courtesy of the New York State Archives.*

Chain hoist, ca. 1930. New York State erected shops and dry docks to help maintain the canal, the state fleet, and to provide places for ships to be repaired. This chain hoist came from a Waterford masonry shed at the Waterford yard in Saratoga County. *New York State Museum Collection, H-2009.5.1.*

Toy steam shovel, ca. 1935. The steam shovel was a novelty to many of the residents in the path of the new canal. In Waterford, residents came out by the hundreds on Sundays to watch the steam shovel digging the channel. *New York State Museum, H-1992.40.7.*

Main Street Lift Bridge, Albion, Orleans Co., NY, ca. 1960, J. Erwin Porter (American, 1903–1981), pastel and watercolor on paper. *New York State Museum, J. Erwin Porter Collection, H-1984.91.36.*

After a career in the advertising industry, J. Erwin Porter left to pursue painting full-time in 1960. Born in the canal town of Medina, Porter began an "Along the Canal" series, focusing on canal structures, both old and new, working and abandoned. The series became a traveling exhibition, which was shown through the 1960s.

Lock No. 2—Erie Canal, Waterford, NY, 1936, Aarne Parker (American, 1902–1995), watercolor on paper. *New York State Museum, H-2016.19.1.*

Parker depicted Lock No. 2 of the Barge Canal, which was the second complete enlargement of the Erie Canal, finished in 1918. In comparing his work with the period photograph (below) from a similar vantage point, we can see that Parker painted the lock structure as he observed it but took some liberties with the buildings in the background.

Lock No. 2, Waterford, NY, ca. 1940–1950, George N. Michon, photographer. *New York State Museum, 1990.11.513.*

In the early twentieth century there was a large influx of Italian immigrants to the canal corridor, drawn by the many employment opportunities in canal, railroad, and highway contruction. A large number of the laborers who built the Barge Canal were Italian immigrants.

The contractors relied on the "padrone system." A *padrone*, usually an Italian immigrant, would recruit Italian laborers for the contractor; in return, the padrone received a portion of their wages. Many immigrant laborers hoped to eventually return to Italy, while others remained in their new home.

Living and working conditions for the laborers were dependent on the contractor and location. For those residing in contractor-provided shanties, the environment could be very poor. Padrones, or at times contractors, in remote areas controlled the camp store and access to food, often leaving laborers with little money left to send home.

(left and below) Camp life. During the construction of the canal, the poor state of the labor camps and poor relations with local communities led to various reform efforts. It was decided that most problems occurred because of the communication barrier, so English lessons were offered. The laborers who worked near towns and villages tended to have better living conditions than those employed in rural areas.

"The Construction Camps of the People: The Findings of an Automobile Tour of Investigation of Camp Conditions Along the Line of New York State's New Barge Canal and New York City's New Aqueduct," *The Survey*, January 1, 1910.

Barge Canal labor sign, ca. 1910. Written in Italian, this sign is a job advertisement for work on the Barge Canal. The sign was found in a barn near Utica, where a large number of Italian immigrants found employment on the canal and subsequently stayed. Translated, it reads: "Workers for road work and Barge Canal work are provided. For information go to the office of John Zuccarelli, General Manager." *New York State Museum, H-1998.12.1.*

Postcards, ca. 1915. Italian postcards, sold by George Michon in his general store in Waterford, Saratoga County. Michon marketed to the large Italian population who arrived there and worked on the construction of the canal. *New York State Museum, H-1990.11*.

BARGE CANALLERS

There is no place on this modern waterway for the old-time "canal tough." He is not needed to preserve the romance of the canal. A different type—I was going to say, a more polished type—is necessary for a broader and more comprehensive canal movement. It will be composed of men who understand modern business conditions and demands, and who will find their work both pleasant and profitable.

—Charles E. Ogden, 1923[2]

When the Barge Canal opened, many of those working on the old canal transitioned to the new one. While families still owned, operated, and lived on canal boats, nationwide progressive trends meant that children had to attend school and could not spend their days working in a factory or on a canal boat. As a result, fewer families remained on the canal.

(pages 336–340) Various views of Barge Canallers, photographs, twentieth century. *New York State Museum H-1988.80.1.3227, H-1997.13.71, H-1997.13.72, H-1993.14.61, H-2009.10.2a, H-2015.37.14, H-2015.37.18, H-1990.11.015.*

URGER

C.C.BROTHERS

Evamay Mosseau Wilkins (1920–2006)

Evamay joined her parents on their family barge as soon as she was baptized. She lived the first ten years of her life on New York's waterways, spending the winters docked at Pier 6 in New York City. Her father and grandfather had worked on the boats, and she was born with a love of the water. After marrying Herbert Wilkins, the couple spent two years on the canals and eventually settled in Waterford to raise their family.

Evamay Wilkins and her husband pose on board a boat (ca. 1940). Images from Wilkins Family Album, photographs, ca. 1925 and 1940. New York State Museum.

Evamay Wilkins (on the right) and her siblings in New York City (ca. 1925). Images from Wilkins Family Album, photographs, ca. 1925 and 1940. *New York State Museum.*

Washtub and washboard, ca. 1940. This washtub and washboard were used by Evamay Wilkins on the barge Mary Chapman. *New York State Museum, H-1993.51.1 and .3.*

Lock controller, ca. 1915. When the Barge Canal opened, it was required that employees be trained to operate and repair the sophisticated machinery. Most of the original equipment used to operate the Barge Canal locks and other structures on the canals are still in use today. *New York State Museum, H-1987.77.1.*

Canal lock operator's booth, ca. 1915. This canal booth once stood at Lock 16 near Mindenville, Montgomery County. *New York State Museum H-1987.54.1 or .2.*

Diver's helmet, ca. 1945. B. T. Sweeney, a former canal section superintendent stationed in Utica, wore this diving helmet for inspections and repairs between 1946 and 1958. The complete diving suit and accompanying equipment are in the collections of the New York State Museum. *New York State Museum, H-1977.87.*

Unidentified Diver, photograph, ca. 1920–1930s. An unidentified diver takes a break from inspecting canal infrastructure. Divers are still used today to inspect the canal. *New York State Museum, H-1988.80.4151.*

Canal inspector badges, ca. 1915–1950. Fred Lindsey Sr., superintendent of operation and maintenance, owned these badges. Lindsey designed some of the electrical systems used to operate the locks. The image below shows Lindsey with some of the electrical systems that he designed. In the bottom left image, Lindsey (one in from the right) appears to be on board the Inspector II with other canal officials, possibly on an inspection tour of the canal. *New York State Museum, 1994.43.2-3, images 1994.42.5-6.*

Barge Canal buoy lantern, ca. 1920. Since the Barge Canal made use of rivers and lakes, the boating channel had to be marked out with lanterns that hung on buoys placed along the edges of the channel. *New York State Museum, H-1973.163.1.*

SERIAL NUMBER 251705

ISSUE NUMBER 3

UNITED STATES DEPARTMENT OF COMMERCE

BUREAU OF NAVIGATION AND STEAMBOAT INSPECTION

LICENSE

TO OPERATE OR NAVIGATE VESSELS NOT MORE THAN SIXTY-FIVE FEET IN LENGTH PROPELLED BY MACHINERY, AND CARRYING PASSENGERS FOR HIRE, AND VESSELS OF FIFTEEN GROSS TONS OR LESS, PROPELLED IN WHOLE OR IN PART BY GAS, GASOLINE, PETROLEUM, NAPHTHA, FLUID, OR ELECTRICITY, AND CARRYING PASSENGERS FOR HIRE.

Earl B. Clark

is hereby Licensed under the provisions of Act of Congress ... approved June 9, 1910, ... Steamboat Inspection ... five years from ... more than sixty ... for hire, and ... by gas, gasoline, ... for hire.

DEPT. OF TRANSP., U.S. COAST GUARD, CG-5205 (4-70)

FILE NO. ---

SERIAL NUMBER 000123

ISSUE NO. 12-12

UNITED STATES COAST GUARD

CHIEF ENGINEER

LICENSE

This is to certify that EARL B. CLARK *having been duly examined and found competent by the undersigned, is licensed to serve as Chief Engineer of United States* *** MOTOR *** *Vessels of any horsepower*

for the term of five years from this date.

Given under my hand this 20TH *day of* SEPTEMBER, *1982*

NEW YORK, N.Y.

ROLAND H. BOUGHTON, COMMANDER, USCG

Officer in Charge of Marine Inspection

By direction

Tug crewmen OK pact

NEW YORK (AP) — Tug boat crewmen voted overwhelmingly Wednesday to accept a new contract ending their 88-day strike in the nation's biggest port.

Most of the 2,800 union members, from captains to deckhands, packed the grand ballroom of the Waldorf-Astoria hotel and approved a 34½-month agreement that is retroactive to April 1.

The pact will raise pay 32 percent, delivering another blow to President Carter's wage guidelines.

Capt. Joseph O'Hare, president of Local 333, United Marine Divison of the International Longshoreman's Association, instructed his members to re-man 250 tugs, motorized barges and coastal tankers at midnight.

Where vessels were ready for immediate operation, crewmen "can return this afternoon," O'Hare said.

The first target was the resumption of escort and docking service for giant container ships that use such facilities as the Port Authority terminals in Po... Newark and Port Eliz... on the New Jersey side ... harbor.

The Sanitation Department said it expected the first pair of Moran tugs with their regular Local 333 crews to resume moving garbage between Staten Island and the other boroughs at 6 a.m. Thursday.

The U.S. Coast Guard said it would continue using two of its harbor tugs to handle that chore through Wednesday, and 15 municipal ferryboat employees temporarily assigned to operate three chartered tugs were expected to do the same. However, the ratification was followed quickly by the withdrawal of the Coast Guard cutter Tamaroa from its emergency operation, hauling sludge barges to ocean dumping sites from sewage plants in northern New Jersey.

Mechanical street sweeping, a casualty of the tug strike when operators had to be reassigned to trucking garbage to Brooklyn landfills, was to remain confined to Manhattan and Queens this week. A later resumption of sweeping in all boroughs, with resultant reimposition of alternate-side parking restrictions, was held in abeyance with a possibility that the gasoline shortage may force a decision Thursday to suspend of all such parking restrictions.

"It will be a long time before they test us again," O'Hare said of the tugboat industry, drawing cheers from his members. "We were tested by management, and we won. I thank you all!"

Identical agreements with members of the Marine Towing & Transportation Employers Association and two big firms — Moran and Bushey — that broke ranks and settled separately were worked out with the aid of Robert E. Kennedy, maritime coordinator for the Federal Mediation and Conciliation Service.

O'Hare said his union "won everything we asked for," including the right to reopen the contract if any of its provisions are invalidated.

That possibility and a potential renewal of the strike was already posed by a dispute over the scope, or geographical limits of the contract. Those terms were put into writing for the first time, despite employer resistance.

The scope clause recognized Local 333 members as having jurisdiction over coastal towing extending all along the Upper Atlantic Coast and inland on rivers and canals to the Great Lakes. That claim has been challenged by the Seafarers International Union and the Marine Engineers Beneficial Association. Results of a consequent AFL-CIO raiding hearing are expected shortly.

... has previously been linked to Mexico City.

Tug, barge crews ratify pact, end 88-day NYC port strike

NEW YORK (UPI) — Striking tugboat and barge crewmen Wednesday unanimously ratified a new contract and ended their 88-day walkout that had crippled activity in New York harbor.

"The contract was approved and we're going back to work this afternoon," said Capt. Joseph O'Hare, president of local 333 of the Maritime Division of the International Longshoremen's Association.

The new contract provides for a 32 percent wage increase over three years and job security for union members who work on ocean-going tugs and barges along the Atlantic Coast.

The latter provision, known as "Scope," gives the union jurisdiction on tugs operating on the East Coast between Norfolk, Va. and Eastport, Me.

A rival union, the Seafarers and Marine Engineers, has gone to court in their fight with the Longshoremen over jurisdiction of long-distance towing jobs on the East Coast.

If the Longshoremen lose the jurisdiction battle, the towing companies agreed to reopen the contract.

Albert Cornetti, secretary-treasurer of the union, said the end of the three-month strike could help ease the gasoline crunch in the metropolitan area.

"Some oil companies have been saying that because of us, 40 percent of oil [for the metropolitan New York and northern New Jersey area] hasn't been moving," Cornetti said. "Now that we are back, let's see what happens."

The smaller tugboat firms reached tentative agreement last week, but the two largest companies, Moran Towing and Transportation Co. and Ira Bushey and Sons, refused to make the same offer because it objected to the "Scope" clause.

Earl B. Clark worked as a tug engineer on the Barge Canal for most of his life. Unions played a significant role in the lives of the crews in the twentieth century. At least two major strikes crippled the Hudson-Erie transportation network in 1946 and 1988. Earl Clark saved these articles in his personal papers regarding the 1988 strike. *New York State Museum, H-XX.569.1.13, H-XX.569.1.14, H-XX.569.1.1, H-XX.569.1.25, H-XX.569.1.22.*

Federal Control during World War I

As the United States prepared to enter World War I, the federal government feared the nation's transportation network was not prepared to move vast quantities of supplies and materiel, not to mention troops, to Europe. In New York State, workers hurried to complete the Barge Canal.

As the nation's railway system became overburdened by the war effort, the United States Railroad Administration (USRA) began studying the ability of canals to alleviate rail congestion. The USRA assumed control of shipping along the Barge Canal, while New York State was responsible for its operation and maintenance. The USRA was made up of railway men and its policies favored the rails, so as not to give an edge to the new canal. Due in part to those policies, the expense of shipping by rail or canal was the same during the war, so the Barge Canal remained underutilized throughout the war.

Concrete Barge, George N. Michon, photograph, ca. 1918. The USRA contracted all available ships that could be used along the Barge Canal but failed to efficiently use them. All steel went to the war effort and the federal government ordered the construction of concrete canal boats. These barges were not suited for the canals: one knock into a dock or lock and the concrete could crumble. *New York State Museum, Michon Collection, H-1990.11.253.*

“Nation’s Canals May End Freight Jam,” newspaper headline, *New York Sun* (New York City), March 17, 1918. This headline from the March 17, 1918, *New York Sun* urges the use of the New York State Barge Canal to alleviate shipping congestion along the nation’s railways. *Courtesy of Chronicling America, Library of Congress.*

16 THE SUN, SUNDAY, MARCH 17, 1918.

Nation’s Canals May End Freight Jams

Could Handle Coal to Great Advantage Say Traffic Experts, Especially for New York and the East

Cost Far Less by Water, and Transit Time, Too, Is Cut Because of Present Railroad Congestion

By S. C. MEAD, Secretary of the Merchants Association of New York.

S. C. Mead, Secretary of the Merchants Association.

A Lockage of Old-Sized Canal-Boats, photograph, 1919. A soldier of the New York Guard or National Guard stands sentry at Lock 3 in Waterford, Saratoga County, during World War I. The soldiers were tasked with protecting the state’s infrastructure from potential sabotage. *State Engineer and Surveyor’s Annual Report, 1919, New York State Museum.*

Make Every Minute Count, poster, ca. 1917. With the United States' entry into World War I, the Barge Canal faced a shortage of ships capable of hauling cargo. As a result, advocates for the Barge Canal turned to the US Emergency Fleet Corporation for assistance. *Courtesy of the Library of Congress.*

Some Backing, James Montgomery Flag, poster, ca. 1917. With the withdrawal of the New York National Guard in August 1917, the New York Guard was established. The upstate troops of the Second Regiment guarded key infrastructure, including the Barge Canal. *New York State Museum, H-1978.182.1.*

Boats of the Barge Canal

When the new waterway was completed in 1918, there was already a shortage of boats. The United States' entry into World War I redirected materials and shipbuilders' focus toward the war effort, so the old wooden boats stayed in use.

In 1921 the state regained control of the canal and boat building began in earnest. A new style of self-propelled metal ships designed specifically for the Barge Canal's dimensions were produced. At that point, old wooden boats, metal barges, tugboats, and the new motor ships were all in use on the canals.

The State has a fleet of vessels referred to as the "state canal's floating plant." This fleet is used to maintain the canal system by performing various tasks, such as placing buoys, dredging, moving barges, placing docks, facilitating repairs, conducting inspections, and much more. Today the New York State Canal Corporation operates a fleet of about fifty vessels.

Wooden Boats Enter Lock 2, Waterford, George N. Michon, photograph, ca. 1920. By the late 1930s most wooden canal vessels were gone or abandoned along the shore, skeletons of a bygone era. *New York State Museum, Michon Collection, H-1990.11.225.*

Day Peckinpaugh, Little Falls, photograph, 1921. The *Day Peckinpaugh* was the first boat built specifically for the Barge Canal dimensions and was the last one still in use when it retired in 1994. Roughly one hundred of these vessels plied the Barge Canal in its heyday, from the 1920s through the 1960s. *New York State Museum, Stellato Collection, H-1993.14.*

Marine radar antenna from the *Day Peckinpaugh* motorship, second half of the twentieth century. Radar was used to help ships navigate in large bodies of water and in ports. *New York State Museum, H-2005.23.*

Model tug and barge, made by Liberty Dry Dock, Inc., Ship Builders and Repairers, Brooklyn, New York, ca. 1950. This model shows an oil barge and tugboat in a Barge Canal lock, a common site on the Barge Canal in the mid-1900s. *Courtesy of the Canal Society of New York State.*

Model of Hanley Barge, artist unknown, ca. 1930. The New York City–based Hanley Line operated a small fleet of tugs and barges in the 1920s and 1930s. Family run, they worked New York Harbor as well as the Barge Canal. Barges such as this were typical sights on the Mohawk River when commercial traffic dominated the waterway. This model was once on display in the company's New York City office. *New York State Museum, H-1991.35.1.*

Tug bitts, 1921. Tug bitts hold the barge to the tug while towing. These bitts were recovered from the tug *Coyne Sisters* (below), which was built in 1921 and sank in the Syracuse Barge Canal harbor in 1973. *New York State Museum, H-2001.49.1.*

Coyne Sisters tugboat, George N. Michon, ca. 1940. *Coyne Sisters* tug in Waterford, Saratoga County. Note the tug bitts on each end of the tug. *New York State Museum, Michon Collection, H-1990.11.045.*

Landscape with Barges, ca. 1950, Geoffrey Biggs (American, born England, 1908–1971), oil on canvas. *Arkell Museum at Canajoharie.*

Biggs was a commercial artist whose paintings were featured in popular periodicals, including *Collier's*, *The Saturday Evening Post*, and *Good Housekeeping*. He was also commissioned for illustrations by numerous advertising agencies. His home was located along the canal in the village of Palatine Bridge and is visible in the foreground. In the middle ground is the Beech-Nut Factory in Canajoharie. The houses under construction, the large transformer, the factory, and the barges and train speak to a bustling post-wartime economy.

(right and pages 354–355) Various images of the *Inspector II*, photographs, ca. 1920–1960s.

The *Inspector II* was a yacht used by state engineers and elected officials to conduct annual inspections of the canal, a process still conducted twice each season today. It was also the governor's boat, and Franklin D. Roosevelt made several trips on the canal in summer 1930. *New York State Museum, H-1988.80.1.2375. Courtesy of the New York State Archives 17672-92.*

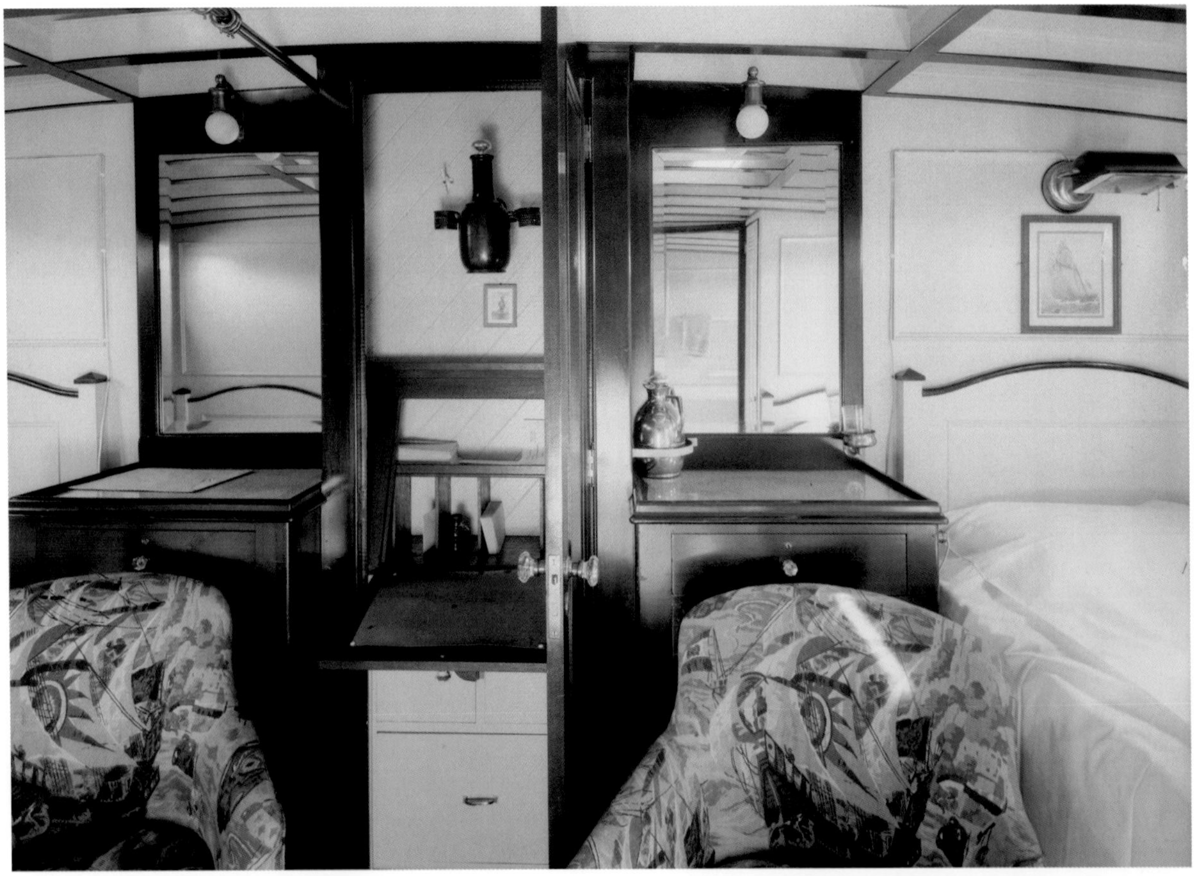

Syracuse China service with seal of the State of New York, ca. 1920s. China set used on the boat Inspector II. *New York State Museum, H-1988.15.1.1-.61.*

Engine operator telegraph from State tug *Reliable*, 1934, photograph ca. 1940. The captain, in the pilothouse, used this device to send a signal to the engineer, who was in the engine room below deck, as to the gear in which to engage the engine. *Courtesy of New York State Canal Corporation. Image New York State Museum, H-1988.80.1.3248.*

Steering and propulsion controls from state derrick boat *Tenkenas*, 1929, photograph, May 1951. Derrick boats are equipped with cranes to dredge and place buoys. The *Tenkenas* and her sister ship, *Ward's Island*, were built in 1929 as New York City ferry boats and later converted by the State for Barge Canal service. The image of the *Tenkenas* shows the boat working on Erie Canal Lock 10 in May of 1951. *New York State Museum, H-1976.271.1-2. Courtesy of the New York State Archives.*

Sign from State tug *Jas. K. Averill*, ca. 1911. The *James K. Averill* was built in 1911 or 1912 at Champlain, New York. New York State purchased the tug in 1922, and she was the last coal-burning tug in the fleet when decommissioned in the 1960s. The small brass plate was removed from the original engine boiler. *New York State Museum, H-1993.48.1.*

State Tug *Jas. K. Averill*, George N. Michon, photograph, ca. 1920s. The *James K. Averill* in dry dock at Waterford, Saratoga County. *New York State Museum, Michon Collection, H-1990.11.006.*

Life jacket from the *Governor Cleveland* (below), twentieth century.

The low-slung *Governor Cleveland* has been a part the fleet since 1928. The vessel was originally used as an ice breaker and is still used today as a tug for multiple purposes. *New York State Museum, H-1994.28.1, New York State Museum, Michon Collection, H-1990.11.88.*

Brass nautical three-chime steam whistle, ca. 1911–1930. This brass steam whistle is from the Dipper Dredge #3, also known as the *St. Johnsville*. The vessel is listed on the National Register of Historic Places. Built in 1911, the dredge was the last steam-operated vessel in the fleet. *Courtesy of the New York State Canal Corporation.*

Dipper Dredge #3, photograph, July 1961. The whistle in this photograph is hard to make out because it was painted black so that the brass would not attract thieves. After it was removed from the vessel, the black paint was stripped. The steam-powered vessel was used to dredge the canal, and the whistle was used to signal to other vessels and crew. *Courtesy of the Canal Society of New York State, Baxter Collection.*

COMMERCE AND INDUSTRY ON THE CANAL IN THE TWENTIETH CENTURY

The wartime policies of the United States Railroad Administration likely slowed canal development, and the canal struggled to regain lost commerce from the railroad. Still, commerce grew as the larger ships carried grains, coal, petroleum, flour, iron ore, and bricks. Tonnage peaked in 1951 but never reached levels envisioned by the Barge Canal's promoters. With the opening of the St. Lawrence Seaway in 1959, ships could travel from the Great Lakes to the Atlantic Ocean. While petroleum and other products continued to be shipped on the canal into the late 1980s, commercial traffic soon became a novelty instead of the norm.

The canal corridor thrived into the early twentieth century, as industries were able to use canals, rails, and trucks to transport materials. After World War II, many of the large-scale industries moved or went out of business, especially in Rochester and Buffalo. Those communities that adapted over the years to new technology-based commercial opportunities have found success, if even only for a short time, but the heyday of canal communities has passed.

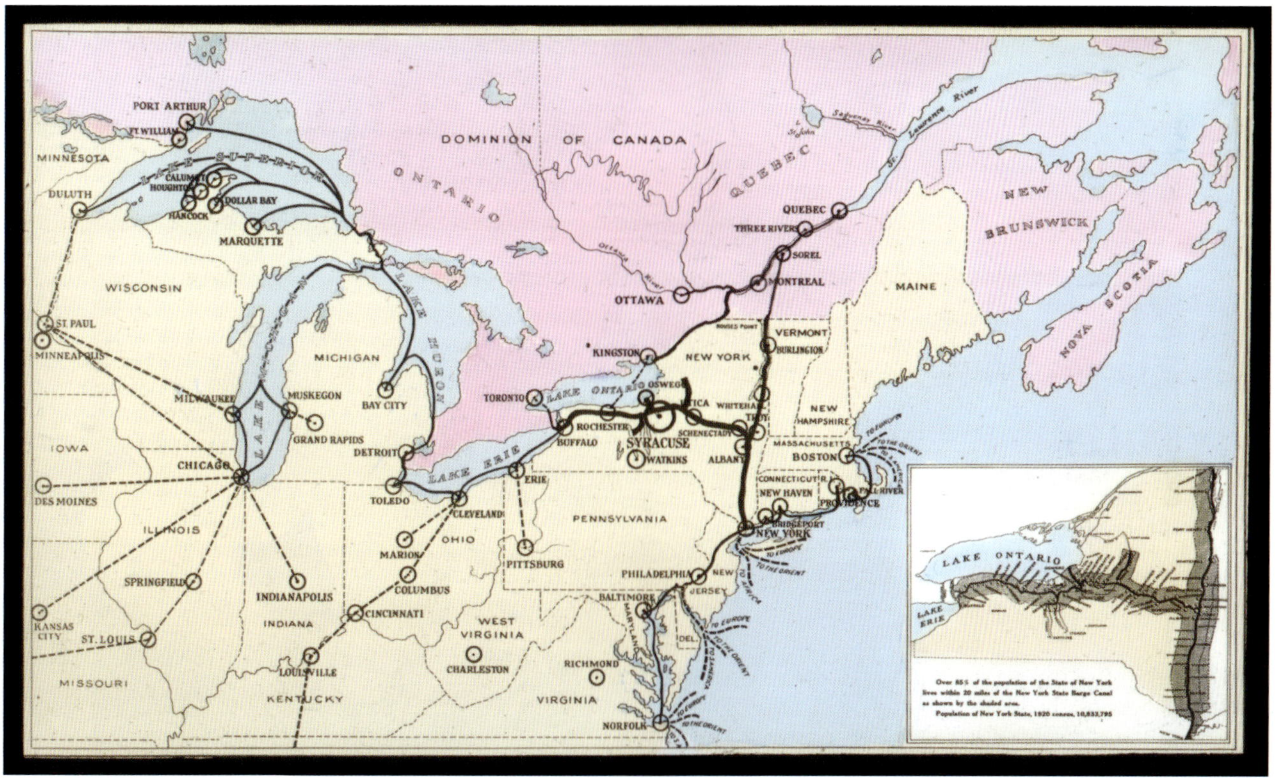

Map showing scope of shipping operation over the inland waterways of the eastern United States and Canada, tributary to the N.Y. State Barge Canal, map, ca. 1925. Map prepared by the Inland Marine Corporation showing the scope of its shipping operations over the inland waterways of the eastern United States and Canada. *Courtesy of the New York State Archives, NYSA_A3045-78_7322.*

(above and top of page 363) Various views of a grain boat being unloaded at Barge Canal terminals, photographs circa twentieth century. *Courtesy of the New York State Archives, 17672-92 (slides).*

Large grain scoops, like this one from the Gowanus Grain Elevator in New York City, were used in warehouses and grain elevators to push the grain toward the marine leg conveyor to lift the grain out of the hull of a boat or the storage area of the warehouse. *New York State Museum, H-1990.103.1.*

Grain shovel, stamped "N.Y. State Grain Elevator," ca. 1920. *New York State Museum, H-1990.103.2.*

New York State Canal Warehouse, Brooklyn, photograph, ca. 1920. By 1900 railroad companies owned many terminals and warehouses along the Great Lakes and in Buffalo and New York City. They used this extensive network to control rates. In order to compete with railroad-owned warehouses, the State built warehouse terminals along the canal route. *New York State Museum, 2005.43.86.*

Standard Oil Tanks in Amsterdam, photograph, 1922. The Standard Oil Company operated tanks at multiple communities along the canal system, including Amsterdam, New York. *Courtesy of the New York State Archives, 17672-92.*

Standard Oil Barge in Amsterdam, photograph, 1921. *Courtesy of the New York State Archives, 17672-92.*

Sign at Lock 9, photograph, 1922. New York initiated a "Ship by Canal" campaign, using billboards like this to attract shippers to the new waterway. The Department of Public Works' canal traffic agent connected producers with carriers. *Courtesy of the New York State Archives, 17672-92.*

Beech-Nut Factory, ca. 1920, unknown artist, American School, oil on canvas. *Arkell Museum at Canajoharie.*

In 1891 the Imperial Packing Co. was built along the canal in Canajoharie to produce Beech-Nut smoked ham. By 1899 the company was incorporated as the Beech-Nut Packing Company and diversified its products in the first decades of the twentieth century to include confections, coffee, condiments, gum, peanut butter, baby food, and other packaged foods. The plant expanded, and Beech-Nut became a major source of jobs and prosperity in the village. In 2009, after 118 years of business in Canajoharie, Beech-Nut closed its flagship plant entirely and moved operations (now just baby food) to nearby Florida, New York.

General Electric Company

The General Electric Company in Schenectady was issued a contract to manufacture all electrical components for the New York State Barge Canal. In addition to the contracts for the canal's construction, GE looked to use the Barge Canal to ship a wide variety of its manufactured products.

Tug *Alice R* and Barges *Acacia* and *Jessie* at Schenectady, Lighterage Dept., General Electric, photograph, ca. 1918. The General Electric Company had its own dock and fleet on the canal. During World War I, when shipping was scarce, General Electric purchased and refitted three Great Lakes schooners for use on the Barge Canal, including the *Acacia* and *Jessie*, pictured above. *New York State Museum, H-1997.13.97.*

Electric motor, ca. 1916. Weaver Building Supply Company in Hudson used this General Electric motor to operate woodworking machinery. The stretch between Schenectady and the Hudson River opened in 1916, and General Electric was able to take advantage of the early opening to ship its products. *New York State Museum, H-1970.129.1.*

John E. Matton & Sons Shipyard

Established in 1900 by John E. Matton along the old Champlain Canal in Waterford, Saratoga County, the company moved in 1916 to a strategic location on the Hudson River in Cohoes, just south of the entrance to the newly opened Barge Canal. All traffic passed the shipyard, which flourished, constructing barges, tugboats, and other types of vessels until 1983. Throughout the company's existence, they operated the only privately owned dry dock between Cohoes and Buffalo.

Matton's Shipyard on Old Champlain Canal, photograph, ca. 1910. Matton's original location was on the Old Champlain Canal in Waterford, Saratoga County. *New York State Museum, H-1990.11.484.*

Aerial view of Matton's Shipyard, photograph, twentieth century. Note the floating dry dock. Today, the former shipyard is part of Peebles Island State Park. *New York State Museum, H-1997.13.116.*

World War II Wood Subchaser Launched at Matton's, photograph, ca. 1943. *New York State Museum, H-1997.13.126.*

Canal, Railroad, and Highway, photograph, ca. 1930–1940s. This image depicts three modes of transportation moving through the Mohawk Valley. In the 1950s the New York State Thruway would cut through the Mohawk Valley, bringing more competition for the Barge Canal. *New York State Museum, H-1988.80.1.2369.*

Beech-Nut gum advertisement, 1940. The Beech-Nut Company in Canajoharie is an example of one of the many companies that opened along the canal and continued to operate into the twentieth century. As was common practice, the company embraced the canal and railroad in their advertising pieces to demonstrate its ability to ship products, without explicitly stating it. *Arkell Museum at Canajoharie. Gift of Cathy Blackburn, 2007.*

Canal Town Veteran, John C. Menihan, two-color lithograph, ca. 1945–1950. This lithograph depicts a house, with its sagging front porch, falling into decay and disrepair. Many canal communities suffered with the loss of jobs during the second half of the twentieth century. *Memorial Art Gallery, 2011.31.*

PART V

Today's Erie Canal

THE CANAL'S LEGACY: ART, ADVERTISING, AND COMMUNITY PRIDE

For two hundred years, the Erie Canal has contributed to shaping the state and the nation. The canal's legacy is visible all along the corridor—from the communities that took root with the canal's emergence to the remaining buildings and warehouses used by canallers and businesses.

Many canal stories would not be known if not for the authors, artists, and promoters who were inspired by the canal in its heyday. Authors such as Walter Edmonds and Samuel Hopkins Adams wrote iconic books featuring folktales from the canal in the nineteenth century. The canal inspired photography, paintings, poetry, and music that add to the legacy that we have inherited today.

Swimming Demonstration in Erie Canal, Ilion, photograph, ca. 1912. Community events, like this swimming demonstration, have been bringing locals to the canal for generations. New York State Museum, H-1980.80.1.882.

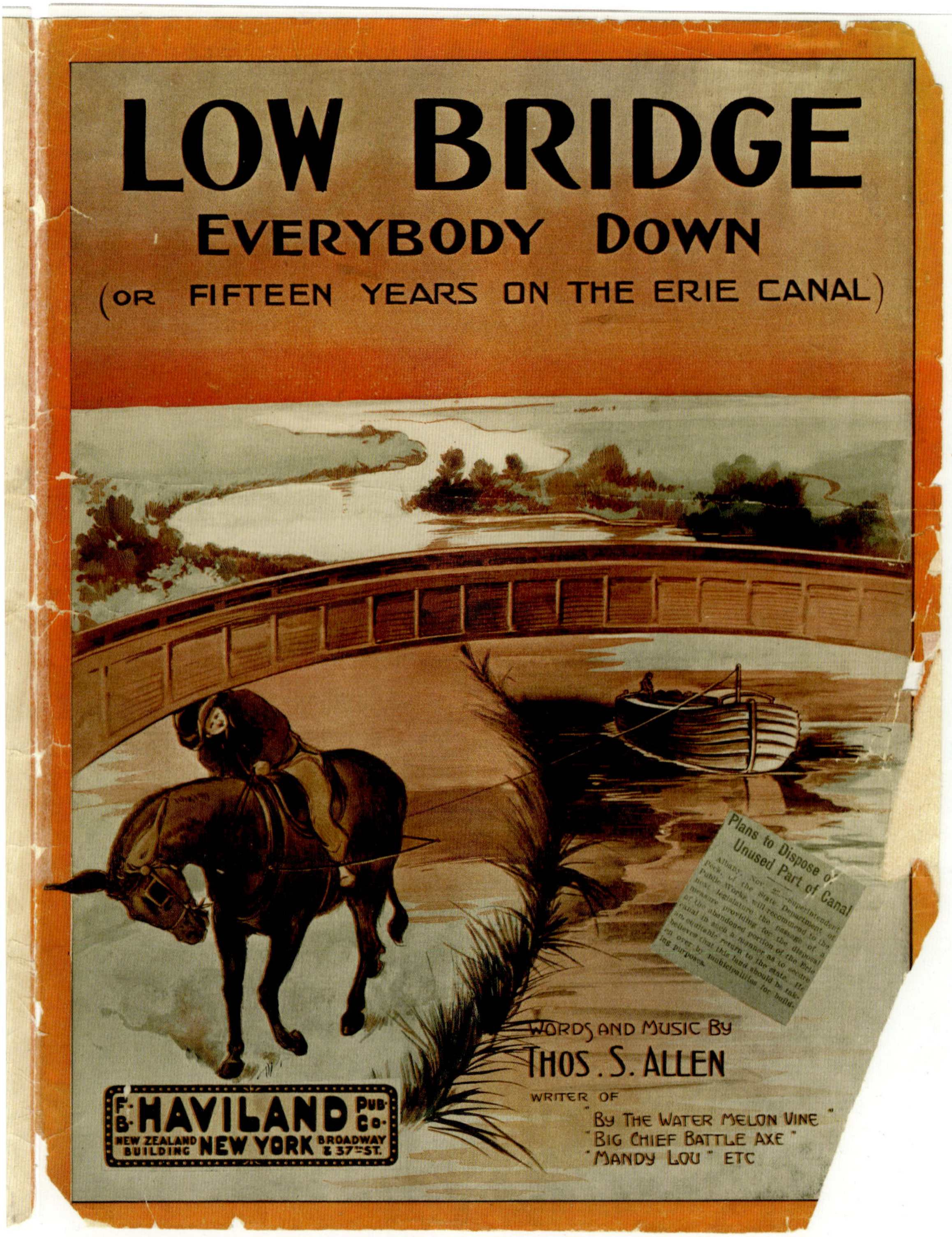

"Low Bridge! Everybody Down (or Fifteen Years on the Erie Canal)," Thomas S. Allen, sheet music, 1913. Today's best-known canal song was probably never sung on the canal. It was written in the early 1900s by a professional songwriter as a nostalgic look back at the old canal. *New York State Library, Manuscripts and Special Collections, 96-c761.*

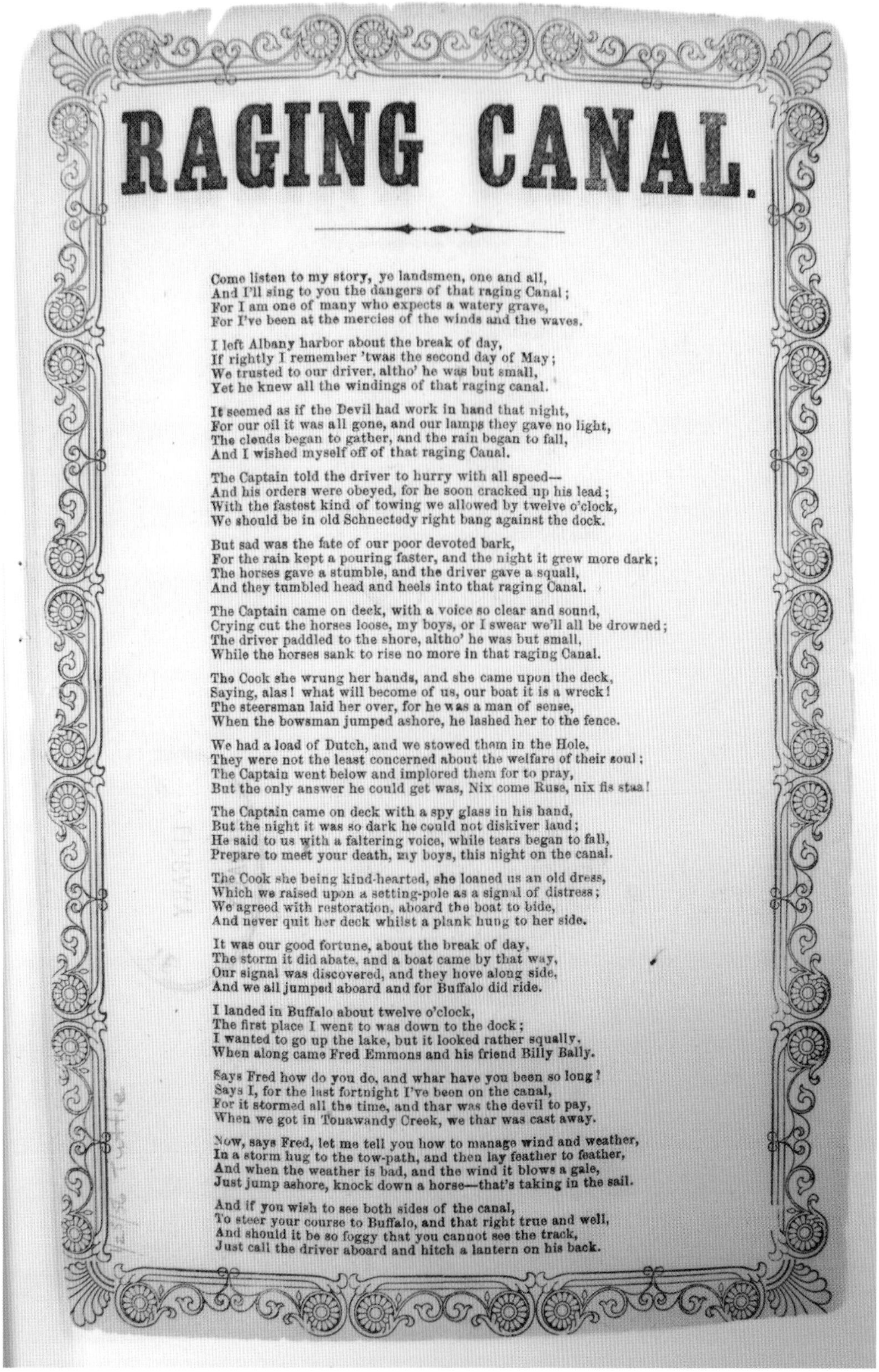

RAGING CANAL.

Come listen to my story, ye landsmen, one and all,
And I'll sing to you the dangers of that raging Canal;
For I am one of many who expects a watery grave,
For I've been at the mercies of the winds and the waves.

I left Albany harbor about the break of day,
If rightly I remember 'twas the second day of May;
We trusted to our driver, altho' he was but small,
Yet he knew all the windings of that raging canal.

It seemed as if the Devil had work in hand that night,
For our oil it was all gone, and our lamps they gave no light,
The clouds began to gather, and the rain began to fall,
And I wished myself off of that raging Canal.

The Captain told the driver to hurry with all speed—
And his orders were obeyed, for he soon cracked up his lead;
With the fastest kind of towing we allowed by twelve o'clock,
We should be in old Schnectedy right bang against the dock.

But sad was the fate of our poor devoted bark,
For the rain kept a pouring faster, and the night it grew more dark;
The horses gave a stumble, and the driver gave a squall,
And they tumbled head and heels into that raging Canal.

The Captain came on deck, with a voice so clear and sound,
Crying cut the horses loose, my boys, or I swear we'll all be drowned;
The driver paddled to the shore, altho' he was but small,
While the horses sank to rise no more in that raging Canal.

The Cook she wrung her hands, and she came upon the deck,
Saying, alas! what will become of us, our boat it is a wreck!
The steersman laid her over, for he was a man of sense,
When the bowsman jumped ashore, he lashed her to the fence.

We had a load of Dutch, and we stowed them in the Hole,
They were not the least concerned about the welfare of their soul;
The Captain went below and implored them for to pray,
But the only answer he could get was, Nix come Ruse, nix fis staa!

The Captain came on deck with a spy glass in his hand,
But the night it was so dark he could not diskiver land;
He said to us with a faltering voice, while tears began to fall,
Prepare to meet your death, my boys, this night on the canal.

The Cook she being kind-hearted, she loaned us an old dress,
Which we raised upon a setting-pole as a signal of distress;
We agreed with restoration, aboard the boat to bide,
And never quit her deck whilst a plank hung to her side.

It was our good fortune, about the break of day,
The storm it did abate, and a boat came by that way,
Our signal was discovered, and they hove along side,
And we all jumped aboard and for Buffalo did ride.

I landed in Buffalo about twelve o'clock,
The first place I went to was down to the dock;
I wanted to go up the lake, but it looked rather squally,
When along came Fred Emmons and his friend Billy Bally.

Says Fred how do you do, and whar have you been so long?
Says I, for the last fortnight I've been on the canal,
For it stormed all the time, and thar was the devil to pay,
When we got in Tonawandy Creek, we thar was cast away.

Now, says Fred, let me tell you how to manage wind and weather,
In a storm hug to the tow-path, and then lay feather to feather,
And when the weather is bad, and the wind it blows a gale,
Just jump ashore, knock down a horse—that's taking in the sail.

And if you wish to see both sides of the canal,
To steer your course to Buffalo, and that right true and well,
And should it be so foggy that you cannot see the track,
Just call the driver aboard and hitch a lantern on his back.

"Raging Canal," poem, date unknown. Various versions of this popular poem existed in the 1800s. *Courtesy of the New York State Library, Manuscripts and Special Collections, SCO BD 1529.*

(pages 374–375) Various images of the Erie Canal's 150th anniversary celebrations, photographs, 1967. Communities along the canal system held celebrations for the 150th anniversary of the Erie Canal. Top image shows a float used in the Rome celebration and the New York State Council on the Arts–supported museum barge that traveled the canal system. *New York State Museum, H-1988.80.1.1150, H-1988.80.1.3175, H-1988.80.1.1125.*

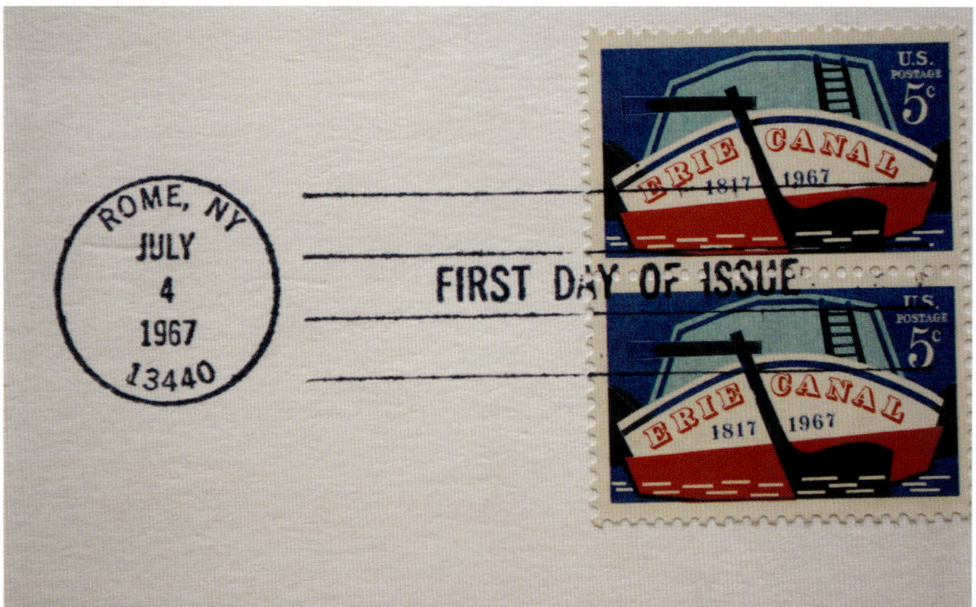

Erie Canal 150th anniversary stamp, 1967. *New York State Museum, Barben Collection, H-1988.79.*

Bicentennial Barge, photograph, 1976. For the national bicentennial celebration in 1976, the state produced a floating museum that traveled to communities along the canal system. *New York State Museum, H-97.13.93.*

Erie Canal at Little Falls, William Rickarby Miller, oil on canvas, 1884. Nostalgia for the early days of traveling by packet boat had already set in by 1884. This study is based on an earlier work by the artist that was published as a woodcut print in *Holden's Dollar Magazine*. Miller produced multiple paintings from different views of this spot based on a study he did in 1848. *New-York Historical Society, 1949.4.*

A View on the Erie Canal Near Syracuse, mid-twentieth century, Frannie Hotchkiss (American, twentieth century), oil on canvas. Amateur artists also found Erie Canal subjects compelling. Nothing is known about Frannie Hotchkiss, nor have other works by her surfaced. Here she depicted a quiet, twentieth-century view of the canal with the aging buildings contrasted to the lush landscape. *Erie Canal Museum.*

Erie Canal at Canastota, 1935, John W. Taylor (American, 1897–1983), oil on canvas. Taylor portrayed the old Erie Canal in the village of Canastota, several decades after the new Barge Canal passed well to the north of the village. The painting shows the old canal bed in the center of town, at that point being used by boys for fishing. The buildings, which would have originally faced the canal, seem to have been reoriented toward business on the other side. *Arkell Museum at Canajoharie, gift of Bartlett Arkell, 1945.*

View of Canajoharie from a 19th-Century Print, 1944, Esta Cosgrave (American, ca. 1900–1952), oil on panel. In 1948, an article on Cosgrave appeared in *Life* magazine, calling her "ingenious" for her copies of eighteenth- and nineteenth-century portraits substituting the faces of friends and family for the originals. Here she based her painting on a print by John W. Barber (shown below) that appeared in the 1842 publication *Historical Collections of the State of New York* by Barber and Henry Howe. Cosgrove enlivened the severity of the print with her choice of muted, solid colors, resulting in a more folk art–like image. *Arkell Museum at Canajoharie, gift of Bartlett Arkell, 1944.*

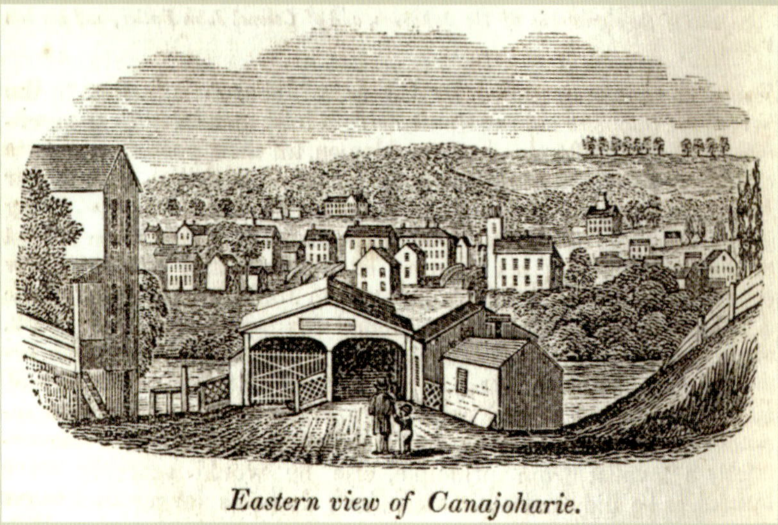

Eastern View of Canajoharie, 1842, John Warner Barber (American, 1798–1885), wood engraving, published in *John Warner Barber and Henry Howe, Historical Collections of the State of New York* (New York: S. Tuttle, 1842). *New York State Library, Manuscript and Special Collections, 974.7 B23a3.*

Canal Town Veteran, ca. 1945–1950, John C. Menihan (American, 1908–1992), two-color lithograph. Menihan's style of expressive realism often focused on subjects near his lifelong home of Rochester. This work represents the architectural legacy of the Erie Canal's heyday, visible in the Vernacular Greek Revival homes that dot canal towns today. Although these homes were built when the canal was thriving, business was booming, and new wealth streamed into the area, Menihan's view shows a neglected, sagging structure left behind by progress. *Memorial Art Gallery, 2011.31.*

Departure of a Packet Boat (on the Erie Canal), 1939, Henry Schnackenberg (American, 1892–1970), oil on canvas. *Arkell Museum at Canajoharie, gift of the artist, 1944.*

This study for one of two murals at the Amsterdam, New York, Post Office depicts a packet boat leaving Fort Hunter, west of the city. Like many works of art commissioned under President Franklin D. Roosevelt's New Deal in the 1930s, the subject nostalgically celebrates the prosperous past of the local area. The carefully arranged composition centers upon the boatman casting off, surrounded by groupings of idealized figures.

Edward Lamson Henry (American, 1841–1919), sketchbooks, late eighteenth–early nineteenth century, (above) *A Canal Lock*, (facing page) *On the Canal*, (page 382) *Canal Office. New York State Museum, H-1940.17.2229, H-1940.17.2470, H-1940.17.2530, H-1940.17.2531.*

Henry was known for his nostalgic images often depicting pre–Civil War America and based on his meticulous study of period costume, architecture, household furnishings, and modes of transportation. These sketchbooks include some of his drawings made in preparation for a group of paintings of canal subjects. The New York State Museum has the largest collection of Henry's work—drawings, watercolors, and oils in addition to sketchbooks—given in 1940 by his family.

a Canal Lock

CANAL OFFICE

"Erie Brand Chipped Beef, Beech-Nut Packing Co.," packing label, twentieth century. Nostalgic use of the Erie Canal in marketing continues up into the twenty-first century. *New York State Museum, H-1991.23.2.*

Souvenir tin, 1937. The 1937 Beech-Nut Christmas Box was decorated with historic images of the Mohawk Valley and included an assortment of Beech-Nut products, such as coffee, cream crackers, cheese wafers, oven-baked beans, tomato juice, jelly, peanut butter, and various flavors of gum and mints. Beech-Nut was founded in 1891 and continues part of its operation in the Mohawk Valley today. *New York State Museum, H-1983.16.4.*

"Barge Canal Bridge, Sylvan Beach," sewing kit, ca. 1920. In the late nineteenth and early twentieth centuries, Sylvan Beach in Verona, on Oneida Lake, was a tourist destination, including amusement parks. This souvenir sewing kit came complete with a view of the new Barge Canal Bridge that crossed over the lake. The Barge Canal channel went through the lake as opposed to bypassing it as the earlier Erie had done. *New York State Museum H-1970.44.4.*

Firefighter's delegate pin, 1918. This delegate's pin is from the New York State Firemen's Convention held in Lockport, August 20–22, 1918. The pin features the new Lockport flight with the two Barge Canal Locks next to one set of the old enlarged locks. *New York State Museum, H-1987.28.87.*

"York State Print" dress and bolero originally worn by Grace Hudowalski, 1949. Grace Hudowalski worked for the New York State Commerce Department from 1945 to 1961. She started as a publicity writer and worked her way up to travel-promotion supervisor. She often played the role of public salesperson for the state, attending trade shows, speaking regularly on the radio, and appearing on television. She wore this special dress made by the Celanese Corporation of America, based in New York City, depicting travel scenes, including the canal, to promote tourism and commerce in New York State. *New York State Museum, H-1988.15.2, H-1988.15.3.*

Grace Hudowalski in "York State Print" dress, Celanese Corporation of America, photograph, 1949–1950. *New York State Museum, H-1988.15.2.4.*

ON THE ERIE CANAL - Grace Hudowalski of the Travel Bureau models a dress made of the new Celanese New York State prints. This cloth carries scenes from the old Erie Canal. The Travel Bureau was helpful to the artists designing a whole series of patterns for this cloth.

THE ERIE CANAL TODAY

The purpose of the Erie Canal was always commercial, but since the 1980s there has been a new movement focused on the quality of life for canal communities and promoting heritage tourism, bringing canal history to the forefront of the communities' self-expression with festivals, public art projects, and interpretive signage. Today, recreational boaters from around the world use the New York State Canal System for leisure. New visitor centers, public docks, boat rentals, tours, and bike paths line the canals and invite tourists to learn about the past. But the canal continues to be a utility, too. It is a source of irrigation for farms, hydro-electric power, and drinking water for communities along its route.

Bronze plaque, 2016. Thanks to the efforts of the Erie Canalway National Heritage Corridor, the New York State Barge Canal system is now on the National Register of Historic Places and has been designated a National Historic Landmark. The designation bestows national recognition, makes certain grants available to entities within the district, and helps provide protection from development. *Erie Canalway National Heritage Corridor, The William G. Pomeroy Foundation.*

Tugboat *Urger*. Today the canal system is operated by the New York State Canal Corporation. Its flagship vessel is the 1901 tugboat *Urger*. The *Urger* is listed on the National Register of Historic Places and is one of the oldest operating tugboats in the United States. The vessel retired from active service in 1986. In recent years it has traveled the corridor as a floating ambassador and provides educational programming for schools and adults. *New York State Museum, H-2005.43.067.*

Fairport Landing in the Evening, photograph, Keith Boas, 2016. Communities like Fairport in Monroe County have cultivated the canal as an economic resource by investing in its waterfront, attracting visitors and new businesses, and in turn improving the quality of life for residents. *Courtesy of the Erie Canalway National Heritage Corridor.*

CONCLUSION

> **Should your noble but stupendous plan of uniting Lake Erie with the Hudson, be carried into effect, you have to fear no rivalry. The commerce of the immense extent of country, bordering on the upper lakes, is yours for ever, and to such an incalculable amount as would baffle all conjecture to conceive. Its execution would confer immortal honour on the projectors and supporters, and would in its eventual consequences, render New-York the greatest commercial emporium in the world . . .**
>
> **—William Weston, English engineer, upon reviewing the plans for the Erie Canal, ca. 1817[1]**

William Weston's opinion was important to the legislators who would be voting on the Canal Bill in 1817. The well-respected professional engineer had knowledge of the terrain and experience building canals. Not only did he think it was possible, he painted a glorious picture of what was to follow in the wake of a new canal. His prediction was largely correct; the commercial success the canal fostered solidified New York as the Empire State. Looking at his words today, we can say he did not go far enough in his prediction, that is, the construction of the canal and its enterprising waters proved to be much more than commercial.

The building of the canal by New York State set the precedent for what was possible under the federal Constitution. The State raised funds, acquired land, constructed and operated the waterway, in the name of progress for the public good. New York's construction of the Erie Canal helped to inaugurate a philosophy of an expansive role for government that impacted the everyday lives of individual citizens in ways that had not previously been envisioned.

The canal also served as the information superhighway, moving not only goods and people along its course but, with them, news and ideas. This influence was so significant and the impact on people's lives so immense that it has been compared to the internet and its impact on commerce, society, and culture today.

Despite the downturn in commercial use of the canal in the second half of the twentieth century, New Yorkers continue to seek ways to reinvent the canal and maintain its relevance in the present and future. Organizations such as the Erie Canalway National Heritage Corridor (ECNHC), the New York State Canal Corporation, the Canal Society of New York State, and others are working to bring the canal system's heritage along with recreational and commercial opportunities to the public.

In 2017 the Erie Canalway National Heritage Corridor conducted a study, reporting that canal-related events attracted 3.3 million visitors that year. Leisure seekers and heritage tourists converged on canal sites for boat tours, bicycle and paddle-sport rentals, and historic site and museum tours—and in doing so generated a $1.5 billion economic impact. Similar studies conducted over the past decade further underscore the trend and also show that non-tourism activities, like hydropower and irrigation, also generate billions of dollars—upwards of $6 billion—each year.[2]

These studies make it clear that the canal is once again a strong partner in the economy. New events and amenities continue to be added each year along the canal corridor, and the future looks bright!

Even though Weston included "for ever" in his prediction, it would have been impossible for him to envision the advances in technology that overtook the canal. Likewise, it would have been impossible for him to foresee the exciting reinvention of the canal that is taking place today—setting the stage for another two hundred years on the enterprising waters of New York's Erie Canal.

NOTES

INTRODUCTION. ENTERPRISING WATERS: NEW YORK'S ERIE CANAL

1. David Hosack, M.D., F.R.S., *Memoir of De Witt Clinton: With an Appendix, Containing Numerous Documents, Illustrative of the Principal Events of His Life* (New York: J. Seymour, 1829), 347.

PART I: BEFORE THE CANAL

1. Samuel S. Forman, December 25, 1803. Personal letter to James and McGabe from Samuel S. Forman, in *Forman's Letterbook*, Samuel S. Forman Correspondence, Fairchild Collection, New York Public Library.
2. Christopher Colles, *Proposal for the Speedy Settlement of the Waste and Unappropriated Lands on the Western Frontiers of the State of New York* (New York: Samuel Loudon, 1785).
3. Hosack, *Memoir*, 278.
4. *Hosack, Memoir*, 278–279.

PART II: CLINTON'S DITCH

1. Jesse Hawley, *An Essay on the Enlargement of the Erie Canal* (Lockport: Courier Office, 1840), 14.
2. "Toasts Drunk at the Dinner Given to DeWitt Clinton, at Stewart's Hotel, in This City, on the 4th Instant," *Pittsburgh Gazette, Friday Morning, August 12, 1825.*
3. Carol Sheriff, *The Artifical River: The Erie Canal and the Paradox of Progress, 1817–1862* (New York: Hill & Wang, 1996), 101.
4. Cadwallader D. Colden, *Memoir, Prepared at the Request of a Committee of the Common Council of the City of New York, and Presented to the Mayor of the City, at the Celebration of the Completion of the New York Canals* (New York: W. A. Davis, 1825), 14.
5. Colden, *Memoir*, 57.
6. Colden, *Memoir*, 64.
7. Colden, *Memoir*, 22.
8. Unknown, "The Great Water Highway through New York State, 1829," in *Life and Manners in the United States*, ed. Warren S. Tryon (Chicago: University of Chicago Press, 1952), 104–114, http://www.eriecanal.org/texts/Mirror.html (accessed January 30, 2018). In this quotation its author has exaggerated the boat dimensions.
9. Martha Robbins Juckett, *My Canaling Days, 1897–1907*, edited by Dorothy M. Parker (Whitehall: Historical Society of Whitehall, The Whitehall Independent, 1985 rpt.), 6–7.
10. Clifton Johnson, "A Canal-Boat Voyage on the Hudson," *The Outlook*, October 1, 1898, 317.
11. Richard G. Garrity, *Recollections of the Erie Canal* (Tonawanda: The Historical Society of the Tonawandas, 1971), 33.
12. Captain Basil Hall, Royal Navy, *Travels in North America in the Years 1827 and 1828* (Philadelphia: Carey, Lea & Carey, 1829), 66.
13. Alexander Stewart Scott, "*1826 Travel Journal of Alexander Stewart Scott," unpublished, 123.* Collection of the New York State Library, Manuscripts and Special Collections, BD13145.

14. Theodore C. Belgen, ed., "Peter Testman's Account of His Experiences in North America," *Minnesota History* 6, no. 2 (1925): 98.
15. Nathaniel Hawthorne, "The Canal Boat," *New-England Magazine*, vol. 9, December 1835, 398–409.
16. H. Niles, ed., "The Erie Canal: Meeting of the Waters from the Commerical Advertiser of October 11, 1823," *Niles' Weekly Register*, October 18, 1823, 110.

PART III: THE ENLARGED CANAL

1. Governor Roswell P. Flower, September 4, 1893, speech to Chicago's "Sons of New York" reception, in General Managers of the Exhibit of the State of New York at the World's Columbian Exposition, *Report of the Board of General Managers of the Exhibit of the State of New York at the World's Columbian Exposition* (Albany: James B. Lyon, state printer, 1894).
2. Hosack, *Memoir, 450.*
3. Morris Bishop, "The Journeys of Samuel J. Parker," *New York History* 45, no. 2 (1964): 135–150.

PART IV: THE BARGE CANAL

1. New York (State) Commerce Commission, *Report of the New York Commerce Commission, Volume 1* (Albany: James B. Lyon, state printer, 1900).
2. Charles E. Ogden, "A Modern Canal Voyage from Lake Erie to the Hudson," *The American Review of Reviews* (January 1923): 61–64, http://www.eriecanal.org/texts/ARR-1923/ARR-1923.html#Ogden (accessed October 8, 2015).

CONCLUSION

1. Hosack, *Memoir, 415.*
2. CHA Design/Construction Solutions with assistance of Jacob Civil Consultants, Inc and A. Strauss-Wieder, Inc. 2014. *New York State Canal Corporation Report on Economic Benefits of Non-Tourism Use of the NYS Canal System*. Economic Impact Study, Albany, NY: New York State Canal Corporation. Accessed May 16, 2018. http://www.canals.ny.gov/economic-benefit-report.pdf.

BIBLIOGRAPHY

Anderson, Patricia. 1984. *The Course of Empire: The Erie Canal and the New York Landscape, 1825–1875.* Rochester: Memorial Art Gallery of the University of Rochester.

Belgen, Theodore C., ed. 1925. "Peter Testman's Account of His Experiences in North America." *Minnesota History* 6, no. 2: 98.

Biron, Gerry. 2012. *A Cherished Curiosity: The Souvenir Beaded Bag in Historic Haudenosaunee Art.* Brainerd: Bang Printing.

Bishop, Morris. 1964. "The Journeys of Samuel J. Parker." *New York History* 45, no. 2: 135–150.

Bitz, Bob. 2012. "A Review of the History of The New York State Agricultural Society." *New York Agricultural Society.* July. http://www.nysagsociety.org/wp-content/uploads/2013/07/a_review_of_the_history_of_the_nys_ag_soc.pdf. Accessed January 10, 2018.

CHA Design/Construction Solutions with assistance of Jacob Civil Consultants, Inc., and A. Strauss-Wieder, Inc. 2014. *New York State Canal Corporation Report on Economic Benefits of Non-Tourism Use of the NYS Canal System.* Economic impact study. Albany: New York State Canal Corporation. http://www.canals.ny.gov/economic-benefit-report.pdf. Accessed May 16, 2018.

Cohn, Arthur B. 2003. *Lake Champlain's Sailing Canal Boats: An Illustrated Journey from Burlington Bay to the Hudson River.* Basin Harbor: Lake Champlain Maritime Museum.

Colden, Cadwallader D. 1825. *Memoir, Prepared at the Request of a Committee of the Common Council of the City of New York, and Presented to the Mayor of the City, at the Celebration of the Completion of the New York Canals.* New York: W. A. Davis.

Colles, Christopher. 1785. *Proposal for the Speedy Settlement of the Waste and Unappropriated Lands on the Western Frontiers of the State of New York.* New York: Samuel Loudon.

Cross, Whitney R. 1950. *The Burned-Over District: The Social and Intellectual History of Enthusiastic Religion in Western New York, 1800–1850.* Ithaca: Cornell University Press.

D'Ambrosio, Paul S., and Charlotte M. Emans. 1987. *Folk Art's Many Faces: Portraits in the New York State Historical Association.* Cooperstown: New York State Historical Association.

Elliott, Dolores N. 2003. "Two Centuries of Iroquois Beadwork." *BEADS: Journal of the Society of Bead Researchers,* 3–22.

Eric Mower and Associates. 2008. *New York State Canal Corporation 2007 Conversion Study.* Marketing study. Albany: New York State Canal Corporation.

Flemming, James. 1892. "Shifting Device of Elevators." Buffalo, New York, United States of America Patent 487,559. December 6.

Forman, Samuel S. December 25, 1803. Personal letter to James and McGabe from Samuel S. Forman. In *Forman's Letterbook,* Samuel S. Forman Correspondence, Fairchild Collection. New York Public Library.

Garrity, Richard G. 1971. *Recollections of the Erie Canal.* Tonawanda: The Historical Society of the Tonawandas.

General Managers of the Exhibit of the State of New York at the World's Columbian Exposition. 1894. *Report of the Board of General Managers of the Exhibit of the State of New York at the World's Columbian Exposition.* Albany: James B. Lyon, state printer.

Hall, Basil, Captain, Royal Navy. 1829. *Travels in North America in the Years 1827 and 1828.* Philadelphia: Carey, Lea & Carey.

Hauptman, Laurence M. 1999. *Conspiracy of Interests: Iroquois Dispossession and the Rise of New York State.* Syracuse: Syracuse University Press.

Hawley, Jesse. 1840. *An Essay on the Enlargement of the Erie Canal.* Lockport: Courier Office.

Hawthorne, Nathaniel. 1835. "The Canal Boat." *New-England Magazine* 9 (December): 398–409.

Hayes, W. Parker, Jr. 2002. "Fritz Vogt's Rural America." *Antiques and the Arts Weekly*, May 28.

Hosack, David, M.D., F.R.S. 1829. *Memoir of De Witt Clinton: With an Appendix, Containing Numerous Documents, Illustrative of the Principal Events of His Life.* New York: J. Seymour.

Johnson, Clifton. 1898. "A Canal-Boat Voyage on the Hudson." *The Outlook*, October 1.

Juckett, Martha Robbins. 1985. *My Canaling Days, 1897–1907.* Ed. Dorothy M. Parker. Whitehall: Historical Society of Whitehall, The Whitehall Independent, rpt.

Koeppel, Gerard. 2009. *Bond of Union: Building the Erie Canal and the American Empire.* Cambridge: Da Capo Press.

Larkin, F. Daniel, Julie C. Daniels, Jean West, eds. 2001. *Erie Canal, New York's Gift to the Nation: A Document-Based Teacher Resource.* Peterborough: Cobblestone Publishing Company.

Level 7 Market Research. 2018. *Canal Event Analysis, 2017.* Tourism marketing and event study. Waterford: Erie Canalway National Heritage Corridor. https://eriecanalway.org/application/files/7215/2570/0183/ECNHC_Canal-related_Event_Analysis_2017.pdf. Accessed May 14, 2018.

Little, Nina Fletcher. 1988. *Face to Face: M. W. Hopkins and Noah North.* Lexington: Museum of Our National Heritage.

McGreevy, Patrick. 2009. *Stairway to Empire: Lockport, the Erie Canal, and the Shaping of America.* Albany: State University of New York Press.

Munsell, Joel. 1854. *Annals of Albany, Vol. V.* Albany: J. Munsell.

Munsell, Joel. 1867. *Collections on the History of Albany from Its Discovery to the Present Time, with Notices of Its Public Institutions, and Biographical Sketches of Citizens Deceased Vol. II.* Albany: J. Munsell.

New York (State) Commerce Commssion. 1900. *Report of the New York Commerce Commission, Volume 1.* Albany: James B. Lyon, state printer.

Niles, H., ed. 1823. "The Erie Canal: Meeting of the Waters from the Commerical Advertiser of October 11, 1823." *Niles' Weekly Register*, October 18, 110.

Ogden, Charles E. 1923. "A Modern Canal Voyage from Lake Erie to the Hudson." *The American Review of Reviews* (January): 61–64. http://www.eriecanal.org/texts/ARR-1923/ARR-1923.html#Ogden. Accessed October 8, 2015.

Phillips, Ruth B. 1998. *Trading Identities: The Souvenir in Native North American Art from the Northeast, 1700–1900.* Seattle: University of Washington Press.

Schultz, Christian. 1814. *Travels on an Inland Voyage through the States of New-York, Pennsylvania, Virginia, Ohio, Kentucky and Tennessee and through the Territories of Indiana, Louisiana, Mississippi and New-Orleans Vol. I* [microform]. New York: Isaac Riley.

Scott, Alexander Stewart. 1826. "1826 Travel Journal of Alexander Stewart Scott." Unpublished. Collection of the New York State Library, Manuscripts and Special Collections, BD13145.

Shaw, Ronald E. 1966. *Erie Water West: A History of the Erie Canal, 1792–1854.* Lexington: University of Kentucky Press.

Sheriff, Carol. 1996. *The Artifical River: The Erie Canal and the Paradox of Progress, 1817–1862.* New York: Hill & Wang.

Staff of the Canal Museum. 1981. *A Canal Boat Primer on the Canals of New York State.* Syracuse: The Canal Museum.

The Transferware Collectors Club, Winterthur Museum, and Historic New England. n.d. *Patriotic America: Blue Printed Pottery Celebrating a New Nation.* http://www.americanhistoricalstaffordshire.com/. Accessed December 4, 2017.

Trollope, Frances Milton. 1832. *Domestic Manners of the Americans.* London: Whittaker, Treacher.

Unknown. 1952. "The Great Water Highway through New York State, 1829." In *Life and Manners in the United States*, edited by Warren S. Tryon, 104–114. Chicago: University of Chicago Press. http://www.eriecanal.org/texts/Mirror.html. Accessed January 30, 2018.

Whitford, Noble E. 1906. *History of the Canal System of the State of New York: Together with Brief Histories of the United States and Canada.* Albany: Brandow Printing Company, state legislative printer.

Wyld, Lionel D., ed. 1967. *40' x 28' x 4': The Erie Canal—150 Years.* Rome: Oneida County Erie Canal Commemoration Commission.

INDEX

Entries that refer to material from either figures or figure captions have an "f" following the page number.

Barge Canal, continued on next page